Principles of Psychotherapy

Second Edition

Irving B. Weiner

John Wiley & Sons, Inc.
New York • Chichester • Weinheim • Brisbane • Singapore • Toronto

Copyright © 1998 by John Wiley & Sons, Inc. All rights reserved.

Published simultaneously in Canada.

Library of Congress Cataloging-in-Publication Data:
Weiner, Irving B.
    Principles of psychotherapy / Irving B. Weiner. — 2nd ed.
        p.   cm.
    Includes bibliographical references and indexes.
    ISBN 0-471-19128-0 (cloth : alk. paper)
    1. Psychotherapy.   I. Title.
    [DNLM: 1. Psychotherapy.   WM 420 W423p 1998]
    RC480.W373   1998
    616.89′ 14—dc21
    DNLM/DLC
    for Library of Congress   97-50225

Printed in the United States of America.

10 9 8 7 6 5 4

Preface

L IKE THE first edition of *Principles of Psychotherapy*, this revision is addressed to psychotherapy practitioners and is primarily a manual of principles for conducting psychotherapy in clinical practice. As before, the text provides detailed guidelines for conducting psychotherapy from the initial evaluation interviews through the termination phase of treatment. These guidelines are amplified throughout with illustrations of what therapists should consider saying and doing in various circumstances.

The revised edition resembles its predecessor in style, structure, and organization, but its text has been almost completely rewritten to reflect clinical thinking and cumulative knowledge in the late 1990s. Older but still relevant themes and issues are presented in modified ways that draw on conceptual and empirical advances since the first edition appeared. New developments in theory and research are integrated within the discussions of how to do psychotherapy, as is attention to such contemporary topics as ethical awareness, multicultural sensitivity, brief therapy, and the impact of managed care. Bearing witness to the currency of the revised text, only works of historical significance are carried over from the bibliography of the first edition, and the vast majority of the more than 400 references cited have appeared since 1985.

Despite advances in theory and research, on the other hand, many of the basic scholarly and professional issues with which psychotherapists must be concerned remain largely as they were in 1975. Hence the remainder of this Preface to the second edition of *Principles of Psychotherapy* expresses many of the same thoughts that were noted originally as having influenced the conceptualization and preparation of the book. To begin with, this guide for conducting psychotherapy closely follows indications from available research wherever possible. Without digressing from the clinical presentation to review relevant empirical findings, each chapter indicates the major data sources on which the discussion is based. Where adequate research studies bearing on proposed guidelines do not yet exist, clinical experience provides the basis of the recommendations made. Transcending both the supporting research and clinical evidence, there is an emphasis throughout the presentation on the importance of conducting psychotherapy within a conceptual framework that embraces the goals of the treatment and the possible strategies and tactics for achieving these goals. It is from such a framework that therapists can most effectively deduce appropriate and incisive ways of intervening on their patients' behalf.

This balanced approach to clinical and research guidelines for the practice of psychotherapy provides counterpoint to a regrettable but persistent gap between them. As readers familiar with current scientist-practitioner debates will recognize, the following observations in the Preface to the 1975 edition are equally applicable today, if not more so:

> Psychotherapy practitioners at times recommend their procedures as if personal conviction were equivalent to validity, while psychotherapy researchers sometimes present their data as if significant research results were an end in themselves, rather than only a means toward developing improved treatment procedures. The resulting dialogue has not always been friendly. Psychotherapy researchers have accused practitioners of ignoring or failing to comprehend the implications of empirical findings and of participating in a fraternity of "believers" who reinforce each other's dedication to their hallowed practices and disregard any data to the contrary. Practitioners have in turn accused researchers of failing to appreciate the complexity of real-life clinical interactions, and of designing experimental studies more with an eye to making them manageable than with adequate attention to making them reflect faithfully the transactions occurring within psychotherapy.

Now as in the 1970s, both of these accusations have some basis. In every field of endeavor, the applications of knowledge lag behind advances in theory and research, and so it is with psychotherapy. At the same time, sophisticated psychotherapy researchers readily admit to many unresolved difficulties in translating the intricacies of clinical interactions into meaningful operational definitions for investigative purposes. Yet the shortcomings of both practitioners and researchers should not obscure their substantial contributions to psychotherapy and the complementarity of their efforts. Hypotheses for research study emerge from the clinical practice of psychotherapy, and it is in the success and failure of clinicians' efforts that the conclusions from such studies must finally be examined for their utility. Clinical practice that is neither subjected to nor influenced by research studies can lead down many blind alleys and detract both from the pursuit of knowledge and from the delivery of responsible clinical service.

Lack of unequivocal documentation, however, should not dissuade clinicians from employing procedures they expect with reasonable certainty to benefit troubled people who have sought their help. Cumulative clinical wisdom must be given its just due, lest uncertainty produce a paralysis of action. In the absence of empirically documented procedures for meeting every contingency, psychotherapists must frequently turn for guidance to conceptual formulations and to the advice of experienced clinicians who have found certain techniques consistently helpful in their work.

To be systematically learned, taught, and practiced, psychotherapy must be grounded in a theoretical perspective on the nature of personality functioning and behavior change. A psychodynamic view of the psychotherapy process provides the primary theoretical context for the selection and discussion of topics in this book. Whatever theoretical perspective commands their primary allegiance, however, psychotherapists will benefit from some degree of eclecticism. Useful contributions to understanding the ingredients of effective psychotherapy have emerged within numerous theoretical contexts, and research evidence supports hypotheses derived from many different theories of psychotherapy.

Accordingly, although the chapters that follow reflect primarily a psychodynamic point of view, they also stress numerous principles of psychotherapy central to other approaches: that psychotherapy is an interpersonal process defined by the nature of the communication taking place within it; that the capacity of therapists to create a climate of warmth, respect, trust, and genuineness has considerable bearing on the outcome of the treatment; that psychotherapy is essentially a learning situation in which the amount of benefit people derive depends on how extensively they can learn to understand and control their behavior; that the goals of psychotherapy include positive behavior change in addition to increments in self-understanding and self-control; and that positive behavior change is measured both in relief from emotional distress and in progress toward fuller utilization of potentials for productive work and rewarding human relationships.

It is widely recognized that the agents of change in psychotherapy include both general and specific factors. General factors promoting change in psychotherapy reside largely in the treatment relationship and more particularly in (a) the opportunity it provides patients to express themselves and (b) the extent to which it fosters an atmosphere of candid self-observation, expectation of change, and amenability to the therapist's efforts to facilitate such change. Specific factors promoting change consist of the technical procedures employed by therapists to foster change and facilitate progress toward the goals of the treatment. A good working alliance and sound therapist technique are thus complementary change agents in effective psychotherapy. Inept technical procedures limit or negate the benefits that might otherwise derive from an open and trusting patient-therapist relationship, whereas the most polished technical skills are of little avail in the absence of a treatment climate that nourishes receptivity to them. For this reason, the general (relationship) and specific (technique) aspects of promoting personality and behavior change through psychotherapy are intertwined throughout this presentation.

The book is organized in four parts. Part One begins with consideration in Chapter 1 of the nature and goals of psychotherapy. Chapters 2 and 3 address the characteristics of patients and therapists, respectively, with particular attention to the bearing of these characteristics on treatment outcome. Chapter 4 presents an overview of the psychotherapy process, which is then elaborated in the remaining chapters of the book.

Part Two concerns the initial phase of psychotherapy and includes chapters on the evaluation and assessment of persons who seek psychotherapy (Chapter 5); on the role of the treatment contract in psychotherapy and procedures for establishing it (Chapter 6); and on methods of conducting psychotherapy interviews in ways that maximize patient participation in the treatment process (Chapter 7).

Part Three turns to the middle phase of psychotherapy and delineates methods for communicating understanding through interpretation (Chapter 8); for recognizing and minimizing interferences with communication that constitute resistance to the treatment process (Chapter 9); and for identifying and utilizing intercurrent influences exerted on the course of therapy by the treatment relationship, in both its transference (Chapter 10) and countertransference (Chapter 11) aspects.

In Part Four of the text, attention is given to determining when an appropriate termination point has been reached and bringing the therapy to an effective end (Chapter 12).

Finally, I would like to acknowledge with deep gratitude the guidance I received from my two main mentors in psychotherapy, Edward Bordin and Paul Dewald. Their sage teaching and sensitive grasp of the human condition are, I hope, adequately reflected in the pages of this book.

IRVING B. WEINER

Tampa, Florida

Contents

PART ONE

INTRODUCTION

CHAPTER 1

The Nature and Goals of Psychotherapy

PSYCHOTHERAPY IS an interpersonal process in which therapists communicate to their patients that they understand them, respect them, and want to be of help to them. Most of the procedures used by trained professionals to treat people with psychological problems involve understanding, respect, and helpfulness, but psychotherapy is unique by virtue of the intentional effort of therapists to communicate their understanding of a patient's difficulties and to help him or her share in this understanding. Whereas other mental health treatment methods such as drug therapy, behavior shaping, and environmental manipulation may imply to patients that their problems are being understood, this implicit communication is only a peripheral feature of the method, intended at most to facilitate the psychotherapeutic effects expected from the drugs, behavior shaping, and manipulations. In psychotherapy, on the other hand, the communication of person-related understanding is explicit and constitutes the central feature of the method.[1]

Yet psychotherapy and most other current methods for treating emotionally troubled people are not mutually exclusive. Sophisticated use of somatic, reinforcement, and manipulative therapies usually includes some explicit communication to patients of where their difficulties appear to lie and in what ways the treatment procedures are expected to prove helpful. When therapists are communicating this kind of understanding to their patients and involving them as active agents in their treatment, they are providing psychotherapy. When therapists shift their

3

focus from the communication of person-related understanding to telling their patients what to do or altering their body chemistry or their environment, they are engaging in treatment procedures that are not psychotherapy, though they may prove psychotherapeutic. In actual practice, the treatment of people with psychological problems frequently combines aspects of psychotherapy with aspects of other psychotherapeutic methods. The more therapists concentrate their efforts on explicitly communicating understanding, the more appropriate it is to label what they are doing as psychotherapy; the less their focus is on communication, the more their work should be called something else.

Defining psychotherapy as the communication of person-related understanding, respect, and a desire to be of help raises the question of whether psychotherapy can be conducted by someone who has not been trained as a psychotherapist. For example, can the special kind of communication that constitutes psychotherapy take place between two friends discussing a problem together? If psychotherapy consists of specific kinds of behavior, it would be illogical to argue that these behaviors constitute psychotherapy when they are performed by a trained psychotherapist but not when they are performed by anyone else. Such an assertion would amount to saying that the same behavior engaged in by different people is not the same behavior. Hence, teaching and learning about psychotherapy as a set of behaviors intended to communicate a special kind of message requires accepting the possibility that these behaviors may emerge in any interpersonal situation.

However, to say that psychotherapy *may* take place inadvertently is not equivalent to saying that it is likely to do so. The likelihood of psychotherapy occurring between two people is in fact considerably enhanced if one of them is a trained and knowledgeable therapist who is following a planned procedure of intervention intended to be of help. Several differences between the professional psychotherapy relationship and other interpersonal relationships account for the greater likelihood that psychotherapy will take place in the former, when a trained professional and a troubled patient have agreed to work together on the patient's problems.

First, the training therapists have received allows them to understand another person's psychological difficulties more fully than any but the most unusually empathic nonprofessional, and it also provides techniques for communicating this understanding in ways the other person can comprehend and accept. Although naturally intuitive individuals may be keenly sensitive to the thoughts and feelings of others, they cannot be expected to translate their sensitivity into the communication of understanding as frequently and as consistently as individuals trained in and dedicated to doing so. Whereas professional therapists typically focus their sessions with patients on significant treatment issues, for example, inherently helpful but untrained people from whom others seek counsel are found to engage primarily in informal conversation and advice giving (Gomes-Schwartz & Schwartz, 1978).

Second, the professional psychotherapy relationship is not a mutual relationship, at least not in the sense that other kinds of ongoing interpersonal relationships tend to be mutual. In psychotherapy, the interests, needs, and welfare of the patient always come first; the therapist rarely asks for consideration of his or her interests, needs, and welfare in return. Unlike a friend or acquaintance, therapists do not inject their own problems and preoccupations into the relationship, do not ordinarily respond to anger and criticism by defending themselves or reciprocating in kind, and do not decide whether to continue the relationship on the basis of how pleasant they find the other person's company.

It is not that professional psychotherapists have no problems and preoccupations, or lack any feelings toward their patients, or fail to experience waxing and waning enthusiasm for a course of treatment. It is rather that their training helps them prevent such human reactions from interfering with their dedication to their task. Trained therapists focus throughout on understanding and helping their patients, and they bring their own feelings and experiences into the situation only when they believe it would facilitate the treatment to do so. By contrast, friends trying to help each other discuss personal problems are found to be much more likely than professional therapists to talk about their own ideas and experiences, and much less likely to express statements of empathic understanding (Reisman, 1986).

Third, there are certain formal commitments and constraints in the professional psychotherapy relationship that seldom characterize other interpersonal relationships. Therapists and their patients agree to meet at specifically designated times on a regular basis and to continue meeting as long as doing so serves the patients' interests. These meeting times are kept as free from interruption as the therapist is able to make them, and, except for chance encounters, patient and therapist do not interact at other times or concerning matters other than a patient's emotional difficulties. These arrangements put a single-minded stamp on professional psychotherapy—helping patients with their problems—that can rarely be maintained in other kinds of relationships between people.

To summarize this point, the training of professional psychotherapists, the nonmutuality of their relationships with their patients, and the formal arrangements they make for ongoing treatment maximize the prospects for their consistently communicating understanding, respect, and a desire to be of help. In interpersonal situations outside professional psychotherapy, on the other hand, the lack of training in understanding and communicating the meaning of human behavior, the absence of formal arrangements for working on a defined problem, and the needs of both parties for their share of being understood, respected, and helped minimize the likelihood that one person will consistently provide psychotherapy to the other.

APPROACHES TO PSYCHOTHERAPY

Although psychotherapy needs to be distinguished from the much broader category of treatment methods that may be psychotherapeutic, the task of doing psychotherapy can itself be approached in several ways. First of all, the communication by one person to another that he or she understands, respects, and wants to be of help is not limited to a two-person situation or any particular setting. It can be communicated by a therapist to several people together, as in group and family therapy, and it can be communicated by more than one therapist at a time, as when cotherapists work together with groups, families, or sometimes even a single patient. It can be communicated to children and adolescents as well as adults and it can be communicated in such diverse locales as clinics, hospitals, schools, and prisons.

Second, there is no single or uniform approach to how human behavior can best be understood and how this understanding can most effectively be communicated. Instead, there are a number of systems or types of psychotherapy based on somewhat different ways of conceptualizing normal and abnormal behavior, most of which fall into the broad categories of psychoanalytic and psychodynamic therapy, behavioral and cognitive-behavioral therapy, and humanistic and experiential therapy. In addition, there are numerous eclectic and integrative approaches to psychotherapy that utilize technical procedures derived from diverse methods or employ an overall formulation that combines concepts from diverse theories.[2]

Aspiring therapists contemplating the vast array of theories and methods that characterize the field of psychotherapy should find it helpful to keep in mind two extensively replicated and thoroughly documented findings in the psychotherapy research literature. First, there is little evidence to suggest that any particular school, method, or modality of psychotherapy produces generally better results than any other. Individual patients may be more amenable or responsive to one type of psychotherapy than another, as a function of their personality style and preferences, and some may derive unique benefit from certain technical procedures, as a function of their specific symptomatology. Generally speaking, however, across a wide range of patients and patient problems, the commonly used psychotherapies are found to be roughly equivalent in their behavioral outcomes (Lambert & Bergin, 1992, 1994; Luborsky, Singer, &

Luborsky, 1975; Norcross, 1988; Shapiro & Shapiro, 1982; Smith, Glass, & Miller, 1980).

Second, there is considerable evidence to indicate that the major approaches to psychotherapy are generally beneficial and prove substantially more helpful to people with psychological problems than receiving no treatment or a placebo intervention. Not everyone is helped by psychotherapy, and close to 10% of patients are found to deteriorate during the course of treatment. However, the data show that the average person treated with psychotherapy is better off than 80% of no-treatment control participants in research studies, and there is good reason to believe that patients who improve in psychotherapy tend to maintain their improvement for extended periods (Lambert & Bergin, 1992, 1994; Lipsey & Wilson, 1993; Seligman, 1995; Shadish et al., 1997; Whiston & Sexton, 1993). The general effectiveness of psychotherapy has been amply demonstrated for children and adolescents as well as for adult patients (Kazdin, 1990; Weisz & Weisz, 1993), and there is little basis for challenging the following conclusion offered by Lambert (1991) in introducing a comprehensive review of programmatic research studies in psychotherapy: "So strong is the evidence favoring the general effectiveness of therapy that this question is no longer of interest in many psychotherapy studies" (p. 2).

With this information about the general equivalence and effectiveness of diverse psychotherapies in hand, therapists should be wary of parochial assertions that one form of psychotherapy is inherently superior to others or has a monopoly on the truth. Although ever an advocate for his own preferred methods, S. Freud (1904/1953e) appears to have anticipated an ecumenical spirit when he expressed the following opinion: "There are many ways and means of practicing psychotherapy. All that lead to recovery are good" (p. 259). As matters have turned out, the comparable results demonstrated by many different approaches in psychotherapy have in fact led in contemporary times to an increasingly open exchange of ideas among adherents to different schools of thought, enhancement of cross-disciplinary collaboration, and the emergence of important new lines of pantheoretical conceptualization and research.[3]

As noted in the Preface, the text of this book addresses psychotherapy primarily from a psychodynamic perspective but stresses principles that are applicable to numerous other approaches to psychotherapy as well. These psychodynamic principles are relevant to any form of therapy that is intended at least in part to help people expand their self-awareness and to utilize the patient-therapist relationship toward this end. Significant in this regard is that diverse schools of psychotherapy demonstrate numerous similarities in the general atmosphere and sense of purpose they create and in aspects of the treatment relationship they promote, and there is broad agreement that both an adequately conducive atmosphere and appropriately employed technical procedures play a part in promoting positive change in psychotherapy.[4] Accordingly, the principles of psychotherapy presented in this book concern ways of employing both a positive treatment relationship and specific methods of intervention to achieve the goals of treatment.

GOALS OF PSYCHOTHERAPY

The goals of psychotherapy are to relieve patients' emotional distress, assist them in finding solutions to problems in their lives, and help them modify personality characteristics and behavior patterns that are preventing them from realizing their potential for productive work and rewarding interpersonal relationships. In terms similar to these, Strupp (1996b), refers to psychotherapy as "the use of a professional relationship for the relief of suffering and for personal growth" (p. 1017). There are many possible routes to such goals, including treatment procedures other than psychotherapy and fortuitous life experiences that improve a person's emotional state and expand his or her opportunities to find self-fulfillment. As noted, the defining characteristic of psychotherapy as a route to symptom relief and positive personality and behavior change is helping people understand themselves better as a vehicle for pursuing these goals.

At times, the methods of psychotherapy have been confused with its goals, leading to the misperception that this form of treatment is focused on helping people understand themselves to the neglect of adequate attention to how well they are adapting to the demands of their everyday lives. Increased patient self-understanding promoted by effective therapist communication is the means by which successful psychotherapy proceeds, but it is not a goal of the treatment. Insight in psychotherapy is merely the means to the end of improved adaptation sought by the patient, and insight in the absence of symptom relief and positive behavior change should not be considered a satisfactory treatment outcome. Enhanced self-understanding without improved adaptation indicates either (a) that the insights achieved have not been relevant to the patient's needs and problems or (b) that certain resistances to behavior change remain to be identified and understood. In either case, further or more incisive treatment is indicated, and the patient may require a different therapist or a different form of therapy.

The goals of psychotherapy are discussed in more detail in Chapter 12, which deals in part with identifying when an appropriate termination point has been reached. The following three chapters in Part One examine further the three central elements of psychotherapy: the patient who comes for help, the therapist who attempts to provide this help, and the treatment process to which both of them commit themselves.

NOTES

1. This approach to defining psychotherapy and distinguishing it from the broader category of what may be therapeutic is elaborated by Reisman (1971) in *Towards the Integration of Psychotherapy*. Reisman's careful synthesis of relevant considerations provides an excellent guide to the essential nature of psychotherapy. As more recently reviewed by Zeig and Munion (1990), there exists a vast array of definitions and perspectives on the nature of psychotherapy. The particular definition offered here, with its focus on the communication of person-related understanding, shares much in common with contemporary definitions proposed by Garfield (1995, Chapter 1), Marmor (1990), Strupp and Butler (1990), and Wolberg (1988, Chapter 1).

2. Descriptions and comparative reviews of approaches to psychotherapy are provided by Bergin and Garfield (1994a, Chapters 10–12); Bongar and Beutler (1995); Dobson (1988); Freedheim (1992, Chapters 4–8, 17–20); Gurman and Messer (1995); Hersen, Kazdin, and Bellack (1991, Chapters 28–33); Kuehlwein and Rosen (1993); Lietaer, Rombauts, and Van Balen (1990); Mahoney (1995); Mahrer (1996); Messer and Warren (1995); Mitchell and Black (1995); Stricker and Gold (1993, Chapters 5–11); Turner, Calhoun, and Adams (1992); Wachtel and Messer (1997); and Wallerstein (1995).

3. This historical development and its implications for an integrated theory of psychotherapy are reviewed by Beitman, Goldfried, and Norcross (1989) and Castonguay and Goldfried (1994).

4. Threads of communality running through many different approaches to psychotherapy as well as differences among them have been widely reviewed and discussed by such authors as Arnkoff, Victor, and Glass (1993); Beitman (1987, 1992); Garfield (1995, Chapter 6); Greencavage and Norcross (1990); Miller, Duncan, and Hubble (1997); Orlinsky and Howard (1987); Weinberger (1993); and I. Weiner (1991).

CHAPTER 2

The Patient

THERAPISTS SHOULD not assume that people who consult them know what psychotherapy consists of, are prepared to undertake it, and should receive it. Far from being assumed, these matters need to be explored before initiating psychotherapy. For all prospective patients, it is important to determine how, why, and with what preconceived notions they have come; the hopes and fears they bring into the treatment situation; and the implications of their personal characteristics for their likelihood of benefiting from psychotherapy.

HOW PEOPLE COME TO PSYCHOTHERAPY

People come to psychotherapy primarily on referral from a physician, an agency or organization in the community, or as self-referred. Some physician-referred patients have specifically asked their doctor for help with a personal or psychological problem, whereas others have presented somatic complaints that the physician considers to have a psychogenic component. Patients who come self-referred sometimes have decided entirely on their own to seek psychotherapy, but more commonly they have come to this conclusion after discussing a problem or concern with someone close to them, such as a spouse, clergyperson, or friend.

Community agencies and organizations that frequently refer people for psychotherapy include family service centers, welfare programs, schools, courts, and places of business. Agency and organization referrals often bring people to psychotherapy on something less than a voluntary basis. Widespread public recognition and acceptance of psychotherapy has made seeing a psychotherapist a common condition of receiving a suspended sentence following a criminal conviction, being allowed to return to school after a suspension or expulsion, continuing to receive public assistance, or retaining a job or position of trust subsequent to some episode of inappropriate conduct.

Such involuntary entry into psychotherapy is less immediately apparent in physician-referred and self-referred patients than among people referred by agencies, but it nevertheless occurs. For example, a married person may insist that his or her spouse enter psychotherapy as a condition of continuing their marriage, and a physician may prescribe psychological treatment as a requirement of continuing to serve as the patient's primary health care provider. These types of involuntary entry into psychotherapy do not preclude successful treatment, but whether people are coming voluntarily or under duress can influence their response to psychotherapy. Determining the conditions under which patients come to psychotherapy therefore needs to be included in their initial evaluation for treatment, as is elaborated in Chapter 5.

WHY PEOPLE COME TO PSYCHOTHERAPY

However people come to psychotherapy, they come for many different reasons. Some are troubled by distressing symptoms, such as anxiety, depression, phobias, compulsions, or difficulty thinking clearly. Some are experiencing problems in living, such as work inhibition, school failure, marital discord, or social isolation. Some feel generally dissatisfied with their lives or disappointed with themselves for not having become the kind of person they would like to be. These common reasons for seeking psychotherapy on a voluntary basis parallel the major goals of psychotherapy identified in Chapter 1: symptom relief, problem resolution, and life satisfaction enhancement.

Despite sharing one or more of these common concerns, prospective patients vary considerably in the extent of their psychological distress, and some consult a psychotherapist for reasons other than being particularly troubled. Relatively untroubled people seek psychotherapy on occasion out of curiosity about what it is like, or because they regard being in psychotherapy as a status symbol or "an in thing to do," or believe that psychotherapy can make their already productive and rewarding life style an even better one. People in training to become therapists often enter treatment as a consequence of being required or encouraged to experience psychotherapy firsthand from the perspective of being a patient. Nevertheless, there is no basis in fact to the presumption that psychotherapy is a self-indulgent luxury for people who do not in reality have many problems. To the contrary, survey data reported by Olfson and Pincus (1994) indicate that users of psychotherapy, compared with the general population, have more health problems and higher rates of work inhibition.

As an additional possibility, people may come to psychotherapists not because they want to become engaged with them in some way, but because they do *not* want psychotherapy. These are people who look to the therapist not for help with psychological problems, but instead for absolution that they have no significant psychological problems or that whatever problems they have are being caused by other people or by environmental circumstances. Prospective patients who want to be told they do not need help are very often people for whom psychotherapy has been mandated. Armed with a therapist's clean bill of health, they could then report to their referring probation officer, school official, or spouse, "I'm all better now" or "See, it's not my problem, it must be yours."

Sometimes, a psychotherapist's most appropriate response to an involuntary patient will be to indicate no need for treatment, while at other times initially unmotivated patients can and should be helped to undertake therapy addressing their psychological problems. To proceed effectively in either of these directions, therapists must first ascertain why a particular person has come to see them.

PRECONCEIVED NOTIONS BROUGHT TO PSYCHOTHERAPY

Except for psychotherapists themselves and patients who have previously been in psychotherapy, most people arrive at a therapist's office with limited information and many preconceived notions about what to expect. Self-referred patients are particularly likely to be uninformed, unless they have been briefed by a friend or spouse who has been in psychotherapy. Even without such briefings, however, self-referred patients rarely come without preconceptions, although they may deny having any prior knowledge about psychotherapy. With the visibility of psychotherapy in the movies, on television, and in magazines and books, very few people remain innocent of at least literary or theatrical versions of what transpires between patients and therapists.

Among people referred for psychotherapy by a physician, agency, or organization, many are likely to have been prepared by some discussion of their need for psychological treatment. Patients referred in these ways do not necessarily come better informed about psychotherapy than patients who are self-referred, however. Referring persons may have reservations about psychotherapy or know very little about it themselves, and their preparation may consequently provide a potential patient with little useful information. Additionally, in their efforts to encourage the patient to accept a referral for psychotherapy, referring persons may foster misconceptions about how rapid, painless, and curative the treatment process is.

The preconceived notions people bring to psychotherapy usually include expectations of what the treatment will consist of and what it will accomplish. Some patients come expecting to talk about themselves and be listened to, whereas others expect to be medicated, hypnotized, advised on how to lead a better life, or presented with a detailed analysis of their psychological makeup. Some patients anticipate that psychotherapy will be an ongoing process involving regular sessions for some indefinite period of time, whereas others anticipate that a few visits will meet their needs. Some patients come to psychotherapy expecting it to relieve them of distressing symptoms, whereas others expect it to help them understand themselves better.

As a further set of varying preconceived notions, some people approach a first visit with the expectation that they are entering psychotherapy and will continue to work with that therapist; others view the initial sessions as an evaluation period to determine whether they should enter psychotherapy and, if so, with whom; and still others begin with no expectations regarding psychotherapy or the particular therapist, but rather see the first meeting solely as a diagnostic consultation for the benefit of a referring physician or agency. Like the how and why of a patient's coming to psychotherapy, all such notions about it need to be explored before undertaking treatment, particularly since success in psychotherapy depends in part on congruity between what patients expect and how their therapist plans to treat them (see Chapter 5).

HOPES AND FEARS ON BEGINNING PSYCHOTHERAPY

People rarely enter psychotherapy without mixed feelings about doing so. Even highly motivated patients often have some reservations about undergoing psychological treatment, and even involuntary patients usually harbor some interest in the possibility of being helped. Such ambivalent attitudes are seldom expressed in the early stages of psychotherapy, at least not spontaneously. Highly motivated patients hesitate to air their reservations for fear of diminishing the therapist's interest in working with them, and involuntary patients resist giving others the satisfaction of knowing that they see any possibility of benefiting from psychotherapy.

What most patients hope for when they begin talking to a psychotherapist is to feel better as soon as possible. Consistent with the basic reasons why people come to psychotherapy, "feeling better" for some means relief from specific symptoms, for some it means resolution of certain problems, and for others it means achieving a greater sense of self-satisfaction and purpose in life. Whatever "feeling better" means, it is a hope shared alike by motivated patients and by those who come to psychotherapy under duress and deny (at least initially) any symptoms, problems, or shortcomings. That other people regard involuntary patients as needing psychological help can be taken as presumptive evidence that their life circumstances are causing them difficulty. Psychotherapy may not be a means of improving these circumstances, but involuntary patients certainly can (and do) hope it might be.

As for feeling better quickly, almost all patients who enter psychotherapy hope for rapid or magical improvement. Even those who recognize that a satisfactory outcome usually requires months or even years of work may still feel disappointed when the first few sessions do not produce noticeable change. Additionally, many people begin psychotherapy with the hope that it will solve all their emotional problems completely and permanently. When therapists appreciate that their patients are likely to have such hopes, whether expressed or not, they are better prepared to discuss with them the goals of the treatment and its possible outcomes.

Patients' fears may be less apparent than their hopes when they consult a psychotherapist, but apprehension in some form or other is almost certain to be present. Some patients are afraid of being considered crazy or dangerous and put in a hospital. Some fear being embarrassed and humiliated about revealing their innermost secrets to a total stranger. Some are fearful of learning terrible things about themselves or their past that they were better off not knowing. Some are concerned that entering psychotherapy will undermine their independence as a person, interfere with their creativity, or change them and their life in other undesirable ways. And many people, in contrast to those who see psychotherapy as a status symbol, worry about the social stigma of being a "mental" patient.[1]

Concerns about being crazy, bad, or too dependent put voluntary patients in a particularly difficult bind when they come for a first meeting with a therapist. On the one hand, they are motivated to put their best foot forward and to demonstrate that they are sane, competent, and worthwhile people capable of managing their own affairs. On the other hand, they are motivated to reveal enough of their emotional problems to ensure that the therapist will recognize and respond to their need for help. An accurate assessment of a potential patient's current status and need for help accordingly depends on the therapist's sensitivity to the influence that such conflicting motivations may have on how patients present themselves in an initial visit.

PATIENT CHARACTERISTICS
AFFECTING OUTCOME

In earlier times, considerable attention was paid to selecting patients for psychotherapy and developing criteria for identifying "good candidates" for treatment. The search for acceptable psychotherapy patients has typically involved the presumption that most failures in treatment can be laid at the patient's doorstep. Presently, however, clinicians generally recognize that most types of people can be helped by psychotherapy and that a diverse repertoire of demonstrably effective methods is available for providing this kind of help. Accordingly, therapists should forsake selecting patients for psychotherapy in favor of choosing treatment techniques that are suited to each patient's needs and capacities. Patients for whom an indicated treatment approach does not fall within the therapist's competence or interests should be referred to a colleague better prepared to conduct the appropriate therapy. People seeking help should not be obliged to suit the preferences of any one therapist or fit the mold of any particular form of treatment. They should instead have access to a wide range of treatment methods and therapists qualified to apply them.

Nevertheless, clinical and research studies summarized by Lambert (1991) and Stricker (1995a) indicate (a) that failures in psychotherapy are not the property of any particular approach or individual practitioner and (b) that patients who do poorly in one form of therapy usually do poorly in other types of treatment as well. As these findings suggest, the personal characteristics that patients bring into the treatment situation have a substantial bearing on psychotherapy outcome. Numerous contributors to the psychotherapy literature argue in fact that the personality style of patients and the way they approach and participate in psychotherapy are the most potent determinants of whether and how they change in response to various types of intervention. Commonly suggested as being next in importance are the nature of the relationship patients form with their therapist and the technical procedures that are employed in their treatment.[2]

The nature of the psychotherapy relationship is partly in the hands of therapists to determine, and the techniques they employ are solely theirs to select. These aspects of how therapists should conduct themselves in treatment sessions occupy most of the following chapters. To conclude the present consideration of patient characteristics associated with change in psychotherapy, the following discussion identifies some qualities in people that are generally related to outcome, some qualities that are occasionally related to outcome, and some that are generally unrelated to outcome.

CHARACTERISTICS GENERALLY RELATED TO OUTCOME

Available data indicate that the following three patient characteristics can be expected to increase a person's likelihood of benefiting from psychotherapy:

1. *The patient comes to psychotherapy with reasonably intact personality integration but a high level of subjectively felt distress.* Clinical observations and research studies have documented that the patients who are most likely to improve in psychotherapy are those whose personality functioning is the most adequate to begin with. Psychological good health and abundant ego strength predict improvement in psychotherapy, whereas initial severity of disturbance is linked with less positive outcome. Although limited personality resources do not necessarily preclude successful psychotherapy, they place special demands on the quality of the treatment and the skill of the therapist to achieve a good result.

Along with being psychologically healthy in general, patients profit most from psychotherapy when they are experiencing emotional distress in relation to current events in their lives. Within limits, the more anxious and upset people are when they enter psychotherapy, the more likely they are to continue in it, the sooner they are likely to respond to it, and the more benefit they are likely to receive from it.[3] Felt distress is one of three patient characteristics most widely regarded as common factors promoting change in all forms of psychotherapy (Greencavage & Norcross, 1990); the other two are patient motivation and expectation of change, which are discussed next.

Before proceeding, however, it should be noted that the implications of adequate personality functioning for positive outcome in psychotherapy have sometimes been taken to mean that psychotherapy works best with patients who need it least, or that the ideal candidate for psychotherapy is someone who has no psychological problems at all. If given credence, such ill-conceived impressions can jeopardize the status of psychotherapy as a necessary and valuable form of treatment for distressed people and as a legitimate health cost. The absurdity of thinking about psychotherapy patients in this way is apparent in an analogy to surgical patients: Those who are in the best general physical condition enjoy the best prospects for an uncomplicated recovery, assuming they need the surgical treatment, and the prognosis for someone who does not need surgery is an irrelevant consideration. Prognosis in psychotherapy must similarly distinguish between generalized personality disturbance and specific psychological problems. The people who will profit most from psychotherapy are those who need and want it because they are having problems in their lives but have nevertheless been able to continue functioning reasonably well. Moreover, there is ample evidence that psychotherapy can bring positive changes to the lives of most patients even among those with serious mental illnesses that have run a chronic or recurrent course and required hospitalization (see

Coursey, Keller, & Farrell, 1995; Karon & Vandenbos, 1981; Scott & Dixon, 1995; Stone, Albert, Forrest, & Arieti, 1983).

2. *The patient is motivated to receive psychotherapy, hopes to change how he or she is feeling or behaving, and expects that the treatment will help to accomplish this change.* Considerable evidence has accumulated to demonstrate that the more positive the attitudes and expectations with which patients enter and pursue psychotherapy, the more likely they are to benefit from it. Most experienced clinicians accordingly regard it as an important task of the therapist to nourish expectations of receiving help and to provide success experiences in the treatment that sustain these hopes. Even before they attempt to have an impact on their patients, however, therapists can anticipate that those who have eagerly sought treatment and arrive on their doorstep already primed for an active collaboration with them are more likely to have a positive outcome than those who lack these indications of motivation.[4]

Although initially strong motivation, high hopes, and positive expectations enhance the likelihood of a patient's benefiting from psychotherapy, none of these is essential for a good response. The committed or involuntary patient, the pessimistic patient, and the skeptical patient can all benefit from psychotherapy if the therapist is sufficiently skillful to get them involved in and enthusiastic about the treatment process. However, because getting treatment underway is less difficult if therapists do not have to surmount any major obstacles to change, patients who come to therapy already motivated, hopeful, and optimistic will have better prospects for improvement on the average than those who do not.

3. *In therapy, the patient is a likable person with good capacity for expressing and reflecting on his or her experience.* Patients who are hostile and negativistic and who exude unpleasantness and distrust can make their therapist's task difficult and sometimes distasteful. Try as they may to prevent negative reactions to unappealing patients from influencing their conduct of the treatment, few therapists can succeed entirely in avoiding some anger or annoyance and concealing such feelings from the patient. Such negative reactions can diminish therapists' effectiveness as well as become apparent to their patients. Sensing therapist displeasure with them, patients who provoke negative reactions to themselves are consequently at risk for poor outcomes in psychotherapy (Arnkoff et al., 1993; Binder & Strupp, 1997; Freemont & Anderson, 1988; Garfield, 1994; Mohr, 1995). Conversely, the more therapists regard their patients as appealing and worthwhile human beings, the more readily they will be able to display toward these patients the interest and respect that, as discussed in

Chapter 3, contribute to a helpful treatment relationship. Likability tends to predict good outcome, then, because it increases patients' prospects for having their therapist work effectively and hold them in positive regard.

The capacity of patients to express and reflect on their experience is perhaps the most obvious of the patient characteristics associated with improvement in psychotherapy. Therapists' understanding of a patient derives from what the person is able to communicate to them; the more fully patients can express themselves, the more information therapists have to work with in the treatment. Patients' progress in treatment depends in turn on their being able to ponder what the therapist says in light of their own self-observations; the more fully patients can reflect on what is said to them, the better use they can make of the therapist's comments in pursuing the goals of the therapy.[5]

How well patients can express and reflect on their experience, together with their previously mentioned level of active and motivated collaboration, defines the quality of their participation in therapy, and there is reason to believe that the quality of a patient's participation may well stand as the most important single determinant of outcome in psychotherapy (Orlinsky, Grawe, & Parks, 1994). It is those patients who in high hopes cooperate with the treatment procedures, communicate openly with the therapist, and take on diverse aspects of the patient role who are most likely to benefit from and who benefit most from psychotherapy. As in the case of instilling motivation and involvement in an initially reluctant or unengaged patient, therapist skill has considerable bearing on whether and how effectively people who come for help embrace the patient's role. Therapist qualities that contribute to such skill are discussed in Chapter 3, and the subsequent chapters of this book are mostly concerned with technical proficiencies by which therapists can establish, maintain, and utilize a good working relationship to meet the needs of their patients.

CHARACTERISTICS OCCASIONALLY RELATED TO OUTCOME

Two additional patient characteristics occasionally help to predict improvement in psychotherapy, although neither carries the weight of the three generally predictive characteristics just discussed. First, people who have previously demonstrated competence in life situations tend to have relatively good prospects for benefiting from psychotherapy. Competence in this respect overlaps somewhat with intact personality integration, but it refers more specifically to what people have been able to accomplish in their lives. Other things being equal, people who have been successful in utilizing their talents and opportunities to achieve academically, vocationally, and socially are similarly likely to achieve good results in psychotherapy. This point is made by Dewald (1971) in the following way:

> The more an individual has had a general pattern of persistent effort in a goal-directed fashion, and of success in the various ventures he has undertaken, the more likely will he be to sustain his effort during the course of the treatment, and ultimately to achieve some measure of success. (p. 116)

Second, people with average or better intelligence and intellectual skills tend to derive more benefit from psychotherapy than those who are less well endowed. Especially with respect to the centrality in psychotherapy of verbal communication and exchange of ideas, facility with language and concept formation is likely to foster progress in this form of treatment (Garfield, 1994). However, this patient characteristic should be applied very cautiously in estimating prognosis in the individual case. Although there may be a modest positive relationship between intelligence and progress in psychotherapy, a high level of intelligence has not been found necessary for effective psychotherapy to take place.

CHARACTERISTICS GENERALLY UNRELATED TO OUTCOME

Generally speaking, demographic characteristics such as age, sex, race, marital status, and social class are unrelated to outcome in psychotherapy and bear little or no relationship to whether people will benefit from it. Of these, age, race, and social class call for further comment, because each has at times been proposed as a predictor of psychotherapy outcome.

Age

There is a slight tendency for younger patients to profit more from psychotherapy than older patients, presumably because they are less set in their ways, have made fewer fixed commitments and irreversible decisions, and can look ahead to greater freedom to reconsider their perspectives, realign their priorities, and point themselves in new directions. On balance, however, research findings provide little support for estimating patients' response to psychotherapy on the basis of their age (Garfield, 1994), and effective psychotherapy with older people is extensively described in the literature.[6]

Race

Attention to the psychological problems of minority groups has included concerns (a) that African American, Hispanic, and Asian American patients, especially those whose first language is not English, come to psychotherapy with needs and attitudes different from those of native English-speaking Anglos; (b) that new theories and methods are necessary to achieve therapeutic success with these patients; and (c) that favorable outcome requires patients' therapists to come from the same minority group as they do. Contrary to these concerns, however, most research findings indicate otherwise. The needs for which minority group members seek psychotherapy and the attitudes they bring to it vary on an individual rather than a culturally determined basis and are indistinguishable from the needs and attitudes of the majority population; current theories and methods, if appropriately tailored to meet the needs of the individual patient, are as applicable to minority as to majority group members; and therapists' race is relevant to outcome only to the extent that it influences their capacity to empathize with a particular patient and to sustain positive regard for him or her. Hence, as long as racial differences do not prevent their therapist from understanding them, appreciating their cultural context, and considering them a worthwhile person, patients' ethnic origins will not predict their likelihood of benefiting from psychotherapy.[7]

As this last observation implies, however, psychotherapy with minority group patients may founder if therapists, through lack of cultural sensitivity, fail to establish a good working relationship with them. Although minority group patients on the average are as likely as anyone else to benefit from psychotherapy once they become engaged in it, research reviewed by Garfield (1994) and noted by many of the authors mentioned in Note 7 indicates that minority group members are somewhat more likely to drop out early and spend less time in psychotherapy than patients in general.

Social Class

Traditional lore suggests that psychotherapy is a treatment of choice only for members of the middle and upper socioeconomic groups, whereas working-class people lack the necessary sophistication, introspectiveness, psychological-mindedness, and verbal capacity to participate effectively in psychotherapy. As a consequence, middle- and upper-status individuals have been more likely to be referred for psychotherapy and have been expected to do better in psychotherapy than low-status individuals (see Garb, 1997). Contrary to this view, however, research reviews past and present concur that no systematic relationship has ever been demonstrated between socioeconomic status and treatment outcome. Like minority group membership, lower socioeconomic status is associated with tendencies toward early dropout and brief treatment duration. In common with those from minority cultures, however, blue collar and economically disadvantaged patients who become engaged in psychotherapy profit from it just as frequently and just as much as patients who are financially and educationally better off, and there is no relationship in the United States between income level and use of psychotherapy (Garfield, 1994; Jones, Hall, & Parke, 1991; Lorion, 1973, 1978; Olfson & Pincus, 1994; Wierzbicki & Pekarik, 1993).

Once again, then, the responsibility falls to therapists, whatever their persuasion, to be sensitive to the context in which their patients live and work and to meet their needs in ways that engage them productively in the tasks of their treatment. Whatever patients' demographic characteristics, just as with respect to the quality of their participation in the treatment, therapists have an opportunity to provide conditions that enhance the likelihood of their progressing toward a positive outcome. In this sense, many of the patient variables discussed in this chapter are interactive with the nature of the treatment alliance the therapist is able to establish. The next chapter turns to therapist characteristics that contribute to this result.

NOTES

1. Kushner and Sher (1991), in reviewing treatment fearfulness, argue convincingly that concerns about being in psychotherapy are not fully appreciated by mental health professionals and constitute a barrier to people seeking psychological help as frequently as they should. Shay (1996) observes that men in particular may have some culturally determined aversion to situations such as psychotherapy in which exposure and intimate sharing are expected.

2. The critical importance of the patient's contribution to psychotherapy outcome is elaborated by Bergin and Garfield (1994b), Blatt and Felsen (1993), Lambert (1991), and Miller et al. (1997, Chapter 3).

3. Empirical evidence regarding the positive prognostic implications of psychotherapy patients being generally well integrated but also in acute distress is presented and reviewed by Garfield (1994); Kopta, Howard, Lowry, and Beutler (1994); Luborsky et al. (1993); Mohr (1995); Mohr et al. (1990); and Wallerstein (1986). Research with the Rorschach Inkblot Method has provided some valuable confirmation of both of these prognostic patient characteristics. Numerous studies have indicated that a high score on the Rorschach Prognostic Rating Scale, which is basically a measure of ego strength, is a powerful predictor of benefiting from psychotherapy (Meyer & Handler, 1997). As for acute distress, patients whose Rorschach protocols show low levels of manifest psychological disturbance on the Rorschach have been found to be more difficult to treat

and more likely to terminate prematurely than patients who initially give more numerous test indicators of current psychological upset (Colson, Eyman, & Coyne, 1994; Hilsenroth, Handler, Toman, & Padawer, 1995). In a similar vein, a direct relationship has been found between the extent to which patients entering psychotherapy report complaints of anxiety and depression on the Minnesota Multiphasic Personality Inventory-2 (MMPI-2), as measured by the Anxiety and Depression content scales, and the amount of improvement they show (Chisholm, Crowther, & Ben-Porath, 1997).

4. The classic work on the role of expectations in promoting positive change in psychotherapy was published by Frank in 1961. A third edition of this book is now available (Frank & Frank, 1991), and contemporary data concerning the therapeutic import of patient attitudes and expectations are discussed by Mohr (1995), Orlinsky et al. (1994), Seligman (1995), Weinberger (1995), and Whiston and Sexton (1993).

5. The capacities people have to observe themselves, reflect on their experiences, and become self-aware has frequently been labeled in personality theory and research as their level of "psychological mindedness." Researchers have found that low scores on measures of psychological mindedness predict early dropping out from psychotherapy, whereas high scores are likely to be associated with successful treatment (McCallum & Piper, 1997; Piper, Azim, McCallum, & Joyce, 1991).

6. For representative discussions of psychotherapy with older people, see Hinze (1987); Knight (1996); Knight, Kelly, and Gatz (1992); Nemiroff and Colarusso (1985); Teri and Logsdon (1992); and Zarit and Knight (1996).

7. Relevant concepts and research concerning the import of racial characteristics and ethnicity in psychotherapy outcome are presented by Acosta, Yamamoto, and Evans (1982); Aponte, Rivers, and Wohl (1995); Carter (1995); Casas (1995); Comas-Díaz and Greene (1994); García and Zea (1997); Holmes (1992); Mays and Albee (1992); Perez Foster, Moskowitz, and Javier (1996); Ponterotto, Casas, Suzuki, and Alexander (1995); Ramirez (1991); Sue, Fujino, Hu, Takeuchi, and Zane (1991); and Zayas, Torres, Malcolm, and DesRosiers (1996).

CHAPTER 3

The Therapist

PSYCHOTHERAPISTS COME from numerous different disciplines and represent diverse training backgrounds. The vast majority of professional psychotherapists are drawn from the specialties of clinical and counseling psychology, psychiatry, and clinical social work, although substantial numbers of marriage and family therapists, mental health counselors, psychiatric nurse clinicians, and pastoral counselors are also presently being trained to provide psychotherapy. How people from different professions become psychotherapists, the nature of the training they receive, and the impact on their lives of committing themselves to this line of work are reviewed by Guy (1987); Guy and Liaboe (1986); Henry, Sims, and Spray (1971, 1973); Kottler (1993); Murphy and Halgin (1995); Sussman (1992); and Wolberg (1988, Chapter 16) and will not be elaborated here. However, mental health professionals and the general public as well should recognize that psychotherapy should be provided only by people who are adequately trained to do so.

Observing that psychotherapy providers should be trained psychotherapists is not a gratuitous statement. Self-anointed experts in human behavior abound, and there is no shortage of people who consider themselves prepared by their own experiences to understand the problems of others. Moreover, psychotherapy can seem deceptively simple after hearing or reading a few things about it: Therapists just listen and give their impressions of what is being said, and patients get better. All too frequently, well-intentioned individuals who are interested in helping others fancy themselves as being able to do so, and charlatans intent on exploiting others hold themselves out as being capable therapists. Such fantasy and pretense jeopardize the well-being of prospective patients who seek psychological help without benefit of attention to the qualifications of its would-be providers.

Psychotherapy is not a benign procedure that either helps people or leaves them unchanged. Ample evidence indicates instead that psychotherapy can be harmful as well as beneficial to patients, and the manner in which therapists conduct treatment, particularly with respect to how often they make errors of omission or commission, has considerable bearing on the likelihood of a good or bad outcome.[1] Persons untrained in psychotherapy may fortuitously conduct interviews in a way that fulfills some of the necessary conditions for a good treatment outcome, and a troubled person may benefit just from talking with someone who listens, even if the listener has little inkling of how best to respond. On the other hand, as noted in Chapter 1, untrained people are unlikely to perform the salutary functions of psychotherapy as well or as consistently as a professional who has been trained to perform them, and it is reasonable to expect that someone who benefits from talking with an uninformed person would have derived greater and more lasting benefit from working with a knowledgeable psychotherapist.

These comments not withstanding, numerous studies seem to have demonstrated that nonprofessional people possessed of good interpersonal skills can in some circumstances and with certain kinds of patients be as helpful in a therapist's role as trained professionals.[2] Such accidental results may be heartening to those who would demean the importance of training psychotherapists. However, benefits provided by untrained people operating as therapists without any formalized conception of what they are doing or why contribute nothing to understanding the psychotherapy process, applying it in uniform ways, and teaching it to aspiring professional therapists. Moreover, as elaborated in the following discussion of what it takes to be a good therapist, contemporary data document that relevant professional experience can make a big difference in the adequacy with which therapists implement specific aspects of the treatment process.

THE ESSENCE OF THE GOOD THERAPIST

Just as considerable effort has been expended to identify the "good patient" for psychotherapy, there have been numerous attempts to define the "good therapist." The 1947 report of the American Psychological Association's Committee on Training in Clinical Psychology offered no fewer than 15 characteristics a psychotherapist should possess (Shakow, 1947). Holt and Luborsky (1958) later expanded this list to 25 desirable qualities in a psychotherapist, and most texts on psychotherapy since that time have noted at least a few essential requirements for being a good therapist. Although of some interest in the abstract, an enumeration of admirable therapist characteristics falls short of addressing whether and how these characteristics contribute to positive outcomes in specific treatment situations. In the same way as the good patient concept is relative to finding the appropriate treatment to meet a particular patient's needs, good therapists are those who prove helpful to the patients with whom they work.

Because psychotherapy is an interpersonal process, the essence of being an effective therapist is possessing interpersonal skills that promote positive outcome in treatment and the ability to display these skills in encounters with patients. Skillful psychotherapists create a helping relationship in which they foster improvement by communicating understanding and respect and by expanding their patients' self-awareness and self-determination. Having abundant interpersonal skills does not ensure capacity to display them in clinical situations, however. Individuals who are intuitively gifted in comprehending personality processes—which is probably true of great novelists and playwrights—may not be able to draw effectively on their sensitivity in the context of a treatment relationship, confronted with a troubled or disturbed person for whom they must bear clinical responsibility. This chapter elaborates the qualities that make psychotherapists effective, first with regard to the interpersonal skills they need to have and then in terms of factors that influence their capacity to employ these skills effectively.

POSSESSING REQUISITE INTERPERSONAL SKILLS

Successful therapists can create a climate in which their patients feel safe, secure, accepted, and understood. From the perspective of patients, this climate provides an interpersonal interaction in which they experience what Orlinsky et al. (1994) call "therapist affirmation" and Weiner and Bordin (1983) referred to earlier simply as "attention from the therapist." In effective psychotherapy, patients experience therapist affirmation and attention by having the opportunity to meet regularly with a professional person who listens to what they say, respects their dignity, and tries to help them. These aspects of a positive treatment climate are known to contribute to improvement in psychotherapy and to depend heavily on therapists' possessing and displaying certain interpersonal skills. Like the positive patient expectations mentioned in Chapter 2, such beneficial therapist qualities are frequently endorsed as a common factor that promotes positive outcome in all forms of psychotherapy.[3]

For research purposes, the requisite interpersonal skills of effective psychotherapists have frequently been translated into the three attributes of therapist *warmth,* therapist *genuineness,* and therapist *empathy.* A brief discussion of what these concepts mean provides some specific indications of how psychotherapists need to conduct themselves so as to create a climate conducive to treatment progress.[4]

WARMTH

Warmth is the means by which psychotherapists provide their patients an atmosphere in which they can feel relaxed, unthreatened, and appreciated for what they are. Warm therapists value their patients as people, regardless of any negative attitudes they may have about a patient's personal characteristics, lifestyle, or behavioral history; they unconditionally accept whatever their patients say or do as something that is part of them and hence worthy of being understood, even while recognizing instances in which legal requirements or ethical considerations may transcend the patient-therapist privilege, as in reporting apparent child abuse; they refrain from passing judgment on their patients' actions or assuming responsibility for their decisions; and they maintain at all times a friendly, receptive, noncontrolling, and nonpossessive stance that preserves the patient's dignity as an autonomous person. By valuing and accepting their patients, without judging or dominating them, therapists display the warmth that patients require to feel safe and secure in the psychotherapy situation and to shed reservations about becoming involved in it.

Expressions of therapist warmth can be illustrated in part by clarifying what warmth is *not.* Although it is through warmth that therapists communicate their interest in a patients's welfare, warmth does not mean sympathy. In responding to a saddening experience in a patient's life, therapists ordinarily should not say, "Oh, that's terrible!" or "I'm so sorry to hear that." Such expressions of sympathy imply some caring, but their warmth is limited by virtue of their presenting possessively the *therapist's* evaluation ("that's terrible") and the *therapist's* reaction ("I'm sorry") to the situation, as opposed to addressing the *patient's* thoughts and feelings. To display respect as well as caring, a warmer response to misfortune would be "That must have been very upsetting for you" (for an obviously devastating experience) or "It sounds like that was upsetting for you" (for a less obviously disturbing experience). These latter responses show the caring that conveys warmth while emphasizing in a nonpossessive way that the treatment relationship is focused on the patient's feelings and attitudes, not the therapist's.

Warmth also does *not* mean that therapists conduct themselves as passive, entirely benign figures who keep the treatment situation as free from anxiety as possible. The therapist's job is to help patients understand themselves better, and the quest for expanded self-awareness is not a painless pursuit. Warm therapists avoid threatening the integrity and dignity of their patients as people, but they do not shrink from challenging the rationality or advisability of a patient's thoughts, feelings, or behavior when it is appropriate to do so. It is a caring person who tries to understand and is willing to confront another person with actions and attitudes that are causing him or her psychological difficulty. Therapists who rarely make an effort to be challenging come across to their patients not as warm and accepting, but as aloof and uncaring.

What warm therapists do, then, is evaluate and challenge their patients' statements and actions when necessary, in an effort to be helpful. What they do not do is denigrate the patient as a person. There is considerable difference between saying to a patient, "That was a dumb thing to do" (which, if properly expressed at a propitious moment, can be a warm and constructive observation), and saying, "You certainly are dumb" (which is a personal attack that conveys no warmth and could be therapeutically effective only under very unusual circumstances). The concept of accepting patients without conditions, which Rogers (1951, 1957) referred to as "unconditional positive regard," means that the therapist respects the patient's right to be the person he or she is, but does not necessarily respect everything the patient thinks, says, and does.

Finally, although warmth should not be possessive, as it is if the therapist assumes responsibility for deciding how patients must feel and what is best for them, it cannot be impersonal either. For a therapist to say, "Here's what I'd like you to do" is caring but possessive, in that it strips the patient of responsibility for determining his or her own course of action. Although such a comment may serve the purpose of some forms of psychological treatment, especially in the case of severely distraught or marginally capable people who need such directive management, it seldom constitutes effective psychotherapy. Yet to convey warmth, therapists do need to inject themselves as a person into the treatment situation and use personal pronouns. Thus to say, "It seems to me that you didn't handle that situation as well as you might have" or "I think there may be something on your mind that you prefer not to talk about" expresses that the therapist, without intruding on the prerogatives of patients to do as they wish, is using his or her own observational skills and personal impressions in the effort to be of help. Therapists who confine themselves to impersonal language communicate an objectivity that patients often perceive as detachment and indifference.[5]

GENUINENESS

To derive maximum benefit from psychotherapy, patients must be able to present their thoughts and feelings in an open, truthful, and nondefensive manner. To some extent, patient candor is facilitated by therapist warmth, which promotes a sense of trust and security in the treatment situation. Beyond feeling safe, however, patients find it difficult to be open and truthful unless they perceive their therapist as relating to them in an open and truthful fashion. Therein resides therapist genuineness, which consists of engaging with patients in a direct personal encounter, rooted in honesty and free from artificiality.

For therapists, being genuine means simply being themselves, that is, being authentic people who say only what they mean and do only what is comfortable and natural for them to do. S. Freud (1915/1958d, p. 164) was emphatic that "psycho-analytic treatment is founded on truthfulness," and he warned that therapists who are caught in a lie by a patient can never again generate the level of trust necessary for that patient to confide in them fully. As part of being truthful, therapists must avoid trying to sound definitive when they lack conviction, or uncertain when they have a definite opinion. Except for those therapists who are consummate actors, their patients will recognize such discrepancies between what they are saying and what they think and will identify them as ungenuine individuals who are not to be trusted.

Patients also quickly identify when therapists are behaving in ways that are unnatural for them. Customarily somber therapists who decide a patient needs an additional show of warmth and force themselves to smile are being ungenuine. A forced smile, which most patients will recognize immediately, bears eloquent testimony to therapist insincerity, not genuine warmth. Warmth is meaningful only when it is expressed by people who are being true to themselves. Similarly, therapists who attempt to improve communication with a patient by talking in the patient's vernacular, when they cannot do so comfortably, will appear ungenuine. Anyone not trained in the performing arts who makes a conscious effort to use profanity, slang, dialect, pedantic words, or technical terms that are not ordinarily a part of his or her speech will struggle and falter in ways that communicate phoniness and pretense.

On the other hand, being genuine does *not* mean that therapists must express every feeling they have and disclose all their personal concerns. What it means is that any feelings therapists do express are sincere and congruent with their inner experiences, and that any concerns they choose to disclose represent a real aspect of themselves. Furthermore, although there are times when openness and self-disclosure by therapists may facilitate the treatment, instant intimacy can be as ungenuine as exaggerated distance from a patient. Patients have difficulty identifying the real person in therapists who hide behind a professional facade and never deviate from an impersonal stance; they will similarly see as unreal therapists who begin in a first session to describe their own personal life or express some innermost concerns or unresolved conflicts. Even patients who are prepared to be very open and hope that their therapist will be forthcoming as well know that people ordinarily need to get to know each other a bit before they share deeply personal experiences, and premature self-disclosure by their therapist will strike them as being unnatural and insincere.

EMPATHY

Empathy is the ability to put oneself in other people's shoes and comprehend their needs and feelings. In psychotherapy, empathic understanding consists of the therapist's special sensitivity to the meaning of what a patient says and does. Empathic therapists are able to perceive their patients' thoughts and feelings accurately and recognize what they signify both for what a patient is experiencing at the moment and also for what may lie outside the patient's conscious awareness. Theodore Reik (1948) captured the essence of empathy when he titled a classic book on therapist sensitivity *Listening with the Third Ear.*[6]

Therapist empathy serves the work of the psychotherapy relationship by facilitating the communication of accurate understanding that helps patients broaden their self-awareness and understand themselves better. Empathy can run aground on many shoals, such as misinterpretation of a patient's thoughts and feelings, failure to listen attentively, preoccupation with making judgments and giving advice, or excessive attention to the content rather than the meaning of a patient's verbalizations. Each of these errors represents a missed opportunity for therapists to empathize with their patients and help them amplify their self-awareness.

To be effectively empathic, therapists must be able not only to understand their patients but also to communicate this understanding in ways that patients can understand and accept. As with therapist warmth and genuineness, then, a gap may exist between what therapists recognize and what they are capable of expressing clearly and helpfully. Highly psychologically sensitive individuals cannot become good therapists until they learn techniques for establishing a good working relationship with patients and for helping patients share in the understanding they gain of them.

Research findings indicate that the effective therapist is one who is friendly, interested, natural, and understanding, whereas the less effective therapist is one who seems less friendly, less caring, somewhat stilted, and not very perceptive. To feel accepted as a person worthy of respect and to receive the undivided attention of a trained and insightful professional who is bringing his or her every skill to bear on their behalf rarely fails to foster patients' feeling better about themselves, optimistic about the potential benefit of their treatment, and enthused about participating in the work of the therapy.

Accordingly, therapist expressions of nonpossessive warmth, genuineness, and accurate empathy contribute to positive outcomes in psychotherapy, whereas therapist manifestations of aloofness, detachment, artificiality, and insensitivity limit the progress their patients are likely to make. Moreover, the positive impact of beneficial therapist qualities on the course of psychotherapy and the specific contribution of therapist warmth, genuineness, and empathy to patient improvement hold true in many different types of psychotherapy, for many different kinds of patients, and in both individual and group psychotherapy.[7] Because therapist effectiveness depends so heavily on interpersonal skills, Binder and Strupp (1997) and Stein and Lambert (1995) argue that more attention should be given than customarily has been the case to selecting students for professional training programs in psychotherapy in part on the basis of their interpersonal skills and including methods of enhancing such skills in the training they receive.

DISPLAYING INTERPERSONAL SKILLS

The capacity of therapists to display the interpersonal skills that contribute to good outcome in psychotherapy depends primarily on three factors: (a) the extent to which their training and experience have taught them how to communicate warmth, genuineness, and empathy to their patients; (b) the extent to which they are free from neurotic difficulties that interfere with their ability to respond to their patients' needs; and (c) the extent to which their interaction with a particular patient promotes their potential for being helpful to that patient.

TRAINING AND EXPERIENCE

As stated earlier, therapist skill makes considerable difference in psychotherapy outcome. Research by Luborsky and his colleagues (Luborsky et al., 1986; Luborsky, McLellan, Diguer, Woody, & Seligman, 1997; Luborsky, McLellan, Woody, O'Brien, & Auerbach, 1985) demonstrates that therapists differ considerably in how successful they are both in working with similar types of patients and in working with caseloads comprising a range of patient problems and characteristics. These wide differences in effectiveness are generally regarded by psychotherapy researchers as stemming from differences in therapist skill, especially skill in displaying facilitative personal qualities and managing the patient-therapist relationship (Beutler, Machado, & Neufeldt, 1994; Orlinsky et al., 1994; Strupp, 1996a).

This chapter began by pointing out that psychotherapy should be conducted only by people who are trained to conduct it. Being a warm, genuine, and empathic person provides a good basis for becoming an effective therapist, but this basis is only a beginning. To be fully effective, therapists need a thorough education in the nature of personality processes and extensive training in the techniques of psychotherapy. Only with a solid grasp of personality processes and a polished repertoire of technical skills can therapists make informed decisions about what they should actually do: when they should express empathic understanding and when they should they express warmth, for example, and how much of either they should express at a particular time for a particular patient, and with what words or gestures they should express it.

In contrast to what has just been said, a regrettably perpetuated myth holds that professional preparation plays little or no role in being able to conduct effective psychotherapy. Christensen and Jacobson (1994), for example, drawing on the research reviews mentioned earlier, conclude, "Under many if not most conditions, paraprofessionals or professionals with limited experience perform as well as or better than professionally trained psychotherapists" (p. 10). As elaborated by Beutler (1997) and Seligman (1996), however, the supposed research basis for this conclusion consists largely of studies that are misleading in two respects. First, these studies equate "experience" with the passage of time and consequently designate therapists as more or less experienced without adequate attention to the kinds of experience or training they have had during that time. Second, these studies measure outcome mainly in situations involving brief treatment conducted according to the specific guidelines of a treatment manual and provided to relatively well-functioning patients who have relatively few problems.

Despite persistent negativism in some quarters concerning the value of training and experience, broadly based studies representative of actual clinical practice have yielded abundant evidence that professional training and relevant experiences of therapists are positively associated with good outcome in psychotherapy.[8] The weight of evidence does indicate that therapists with relatively little professional preparation may provide as much benefit to patients as better trained and more experienced therapists in simple cases in which they follow a treatment manual and provide brief therapy after a more fully qualified clinician has evaluated the patient and determined that such treatment would be appropriate. In the real world of clinical practice, however, such cases rarely occur. Most psychotherapists deal most of the time with substantially distressed or dysfunctional people whose problems are multiple and complex, for whom a careful diagnostic evaluation must precede treatment planning, and whose treatment needs go beyond the provisions of any manual. It is in these cases that therapist experience and training make a difference and become important predictors of patient progress.

Research has also confirmed specific ways in which good training and relevant experience contribute to therapists being able to display beneficial personal qualities in treatment. For example, the more training and experience they have had, the more likely therapists are to be flexible in applying their skills as changing circumstances require (Tracey, Hays, Malone, & Herman, 1988); to be skillful in implementing complex therapy procedures that facilitate the patient-therapist relationship (Holloway & Neufeldt, 1995); to be able to avoid saying things to patients that they later regret (Brody & Farber, 1996); to be rated highly by their patients for their interpersonal skills (Mallinckrodt & Nelson, 1991); and to rate their own skill level highly (Levenson, Speed, & Budman, 1995). Of further particular interest, specific training in cultural diversity has been found to increase therapists' sensitivity, enhance their ability to display interpersonal skills, and contribute to their feeling competent in working with minority group patients (Allison, Echemendia, Crawford, & Robinson, 1996; Yutrzenka, 1995).

FREEDOM FROM NEUROTIC DIFFICULTIES

To conduct psychotherapy effectively, therapists must be free from neurotic difficulties that interfere with their responding openly and flexibly to the needs of their patients. To be free from interfering neurotic difficulties, therapists must first of all be keenly aware of their own personality dynamics, particularly what tends to make them angry or anxious, how they feel about the important figures in their life, and why they behave as they do in various situations. Only with a high level of self-awareness can therapists differentiate adequately between the implications of a patient's behavior and their own reactions to that behavior. Although therapists can often glean valuable information about what is going on in the treatment by pondering their personal thoughts and feelings during a session (as discussed in Chapter 11), they can do so only if they recognize that how they are reacting may not necessarily be warranted by what the patient has said or done.

Therapists who lack self-awareness tend to interpret what they observe within their own frame of reference, which can seriously handicap their efforts to help their patients understand themselves better. For example, a female therapist who has not fully resolved underlying gender role concerns about being a professional person may become angry at a male patient who tells her, "The suit you're wearing today looks a little mannish," and she may then proceed to interpret the patient's behavior as an expression of hostility. In doing so, she may miss a subtle indication that for some important reasons this patient is more comfortable with men than with women and wishes the therapist were a man, or at least more masculine, in which case his comment on her appearance was intended as a compliment rather than a criticism. The therapist in this example would have been better prepared to recognize the meaning of her patient's behavior if she had been able to avoid or at least understand her own anger in response to it.

In addition to preventing any underlying attitudes or unresolved conflicts and concerns from clouding their objectivity, therapists must also refrain from using a psychotherapy relationship to gratify inappropriate personal needs. Psychotherapists can appropriately seek and expect certain gratifications in their work, such as the opportunity to be of help, to learn more about human behavior, to be respected for their integrity, and to be paid for their time. On the other hand, if therapists feel compelled to bolster their own self-esteem by dominating or depreciating their patients, if they have sadistic needs that lead them to be cruel or dependent needs that lead them to curry favor, if they have sexual needs that result in their acting seductively, or if they have fears of failure that cause them prematurely to discharge patients who are progressing slowly, then their behavior is being governed by inappropriate personal needs that prevent them from giving the necessary priority to their patients' needs.[9]

The personality requirements for being an effective psychotherapist do not mean that competence graces only those who are paragons of psychological adjustment, free from any neurotic symptoms, eccentric preferences, or life problems. Rather, it means that whatever warps therapists may have in their personality and whatever adjustment difficulties they are having in their lives, these neurotic elements either (a) do not interfere with their objectivity and commitment to their patient's needs in the psychotherapy situation or (b) are sufficiently within their self-awareness and self-control for them to recognize and counteract promptly any such interference that may arise with their ability to comprehend and address their patient's needs (see Chapter 11).

Long-standing traditions suggest that therapists must undergo psychotherapy themselves in order to attain sufficient objectivity, commitment, self-awareness, and self-control to function effectively in their work. Postgraduate training programs in psychoanalysis and psychotherapy generally require a treatment experience, and surveys indicate that 75% to 85% of psychologists interested in psychotherapy have undergone individual treatment, although mostly for purposes of personal enrichment rather than relief of any symptoms (Guy, Stark, & Poelstra, 1988; Holzman, Searight, & Hughes, 1996; Mahoney, 1997; Mahoney & Craine, 1991). Nevertheless, any unqualified assertion that personal therapy is necessary confuses the goal of being an effective therapist with the means of becoming one. The goal is for therapists to be free from neurotic interferences with their work, and, for therapists whose effectiveness is hampered by neurotic difficulties, personal psychotherapy may be a necessary means of acquiring competence in their work. On the other hand, for therapists already prepared by their personal capacities and prior experiences to understand and meet the needs of their patients adequately, personal psychotherapy may be irrelevant except as an educational experience. Generally speaking, however, research findings have not yet demonstrated any consistent relationship between how well patients do in psychotherapy and whether their therapist has had any therapy (Clark, 1988; Garfield, 1995, Chapter 4; Greenberg & Staller, 1981).

THERAPIST-PATIENT INTERACTION

Whatever their level of training, experience, and freedom from neurotic needs, therapists rarely work equally well with all patients. Therapists can expect instead to be more sensitive to the difficulties of some kinds of patients than others and more interested in helping some kinds of people than others. In addition to learning in the course of their experience what types of treatment techniques they prefer and implement most comfortably, therapists typically come to recognize what types of patients and patient problems they treat most effectively. Even when therapists find it difficult to make such judgments about their clinical functioning, they should keep in mind that optimal psychotherapy outcome requires the matching of patients with therapists who can best communicate interest, understanding, and respect to them. In this sense, then, the interpersonal skills of therapists are dyadic variables that are influenced by the nature of their interaction with a particular patient as well as by their intrinsic qualities and the training they have received.

In fact, not only most beneficial personal qualities of therapists but also many of the patient characteristics associated with positive outcome in psychotherapy are interactive variables. As noted in Chapter 2, whether patients become active and motivated participants in their psychotherapy and expect to benefit from it depends in part on their therapist's ability to kindle their hope and nourish their involvement. Likewise, how well therapists convey nonpossessive warmth, genuineness, and accurate empathy in working with particular patients depends in part on how these patients conduct themselves in their treatment sessions and also some of the basic characteristics they bring into the psychotherapy.

As examples in this last regard, some psychotherapists work more effectively with certain age groups (children, adolescents, adults, the elderly) than others. Some achieve better results on the average with male than female patients, or vice versa. Some therapists have more of a flair than others for working constructively with patients who are angry, assertive, bombastic, and frequently in trouble because of their conduct; some therapists have more of a special talent than others for being helpful to passive, timid, quiet patients whose difficulties involve withdrawal and avoidance. These and other types of interactive differences do not mean that therapists cannot or should not treat patients for whom they have no particular flair or special talent. What these differences mean is that therapists need to know enough about themselves and their skills to distinguish among cases in which being a good therapist will come easy for them, cases in which they will have to be especially alert and work especially hard to conduct the treatment effectively, and cases they should refer to a colleague better equipped to respond helpfully to this particular type of patient or problem.

Despite these observations about the benefits of a therapist-patient match that promotes both patient and therapist contributions to progress in treatment, little success has yet been achieved in validating any specific criteria on which to base such a match. Efforts to match patient and therapist according to their gender, values, and cognitive style have not yielded any improvement in treatment results compared with unmatched dyads. The closest that research has come to yielding any dependable results in this respect is a suggestion that a moderate initial degree of similarity in values is associated with better outcome than patient and therapist being either very much alike or very different from each other in their values.[10] In the absence of data to amplify the specific bases on which most therapists are likely to work more effectively with some patients than others, all that can be said is that the match between therapist and patient is important to the extent that it influences the degree to which a particular therapist can communicate effectively with a particular patient.

On the other hand, a great deal can be said about how critically important the quality of the patient-therapist relationship is to treatment outcome and how essential it is for therapists to be skillful in fostering an advantageous relationship. Among numerous factors that have been put forward as potential sources of benefit common across diverse types of psychotherapy, the one most widely endorsed is the development of a "working alliance" (Greencavage & Norcross, 1990). Coined by Greenson (1965b) in the context of psychoanalysis and later elaborated by Bordin (1979, 1994) as a concept applicable to psychotherapy in general, the working alliance refers to (a) a mutual understanding and agreement between patient and therapist concerning the goals of the therapy, (b) a shared commitment to the treatment tasks necessary to achieve these goals, and

(c) a sufficient bond of attachment between them to sustain their collaboration in resolving strains that inevitably arise during the course of psychotherapy.

The working alliance thus constitutes an interactive process that, by virtue of its influence on the quality of both the patient's and the therapist's participation in a psychotherapy relationship, has substantial bearing on treatment outcome. With few exceptions, the stronger the working alliance, from the beginning through the end of treatment, the more likely patients are to remain in psychotherapy, apply themselves to it, and benefit from it.[11] As for the skills therapists need to foster an effective treatment relationship, working alliance theory amplifies the point made repeatedly in this chapter that merely possessing admirable personal qualities is of little avail in the absence of proficiency in employing them. Psychotherapy practitioners and researchers widely agree that a successful therapeutic alliance depends on the therapist's skillful selection and application of technical procedures and that skill as a psychotherapist consists in the final analysis of a salutary integration of beneficial personal qualities and proficiency in specific techniques for communicating warmth, genuineness, and empathic understanding (see, e.g., Addis, 1997; Jones, Cumming, & Horowitz, 1988; Strupp, 1995).

As defined in Chapter 1, psychotherapy consists of the communication of understanding, respect, and a wish to be of help. Chapter 2 notes that the patients most likely to benefit from this particular form of treatment are those who are motivated to receive it, have reasonably intact personality integration but a high level of felt distress, and are likable people with good capacity for reflection and self-expression. The present chapter identifies the effective psychotherapist as one who can display high levels of warmth, genuineness, and empathy.

Yet it needs to be recognized that psychotherapy may not be *effective* psychotherapy. Psychotherapy is defined by the communication of understanding, respect, and a wish to be of help, irrespective of whether a patient benefits from receiving this communication. Whether psychotherapy will be effective psychotherapy in a given instance depends on (a) whether the patient's needs are suited for psychotherapy as opposed to some other form of treatment; (b) whether the match between the patient and therapist facilitates their being able to collaborate in forming a strong working alliance; and (c) whether therapists are proficient in judging how, when, and to what degree they should express understanding and warmth.

The proficiency of therapists in judging what they should try to communicate to a particular patient, when they should communicate it, and what words they should use constitute their technical skill. Following a brief overview of theory and process in psychotherapy in Chapter 4, the remaining chapters of this book concern the technique of psychotherapy and elaborate principles of conducting psychotherapy interviews during the initial, middle, and final phases of a treatment relationship. Some approaches to psychotherapy have focused largely on technical skill with little attention to the personal qualities of the therapist. Others have stressed the personal interest and warmth of the therapist as the major agent of change in psychotherapy and have minimized the importance of technique. As emphasized in the present chapter, however, most psychotherapy practitioners and researchers concur that effective psychotherapy requires a balanced combination of interpersonal and technical skills.

Technical mastery is useful in the hands of therapists who can foster a good personal relationship with their patients, a relationship that induces their patients to listen to, understand, and trust in what they are trying to communicate, no matter how painful the message may be. Without such a relationship, the most brilliant insights and deftly turned phrases fall on deaf ears. Likewise, therapists' interpersonal skills can be turned to their patients' fullest advantage only if they have sufficient knowledge of personality dynamics and treatment techniques to build self-understanding on the foundation of a solid working alliance. Good therapists are neither a good friend nor a good technician; they are a little of both, in a combination distilled from their personal qualities and their professional training.

NOTES

1. Research concerning the potential of psychotherapy to harm as well as benefit patients is discussed by Lambert and Bergin (1994), Grunebaum (1986), and Mohr (1995). For more extensive analyses of success and failure in psychotherapy, books by Chessick (1971); Mays and Franks (1985); and Strupp, Hadley, and Gomes-Schwartz (1977) are recommended.

2. For reviews of this work, see Berman and Norton (1985); Christensen and Jacobson (1994); Durlak (1979); and Hattie, Sharpley, and Rogers (1984).

3. For general commentary and data concerning the common prognostic significance of therapists' providing an accepting treatment climate, see contributions by Greencavage and Norcross (1990); Henry, Schacht, and Strupp (1990); Lambert and Bergin (1994); Orlinsky et al. (1994); and Strupp (1989). The psychotherapy literature reflects wide agreement with Strupp that "The first and foremost task of the therapist is to create an accepting and empathic context" (p. 718).

4. The significant role of therapist attention in promoting behavior change was first elaborated by Carl Rogers (1951, 1957) in the context of

client-centered therapy, and it was Rogers' formulations that spawned pioneering research on the concepts of therapist warmth, genuineness, and empathy. These formulations have continued over the years and to the present day to enrich understanding of the psychotherapy process and yield significant research findings (see, e.g., Eckert, Abeles, & Graham, 1988; Meissner, 1991; Patterson, 1984; Rogers, 1974; Stubbs & Bozarth, 1994).

5. For a classic contribution on the nature of warmth as a therapist quality and as a personality characteristic the reader is referred to Raush and Bordin (1957).

6. The role of empathy in psychotherapy is reviewed in detail by Bohart and Greenberg (1997) and elaborated from a clinical perspective by Berger (1987). Research reported by Lafferty, Beutler, and Crago (1989) documents that relatively ineffective therapists show lower levels of empathic understanding than their more effective colleagues, and that patients of relatively ineffective therapists are likely to feel less understood by their therapists than patients being treated by more effective therapists.

7. Empirical findings in this regard are reviewed by Beutler et al. (1994), Lambert (1991), Lambert and Bergin (1994), and Orlinsky et al. (1994). Orlinsky et al. conclude that more than 40 years of research involving hundreds of studies of process and outcome in psychotherapy have established several facts, with one of them being the following: "The therapist's contribution toward helping the patient achieve a favorable outcome is made mainly through empathic, affirmative, collaborative, and self-congruent [i.e., genuine] engagement with the patient" (p. 361).

8. The importance of good training and appropriate experience in promoting therapists' contribution to progress in treatment is elaborated by Beutler and Kendall (1995); Burlingame, Fuhriman, Paul, and Ogles (1989); Crits-Christoph et al. (1991); and Stein and Lambert (1995).

9. These examples of neurotically determined therapist behavior are presented mainly to illustrate psychological rather than professional aspects of poor psychotherapy practices. Further information about the kinds of stresses and personal problems experienced by psychotherapists, and about stress-reducing factors that help them continue to function effectively, is provided by Coster and Schwebel (1997), Mahoney (1997), and Sherman (1996). Nevertheless, when such ill-advised practices constitute incompetence or escalate to the point of patient abuse, mismanagement, and sexual exploitation, they violate the ethical standards of established mental health professions. All psychotherapists should be familiar with and mindful of the statutory and professional codes of conduct to which

they are responsible, such as the *Ethical Principles of Psychologists and Code of Conduct* promulgated by the American Psychological Association (1992). Comprehensive discussions of ethical issues in psychotherapy are provided by Bersoff (1995); Chodoff (1996); Conte, Plutchik, Picard, and Karasu (1989); Koocher (1995); Lakin (1991); Pope, Sonne, and Holroyd (1993); Smith and Fitzpatrick (1995); and Thompson (1990).

10. Reviews and research findings concerning patient-therapist matching are presented by Cavenar and Werman (1983); Garfield (1994); Hunt, Carr, Dagadakis, and Walker (1985); Kelly (1990); Kelly and Strupp (1992); and Mogul (1982).

11. Horvath and Greenberg (1994) provide a comprehensive overview of the working alliance concept and its relevance to diverse types of psychotherapy. Research findings documenting the contribution of a strong working alliance to treatment efficacy are discussed by Horvath and Symonds (1991); Saunders, Howard, and Orlinsky (1989); Weinberger (1995); and Whiston and Sexton (1993).

CHAPTER 4

Theory and Process
in Psychotherapy

T O FUNCTION effectively as psychotherapists, clinicians must work within the context of a cohesive theory of personality and an over-all conception of the psychotherapeutic process. Planned interven-tion always promises more productive results than accidental behavior, and therapists can do their job best if they operate with a set of principles that help them formulate what is happening in the treatment and what their next move should be. The principles of psychotherapy presented in this book are derived from dynamic personality theory, from the distinc-tion between uncovering and supportive psychotherapy, and from the complementary roles of strategy and tactics in conducting psychotherapy.

DYNAMIC PERSONALITY THEORY

Dynamic personality theory is most clearly represented by, although not limited to, psychoanalytic approaches to understanding human behav-ior.[1] Three elements of dynamic personality theory that are especially relevant to formulating and implementing psychotherapy are the notion of the unconscious, the notion of conflict and defense, and the notion of an experiencing self and an observing self.

THE UNCONSCIOUS

The notion of the unconscious refers to the fact that people can have thoughts and feelings of which they are not fully aware. Thoughts and feelings existing outside conscious awareness often exert powerful influences on a person's behavior, and some of the reasons people behave as they do may be entirely unknown to them.[2] For example, a man may find to his puzzlement and consternation that he is slacking off in his work just when he is coming up for promotion, and he may have no idea that his declining performance is being influenced by underlying concerns he has about becoming a more successful person than his father was.

Behavior determined by largely unconscious influences is not necessarily self-defeating, however. A woman who chooses a husband without realizing that he bears many resemblances to her father, whom she loves dearly, may make an excellent choice that she will never regret. On the other hand, the more people's behavior is determined by influences that they neither recognize nor appreciate, the more prone they are to develop psychological problems and have adjustment difficulties. It is precisely because they are not available for conscious consideration that the unconscious determinants of behavior are potential sources of emotional upset and problematic conduct. Sorting out their feelings and weighing alternative perspectives are the means by which people decide on courses of action that are consistent with their needs and tailored to realistic constraints. When important feelings and attitudes are not sufficiently conscious to participate in such decision making, then possibilities increase for people to behave in ways that are not fully satisfying to them or appropriate to their circumstances. Thus a woman motivated by unconscious fears of sexual intercourse may avoid having relations with her husband even though she consciously feels frustrated by the lack of physical intimacy in her marriage and concerned about her husband's losing interest in her.

The significance of what is unconscious can also be conceptualized by distinguishing between the *manifest* and *latent* content of behavior. The manifest content of behavior consists of what is readily observable, whereas the latent content consists of the underlying meanings of observable behavior. Distinctions between the manifest and latent content of behavior often become apparent in psychotherapy and provide useful information about a patient's motivations. For example, suppose a session with a female patient begins late because the therapist was unavoidably detained, and the patient arrives late for the following session with the explanation that she was delayed by heavy traffic. Perhaps this woman was in fact involved in a traffic jam and is not aware of any other reason for her being late. Yet the latent content of her tardiness could well involve anger at the therapist and an unconscious wish to repay the disrespect of having been kept waiting previously. In the patient's unconscious, there may be no such word as "unavoidable"; instead, from the unreasonable perspective of the unconscious, an inner voice may be saying to the therapist, "If you really cared about me, you would not have allowed anything to detain you, and you would have been on time." That such an expectation is unreasonable and should not be used as a measure of the therapist's interest and commitment illustrates how unconscious influences can lead people astray. Should such latent content be implicated in a late-arriving patient's actions, careful exploration will usually turn up some corroborating evidence. Thus for this patient, it may turn out that the traffic was really not much worse than usual, but the patient "somehow" managed not to leave for the appointment until 10 minutes later than she customarily does.

As this example shows, one of the ways in which psychotherapy proceeds is by making the unconscious conscious. By identifying the unconscious determinants or latent contents of their patients' behavior and helping them become aware of these underlying influences, therapists expand their patients' self-awareness. Expanded self-awareness allows people to subject their underlying needs, attitudes, conflicts, and concerns to conscious control, which then makes it possible for them to evaluate and deal with these influences more constructively than they could when they had little idea of what they were or how they were having an impact on them.

CONFLICT AND DEFENSE

Conflict and defense in dynamic personality theory refer to aspects of behavior that may be motivated more by needs to avoid anxiety than by the pursuit of self-fulfillment. This model of ineffective behavior presumes that people may have unconscious wishes that run counter to what is possible or what they consider proper, and that such conflicts may generate anxiety. Thus a man who is sexually attracted to other men but views homosexuality as unacceptable may become highly anxious in situations that put him in close proximity with other men, such as a locker room or an Army barracks. As another example, a woman who unconsciously hates her mother but consciously considers it the moral duty of a woman to love her mother may feel very uncomfortable in her mother's presence.

Because anxiety is a painful affect, people tend to defend against it by behaving in ways that prevent it from being directly experienced as subjectively felt distress. To continue with the preceding examples, a latently homosexual man with strong conscious aversion to homosexuality may defend against anxiety about his own masculinity by becoming a Don Juan, preoccupied with demonstrating his sexual prowess as often and with as many women as possible, or by becoming a hypermasculine individual constantly intent on displaying his strength, bravery, and capacity to be a "man among men." A woman with underlying hostility toward her mother may minimize the discomfort these feelings cause her by keeping away from her mother as much as possible (leaving the field) or by bending over backward to be kind and loving toward her mother (reaction formation).

Sometimes such defensive maneuvers succeed in easing the anxiety stemming from a conflict without creating serious new conflicts. At other times, however, a defensive maneuver may take the form of symptoms or maladaptive behaviors that are in turn anxiety provoking and cause adjustment problems. A man with a Don Juan complex may become distraught at being unable to settle down with and be satisfied with one woman, and a woman who is repressing hostility toward her mother and relying on reaction formation to present a loving facade may find herself getting a headache whenever she and her mother are together for an extended period.

Because the origins of their conflicts are unconscious, neither of these two people will understand why they are behaving as they are or experiencing the symptoms they have, but both are likely to want to live more comfortably than they are. The therapist's task consists of helping such people recognize the defensive quality of their behavior and explore the underlying needs or wishes they are defending against. Psychotherapy contributes to people bettering their lives by identifying and resolving concerns that have arisen outside their conscious awareness, thus increasing their potential for conscious control of their behavior.[3]

THE EXPERIENCING SELF AND THE OBSERVING SELF

In dynamic personality theory, people are viewed as having capacities to experience themselves and to observe themselves. Although everyone is capable of both types of activity, individuals vary in the degree to which their personality style favors one or the other. Some people are primarily *experiencers;* they do what they do and feel what they feel without much pause for taking stock of themselves. Other people are primarily *observers;* they ponder the implications of what they think and do without having much inclination toward spontaneous expression in thought or deed. Self-experiencing and self-observing exist on a continuum, neither end of which is conducive to good adjustment. Total experiencers are prone to impulsive, inconsiderate, and poorly planned behavior involving little introspection; total observers are subject to excessive self-evaluation and self-consciousness and a paralysis of action or reaction.

Psychotherapists need to have both experiencing and observing aspects of their patients' personality operable, and they need to be able to foster shifts between these portions of the ego as occasions demand. Patients who only observe themselves produce abundant reflections on their experience but do not report the kinds of spontaneous thoughts and feel-ings that offer clues to new or different ways they might experience themselves. Patients who only experience themselves produce abundant fresh material concerning what they are thinking and feeling but are un-able to participate with their therapist in reflecting on and searching for the meaning of what they are experiencing.

Progress in psychotherapy requires a flexible split between patients' experiencing self and their observing self, which is an aspect of personal-ity functioning originally described by Sterba (1934) as an "ego split." They must be able to relate what they are thinking and feeling sponta-neously and with minimal self-consciousness. Yet with their therapist's help, they must also be able to take distance from themselves, to sit back and look at their behavior as phenomena that can and need to be under-stood. Psychotherapy is in many ways a learning process in the sense that patients' progress is closely tied to their becoming knowledgeable about themselves. Experiencing oneself facilitates such learning, but for learn-ing to take place self-experience must be balanced by self-observation.[4]

UNCOVERING AND SUPPORTIVE PSYCHOTHERAPY

Uncovering and *supportive* describe two approaches to psychotherapy that differ in the degree to which attention is focused on unconscious deter-minants of a patient's behavior. In uncovering psychotherapy, which is also referred to as "insight," "expressive," or "exploratory" psychother-apy, the aim is to help patients achieve some reorganization or restructur-ing of their personality by helping them recognize and articulate their unconscious conflicts and concerns. In supportive or "suppressive" psy-chotherapy the aim is helping patients deal more effectively with their real-world problems without delving into their unconscious conflicts and concerns. Some uncovering with accompanying personality change may occur in the course of successful supportive psychotherapy, but such accomplishments are secondary to the primary intent of the supportive approach.

Despite this difference in aims, uncovering and supportive psychother-apy share many features. In both, the overriding purpose is to expand patients' self-awareness to allow them to enjoy a more comfortable and more satisfying life. Uncovering psychotherapy seeks to bring many pre-viously unconscious thoughts and feelings into a patient's awareness, whereas supportive psychotherapy focuses on increased understanding and control of thoughts and feelings of which the patient is already at least dimly aware.

Additionally, the course of both uncovering and supportive psychotherapy proceeds largely through interpretive comments by the therapist about what the patient says and does. These interpretations may point out connections between past experiences and current behavior (genetic interpretations), they may identify relationships among current events in the patient's life (here-and-now interpretations), or they may address aspects of the ongoing therapy process (resistance and transference interpretations). What distinguishes the two approaches is that in uncovering psychotherapy the interpretations more often pertain to patients' personality style as well as the content of what they are saying, whereas in supportive psychotherapy, therapists focus more exclusively on content without challenging a patient's personality style.[5]

To appreciate the implications of this distinction, therapists need to recognize that any interpretive comment they make constitutes a challenge. As elaborated in Chapter 9, interpretations suggest to patients some new or different way of looking at their experiences, and they accordingly always imply that the patient's current views are faulty or mistaken in some way. In uncovering psychotherapy, these interpretive challenges concern not only the thoughts and feelings patients express, but also their preferred style of coping with problem situations and the characteristic defensive maneuvers that define their personality style. In supportive psychotherapy, the patient's personality style is accepted as it is, and interpretations are concentrated on thoughts and feelings as they are expressed within this style.

To illustrate this distinction between interpreting or accepting a patient's personality style, consider an obsessive-compulsive man who describes in excruciating detail the pros and cons of a decision he is having difficulty making. In uncovering psychotherapy, the therapist may encourage this patient to step back from the decision for the moment and examine his style of decision making, which involves becoming so preoccupied with details that he is unable to reach a reasonable and acceptable solution. This intervention may lead to exploration of why this man needs to be so pedantically careful in dealing with his experience and from there to some resolution of the conflicts that have given rise to what is basically an obsessive personality style. Subsequently, then, this patient's characteristic ruminativeness should diminish, allowing him to make this and other decisions with considerably less vacillation than before.

In supportive psychotherapy with such a patient, the therapist would work instead within the context of this man's obsessive-compulsive style to help him make the decision that has been eluding him. The therapist might, for example, set up an orderly procedure for reviewing the pros and cons bearing on the decision and assigning them some relative weight, so that by increasing his capacity to differentiate among the more and less crucial considerations the patient will be able to reevaluate the choices open to him and arrive at a sensible and satisfying decision.

With respect to practical aspects of conducting psychotherapy, the distinction between uncovering and supportive approaches must be qualified in three important respects. First, uncovering and supportive psychotherapy constitute a continuum and not a dichotomy. Psychotherapy as practiced involves a spectrum extending from a very intensive, uncovering treatment relationship, as in psychoanalysis, to an exclusively supportive relationship; in between these extremes, there exists a broad range of limited or moderate insight approaches. How uncovering or how supportive a particular treatment approach is depends on the extent to which unconscious determinants of behavior are probed and the patient's defensive style is interpreted. Stated the other way around, therapists should decide how extensively to interpret a patient's behavior and personality style on the basis of how uncovering or how supportive they believe the psychotherapy for this patient ought to be. Without such judgments to guide them, therapists may err by flitting randomly between various depths of approach and thereby conduct a chaotic psychotherapy that poorly serves a patient's needs.

Second, uncovering and supportive approaches are not mutually exclusive. Because psychotherapy exists in a spectrum of intensity, effective psychotherapy usually combines efforts to help patients gain insight and efforts to provide them support. Psychotherapy proceeds most closely in concert with patients' needs when therapists operate with some sense of which aspects of a particular individual's personality should be uncovered and which should be supported. Schlesinger (1969) referred to planning in this way to help patients derive maximum benefit from psychotherapy as having a "prescription" for the treatment.[6]

Aside from not being mutually exclusive, prescriptions for some particular blend of uncovering and supportive methods may have to be altered from to time in the course of psychotherapy. During primarily uncovering psychotherapy, for example, circumstances may arise that call for supportive techniques. Patients faced with a crisis or situational difficulty in their lives may temporarily become too anxious or depressed to be able to step back from their distressing experiences and look objectively at themselves—the experiencing self at times of stress may become so absorbing and draining that little attention or energy is left available for the observing self. Should this occur, the therapist may have to suspend temporarily an uncovering focus in the treatment and concentrate instead on supporting the patient through his or her difficulty.

Patients may also experience minicrises during psychotherapy sessions that call for some support and reassurance from the therapist. In the course of exploring painful memories or disturbing impulses, a patient may become so upset that further uncovering at the moment will do more harm than good. In situations of this kind, therapists may find it advisable to stop exploring and comment on obvious and superficial aspects of what is being discussed, which is supportive by allowing patients to regain their composure and reestablish their defenses. Alternatively, the therapist might observe at such times, "I can see this is a difficult thing for you to talk about," which reassures patients that their therapist recognizes and cares about how distressed they are.

In other instances, patients who are being treated with a primarily uncovering approach may indicate that they cannot tolerate the anxiety it produces or that they are unable to maintain a productive balance between experiencing themselves and observing themselves during therapy sessions. Such developments usually mean that the patient's capacity to participate in and benefit from uncovering psychotherapy has been misjudged, and the therapist may then have to shift from a primarily uncovering to a primarily supportive approach for the duration of the treatment.

By contrast, patients whose initial capacities were underestimated or who have been helped to resolve a crisis situation that brought them for help may want and need their prescription for psychotherapy changed from primarily supportive to primarily uncovering. Therapists should anticipate that shifting smoothly from supportive to uncovering psychotherapy may be more difficult to accomplish than the reverse, however. Uncovering psychotherapy is primarily an *investigative* approach, whereas supportive psychotherapy is primarily a *giving* approach. For therapists to become less investigative and more giving is easy for patients to accept, but a therapist who becomes less giving than before is often experienced by the patient as depriving and rejecting.

For this reason, therapists who have initially treated a patient supportively and subsequently decide that an uncovering approach should be started will usually do well to refer the patient to another therapist. This will not entirely solve the problem, since patients who go through such a referral frequently complain to the new (uncovering) therapist that he or she is not doing as much for them and does not seem as interested in them as the former (supportive) therapist. By and large, however, the change from supportive to uncovering psychotherapy is still easier to accomplish when the uncovering therapist is a different person from the supportive therapist.

The third qualification that needs to be made in distinguishing between uncovering and supportive approaches to psychotherapy concerns the value that is assigned to each. Clinicians have at times fallen into the error of extolling uncovering psychotherapy as a thorough and effective

approach for patients who have many personality strengths, while denigrating supportive psychotherapy as a less potent and less desirable alternative for people who are not interested in or not able to tolerate
uncovering psychotherapy. Although more intensive therapy usually produces more change than less intensive therapy, research indicates that the
difference between uncovering and supportive approaches in the amount
of change they produce is less than is often supposed, and furthermore
that no particular kind of change is linked solely to either uncovering or
supportive therapy (Wallerstein, 1989). From a different perspective,
moreover, let it be said that effective psychotherapy should be defined not
by its brand name, but by how well it meets the needs of the patient. In
the abstract, no approach to psychotherapy is better or more desirable
than any other approach. For each patient, there is an approach that
promises to bè best and most desirable for him or her; for some, this best
and most desirable approach may be uncovering psychotherapy, for others
it may be supportive psychotherapy, and for still others it may be group
therapy, family therapy, or a form of psychological treatment other than
psychotherapy.

STRATEGY AND TACTICS IN PSYCHOTHERAPY

To conduct psychotherapy effectively, therapists need to operate with a
sense of both strategy and tactics. *Strategy* refers to the objectives they are
trying to achieve at a particular time, and *tactics* to the specific methods
they are employing to gain these objectives. Strategy may involve such
general objectives as helping patients talk more freely, assisting them in
recognizing the nature and origins of their maladaptive behaviors, or expanding their awareness of alternative ways of thinking or feeling. During a single interview or within a portion of an interview, strategy may
consist of more specific objectives, such as leading patients to recognize
some underlying feelings of inferiority they have or to realize that they
are experiencing anger toward the therapist. Tactics include whatever
therapists may say or do, including questions, assertions, interpretive
comments, facial expressions, or gestures, as a means of implementing
their current strategy.

Having a clear sense of their strategy and tactics means that, at every
point in the course of psychotherapy, therapists know exactly what they
are trying to accomplish and how they are trying to accomplish it. Strategy without tactics is an abstract conception of what psychotherapy
should be like without the necessary therapist operations to make it be
that way; tactics without strategy is a technical exercise that meanders
in the patient's psyche without fostering any systematic progress toward increased self-understanding. For therapists to want their patients

to achieve certain objectives but be unable to help them do so (strategy without tactics) is ineffective psychotherapy, because the objectives, no matter how correctly conceived, will not be attained. For therapists to say the right thing for the wrong reason (tactics with poor strategy) or for no reason at all (tactics with no strategy, as in "It just felt like the thing to say") is unpromising therapy, because it offers little likelihood of the therapist's being able to say the right thing at other times or in other situations.[7]

THE PROCESS OF PSYCHOTHERAPY

Although the actual course of psychotherapy varies greatly from one patient to another, there is a general sequential process in all psychotherapy relationships. The elements of this process may not always appear in the same order or with the same degree of importance, but some awareness of how psychotherapy may generally be expected to proceed aids therapists in knowing where they are in their work with a particular patient and mapping their strategy accordingly.

Psychotherapy begins with patients who come for help and participate with the therapist in deciding whether psychotherapy is the kind of help they should receive. This initial phase of the treatment relationship consists of (a) evaluating the patients' problems and what there is about themselves they would like to change; (b) assessing the patient's needs, motivations, and capacities for psychotherapy or for some other form of treatment; and (c) if psychotherapy is indicated, making a contract to proceed with it. The psychotherapy contract is an explicit agreement between patient and therapist about how their meetings will be arranged, what their respective roles will be in the treatment relationship, and the specific goals toward which they will be working.

Following a period of evaluation and assessment and an agreement on a treatment contract, psychotherapy enters its middle phase. The middle phase is usually the longest phase in psychotherapy, and it is the time when therapists do the major portion of their work in communicating psychological understanding to a patient. During this middle phase, therapists' major tasks consist of helping their patients talk, listening to and coming to an understanding of what their patients are able to reveal about themselves, and making interpretive comments that help their patients share in this understanding.

During the middle phase of psychotherapy, therapists can expect to encounter certain interferences with their efforts to listen, comprehend, and communicate understanding. These interferences or *resistances* constitute a paradoxical reluctance on the part of the patient to participate in the therapy. When resistance occurs, patients who are apparently eager to learn more about themselves and change their behavior become unable or unwilling to talk freely.

Resistances arise from a number of sources, including underlying reservations about being a patient or changing themselves (resistance to treatment), an entrenched personality style that is refractory to being challenged (character resistance), discomfort with a particular subject that is being discussed (resistance to content), and feelings about the therapist that a patient is reluctant to express (transference resistance). All of these forms of resistance disrupt patient-therapist communication, and therapists need to find ways of proceeding through or around them to continue making progress in the middle phase of psychotherapy. At the same time, however, these resistances can provide useful information about a patient's personality style, underlying attitudes, and sources of anxiety.

Transference, which consists of feelings and attitudes that patients experience toward their therapist, is a potential form of interference with patient-therapist communication that merits special comment. Psychotherapy seldom gets satisfactorily underway unless patients have some positive feelings toward their therapist, since such positive regard undergirds their willingness to talk freely and accept interpretations of their behavior. On the other hand, positive feelings toward the therapist, if they become strong enough, can motivate patients to want approval and affection from their therapist more than they want the therapist's help and understanding. Communication then becomes disrupted because patients report primarily what they think will find favor in the therapist's eyes and keep to themselves anything they expect the therapist might disapprove.

As therapy continues, patients also develop negative feelings toward their therapist, primarily for two reasons: first because therapists eventually frustrate their patients by not expressing the affection and approval they would like to receive from them, and second because negative feelings toward important people in the patient's life tend to be stirred up in the course of the treatment and directed, or *transferred,* onto the therapist. Negative transference typically disrupts the communication process by making patients feel angry or dissatisfied with their therapist, and hence unwilling to cooperate with the treatment procedures. Like resistance, however, both positive and negative transference reactions reveal a great deal about patients' inner lives and dispositions to adjustment difficulties, and they often warrant a central portion of the therapist's attention.

One additional interference with the communication of psychological understanding that may complicate the middle phase of psychotherapy stems from the therapist's attitudes. All therapists experience fluctuating positive and negative feelings toward their patients, sometimes in response to something a particular patient has said or done and sometimes as a result of events in their own lives that are affecting their frame of mind. Therapists need to recognize and control such *countertransference* reactions to prevent them from distorting their perception of a patient or adopting incorrect treatment strategies. At the same time, countertransference reactions can be utilized productively if therapists have sufficient knowledge of themselves to find in them clues to latent features of the patient's behavior that may have prompted their reactions.

Interpretation, resistance, transference, and countertransference are the main themes of the middle phase of psychotherapy. When the work of communicating psychological understanding has been achieved as much as is possible or was planned for, that is, when the goals of the treatment have been realized, psychotherapy enters a final phase of termination. Termination consists of reviewing the course of the treatment, tying up loose ends, and contemplating with patients what the future may hold for the patient with regard to personality functioning and life endeavors.

This brief overview of the process of psychotherapy indicates the ground to be covered in this form of psychological treatment. The chapters that follow consider in detail each of these aspects of the initial, middle, and final phases of psychotherapy, with specific attention to the strategy and tactics they require.

NOTES

1. For overviews of dynamic personality theory, the reader is referred to Barron, Engle, and Wolitzky (1992); Blatt and Lerner (1991); Karon and Widener (1995); Maddi (1996); and Westin (1990).

2. Contemporary views on the nature and implications of unconscious mental processes are elaborated by Bowers and Meichenbaum (1984); Epstein (1994); Horowitz (1988, Chapters 8–9); Power and Brewin (1991); and Shevrin, Bond, Brakel, Hertel, and Williams (1996).

3. The role of conflict and defense in shaping personality characteristics and contributing to adjustment difficulties has figured prominently in dynamic approaches to psychotherapy since the inception of psychoanalytic methods. S. Freud (1914/1957b) commented that the theory of defensive operations is "the cornerstone on which the whole structure of psychoanalysis rests" (p. 16). Current perspectives on conflict and defense and their implications for treatment techniques are provided by Beres (1995), Blanck and Blanck (1994), Brenner (1982, 1996), Busch (1995), S. Cooper (1992), Dowling (1991), Gray (1994), Pine (1990), and Willick (1995).

4. In pointing out that the concept of the observing ego has received less attention in the literature than it warrants, Gray (1994) and Glickhauf-Hughes, Wells, and Chance (1996) elaborate several techniques for helping patients improve their skills in observing themselves.

5. Numerous authors have delineated similarities and differences between uncovering and supportive psychotherapy and the technical implications of these differing approaches in phases of the treatment process. Recommended in particular are discussions by Dewald (1971), Oremland (1991), Pine (1984), Rockland (1989a, 1989b), and Werman (1984).

6. The notion of having a "prescription for psychotherapy" has remained viable as a practice guideline and is also reflected in a substantial literature on differential treatment selection. Representative books concerning this matter in general include contributions by Beutler and Clarkin (1990); Frances, Clarkin, and Perry (1984); and Goldstein and Stein (1976). McWilliams (1994) elaborates in detail how psychodynamic conceptualizations of patients' personality characteristics can help therapists choose and focus their style of intervention in ways that meet patients' individual needs.

7. Dewald (1996) discusses in further detail the complementary roles of strategies and tactics in conducting psychotherapy.

PART TWO

THE INITIAL PHASE
OF PSYCHOTHERAPY

CHAPTER 5

Evaluation and Assessment

T HE INITIAL phase of psychotherapy begins with a period of evaluation and assessment in which therapists learn something about a patient and decide whether ongoing psychotherapy seems indicated. Evaluation and assessment are followed by the formulation of a treatment contract, in which patient and therapist agree to work together in psychotherapy and make arrangements for doing so. A final aspect of initiating psychotherapy involves proper conduct of the interview, which consists of therapists helping patients talk freely and become engaged in the process of the therapy. The present chapter addresses the evaluation and assessment of prospective psychotherapy patients, and Chapters 6 and 7 consider the treatment contract and conduct of the interview.

EVALUATING THE PATIENT

The process of evaluating a prospective psychotherapy patient takes place in four steps: (a) identifying the presenting problems, (b) exploring the background of these problems, (c) beginning to understand the patient as a person, and (d) arriving at an adequate working formulation.

IDENTIFYING THE PRESENTING PROBLEM

The first step in evaluating prospective psychotherapy patients consists of identifying the problems that have led them to seek help. Many patients facilitate this task by volunteering why they have requested or agreed to come for a first appointment. Some open the initial interview with complaints of diffuse symptoms or interpersonal problems ("I've been feeling tense and nervous lately, and I've been screaming at my husband and children for no reason and they're really upset with me"); some present specific symptoms that have prompted their seeking help ("The reason I'm here is that I've become impotent and it's bothering the hell out of me"); and some do not mention symptoms or problems at all but instead express general dissatisfaction with how their life is going ("I wanted to talk with someone because I'm just not happy in what I'm doing, in my work or my personal life, and I want to see if I can find some ways to change things before it's too late").

These spontaneous presenting complaints give therapists a good lead in knowing what topics to pursue in an initial evaluation interview. If, however, patients begin with statements that provide few clues to their difficulties and concerns, the therapist needs to direct them toward furnishing such information:

PATIENT: Dr. Smith told me I should come to see you.
THERAPIST: What was that about?

PATIENT: I don't know where to begin.
THERAPIST: You can begin anywhere you like.
PATIENT: You mean you want to hear all about my childhood?
THERAPIST: Well, perhaps you could begin by telling me what led to your coming to see me.

Still other patients do not begin at all, but instead sit quietly and wait for the therapist to open the interview. In this situation, the therapist should inquire directly about the patient's chief concerns. In disagreement with this recommendation, it has sometimes been suggested that initially silent patients should be responded to with silence. Rationales for such initial therapist silence include: (a) It avoids taking a directive stance in relation to the patient; (b) it helps in assessing how willing and able patients are to talk about themselves; and (c) it is a useful measure of how well a patient can tolerate anxiety in an interpersonal situation. However, hearkening back to the discussion in Chapter 4 of strategy and tactics in psychotherapy, extended therapist silence at the beginning of a first interview provides a good example of erroneous tactics based on incorrect strategy.

Although therapist silence can be an effective treatment tactic when employed at the right time, the correct strategy for the beginning of an initial interview is not to test patients' anxiety tolerance, nor to assess their capacity to talk, nor to demonstrate the nonpossessiveness of the therapist. These are all important strategies, but the proper moment for them comes later. At the beginning of an initial interview, the overriding strategy must be to find out what the patient's problem is, and this strategy dictates the appropriate tactic—if patients don't tell you, ask them.

Advantageous technique in an initial interview can be clarified further by looking critically at a sometimes encountered suggestion that the therapist should begin with whatever dynamic implications appear in the patient's opening remarks. Following this approach, the therapist's response to the opening comment "I don't know where to begin" might be "It's hard for you to get started with things." Such an interpretive tactic at the beginning of a first interview is inopportune, partly because it defers the strategy of identifying the patient's current difficulties, and partly because it may interfere with the strategy of establishing a productive working alliance.

Speaking further to prospects for establishing a productive working alliance, the pitfalls of an immediate interpretive focus on personality dynamics are threefold. First, because therapists have only limited knowledge of their patients at this point, they run a high risk of making incorrect interpretations. Erroneous interpretations are generally disadvantageous, as elaborated in Chapter 8; coming in an initial interview, these blunders give patients reason to question how understanding their therapist is and how able to refrain from jumping to conclusions.

Second, because interpretations constitute a challenge, patients who encounter interpretive comments early on are likely to view the therapist as someone who shoots from the hip and may persist in shooting them down at every opportunity. Third, interpretations at the beginning of an initial interview mean that the therapist has undertaken the work of the treatment before the patient has agreed formally to participate in psychotherapy, which is authoritarian and patronizing on the therapist's part. In sum, then, a premature interpretive focus can have the undesirable effects of (a) causing patients to doubt the therapist's sensitivity, (b) interfering with patients developing a sense of security in the treatment relationship, and (c) undermining the therapist's efforts to communicate warmth and respect.

A further cautionary note in beginning an initial interview: Therapists will usually know something about patients' current problems before seeing them because a referral source has provided this information. In these instances, therapists should not play dumb, as by saying, "Perhaps you could tell me what brings you here." They should instead state exactly what the situation is: "Dr. Brown tells me that you've been having some problems you're concerned about." After such an opening remark, the therapist can wait for the patient to elaborate on the problem, without necessarily relating everything that was learned from Dr. Brown. Should patients not take up this cue to begin talking about themselves, the therapist can then add, "Perhaps you could tell me something about it" or "What has it been like for you?"

Prompt acknowledgment of a referral usually helps get the treatment relationship off to a good start. Referred patients know they have been referred, and their therapist's failure to mention this fact may lead them to conclude (a) that the therapist has some prior information about them that is not being acknowledged, which means the therapist is asking questions he or she already knows the answer to and hence is being ungenuine, or (b) that the therapist has no prior information, which means he or she was not sufficiently interested to bother discussing their situation with the referral source. Therapists can easily avoid or repair such inadvertent communication of ungenuineness or disinterest if they are alert to the importance of doing so:

THERAPIST: Why don't you begin by telling me what brings you here.

PATIENT: (with some irritation) Dr. Jones said he had talked to you about seeing me. Didn't he tell you anything about the problem?

THERAPIST: (correcting the therapist error) Yes, he did, and I know it has to do with your relationship with your husband. But I'd like to hear your view of things.

PATIENT: (midway in the first interview) I think that's all there is to say about what's bothering me right now. I guess you know about my past since I was a patient here before.

THERAPIST: I know you were seen in the clinic a couple of years ago, and I've had a chance to look through your records. But I think it would be helpful if you could tell me about yourself in your own words.

EXPLORING THE BACKGROUND OF THE PRESENTING PROBLEMS

After therapists have identified the major problems and concerns that have brought a patient for help, they need next to learn something about the background of these presenting difficulties. If the patient has come with a specific complaint, such as anxiety attacks, the therapist's inquiry likewise needs to be fairly specific: When did the anxiety attacks first begin, how are they manifested, what seems to bring them on, and so forth. When patients begin with a more general concern, the inquiry should take a correspondingly general tack:

PATIENT: I don't know how to deal with people, and that's the big thing I'm worried about.

THERAPIST: Tell me something about your relationships with people.

Whether the initial inquiry into a patient's presenting problems is specific or general, its purpose is to elicit some elaboration of their nature, history, and connection with possible precipitating circumstances. Should patients initially present multiple problems and concerns, therapists may have to be selective in deciding which ones to pursue first and how extensively to pursue them. Faced with a litany of complaints, all of which seem to merit attention, the therapist may be unsure where to begin further exploration. In this circumstance, it is often helpful to ask patients for their opinion: "You've mentioned a number of things you're concerned about; which are the ones that are bothering you the most or that you'd like to talk about first?"

Even when asked, however, some patients may be reluctant or unable to identify their core or most serious problems. They may feel it would be too painful or embarrassing to begin with what is bothering them the most, and they may prefer to start instead with matters that are relatively easy to talk about. As another possibility, they may not themselves know which of their many concerns are most fundamental or serious. Nevertheless, therapists who request such a choice will often get help in selecting the initial topics of discussion, and they will also be communicating warmth and respect. Asking patients for their views about what should be discussed tells them that they will share responsibility for deciding what goes on in the treatment and that they will be accepted as they are without being called on to do more than they are psychologically prepared to do.

As for how extensively to explore aspects of a patient's presenting complaints during an initial interview, two related guidelines often prove helpful. On the one hand, the more it appears that ongoing psychotherapy will follow the initial phase of evaluation and assessment, the less actively therapists should pursue any particular topic in the first interview. Detailed information about a patient's problems is ordinarily not necessary for arranging a treatment contract and will subsequently emerge during the course of the psychotherapy. Moreover, vigorous questioning in the initial phase of psychotherapy to unearth such details may have the unintended effect of inhibiting a patient's spontaneity and giving the impression that psychotherapy consists of a question-and-answer interaction in which the therapist takes the initiative.

On the other hand, the more a patient's presenting complaints suggest an emergency or crisis situation, the more actively and thoroughly therapists need to explore the details of these complaints during a first interview. Intensive assessment in an initial interview is mandatory in particular for patients who are depressed to the point of contemplating suicide, who are struggling with problems of anger management and impulse control that create potential for violence, or who show serious cognitive or emotional difficulties that suggest an impending psychotic breakdown. In these instances, careful assessment of the risk of such consequences, followed as necessary by immediate preventive intervention, takes precedence over planning for ongoing psychotherapy.

Therapists also need to recognize when patients with physical complaints, somatoform disorders, and certain psychological disturbances may need medical evaluation prior to or instead of psychotherapy. Additionally, people embroiled in problematic social situations may be served better by referral to an appropriate community agency or counseling service than by further assessment for psychotherapy. Whenever such possibilities arise, they should be explored thoroughly until the therapist is satisfied that they do not contraindicate psychotherapy as a treatment of choice.

UNDERSTANDING THE PATIENT AS A PERSON

Thus far, the discussion of evaluation has focused on the patient's problems. It is also essential in the initial evaluation to get some understanding of the patient as a person. Most patients provide considerable information about themselves as they describe their current concerns. Just by listening to this description, therapists will usually learn a great deal about patients' family circumstances, their occupations and avocations, their attitudes toward the significant people in their lives, and even their views on how earlier life experiences may have contributed to their present difficulties.

However this may be, therapists will reach a point in the evaluation where they have as much initial information as they need about a patient's presenting problems, and it is then time for them to concentrate on filling in their picture of the patient as a person. This shift in focus may occur imperceptibly, with the therapist merely following where patients lead into talking about themselves. Should patients continue to talk only about their symptoms, the therapist may have to suggest a change of subject: "I think you've given me a pretty good idea of what's troubling you; perhaps you could tell me something about yourself and your background."

When therapists begin to inquire about a patient's background, they must again decide what topics to pursue and how much detail to obtain about them. Knowing what background topics to pursue in a diagnostic interview requires being broadly knowledgeable about normal and abnormal personality development and about the dynamics of interpersonal relationships. Determining how much detail to obtain is a matter of finding a middle ground between too much and not enough. If therapists do not get enough information about the patient as a person, they are not in a good position to assess whether psychotherapy is indicated. On the other hand, if they seek too much information, they risk creating the type of question-and-answer atmosphere that can impede subsequent spontaneity and progress in psychotherapy.[1]

The guiding principle of information gathering in the initial evaluation phase of psychotherapy is to learn enough to arrive at an adequate working formulation of the patient and the patient's problems. The particular amounts and kinds of information required for an adequate working formulation vary among therapists and from one patient to the next. Therapists differ in how definitive they prefer their initial formulations to be prior to proposing a treatment contract, and they also differ in their degree of clinical sensitivity and their knowledge of personality processes. The more therapists can tolerate uncertainty (within the limits of good clinical judgment), and the more sensitive and knowledgeable they are, the less information they will require to complete their initial evaluation of prospective psychotherapy patients.

Whatever the amount and kind of information therapists would like to have initially, the patients they see will vary in how readily they can provide it. Some patients talk more freely and rapidly than others, some keep to the point while others ramble, and some have fewer and more focused concerns than others. Hence, more time is required to complete an initial evaluation in some cases than in others, and no exact number of interviews can be specified for this process. However, it is possible to elaborate further on what needs to be accomplished in arriving at a working formulation.

ARRIVING AT A WORKING FORMULATION

An adequate working formulation in the initial phase of psychotherapy comprises a *clinical* formulation and a *dynamic* formulation. A working clinical formulation consists of traditional diagnostic judgments concerning the patient's psychological condition. Although a highly specific and thoroughly documented diagnosis is not necessary for a working formulation, an initial evaluation is not complete until the therapist has formed three general diagnostic impressions: (a) whether a patient has primarily a psychotic, characterological, neurotic symptom, or adjustment disorder; (b) whether the presenting complaints are primarily psychogenic in origin or are instead suggestive of some somatic or toxic condition that requires medical attention; and (c) whether the patient's psychological difficulties are so slight as not to require psychotherapy or so severe as to call for immediate crisis intervention.

In addition to indicating whether therapists should continue to explore a patient's interest in and capacity to benefit from psychotherapy, the working clinical formulation provides some guidelines for choosing between a primarily uncovering and a primarily supportive approach. Uncovering psychotherapy is most likely to be appropriate for people with neurotic symptom and adjustment disorders, whereas impending or overt psychotic disturbance and entrenched characterological problems are more likely to call for relatively supportive psychotherapy.[2]

A working dynamic formulation consists of a general impression of what patients are like as people and how they got to be that way. Included in this formulation are preliminary conclusions concerning the nature of the conflicts patients are experiencing; the ways in which they customarily defend against the anxiety these conflicts produce; their style of coping with social, sexual, and achievement-related situations; their attitudes toward significant people in their lives and what they perceive the attitudes of others to be toward them; and how their past and present life experiences have contributed to their becoming distressed and seeking help. Expanding these preliminary conclusions into an extensive and definitive dynamic formulation is a tall order, and even at the conclusion of psychotherapy there may be aspects of a patient's personality that have not fully come to light. Initially, however, the working dynamic formulation must be sufficiently certain and complete for therapists to have some sense of the kind of person with whom they will be working and of what the focal points of the treatment are likely to be. Only then can psychotherapy proceed as planned intervention and not as fortuitous tampering.

Thus the working formulation consists of just enough information for the therapist to decide whether psychotherapy might be an appropriate treatment approach to pursue and along what lines the treatment might proceed. Beyond this initial appraisal, however, ongoing evaluation of patients during psychotherapy is essential in guiding the selection of appropriate strategies and tactics. Continuous awareness of alterations in a patient's clinical condition and prevailing dynamics keeps therapists attuned to modifications that are frequently necessary in the treatment plan by which they are in trying to guide their patients toward a more symptom-free and self-fulfilling life.

ASSESSING THE APPROPRIATENESS
OF PSYCHOTHERAPY

When therapists have learned enough about a patient and the patient's problems to arrive at a working clinical and dynamic formulation, their next task is to assess the appropriateness of psychotherapy for meeting the patient's needs. From among numerous guidelines that have been proposed for assessing a person's capacity to participate in and benefit from psychotherapy, the research discussed in Chapter 2 points primarily to three criteria: (a) whether patients are motivated for psychotherapy,

(b) whether they are capable of reflecting and talking about themselves, and (c) whether despite their difficulties they have retained generally well-integrated personality functioning.

As noted in Chapter 2, none of these criteria is essential for effective psychotherapy to take place, and unmotivated, unreflective, untalkative, and poorly integrated people may be helped by psychotherapy. Other things being equal, however, the three variables of motivation, reflectiveness, and personality integration indicate the likely extent to which a patient who needs psychotherapy will be able to engage in and profit from it. An adequate assessment of these variables guides therapists in deciding whether to recommend psychotherapy to people who have come to them for help, or whether instead to recommend some other form of treatment or no treatment at all.

ASSESSING MOTIVATION

Patients' motivation for psychotherapy is best assessed by determining how much acute distress they are experiencing. Generally speaking, the more acutely distressed people are, the more they would like to see changes in themselves and their lives and the more willing they are to bear the burden of being in psychotherapy. In particular, the more dissatisfied patients are with their current psychological state, the more inclined they will be to attend sessions regularly, to talk about themselves even when doing so proves painful or embarrassing, to consider interpretations that they find objectionable even if accurate, and to persevere in the treatment process until an advantageous termination point is reached.

People with masochistic needs may appear to present an exception to distress as an index of wishing to change, because they often complain bitterly about their difficulties while nevertheless finding solace in them. However, careful diagnostic evaluation of masochistic patients usually reveals that most of their complaints relate to long-term problem situations that they have cultivated and endured when other options were open to them, and these complaints do not identify any acute distress. When masochistic individuals do give evidence of acute concerns in addition to their chronic characterological complaints, then their current distress is likely to represent suffering beyond what their masochism requires and to have the same implications for psychotherapy motivation as the acute distress of any other patient.

Level of acute distress can be judged from how much anxiety patients display in relation to their presenting complaints and from what they say in response to two kinds of questions: "How have these problems (symptoms, difficulties, concerns) been affecting your life in general?" and "In what way would your life be different if you weren't having these problems?" How patients answer these questions often illuminates the extent of their wish to change and hence the strength of their motivation for psychotherapy. The more pervasive and distressing the presenting complaints are reported to be, and the more critical the differences anticipated to result from the amelioration of these complaints, the more highly motivated for psychotherapy a patient can be assumed to be.

To illustrate this indirect approach to assessing motivation for psychotherapy, consider the following two responses to the question, "How has this problem been affecting your life in general?":

PATIENT 1:   Well, I worry about it from time to time, and then I get a little irritable or have trouble falling asleep.

PATIENT 2:   It's turned me into a nervous wreck and been ruining everything for me. At work I've been told that I'll be reassigned to a less responsible position if I don't get my act together, at home my wife is out of patience with me and talking about a trial separation, and some of my best friends are starting to avoid me.

The contrast in these two responses is evident between one that indicates passing concern over a mildly disruptive problem and one that indicates considerable anxiety over a problem that is interfering with the patient's work, marriage, and social relationships. Because the impact of the presenting problem on a patient's life in general provides such important clues to the person's level of motivation for psychotherapy, the therapist should be sure to broach this subject if the patient does not bring it up spontaneously. The initial assessment in psychotherapy cannot be considered complete unless it includes some information about patients' subjective attitudes toward their presenting problems and about how these problems are affecting their friendship patterns, their family and love relationships, and their performance in school or at work.

A similarly instructive contrast can be illustrated for responses to the question, "In what way would your life be different if you weren't having this problem?":

PATIENT 1:   I'd be able to relax a little more.

PATIENT 2:   It would be a different world for me. I could feel good about myself again, hold on to my job and maybe even get a promotion, and patch up my marriage.

As in the previous example, the difference is striking between an attitude that indicates only a slight wish for relief from the presenting complaint and one that suggests considerable motivation for change. It is the latter attitude that sustains patients through the arduous and challenging task of learning about themselves in psychotherapy, whereas the former attitude tends to predict minimal investment in treatment, spotty attendance, and premature termination when treatment sessions become difficult or uncomfortable.

At times, these indirect questions can shed more light on a person's motivation for psychotherapy than direct inquiries. Patients asked directly about their attitudes toward entering psychotherapy may voice seemingly clear views one way or the other: "I really want very much to have some psychotherapy and I hope you'll take me on as a patient"; or "Well, I don't really see much need for it, and I think the problems I'm having will work themselves out." Although the first of these comments may in fact reflect strong motivation for psychotherapy and the second comment weak motivation, both personality and situational influences can result in patients' true level of motivation for psychotherapy being quite different from what they say or think it is.

Regarding personality influences, an apparent lack of motivation in patients who would in fact prosper in psychotherapy may derive from the same conflicts that are causing the psychological difficulties for which they are being evaluated. For example, unhappy and unsuccessful people driven by underlying inner voices that tell them they do not deserve to be happy or successful may express reservations about psychotherapy because the idea of receiving help makes them uncomfortable. Other people who are eager to receive help but whose psychological difficulties include powerful fears of failure may express only lukewarm interest in treatment because they anticipate not being able to make a success of it and dread the disappointment of failing as a psychotherapy patient.

As a third example of deceptive expression of disinterest in psychotherapy, most therapists can expect to see a certain number of people who feel a need for treatment but have reservations about becoming a patient. Even though wanting very much to undertake psychotherapy, such potential patients are inclined to reject treatment because they regard patienthood as an admission of weakness or as an embarrassment to themselves or their families. Whenever therapists perceive such mixed feelings about entering psychotherapy, discussing them directly with the patient becomes an important part of arranging the treatment contract (see Chapter 6).

Situational influences sometimes lead to the opposite kind of misleading patient statement, in which very positive attitudes toward entering psychotherapy are expressed by people who do not particularly need it and are not especially likely to work hard at it. People who come under duress, for example, with psychotherapy held over their head as a condition for staying in school, on the job, in the home, or out of jail, may wax eloquent about their interest in psychotherapy to promote their being accepted as a patient. For the same reason, people who have some intellectual curiosity about psychotherapy or regard it as a social badge of merit may attempt to impress a therapist with their terribly urgent need to be treated by him or her.

As a general guideline for therapists to keep in mind, patients who have come of their own volition to get psychological help are more likely to be well motivated for psychotherapy than those who have come at someone else's behest. This index of motivation is far from being infallible, however. Self-referred and psychologically minded patients may seek psychotherapy with little appreciation of how much effort and commitment it requires and rapidly lose their enthusiasm for being in treatment once they find out. Conversely, involuntary patients with little psychological mindedness who need psychotherapy badly may become highly invested in treatment once they sense its potential for helping them.[3]

Although knowing how and why patients have come for psychotherapy may provide some important clues to their level of motivation, therapists should attend to possible differences between what patients say in response to direct inquiries about their motivation and what their true motivation will turn out to be once psychotherapy gets under way. Overall, then, in trying to assess whether prospective patients will remain in and work hard in psychotherapy, therapists should rely primarily on their impressions of how distressed these people are and how much they would like to change.

ASSESSING REFLECTIVENESS

The capacity of patients to reflect and talk about themselves can usually be assessed from their behavior during the evaluation phase of treatment. Do they describe their presenting complaints in relation to themselves as people, or do they enumerate their symptoms as if they were talking about someone else or about no one in particular? Do they volunteer information spontaneously, or, as if on the witness stand, confine themselves to answering the questions asked of them? When answering a question, do they provide abundant detail, or are they forthcoming only with the minimum response consistent with being courteous? As they give details, do they remind themselves of related topics which they then elaborate, or do they merely follow in the direction taken by the interviewer? The more closely a patient's interview style resembles the former rather than the latter of these pairs of alternatives, the more likely he or she is to be sufficiently talkative and reflective in subsequent psychotherapy to derive benefit from it.

For therapists to estimate accurately a patient's ability and willingness to talk, they need to prevent their own initial interview style from becoming too directive. A rapid-fire flow of questions, intended to accumulate as much information as possible, limits opportunity for therapists to learn very much about a patient's capacity for reflection. Except when presenting difficulties identify the type of emergency situation discussed earlier and call for crisis intervention, therapists should conduct their evaluation interviews in a manner that leaves room for patients to pause and contemplate, to bring up ideas spontaneously, and to pursue directions in which their thoughts and feelings may lead (e.g., "You know, what I just said reminds me of something I haven't thought of in years"). Patients who cannot or do not take advantage of opportunities to talk about themselves in unfettered ways have a low probability of being able to participate in and benefit from psychotherapy.

Some additionally useful information about a patient's capacity for reflectiveness can be obtained by occasional use of trial interpretations during the assessment phase of psychotherapy. A trial interpretation is a superficial, relatively nonthreatening reflection or recasting of what a patient is saying. Trial interpretations give patients a sample of how psychotherapy proceeds and at the same time allow the therapist to observe how patients react to having their behavior interpreted. For example, a female patient in an initial interview may talk at one point about feeling anxious at home whenever she and her husband are having company and at a later point about feeling anxious whenever she has to attend an office meeting. Unless there is clear evidence to the contrary, the therapist might observe, as a trial interpretation, "So it appears that one thing that makes you anxious is having a lot of people around, whether at home or at work."

Patients may respond to a trial interpretation negatively, as by ignoring it completely, by acknowledging it grudgingly and with irritation that their story has been interrupted ("Could be . . . who knows?"), or by becoming overtly angry and resistive ("Why would you say a thing like that? What could one thing have to do with the other?"). Patients who respond in these ways to trial interpretations—assuming the therapist has framed a minimally threatening interpretation that is almost certainly correct—are not particularly likely to do well in subsequent psychotherapy. They will have difficulty making a shift from experiencing themselves to observing themselves, and they will be disinclined to consider connections between various aspects of their behavior.

In other instances, patients may respond positively to trial interpretations with interest and curiosity ("Well, you may have a point there; I wonder what one thing has to do with the other?"); with endorsement ("You've got it right, I do have a problem with having a lot of people around, wherever it is"); or even with enthusiasm ("Hey, you know, I never thought of that before, but that would explain a lot of things"). Patients who treat a trial interpretation as something to stop and think about are displaying a readiness to observe themselves. If in addition they accept the interpretation, they are showing an openness to the psychotherapeutic process. If they furthermore appear to welcome having their behavior interpreted, they are responding to the caring and empathy that interpretations convey rather than their threatening aspects. Such indications of self-observation, openness, and enthusiasm for the therapist's efforts predict reflectiveness and willingness to talk in subsequent psychotherapy sessions.

Assessing Personality Integration

The assessment of personality integration proceeds primarily on the basis of listening to what patients say about their past and current life experiences and observing how they go about saying it. Technical guidelines for diagnostic interviewing were referenced earlier in the chapter (see page 61), and the present section calls attention to two useful adjuncts to the diagnostic interview in assessing a patient's personality integration: psychological testing and contacts with people other than the patient.

Psychological Testing

Information gleaned from psychological test data about a patient's attitudes, concerns, capacities, and personality style often prove helpful in planning the course of psychotherapy and evaluating its outcome. Pretherapy test findings can be especially useful in deciding on the appropriate intensity of the treatment, selecting critical treatment targets, and anticipating how patients are likely to react at different points in the treatment process.[4] Decisions about having potential therapy patients tested should be made on the basis of whether initial interviews have given the therapist sufficient information to arrive at a working formulation that provides a comfortable basis on which to proceed. If so, there is little reason for psychological testing, except to establish baseline data against which to monitor change and progress with subsequent retesting. In the absence of a working formulation with which therapists feel comfortable, however, psychological test findings may substantially enhance their understanding of a patient's needs and their preparations for meeting these needs.

Of the three variables involved in assessing the appropriateness of psychotherapy—motivation, reflectiveness, and personality integration—the last one is most likely to require the kind of supplementary information provided by psychological testing. If therapists misjudge a patient's motivation or reflectiveness, subsequent psychotherapy may bog down or require some restructuring, but dire consequences are unlikely. Likewise, if therapists proceed with erroneous conceptions of a patient's personality dynamics, these can usually be adjusted as new information emerges in the treatment, without any seriously adverse effects.

However, should therapists initially overestimate a patient's level of personality integration, the results may be regrettable. When people with minimal capacity to tolerate anxiety and frustration are taken into uncovering psychotherapy and confronted with the ambiguity, lack of structure, and focus on painful experiences that characterize this treatment approach, there is considerable risk of their becoming inordinately upset and dysfunctional even to the point of a psychotic breakdown. As noted in Chapter 3, deterioration effects in psychotherapy can often be laid at the doorstep of an overly ambitious treatment approach conceived in the absence of an adequate evaluation and exceeding a patient's capacities to tolerate and benefit from it. Adequately trained psychotherapists should be able to recognize such personality decompensation as soon as it begins to appear and to appreciate its origin in their having instituted an excessively unstructured form of treatment. They can then take steps to correct their error and avert further breakdown, primarily by becoming more directive and supportive. Far better, of course, is avoiding this type of mistake in the first place.

Whenever therapists remain uncertain about a patient's level of personality integration after they have become satisfied in other respects that psychotherapy seems indicated, they should utilize psychological testing. Thorough personality assessment for clinical purposes by a qualified psychodiagnostic consultant is a specialized and costly procedure. Nevertheless, when appropriately employed to answer critical questions that cannot readily be answered through other means, it is highly cost-efficient. Mistaken treatment strategies based on insufficient diagnostic evaluation can lead to wasted sessions that do little or no good; by providing critical but otherwise missing diagnostic information, psychological testing can help to eliminate fruitless sessions that combine to cost far more in dollars than the psychodiagnostic consultation. Inadequately structured sessions can lead to deteriorating functioning that is enormously distressing to patients and to their therapists as well; by helping to spare patients and therapists this distress and minimizing the risk of such regrettable results as psychotic breakdown, psychological testing can cost far less than the psychological toll of misdirected therapy. At the same time, however, psychological testing should not be used as a replacement for adequate diagnostic interviewing. Therapists who regularly turn to test data for information that could be obtained from interviews are not fulfilling their responsibility to their patients.

Contacts with Others

By contacting other people in patients' lives, therapists can usually obtain information about their social, heterosexual, and work adjustment that a patient has overlooked or been reluctant to mention. However helpful this information may be in constructing a complete case history, considerable caution is advisable in seeking and relying on it.

First, although patients' relatives, friends, and employers may be more objective observers of patients' behavior than they are, the information they provide will not necessarily be more reliable than what patients themselves have to say. People coming for psychotherapy are typically having some interpersonal difficulties, whether as a primary manifestation of their psychological problems or as a secondary consequence of being emotionally troubled. The important people in their lives will be involved in their problems; some will be contributing to the problems, others suffering as a result of them, and all regarding the patient with varying degrees of concern, impatience, sympathy, or annoyance. The impressions these people have of the patient's behavior will be influenced by the role they are playing in this person's problems and by their relationship to him or her as spouse, parent, offspring, friend, or employer. Therapists thus need to proceed cautiously with the information provided, particularly because they are unlikely to know the informants well enough to appreciate their motivations and judge the reliability of what they report.

Second, reliable and useful information that does emerge from talking with people other than the patient may come at the expense of the working alliance. In accord with the previously mentioned principle of limiting the evaluation phase of psychotherapy to gathering just enough information to arrive at an adequate working formulation, talking with other people should ordinarily be confined to situations in which patients are reluctant or unable to provide critical diagnostic information, especially when there is reason to be concerned about a crisis or emergency situation.[5] Like unnecessarily detailed evaluation interviewing, data gathering from other people in the absence of a compelling purpose can convey to patients that therapy has more to do with collecting information than with understanding it. The interest of therapists in talking with others may also imply that they regard patients as incapable of providing adequate information. In addition, knowing that the therapist has discussed their problems with other people can cause patient doubts about the confidentiality of psychotherapy and about how much they can safely reveal. Thus the use of informants can limit the degree to which therapists help their patients feel secure and respected in the treatment relationship.

Third, therapists have little control over what the other people to whom they talk may subsequently say or suggest to the patient. Without malice, and sometimes with, informants may give the patient a distorted report of what transpired between them and the therapist, and such accounts can undermine motivation for treatment, at least with respect to the particular therapist. Consider the following comment from a patient being evaluated for psychotherapy: "My wife says you told her she'd have to be more tolerant of me because I'm just a nasty person by nature and unlikely to change; if that's what you think of me, how can you be any help to me?" Once therapists have permitted such a situation to come to pass, however good their intentions were, they face an uphill struggle in rekindling a patient's enthusiasm for entering treatment with them.

These potential disadvantages of seeking evaluative information from other people in the patient's life can be minimized if therapists anticipate or circumvent them. For example, talking with informants only in a patient's presence allows the person to know exactly what has been said by whom and gives no cause for concern about confidentiality. However, because of concerns about saying something that would be upsetting to the patient or would perhaps invite reprisals from him or her, informants are sometimes unwilling to relate crucial information in the patient's presence. Therapists have little recourse in this situation unless they move to structure the treatment as couple or family therapy. As a further drawback, patients who are present to hear everything that is said about them can still be left wondering why the information they were able to give in private was not sufficient and how they will be able on their own to hold up their end of a psychotherapy relationship. To add one more complication, patients who observe their therapist's interest in what someone else has to say may not appreciate having to share the therapist's attention instead of remaining the sole focus of it.

In light of these considerations, therapists should be circumspect in deciding whether they need to talk with other people about a patient they are assessing for individual psychotherapy. Like psychological testing, informants should not be used as a replacement for adequately interviewing patients themselves, nor should other people be consulted to fill in details about a patient that do not bear significantly on the initial working formulation. Instead, contacts with others should usually be reserved for patients whose level of personality integration is initially uncertain. In common with psychological test data, the most important purpose served by additional informants in the assessment phase of psychotherapy is the identification of patients for whom psychotherapy may be contraindicated by virtue of their personality limitations or crisis condition, and for whom other therapeutic measures should be instituted instead.

COMPLETING THE INITIAL
EVALUATION AND ASSESSMENT

At this point in their work with prospective psychotherapy patients, therapists will be completing their initial evaluation and assessment. They will have identified the presenting problems, learned something about the background of the patient's concerns, filled in their picture of the patient as a person, and arrived at a working clinical and dynamic formulation. They will also have assessed the patient's motivation for psychotherapy, capacity for reflectiveness, and level of personality integration. With this information, which may take from one to several interviews to piece together, therapists are in a position to decide whether psychotherapy appears to be a treatment procedure in which the patient can participate and derive benefit. To complete the initial evaluation and assessment, what remains is to determine whether a patient for whom psychotherapy seems indicated is realistically able to undertake it.

As identified earlier by Dewald (1967), the reality factors in people's lives that most often determine whether they can engage in the work of psychotherapy consist of their having sufficient time, money, and freedom from distraction to do so. With regard to time, will the patient be able to attend sessions regularly when the therapist can make them available, or will responsibilities at home or work prevent him or her from making such a commitment? Will it be possible for the therapy to continue for some length of time, or will it be limited by an imminent move or interrupted frequently by prolonged vacations or business trips? Concerning money, does the patient have adequate personal funds or insurance coverage to meet the cost of ongoing psychotherapy? As for freedom from distraction, is the patient's life situation sufficiently stable to enable him or her to concentrate on the content and significance of treatment sessions?

Patients for whom psychotherapy is appropriate and who have adequate time, money, and concentration to devote to psychotherapy should be encouraged to pursue it. In work with people who could benefit from psychotherapy but are less fortunate with respect to these reality considerations, therapists should be prepared to explore various alternatives. Except in situations calling for brief crisis intervention, patients whose time for treatment is limited will do best to defer psychotherapy until they can arrange to be in one place for an extended period and fit regular sessions into their schedule. People embroiled in a chaotic life situation that is not directly related to their desire to have psychotherapy might also be advised to wait for psychotherapy until their circumstances have stabilized and they can devote sustained attention to their particular goals in psychotherapy. Patients with financial limitations may need help to pursue their eligibility for various kinds of insurance or to become familiar with available low-cost clinics.

The exploration of these practical matters with patients for whom psychotherapy is indicated provides a bridge between evaluation and assessment in the initial phase of psychotherapy and the making of an agreement between patient and therapist about continuing treatment. This agreement constitutes the treatment contract, which is the subject of the next chapter.

NOTES

1. Guidelines for the evaluation interview, together with perspectives on the technique of diagnostic interviewing, are elaborated in numerous books and chapters. Readers are referred in particular to contributions by Craig (1989), Groth-Marnat (1990, Chapter 3), Halleck (1991), Hersen and Turner (1985), Morrison (1995), Othmer and Othmer (1994), Rogers (1995), Trzepacz and Baker (1993), Wiens (1991), and Wolberg (1988, Chapters 22–34).

2. Although this view on conditions usually calling for relatively supportive psychotherapy is widely endorsed, there is an extensive literature concerned with the application of expressive and uncovering methods in the treatment of such psychotic and characterological disorders as schizophrenia and borderline personality disorder. Contemporary books in this regard include work by Akhtar (1992); Chessick (1983); Goldstein (1996); Karon and Vandenbos (1981); Kernberg, Selzer, Koenigsberg, Carr, and Appelbaum (1989); and Stone et al. (1983).

3. In discussing the assessment of intrinsic (a patient's own) and extrinsic (someone else's for the patient) motivations for psychotherapy, Robertson (1988) elaborates the role that therapists can play in helping involuntary patients discover a self-focused purpose for therapy. When adequately instilled, this intrinsic motivation sustains the patient's involvement in treatment after external pressures to receive help have diminished or evaporated.

4. Detailed discussions of the utilization of psychological tests in treatment planning and outcome evaluation are provided by Butcher (1990); Finn (1996); Hurt, Reznikoff, and Clarkin (1991); Maruish (1992); and I. Weiner (1992b).

5. This guideline obviously does not apply when therapists are considering the possibility of recommending couple or family therapy to a patient who has presented initially on an individual basis.

CHAPTER 6

The Treatment Contract

THE TREATMENT contract in psychotherapy is an explicit agreement between patient and therapist to work together toward alleviating the patient's psychological difficulties. To arrive at this contract, patient and therapist need first to agree that treatment is indicated and will be undertaken. Next they need to agree on the objectives of the treatment and on the procedures they will follow in working toward these objectives. Finally, they need to agree on such specific treatment arrangements as the time, place, frequency, and fee for sessions. This chapter concerns the therapist's task in explicating these three aspects of the treatment contract.

AGREEING ON PSYCHOTHERAPY

For psychotherapy to begin well, there must be an explicit agreement between patient and therapist that the treatment is indicated and will be undertaken. As obvious as it may seem, this first step in arriving at a treatment contract is easy to overlook, especially with patients who have been eager and responsive during the initial evaluation interviews. With such patients, it may seem appropriate to assume that they want psychotherapy and are ready to discuss arrangements for it. This assumption has the distinct disadvantage of denying the patient an opportunity to share explicitly in the decision about further treatment. Assumptions and unilateral decisions should generally be avoided in psychotherapy, because they communicate disrespect for a patient's integrity and competence. To show respect, therapists need to offer their patients the choice of accepting or declining to continue in psychotherapy before they propose any specific arrangements for doing so.

Therapists furthermore need to help their patients make an *informed* decision about continuing in treatment. Just as the parties to any contract should have the right of informed consent, patients have rights to certain information before they decide about psychotherapy. They have a right to know how the therapist views their psychological problems and what means he or she recommends for dealing with them; they have a right to know something about the psychotherapeutic process and the nature of the commitment it requires; and they have a right to inquire about the qualifications of the therapist to provide the treatment that is being offered.[1]

RECOMMENDING PSYCHOTHERAPY

Following their initial assessment of a person who has sought their help, therapists need to summarize the impressions they have formed and make some recommendations. This summary should usually be limited to recasting briefly what has been discussed in prior interviews and should not attempt to reconstruct patients' personality development or the origin of their difficulties. Therapists are still working with minimal information at this point, and they risk making errors if they attempt a full reconstruction of the patient's psychological history and symptom formation. Additionally, the more hypotheses therapists elaborate in a summary statement, the fewer hypotheses they leave for patients to arrive at on their own in subsequent psychotherapy. The following summary, presented to a 33-year-old professional man with a classical success neurosis,[2] illustrates the form such a statement might take:

> I think this would be a good point for me to share with you the impressions I have. You came to see me mainly because you were feeling depressed and irritable and generally dissatisfied with the way your life is going. As we've talked, it's become clear that the most likely source of these feelings is your work situation. Everything was going pretty well until you were told you were in line for a promotion. Then your job performance deteriorated, you didn't get the promotion, and your depression, discouragement, and irritability set in. We've also learned that a similar kind of thing has apparently happened to you before, at times when you were on the verge of some success, and you have vivid memories of very high standards of accomplishment being set in your family while you were growing up. Putting all this together, it seems to me that your problem lies in some mixed feelings you have about being successful and some underlying attitudes you have toward people in your life who have been successful. Mostly these are feelings and attitudes that you haven't been fully aware of, but that have nevertheless been preventing you from doing as much with your life as you could or as you would find satisfying. How does all that sound to you?

As this example indicates, there is nothing dramatic or startling about the summary presented at this point. Patients will have realized most of what it contains before coming for help, and the rest of it will have been brought out during the initial assessment interviews. Therapists should nevertheless take pains to construct this kind of summary and present it emphatically. There is considerable difference between having ideas brought out in an initial interview and having them restated in a summary of impressions at the end of an evaluation. Isolated ideas can sometimes be given short shrift and disappear from view, especially if a patient's defenses are geared to repressing them or denying their implications; a summary stands out as a definite conclusory statement by the therapist that is difficult to ignore.

There are several advantages in having the therapist's working formulation stand out as a definite statement. First, accurate and clearly presented summaries provide a convincing demonstration that therapists have taken the trouble to listen carefully and think about what they have heard, that they are capable of understanding the patient's difficulties, and that they regard the patient as entitled to straightforward disclosure of their impressions. Second, good summary statements usually identify specific goals for the patient's treatment and thereby pave the way for subsequent agreement on these goals. Third, vivid and unequivocal summaries help therapists avoid the therapist from the pitfall of implicit understandings.

Implicit understandings about the treatment contract can cause considerable difficulty as psychotherapy unfolds, primarily because they undermine the therapist's capacity to be effective at times when communication in psychotherapy becomes disrupted by the difficulty of the material being discussed or by patients' feelings about the therapy or about the therapist. As elaborated in Chapters 9 and 10, patients experiencing resistance and transference reactions may become temporarily disenchanted with the treatment and raise such complaints as, "You never even asked me if I wanted to get into psychotherapy," or "You never told me what you thought my problem was," or "You never gave me any idea about what this would be like."

Faced with such complaints, therapists should be able to point out that these matters were in fact discussed directly, after which they can address what may be troubling a patient at the moment and clouding his or her recollection of the treatment contract. Therapists who are conducting treatment on the basis of implicit understandings, without having made all aspects of the treatment contract explicit, lack a solid foundation for dealing effectively with these kinds of patient complaints.

The final sentence of this sample summary statement illustrates one further technical recommendation: Therapists should end a summary statement by asking the patient to comment on it. The respect and mutual participation communicated by asking patients for their reactions are obvious, and the responses they give provide additional useful information. If they concur with the therapist's formulation, the eagerness and wholeheartedness with which they agree give some indication of how open and expressive or how defensive and reserved they are likely to be in subsequent psychotherapy. If on the other hand they reject the therapist's formulation, they make clear the necessity for some reassessment. They may not be as prepared to look at themselves as the therapist thought, or the therapist may not have been particularly sensitive to their problems and needs. In the former case, some treatment approach other than psychotherapy may be indicated, and in the latter case additional evaluation or a different therapist may be what is needed.

When a summary statement has been made and acknowledged as correct, a firm and unambiguous treatment recommendation is the next order of business. Like the summary, this recommendation does not require any lengthy exposition, and it certainly does not call for therapists to indicate why each of a number of possible treatment approaches is or is not suited to the patient's needs. Rather, therapists should recommend the treatment of choice as they see it and then answer any questions the patient may raise about other possibilities.

Thus, when psychotherapy appears to be the treatment of choice, the therapist should simply say so: "I think it would be worthwhile for you to have some psychotherapy, and I'd like to talk further with you about what that would consist of." Stated in this way, therapists' recommendations leave little room for doubt about their opinion or about their readiness to be of help, and patients are being told that they will have an opportunity to talk about psychotherapy before being asked to decide about pursuing it.

Under these circumstances patients usually reserve any questions they have about psychotherapy until they have heard more of what the therapist has to say. If procedural questions begin to emerge as soon as a treatment recommendation has been made (e.g., "What exactly is psychotherapy?" "How long will it last?" "How often would I have to come for sessions?"), therapists can indicate that these are among the matters they are about to discuss: "Let me tell you something about psychotherapy, and I think as we talk about it the questions you have will be answered." Similarly, questions that reflect ambivalent feelings about entering psychotherapy ("Do I really need it?") can usually be deferred until the psychotherapeutic process has been discussed in general.

However, when a question such as "Do I really need it?" appears to reflect patients' anxiety about the severity of their condition or denial of the problems they are having, further clarification of the therapist's summary and recommendations may be necessary. With anxious patients, this will involve eliciting and correcting any misconceptions they have of how disturbed they are and how extensively they will have to be treated. With patients who are minimizing their need for help, clarification will involve restating what the apparent problems are and what kinds of difficulties they may continue to cause in the absence of some ameliorative actions.

Under no circumstances, however, should therapists threaten or frighten defensive patients into accepting a psychotherapy recommendation, any more than they should minimize the problems of anxious patients or falsely reassure them. Instead, therapists need always to be guided by respect for the patient and a code of genuineness, which means presenting and reaffirming their summary and recommendation as clearly and directly as they can and leaving the decision about how to respond in the patient's hands. As noted in Chapter 3, only when a patient's circumstances are sufficiently grave to warrant consideration of involuntary hospitalization, or when the patient's actions require some type of reporting dictated by applicable ethical and legal guidelines, should therapists interfere with patients' rights to make their own decisions.

A second patient question that deserves a direct response has to do with other possible treatment modalities. Patients with various kinds of prior information about mental health services may respond to a recommendation for individual psychotherapy by asking about the equal or greater appropriateness of group therapy, relaxation therapy, hypnotherapy, assertiveness training, or psychotropic medication. When such questions arise, psychotherapists should steer a middle course. They must avoid representing psychotherapy as the only treatment that is likely to be of help, because that is seldom the case. Yet they also need to avoid getting into a discussion of the relative merits and possible appropriateness of a wide range of treatment approaches, because doing so can easily become a didactic exercise that sidetracks therapists from describing what they are prepared to offer. Simplicity and directness remain the guidelines to answering such questions: "There are a variety of treatment approaches that have proved helpful to people with problems similar to yours, just as there is usually more than one way to solve any kind of problem. The approach that I use is individual psychotherapy, and this is what I am recommending that you consider."

Many individual psychotherapists practice or at least maintain familiarity with other treatment methods as well. Therapists who conduct group as well as individual psychotherapy, and perhaps also see patients for marital counseling and stress management, may feel that one of these treatment modalities is more suitable for a particular patient than the others and may recommend it. Or, seeing no clear advantage of one method over another, they may elect to describe two or three alternative approaches they are prepared to employ and help a patient choose among them. In other situations, psychotherapists may be sufficiently familiar with a treatment approach they do not use to conclude that it is more clearly indicated than their own approaches, in which case they need to convey this impression to the patient and help arrange referral to a colleague who provides the indicated treatment. Finally not to be overlooked, some patients will not require any further psychological help following the assessment interviews, and for them a no-treatment recommendation will conclude the therapist's summary.

For therapists to choose wisely among these possibilities, they must know more than just how to conduct psychotherapy. They also need to know how to judge whether a patient needs treatment and, if so, whether psychotherapy or some other treatment approach is most likely to benefit the person. This accounts for why psychotherapists who practice independently or take responsibility for the initial evaluation of patients need to have broad clinical training as well as schooling in psychotherapeutic skills.

EXPLAINING THE PROCESS OF PSYCHOTHERAPY

To allow patients to make informed decisions about continuing in psychotherapy, therapists should follow their treatment recommendations with some explanation of the psychotherapy process. A good way to begin this explanation is to ask patients what information or ideas they may already have. Most people come for help with a mixture of accurate and inaccurate notions of psychotherapy, and knowing what these notions are can guide therapists in formulating their description of the treatment process, especially with respect to confirming or correcting preexisting beliefs.

As in recommending psychotherapy, the key to explaining psychotherapy effectively is being explicit and avoiding assumptions. Accordingly, therapists should never accept at face value patients' statements that they know what psychotherapy is all about. No matter how informed they profess to be, they should be asked to spell out their notions, to allow the therapist to assess their accuracy. Furthermore, even patients who can give a thorough and accurate description of how psychotherapy proceeds should have an opportunity to hear the therapist do so. This includes patients who have previously been in psychotherapy; they too need to hear the present therapist's version of what psychotherapy entails, directly from his or her lips. When patients are moved to complain during the middle phase of treatment that they were never adequately informed about what psychotherapy would be like, therapists as already noted cannot respond effectively if the most they can say is "I thought you knew" or "You seemed to have a good idea about it at the beginning."

The explanation of psychotherapy itself can be accomplished in a relatively brief discussion with the patient that covers the following points: (a) In psychotherapy, patients talk about themselves while the therapist listens, facilitates the talking, and helps patients understand the significance of what they say and do; (b) in the course of this talking, thoughts, feelings, and experiences in patients' past and present lives come to light in ways that clarify the nature of their personality and the origin of the difficulties they have been having; and (c) armed with this knowledge, and with the therapist's assistance, patients translate their expanded self-awareness into less disturbing thoughts and feelings and more adaptive and gratifying ways of conducting their lives.

This simplified explanation of how psychotherapy works can usually be elaborated in reference to what has already transpired in the evaluation interviews. In particular, therapists who have made good use of trial interpretations should be able to present an accurate and comprehensible glimpse of psychotherapy with such statements as the following:

> Psychotherapy consists of talking together pretty much as we have been so far, with your doing most of the talking, telling me about your experiences and the things on your mind, and my listening and trying to help you understand yourself better. For example, you mentioned at the very beginning that one of the things you were concerned about was never having met a man that you could feel attracted to, and then later, when I asked you something about your experiences growing up, you recalled how much you idolized your father. From this, we came up with the idea that perhaps one reason you have had difficulty feeling attracted to men is that you could never find one who could live up to your father, and this was a possibility that made sense to you but had never occurred to you before. And that's how psychotherapy operates.[3]

Once therapists have laid before patients a basic outline of the psychotherapy process, they need to consider carefully how much detail to add. A particularly important question is whether they should anticipate interferences with the communication process, as by telling patients that there will be times when they find talking difficult or develop strong positive and negative feelings toward the therapist. As a useful guideline, therapists should explain enough to get patients off to a good start in psychotherapy, but not so much as to leave no room for surprises in the treatment.

More specifically, the information that patients receive about the basic process of psychotherapy, intended to help them make an informed decision about whether to undertake it, should consist of telling them what psychotherapy is like, but not how they will react to it. As elaborated in Chapters 9 through 11, reactions to the psychotherapeutic process can facilitate patient self-understanding, especially if these reactions can be treated as unique individual experiences. If therapists spell out in the beginning how people generally react to psychotherapy, then patients are unlikely to attach much significance to these reactions when they occur.

Suppose, for example, that a patient has become unable or unwilling to talk freely, and the therapist is attempting to explore why this person, who came voluntarily and eagerly for help and up until now has had a lot to say, has suddenly fallen silent. For people who have been told that all patients have trouble talking from time to time and can also be expected to develop strong feelings toward their therapist, the implications for resistance and transference reactions of becoming reluctant to communicate are diluted, and the possibility of making constructive use of these phenomena is minimized. To facilitate uncovering psychotherapy, it is far more advantageous for patients who experience problems in talking or feelings toward their therapist to be puzzled and surprised by them, or at least susceptible to being helped to feel puzzled and surprised. The patient who asks, "Isn't it natural to feel this way in psychotherapy?" or "Don't all patients go through this kind of thing?" should be told "The important thing is that you are having these feelings and reactions right now, and we have to wonder where they came from and what they mean with respect to you as an individual."

While avoiding details about probable reactions to psychotherapy, therapists should add to their initial explanation some indication of the commitment of time that will be required of the patient. First, they need to clarify that sessions will be held regularly according to a fixed and prearranged schedule. Although the exact frequency and time for appointments will not be decided until the discussion moves to a consideration of specific arrangements, patients should be apprised that psychotherapy does not proceed on the basis of their calling for appointments when they have a problem or feel like coming in to talk. Such informal arrangements may be suitable for medication management and some kinds of counseling, but they do not lend themselves well to ongoing psychotherapy, whether relatively supportive or relatively expressive.

Second, therapists are obliged to say something about how long the treatment will last, even though the duration of psychotherapy is difficult to estimate. Aside from its being initially uncertain just how rapidly a person will progress in psychotherapy, patients do not always work toward precisely the goals originally agreed on. Some after achieving their original objectives decide to continue working on other problems or toward deeper self-understanding, and some decide to settle for lesser treatment accomplishments than they originally had in mind.

Unless there is some specific reason or basis for fixing the duration of the treatment (e.g., a clinic policy, a managed care restriction, participation in a research study of time-limited therapy, or the expected departure of patient or therapist), it is best to structure the length of psychotherapy as indefinite and open-ended. At the same time, it should be clearly indicated that the time necessary for substantial progress in psychotherapy is measured in months or years and not in days or weeks. For patients who have difficulty comprehending that the treatment process will take longer than just a few sessions, it is usually sufficient to point out that it has taken a long time for them to become the person they are, and that it will accordingly take some time to understand how they got to be that way and to bring about any changes in how they feel and behave.

Before concluding their explanation of the treatment process, therapists may also have to respond to questions from patients about their prospects for benefiting from psychotherapy. For good reasons, therapists should refrain from holding out any promises of "cure" or marked behavior change; there can be no guaranteed outcome in psychotherapy, and it is insincere for therapists to provide assurances on which they may not be able to deliver. Strupp (1989) has laid down the basis for what therapists can and should say in this regard with the following instructive summary of known facts:

> *Cure* is a term that probably should be stricken from the therapeutic vocabulary. It is rarely to be expected, and whatever its meaning, it rarely occurs. What can be expected are (a) improvements in interpersonal functioning; (b) increases in self-esteem, self-confidence, security, self-respect, and personal worth; (c) greater interest in living, energy, and satisfaction; (d) a greater sense of mastery and competence; and (e) significant diminution of the problems (symptoms) that brought the patient to therapy. (p. 723)

In considering how to respond to patients' questions concerning prognosis, therapists should keep in mind both Strupp's summary of what is known and the positive impact noted in Chapter 2 of patients entering psychotherapy with high hopes for its outcome. To translate all of this into a helpful and accurate response, the following kind of simplified statement will ordinarily suffice:

> It's difficult to know in advance whether psychotherapy will relieve the problems you've been having. However, it is a process that will aid you in understanding yourself better, and it has proved beneficial to other people with problems similar to yours.

PRESENTING THE THERAPIST'S QUALIFICATIONS

After completing their explanation of the treatment process and answering a patient's questions about psychotherapy, therapists are next obliged to satisfy the patient regarding their professional qualifications. This does not mean providing a complete resumé of their training and experience. What it means is that patients have a right to know whether a therapist is qualified to provide the treatment that is being offered and to raise any questions they may have in this regard. In responding to such questions, therapists should differentiate those that concern them as a therapist and those that concern them as a person. Within limits, questions about the therapist as therapist, such as what their discipline is and where they received their education and training, should be answered directly and honestly. However, therapists also need to recognize questions that call for equally direct but less denotative answers.

For example, patients who ask "How many years have you been in practice?" or "How many patients have you treated with problems like mine?" are really not seeking a numerical answer. They have no basis for judging how many years of experience with what kind of patients the therapist should have had, and what they really want to know is whether the therapist will be able to understand and help them. Hence an appropriate response to such questions is, "You're wondering whether I will be able to understand your problems and help you with them, and the best way I can answer your question is to tell you that I have had the experience necessary to be able to work with you; if I did not feel I could be of help to you, I would be referring you to another therapist."

Most patients will be satisfied with such an answer, which tells them what they need to hear. Should patients persist with requests for more specific information about the therapist's credentials, it then behooves the therapist to comment on the unusual nature of their behavior; because as laypersons they have no basis for judging how much training and experience are necessary to guarantee competence, their asking for such detailed information must have some underlying meaning. Perhaps a generalized need to obtain more information than should be necessary to make a decision is one of their neurotic difficulties, or perhaps they characteristically antagonize people by refusing to take what is said to them at face value, or perhaps they are having second thoughts about continuing in psychotherapy or about their ability to be helped. If these or similar motivations underlie their persistent questioning, then no number of years of experience or patients successfully treated will satisfy them concerning the therapist's competence.

In contrast to questions about the therapist as a therapist, questions raised by patients about the therapist as a person should usually not be answered. Even though a good psychotherapy relationship requires therapists to be warm and genuine, to invest themselves as people, and to foster an atmosphere of shared participation in problem-solving, psychotherapy is not a friendship. The problems to be solved are the patient's problems, and the only personal information relevant to working effectively on these problems is personal information about the patient. Patients who need psychotherapy need a trained therapist whose contribution to their welfare will come through his or her interest, understanding, and willingness to help, not through promoting a mutually disclosing acquaintanceship.

Hence, personal questions about the therapist ("Are you married?" "How many children do you have?" "Are you interested in sports?") need to be construed as statements to be understood, not answered. Such personal questions often can be utilized to good effect by asking in return, "How would you like it to be?" or "How would you feel about it either way?" Patients who have asked whether the therapist is married, for example, may then be able to explore feelings they have that only a married or only an unmarried therapist will be able to understand and help them. These are the feelings that are important to discuss, not the patient's manifest interest in the therapist's marital status. Except perhaps for some mild curiosity, patients beginning psychotherapy who need and want treatment are not really concerned about the therapist as a person. They are concerned only with whether the therapist is someone they will be able to confide in and be helped by, and any personal questions they raise are almost certain to reflect such concerns.

When patients in this initial phase of treatment dwell on personal questions or ask directly why the therapist is not talking about his or her own life, a usually effective tactic is simply to point out that the focus of the treatment relationship will be on the patient and the patient's problems. Patients truly interested in psychotherapy will usually accept this explanation, because it is exactly the focus they wish the treatment to have. Those who are not satisfied with a therapist's statement that the focus will be on them, and instead insist that the therapist as well will have to talk about personal matters, may be looking for some excuse not to pursue psychotherapy, or they may be seeking some kind of encounter experience different from what the therapist is prepared to provide. In such cases, further exploration of patients's motivations may be necessary to reevaluate both their wish for help and their expectations of the kind of treatment they will be receiving.

Two other points need to be kept in mind with respect to this issue. First, as is true of virtually every aspect of conducting psychotherapy, there can be no fixed and immutable rules. At some times with some patients, therapists may decide that there is good reason to mention some aspect of their personal life, and they should then do so. Flexibility based on sound clinical judgment, not hard-and-fast rules, is the key to conducting good psychotherapy. Empathic therapists who have a good grasp of personality dynamics and psychopathology will be able to recognize when it is in a patient's best interests to answer a personal question or volunteer some information about themselves.

Second, therapists should not for a moment think that treating their personal life as classified information will preserve their anonymity. The main reason for therapists to deflect personal questions is to keep the treatment focused on the patient, not to shroud themselves in mystery. There is some advantage to limiting how much patients know about their therapist's personal life, in order to maximize latitude for them to form impressions of the therapist on a transference basis. In fact, however, patients almost invariably seek out and absorb considerable information about their therapist.

Patients notice styles of dress and grooming, office decor, a wedding band, diplomas on the wall, books on the shelf, and other clues to the reality of the therapist's personal life, tastes, and interests. Attempting to limit these sources of information by conducting the treatment in a bare, impersonal cell detracts from the therapist's image as an authentic person and serves little purpose. In addition, patients often prove very resourceful in finding out where their therapist lives, determining the therapist's rank and position in a university or agency, and picking up other bits of information from one source or another. The smaller the community or the professional circle in which therapists work, the more their patients learn about them, and even in large metropolitan areas therapists deceive themselves if they believe that careful control of what they say ensures their anonymity as a person. Issues concerning therapist anonymity, self-disclosure, and maximizing latitude for transference are elaborated in Chapter 10.

THE PATIENT RESPONDS

When therapists have finished recommending psychotherapy, explaining the psychotherapeutic process, and answering questions about their qualifications, the time has come for the patient to respond. Patients at this point may accept the recommendation for psychotherapy and indicate their readiness to continue, or they may reject the offer of treatment or express some uncertainty about what they would like to do. The first type of response completes the initial agreement phase of making a treatment contract and leads into a discussion of goals, procedures, and arrangements. The second and third types of response require the therapist to give some additional attention to the patient's attitudes toward receiving psychological help.

Patients who flatly decline further psychotherapy at this point should always be asked the reasons for their decision. Sometimes the reasons given open avenues for further exploration (e.g., "I just don't have any clear picture of how this kind of treatment works or how just talking can really be of any help to me"), and the therapist can then review with the patient any areas of information that may not have been covered sufficiently. At other times, patients may reject psychotherapy in a manner that leaves little room for discussion ("I don't think I need it"; "I appreciate your interest in helping me, but getting into psychotherapy is not something I want to do right now").

When presented with clear and definite rejections of psychotherapy, therapists should have sufficient respect for patients' integrity to accept their wishes. Patients are, after all, free agents. They are free to decline an offer of psychological help no matter how much someone else thinks they need it, just as they are free to decline financial aid or medical care. As in presenting their initial treatment recommendation, therapists need to resist any temptation to cajole or seduce patients into reconsidering a decision not to enter psychotherapy. Glowing portents if psychotherapy is undertaken and dire predictions if it is not are forms of hucksterism that demean both patient and therapist, and they also exaggerate the transcendence of psychotherapy, which is after all not the only solution to everybody's problems.

Emergency situations such as suicidal risk and imminent personality breakdown do of course call for a firm and persistent treatment recommendation. However, such emergencies should be identified and responded to early in the evaluation process, long before work with a patient has reached the point now being discussed. By the time therapists have begun to discuss ongoing psychotherapy with a patient, any emergencies should have been ruled out. Hence a patient's unequivocal rejection of a psychotherapy recommendation deserves to be taken at face value.

Nevertheless, there are steps therapists can take with patients who appear to have potential for benefiting from psychotherapy but decline to undertake it. First, therapists should inquire whether there is any other way they might be of help. Some patients may be convinced that, contrary to the therapist's opinions, they would benefit more from marriage counseling, hypnotic treatment, or social skills training than from psychotherapy, and they may appreciate being recommended to someone else for this purpose. Even when therapists sincerely believe that these other approaches are potentially less beneficial for the patient than psychotherapy, they should avoid pouting at the expense of discharging their professional responsibility. For patients who intend to explore some form of treatment that a therapist does not provide, the least the therapist can do is refer them to a practitioner of this other treatment who is known to be competent.

Second, therapists should help patients who reject a psychotherapy recommendation look to the future. Without being overly dramatic, they can point out that the patient's problems may persist, that the person may at some future time want to reconsider psychotherapy, and that the therapist will remain available and interested in being of help. In this way, therapists can subtly encourage patients to reconsider while leaving the door open for them to return without prejudice. It is not uncommon for initially disinterested patients who are treated in this manner to return for psychotherapy following some subsequent events that convince them of their need for this form of professional assistance.

When patients initially express uncertainty in response to a psychotherapy recommendation, therapists should attempt to explore these feelings and resolve them in favor of a decision to continue. Some people are embarrassed or anxious about being a psychotherapy patient, some may resent being told they need help (even though they have come seeking it), and others may be unsure whether they can meet the time and financial commitments of psychotherapy. Usually such hesitancies about accepting an otherwise appealing psychotherapy recommendation can be worked through satisfactorily if therapists are sufficiently sensitive to recognize them and help patients talk about them.

In concluding this discussion of agreeing on psychotherapy, it is important to keep in mind that good beginnings in psychotherapy require an explicit agreement between patient and therapist that treatment is indicated and will be undertaken. This statement may seem inconsistent with the point made in Chapter 2 that patients who come to the therapist under duress or without much intrinsic motivation are not necessarily incapable of being helped. What happens in fact is that involuntary patients and patients who doubt that treatment is indicated rarely get off to a good start. They may eventually benefit from psychotherapy, but their prospects for doing so hinge on how effectively the therapist can surmount their lack of motivation and generate some interest in being treated. When such interest can be generated, inauspicious beginnings can be turned into commitment to a treatment contract that promotes a successful outcome.

AGREEING ON OBJECTIVES AND PROCEDURES

The psychotherapeutic process is facilitated if the treatment contract includes an explicit agreement between patient and therapist on the objectives of their work together and on the procedures they will follow in attempting to reach these objectives. As elaborated first by Bordin (1979) and confirmed by research referenced in Chapter 3, the therapeutic alliance that makes such a significant contribution to psychotherapy outcome depends for its strength on the degree of agreement between patient and therapist concerning the goals and tasks of the treatment. To therapists who have completed an initial evaluation, provided a summary and treatment recommendation, and obtained a patient's agreement to undertake psychotherapy, it may seem that the treatment objectives and procedures for working toward them are obvious and already known to both parties. Nevertheless, the guideline to remember is that nothing in the treatment contract should be assumed or taken as implicitly understood. Explicit statements of each facet of the contract, no matter how apparently redundant at this point, help resolve any uncertainties or misconceptions held by either party and solidify the foundation for subsequent psychotherapeutic work.

To clarify the objectives of the treatment following a patient's agreement to undertake psychotherapy, the therapist can begin by saying, "Now that we've decided to work together, let's review for a moment exactly what you see as the main objectives we'll be working toward." Patients may respond by summarizing their problems and concerns in much the same manner as they presented them originally, in which case the therapist can simply (a) acknowledge and repeat this summary to give it additional emphasis and (b) move on to talk about procedures and arrangements.

On the other hand, patients may now present objectives or treatment priorities that differ somewhat from those they presented initially. The process of being evaluated in one or more interviews often results in people gaining some new perspectives on themselves and their problems. Concerns that seemed pressing earlier may take on a paler cast after having been discussed briefly, and previously suppressed or denied difficulties may emerge as primary sources of concern. By asking for a summary at the end of the evaluation, after agreement has been reached to continue in psychotherapy, therapists can avoid proceeding on the basis of an outdated view of what a patient most wants to accomplish in treatment.

In addition to facilitating progress in therapy by keeping patient and therapist out of blind alleys, and by promoting a congenial working relationship, an explicit agreement of agreed on objectives also provides an excellent benchmark for judging when the treatment should stop. As discussed in Chapter 12, the therapist's task in terminating psychotherapy is as much a matter of knowing when as how to bring the treatment to an end. Proceeding on the basis of an explicit and mutually agreeable list of specific objectives helps avoid a situation in which psychotherapy drifts aimlessly. Objectives may change during the course of the treatment, but, as long as they remain explicit and mutual, patients and therapists will be able at any time to review together where they stand in relation to reaching the treatment goals.

As for agreeing on treatment procedures, therapists at this point will already have described the process of psychotherapy as part of recommending that a patient consider undertaking it. Patients may have some specific questions they would like to raise now that the discussion concerns psychotherapy for them rather than the nature of psychotherapy in general. Typically, these questions concern specific aspects of the arrangements for the therapy, as discussed next.

AGREEING ON ARRANGEMENTS

When patient and therapist have decided to work together in psychotherapy and have clarified the objectives and procedures of the treatment, the final step in establishing a treatment contract consists of agreeing on specific arrangements for the time, frequency, place, and fee for sessions. Making these arrangements may at times seem a routine matter, and agency policies and dictates of managed care over which the therapist has no control may automatically determine what they will be.[4] Nevertheless, these matters are not inconsequential for the course of psychotherapy, and therapists should keep certain considerations in mind in discussing these arrangements with a patient.

TIME

Specific appointment times for psychotherapy interviews should be arranged to suit the mutual convenience of patient and therapist and should usually involve sessions that are 45 or 50 minutes in length. Limiting the psychotherapy "hour" to something less than a 60-minute session allows therapists a few moments between appointments to reflect, make notes, answer telephone calls, and tend to other personal needs. The most important aspect of making this particular arrangement is communicating that session length will be uniform throughout the treatment. Leaving the time period for sessions free to vary with the nature of the material being discussed incurs several disadvantages. For example, patients struggling with upsetting thoughts that are difficult or embarrassing for them to express may sit quietly or talk about the weather for 15 or 20 minutes and then indicate that they are ending the session because "There's nothing much on my mind today." In the absence of a previously fixed and specified time period for sessions that they can refer to, therapists are in a poor position to help such patients realize there is something unusual about their behavior that constitutes an interference with communication and is not a customary and appropriate feature of the treatment arrangements.

A fixed time period also helps therapists work effectively with patients who are inclined to measure their interest and helpfulness according to how much time they are given. Dependent and narcissistic patients in particular are likely to save material they consider important or captivating for the last few minutes of a session, in the hopes of getting the therapist to extend their time. Unless a fixed session length has been set and adhered to, therapists are hamstrung in such situations. If they allow patients to go on, they gratify their dependency or narcissism without helping them understand it; if they cut patients off, they risk appearing disinterested and unsympathetic.

Operating within a fixed time limit makes it possible for therapists to end sessions without communicating dislike for a patient or disinterest in what the patient is saying. When patients interpret "Our time is up for today" as a rejection, the therapist can remind them that the end of the session is based solely on the agreed time period for their meetings, not on the therapist's feelings or attitudes. Additionally, a fixed session length helps therapists resist being influenced by any feelings or attitudes they do have. All therapists experience temptations to abbreviate dull or difficult sessions and extend productive ones, and the fixed time period protects them against introducing such surplus meanings into session length.

Thus a clear initial statement of a fixed duration for sessions serves two related purposes. First, it promotes a relationship in which the therapist's saying "Our time is up for today" is interpreted to mean simply that the time is up, not as "I don't like you," or "I don't want to spend any more time with you," or "You and your problems aren't very important," or "You're boring me." Second, it provides a definite basis for regarding any such patient impressions as misconceptions that need to be understood. On the other hand, the advantages of fixed-length sessions do not mandate inflexibility. Therapists should always be prepared for unusual situations that seem to call for abbreviated or extended interviews, particularly in the context of relatively supportive psychotherapy.

In fact, moreover, there is nothing sacrosanct about any particular length of time for therapy sessions. The advantages of a fixed duration for interviews and of some breathing space between appointments have compelling face validity, but there are no data to indicate that a 45- to 50-minute hour is either the best or only effective time period. For patients in supportive psychotherapy who have difficulty tolerating a "full-length" session, 30-minute sessions may be indicated. The differential effectiveness of various length "hours" in psychotherapy has not been studied systematically. Hence, even though the 45- to 50-minute hour is the most widely recommended and commonly used time period, there is no basis for considering it inviolate.

FREQUENCY

For the same reasons that psychotherapy should consist of sessions of specified and uniform length, the sessions themselves should be scheduled at regular and fixed intervals. Systematic progress toward self-understanding is difficult to sustain if appointments are made or canceled according to a patient's felt needs for a session. Patients who feel disinclined to talk may be struggling with some difficult material that should be talked about, and patients who feel no need for a session because things are currently going well in their lives may be in a good frame of mind, free from daily pressures, for recalling and thinking productively about past events.

Therapists likewise need some protection from their underlying needs, so that they do not find themselves scheduling additional sessions when patients are presenting interesting material and progressing well, and cutting back on the frequency of the interviews when progress becomes slow or difficult. There may be times when it appears appropriate to alter the frequency of sessions, particularly in relatively supportive psychotherapy, but such alterations should be based on the patient's needs and not on how fascinating or rewarding the therapist's work is.

It is usually helpful to begin discussing the frequency of sessions by asking patients about their expectations in this regard. Some people come for therapy with little idea that regular sessions on at least a weekly basis are likely to be required, whereas others may have the notion that psychotherapy always has to involve daily sessions. By eliciting any misconceptions a patient may have before they propose a particular session frequency, therapists can be prepared to close any gaps in this regard between the patient's expectations and what they are going to suggest.

There are no hard-and-fast rules for the most desirable session frequency. In general, the more intensive the treatment is to be, as defined by how ambitious the treatment goals are and how deep a level of self-understanding is to be sought, the more frequently interviews should be scheduled. Nevertheless, there is no uniform relationship between depth of psychotherapy and frequency of sessions. Some patients work faster and are less rigidly defended than others, whereas others are rather deliberate in their manner of presentation and hesitant to embrace new perspectives. A relatively open and spontaneous patient may work as intensively in once weekly psychotherapy as a relatively restrained and guarded patient can in two sessions per week.

Moreover, there is no direct relationship between how frequently sessions are scheduled and how quickly therapy will be completed. Some patients may expect that, by coming for sessions twice weekly, they will finish treatment sooner than if they are seen just once a week. In fact, however, just the opposite is likely to occur. Patients who have relatively frequent sessions tend to bring up more different issues than patients seen less frequently, to get more deeply involved in these issues, and to require more time to resolve them. Hence, when recommending how frequent the sessions should be, therapists should clarify that the frequency has no necessary bearing on how long the treatment will last.

The actual decision that therapists make concerning session frequency will be determined by their assessment of what seems suitable for helping a particular patient work on the problems that have been outlined and toward the goals that have been agreed on. No particular frequency of sessions has been demonstrated in general to surpass other frequencies in effectiveness (Whiston & Sexton, 1993). However, such general findings mask the likelihood that differing session frequencies are differentially effective with different patients, depending on their needs and the goals of their treatment. As a general rule of thumb, clinical experience suggests that at least weekly sessions are usually necessary to sustain the treatment progress necessary to conduct uncovering psychotherapy and promote significant personality change. The more ambitious the goals of the treatment, the more likely the therapy will be to require sessions on more than a weekly basis. Additionally, the more guarded, rigid, or resistive a patient appears, the more necessary a frequency greater than once weekly may be to attain a given set of goals. Conversely, the more supportive rather than expressive the planned treatment strategies, the more likely it is that the goals of the psychotherapy could be realized with sessions on less than a weekly basis.

PLACE

Therapists making treatment arrangements should state clearly where the sessions are to be held and where the patient is to check in when arriving for them. This advice may seem gratuitous, especially from the perspective of established practitioners conducting psychotherapy in an office with their name on the door. However, it is less gratuitous with respect to psychotherapy being provided by professionals in training, who may not have their own office, and with respect to psychotherapy being conducted in hospital, clinic, and agency settings in which unassigned interviewing rooms are used for treatment and in which a large and complex physical plant may challenge even capable and determined patients to find out where they are supposed to be. A few words of direction from the therapist will be appreciated by patients and may make the difference in their arriving on time for their initial sessions.

With further respect to settings in which an individual private office may not be available, therapists should try to see their patients in the same place each time they come in. People talk about themselves more easily when they feel "at home," and the trappings of a therapist's office take on a familiarity that helps make a patient comfortable. Even a relatively barren interview room has features to which patients become accustomed and that give them a sense of being in a familiar place, such as the type and placement of the furniture, the pictures on the walls, and the view from the window. Constant shuffling among interviewing rooms has a second and more subtle disadvantage for the therapist's image. Patients tend to invest themselves more eagerly in the treatment process if they feel that their therapists, whatever their age or years of experience, are competent professionals who have the respect of their colleagues. Accordingly, it may dampen patients' enthusiasm for their treatment if their therapist appears to be such a low-status person that he or she cannot command a regularly scheduled interviewing room for an ongoing case. Even without having their own office, therapists can avoid this possible interference with treatment progress by putting themselves in the position of being able to say, "We will be meeting each Wednesday at one o'clock, then, and we will have the use of this room for our sessions."

FEES

Opinion is divided concerning whether the payment of a fee is necessary for progress to occur in psychotherapy. Whereas some therapists are convinced on the basis of their clinical experience that a financial sacrifice by the patient is essential for benefits to accrue, others view the fee as incidental to outcome. Relevant research appears to indicate that fees are generally not related to the outcome of psychotherapy but that, in some circumstances, having patients pay something toward the cost of their treatment can have a positive influence on their attitudes toward it (Garfield, 1994; Orlinsky et al., 1994; Whiston & Sexton, 1993).

However this may be, most psychotherapy patients are charged fees and are expected to cover a portion of them out of their own pockets. Some discussion of the fee arrangements must therefore be included in finalizing the treatment contract. Most people find it difficult to discuss money, and therapists are sometimes tempted to talk around rather than about it. Rationalizations for avoiding money talk are readily available ("I want patients to feel that I'm interested in them as a person, regardless of how much money they have or how much they are paying to see me"), and often there is someone else around to whom money matters can be referred, such as the fee clerk in a sliding scale clinic or the gatekeeper in a health maintenance organization.

Whether therapists are setting their own fees or having them set by others, they should without fail make sure that their patients know what the fee will be, consider it fair and acceptable, and have an opportunity to raise questions about it. Although the setting of a fee should not be a bartering affair, therapists must be prepared to discuss fee variations with individual patients based on realistic considerations, just as they are prepared to schedule sessions on a Wednesday rather than a Tuesday for a patient who would have difficulty keeping Tuesday appointments. Explicit discussion of fees provides information to which patients are entitled and also helps communicate that all aspects of their lives are appropriate subjects for discussion in psychotherapy. Money matters play some role in everybody's life, and therapists who omit discussing such an obvious money matter as the fee for their services may inadvertently imply that financial concerns, and perhaps other unspecified subjects as well, should not be brought up in the treatment.[5]

Finally, therapists do well to keep in mind what patients have a right to expect in return for their money. Psychotherapy patients are purchasing the therapist's professional services. They are not purchasing a piece of merchandise with a money-back guarantee if they are not satisfied with it, nor are they accepting a free trial offer. Patients are expected to pay their bills regularly from the beginning of the treatment, assuming that therapists are keeping their part of the treatment contract. Whether patients are getting their money's worth is solely a function of whether they have a qualified therapist who is exercising a conscientious effort to be helpful to them.

NOTES

1. Menninger and Holzman (1973, pp. 15–38) elaborate on how the psychotherapy relationship operates as a two-party contract, and the ethical responsibility of therapists to make patients' rights an integral part of their treatment is discussed further by Hare-Mustin, Maracek, Kaplan, and Liss-Levinson (1979). Readers are also referred to a classic paper by S. Freud (1913/1958), "On Beginning the Treatment," which addresses many of the topics covered in this chapter; to an extended analysis and discussion of Freud's papers on the technique of psychotherapy by Ellman (1991); and to contemporary comments on the details of getting psychotherapy underway provided by Blanck and Blanck (1994, Chapters 15–16) and Jacobs and Rothstein (1990).

2. Although rich in meaning, "success neurosis" is more of a dynamic than a descriptive diagnosis. As such, it is not a formally designated entity in *DSM-IV*. Readers unfamiliar with this classic concept are referred to S. Freud's (1916/1957c) discussion of people "wrecked by success" and to discussions by Canavan-Gumpert, Garner, and Gumpert (1978); Schuster (1955); and I. Weiner (1992a, pp. 279–282) of fears of success.

3. Taken together, this illustrative explanation of the process of psychotherapy and the previous illustration of a summary statement concerning the nature of a patient's problems constitute a rationale for the treatment. As described by Greencavage and Norcross (1990), an explicit rationale that provides patients a plausible explanation of their symptoms or problems and lays out a procedure for ameliorating them constitutes one of the common factors widely acknowledged as contributing to positive outcome in many forms of therapy. Garfield (1994) notes in particular that patients who enter psychotherapy with an accurate sense of their role in it and expectations similar to those of their therapist are relatively likely to continue in and benefit from treatment.

4. External administrative and financial controls on how psychotherapy can be conducted are a reality of contemporary clinical practice. Guidelines imposed by treatment facilities and the benefits provisions of health care insurance coverage presently exert considerable influence on who is seen for what type of psychotherapy for how many sessions of what length and for what fee. These guidelines and benefit provisions do not necessarily conform to principles of effective psychotherapy as demonstrated by research findings and inferred from cumulative clinical experience. The impact of external controls on the work of psychotherapists in a managed care environment is elaborated by Austad and Berman (1991); Barron and Sands (1996); Herron, Javier, Primavera, and Schultz (1994); L. Johnson (1995); Lowman and Resnick (1994); Miller (1996a); and Tuckfelt, Fink, and Warren (1997).

5. For further discussion of issues regarding the setting and management of fees in psychotherapy, see Herron and Welt (1992), Krueger (1986), and Pasternack (1988).

CHAPTER 7

Conduct of the Interview

A s PATIENTS become increasingly comfortable with talking and their therapists become increasingly familiar with them and their concerns, psychotherapy gradually progresses from its initial, preparatory phase to its middle, interpretive phase. To promote such progress, therapists need to conduct the interviews following agreement on the treatment contract in ways that acclimate patients to the methods and procedures of psychotherapy, help them talk productively, and elicit further information about their life experiences and personality functioning.

ACCLIMATING THE PATIENT

No matter how informed patients have been about psychotherapy before coming for help and no matter how perceptively they have endorsed their role as a patient in discussing the treatment contract, they are unlikely to be fully prepared to participate in the treatment. To make the transition from being told about their role to actually filling it, most patients require some continuing education aimed at helping them become acclimated to the psychotherapy situation. A useful beginning in this direction is a capsule review of patient and therapist roles:

> Now that we've made our arrangements to continue working together, let me say something about what our roles will be. Your role will be to talk as freely as you can about yourself and whatever may be on your mind, and my role will be primarily to listen, to help you talk, and to help you understand yourself better.

A brief statement of this kind usually suffices to clarify for patients what their task is and how the therapist intends to respond. Having made such a clear and definitive statement, therapists can refer back to it in helping patients recognize role distortions that they may express from time to time (e.g., "I've been talking a lot lately; it's your turn now"). Likewise, patients who have understood the therapist's explanation of how psychotherapy proceeds may still have specific questions about how they should actually begin, what they should focus on in talking, how they can tell what is important to bring up and what is not, and the like. The therapist can respond adequately to most such questions by briefly amplifying the patient's task:

> The main thing is that you should talk about whatever is on your mind. It's difficult to know in advance whether something will be important or not in understanding more about you, and we can't tell for sure until we've had a chance to discuss it. For this reason, you should try not to censor any thoughts or feelings you may have, but just express them as they come to you.

More often than not, the need for continuing patient education arises frequently in the interviews immediately following agreement on the treatment contract. For example, patients may begin one or more of these early sessions by sitting silently or otherwise indicating their preference for the therapist to open the interview (e.g., "I don't know where to begin"; "What should I talk about today?" "I wish you would ask me some questions"). In response to such beginnings early in psychotherapy, it is helpful for therapists to communicate that the patient, as much as possible, should take responsibility for starting sessions:

> We have been learning something about you and have seen how this emerged from what you were able to say about yourself. It will work best if we continue to begin each time with what may be on your mind, and then take it from there.

This type of response to initial silence ignores any elements of resistance that may be involved. In the initial phase of treatment, therapists need to refrain from jumping on every possible hint of resistance in a patient's behavior. Unless resistances are threatening continuation of the treatment, they are better left alone until, in the middle phase of therapy, they arise after a period of comfortable participation by a patient in the treatment process (see Chapter 9). The initial phase of psychotherapy is a time for educating patients in their role, not offering challenging interpretations of their behavior. Hence, the instructional approach just illustrated is typically the preferable way of responding to patients who have difficulty starting interviews early in the treatment.

Once patients have begun an interview and raised some topics for discussion, they may become uncertain about how to continue and ask for guidance: "Should I tell you more about that?" "There are a number of things I could talk about next, but I'm not sure what you're interested in finding out or what's proper for me to bring up." Like silence, such questions often reflect some resistance to the communication process, such as a wish to change the topic because the subject being discussed is leading toward some distressing or embarrassing material. Such requests for guidance may also have rich implications for patients' personality dynamics and their attitudes toward the therapist. For example, why do they feel a need to ask permission to continue talking, and why do they allude to what the therapist wants to find out rather than to what they themselves want to learn more about, and why are they concerned about being "proper?"

Again, however, the task for therapists in the initial phase of psychotherapy is not to demonstrate their brilliance at picking up subtle clues to the patients' underlying thoughts and feelings, but rather to cement patients' involvement in the treatment process and prepare them for subsequent interpretive work.[1] Hence the focus at this point belongs on instructing patients who express uncertainty about how to proceed, and not on trying to probe the origins of their uncertainty.

The most effective instructional technique with uncertain patients consists of repeating as necessary the basic elements of the "free association" method that define their role: they should talk as freely as they can about whatever comes to their mind; they should try not to censor or withhold any of their thoughts or feelings; and because it is difficult to know in advance what is more or less important to discuss, they should avoid any prejudgments about whether something should or should not be said.[2]

Whenever patients are talking freely in these early interviews, therapists can acclimate them to the treatment process simply by adopting the role they have said they will fill and by displaying the therapist behaviors that contribute to good outcome, as noted in Chapter 3: they listen attentively, they provide an accepting climate in which nothing that is said elicits scorn or censure, and they demonstrate their ability and willingness to help the patient understand the meaning of his or her experiences.[3] As just mentioned, however, this is not yet the time for therapists to demonstrate their empathy in the form of penetrating insights and sweeping interpretations. Instead, they need to accustom patients gradually to the interpretive aspect of the treatment process through occasional clarifications and relatively superficial observations.

These clarifications and observations should consist for the most part of repeating or asking patients to repeat bits of information that seem potentially important ("As I understand it, then, it was the combination of your being criticized about your work and having the criticism come from someone you admire that led to your feeling particularly bad"; "Could you go over that again so I can be sure I have a clear picture of what it was your husband did that made you angry?"). With such occasional interjections, therapists help familiarize patients with how psychotherapy works, while at the same time they demonstrate their interest, attentiveness, and capacity to understand.

An additional aspect of education for psychotherapy involves questions patients may raise about the content of their thoughts and feelings. As patients begin to associate freely and to come up with novel ideas and recollections, they are likely to ask their therapist's opinion of them: "Why did I think about that now?" "What does it mean that I'm feeling angry as I talk about my sister?" "How have I become such a rigid person as I seem to be?" In some instances, when answers to such questions would constitute the type of clarification or superficial interpretation that helps accustom patients to the psychotherapy process, the therapist may offer a direct answer. More commonly, however, it is preferable not to answer such questions, but instead to use them to help patients work toward discovering their own answers.

Two approaches in particular allow therapists to respond to content-oriented questions in ways that foster further self-exploration by the patient. One approach consists of eliciting the patient's own associations ("I wonder what ideas might occur to you about that question"), and the other involves calling attention to the question itself ("Perhaps it would be helpful to look at why that particular question occurred to you at this point"). In addition to encouraging patients to plumb their own mental contents further, these types of response help patients learn that in psychotherapy questions are considered statements to be understood and not necessarily answered.

HELPING THE PATIENT TALK PRODUCTIVELY

Whereas the general process of acclimating patients to psychotherapy helps induce them to talk freely, several more specific technical procedures can be employed to promote productive talking. Productive talking consists of a readiness on the part of patients to elaborate what they are saying, sufficient spontaneity for them to report new feelings and ideas as they arise, and a willingness to continue talking even when it becomes difficult or uncomfortable to do so. The techniques by which patients can be helped to achieve and sustain these elements of productivity comprise various ways of phrasing statements, responding to silences, handling discomfort, and arranging the physical setting for interviews.

PHRASING THERAPIST STATEMENTS

Therapists can foster spontaneous production of material in treatment sessions by attending carefully to how they phrase their statements. Particularly effective in this regard is conducting the interview without asking questions. Although there are times when direct questions are the most suitable means of accessing necessary information, a predominantly inquisitive interview style has several disadvantages for ongoing psychotherapy. First, being inquisitive sets a question-and-answer tone and suggests to patients that their task is simply to answer what the therapist asks them. Second, asking questions implies that the therapist is responsible for determining what subjects are to be discussed and in how much detail. Third, frequent questions give the impression that, once patients have finished answering them all, they will be handed the solution to their problems.

For these reasons, a question-oriented interview style often discourages patients from elaborating their remarks or spontaneously volunteering information on subjects of their own choice, while obscuring the patient's responsibility for producing material and working toward self-understanding. With practice, therapists can learn to avoid taking a questioning or directive stance even when they are trying to elicit a specific bit of information or lead a patient into a particular subject area.

For example, "How did you feel about that?" can be phrased "I wonder what feelings you may have had about that"; "Tell me more about your mother" can be phrased "You've been mentioning your mother but you really haven't told me much about her"; "How old is your father?" can be phrased "You've been talking about your father but you haven't said how old he is"; and so on. Despite the seeming insignificance of these changes in wording, they subtly alter therapists' overt role. Instead of being a questioner, they become someone who listens and clarifies, and instead of leading the discussion, they influence its direction without obviously doing so. Questions ("How old is your father?") call for an answer, whereas statements ("You haven't mentioned your father's age"), no matter how compelling, do not demand any specific answer. To borrow an apt phrase from Sullivan (1954, pp. 19–25), it is as a "participant observer" who can translate questions and directives into observations and clarifications that therapists best facilitate productive talking by their patients.

In addition to avoiding questions and directives, therapists can also foster patient productivity by being concise. Phrasing whatever observations or clarifications appear indicated in as few words as possible helps to keep patients working productively. Lengthy commentaries and elaborate reconstructions of the therapist's impressions impede rather than facilitate progress; they impose a role shift, with the therapist becoming the talker and the patient the listener, and they interrupt the patient's flow of ideas and efforts at self-understanding.

Psychotherapy is not an occasion for speech making. Therapists who find themselves engaging in long-winded interventions should ask themselves two questions. First, are they gratifying needs of their own (e.g., to be in control, to exhibit perspicacity, or to win admiration) at the expense of meeting the patient's needs? If so, a change in style is called for. Second, do they lack sufficient understanding of what they are observing to formulate it concisely? If so, the attempt at formulation should be deferred until they know enough to do a better job of it.[4]

RESPONDING TO SILENCES

To help patients talk productively, therapists must be prepared to deal with periods of silence that inevitably occur during psychotherapy interviews. Patient silences, whatever their origin, represent an obstacle to communication that must be removed or circumvented before progress can be resumed. This particularly is the case when silent patients do not appear actively absorbed in thinking about or trying to find the words for what they will say next, but instead are looking around blankly or squirming uncomfortably at an apparent loss for ideas. Faced with such silences, therapists have four primary options open to them.

First, they can sit silently themselves and wait for the patient to resume talking. Prolonged silences make most patients progressively more uncomfortable and motivate them to talk as a way of relieving their discomfort. In this sense, the interview situation can be likened to a vacuum, which compels being filled, and sooner or later the patient will say something if the therapist does not. However, extended therapist silence should be recognized as a potentially counterproductive tactic. Although consistent with the therapist's role as listener, silence can may make patients too anxious to express themselves clearly or unable even to tolerate remaining in treatment. Prolonged therapist silences can also cause patients to wonder whether the therapist has been paying attention to what they have been saying and is really interested in helping them.

For these reasons, therapists should be cautious about greeting silence with silence, especially in the early phases of treatment. Occasional brief silences educate patients about the treatment process and foster their spontaneity and sense of responsibility for talking. Extended painful silences, on the other hand, occurring before patients are accustomed to their role as talkers and prepared to deal with interpretations of their silence, are more likely to be damaging than helpful. Therapists who sit in stony silence during early interviews, believing that they are properly requiring patients to demonstrate their motivation and assume their responsibility for the treatment, are shirking the responsibility that is theirs for helping patients talk.

Second, therapists can assume responsibility for sustaining the conversation when patients fall silent. Whereas the preceding option of therapist silence is the most radical and anxiety provoking of the four responses to patient silence being discussed here, this second option of taking over responsibility is the most conservative and anxiety-reducing response. In sustaining the conversation, therapists respond to patients who have fallen silent by commenting on what they had been talking about or by suggesting a new topic for them to take up: "You were talking a few moments ago about what it was like when your parents got divorced, and I wonder if there is more you could say about that"; "So far today you haven't mentioned anything about how things are going at work."

Although this means of responding to patient silences avoids the potential disadvantages of therapists also remaining silent, it too has serious drawbacks. When comments or suggestions are offered to sustain conversation following a patient silence of a few minutes or more, they implicitly contradict what therapists are trying to convey about their role in the treatment. That is, they imply that therapists stand ready to indicate what patients should talk about, whether they should elaborate on a topic, and when they should change the subject.

Therapists therefore should use this direct method of ending patient silences only sparingly, usually in just two circumstances. The first occurs when it appears so important to elaborate certain aspects of content or background information that getting this further information takes precedence over instructing patients in their role or exploring their difficulty in talking. In this circumstance, therapists might respond to patients who have fallen silent by encouraging them to continue with the topic they were discussing. The second occurs when silent patients appear to have become so upset about what they had been saying that reducing their anxiety takes precedence over trying to understand its origin. In this circumstance, therapists might choose to change the subject, help patients talk about something they are relatively comfortable with, and defer the upsetting subject for some later time.

As a third option, therapists can ask silent patients for their associations. Asking for associations ("What's going through your mind right now?" "I wonder what thoughts or feelings you may be having") helps to break through a patient's silence without having most of the drawbacks of the therapist's remaining silent or becoming directive. A request or suggestion that patients associate is sufficiently active to let them know the therapist is paying attention and trying to be helpful, while it is sufficiently inactive to leave in the patient's hands the responsibility for deciding how much to say about what.

Because the free association method can help silent patients talk productively without compromising the therapist's role as an interested but nondirective listener, it is generally preferable to remaining silent or attempting to sustain the conversation. Yet all three of these ways of handling silence have in common that they are efforts to circumvent a silence and cause a patient to talk again, rather than to understand the origin and meaning of the silence. Circumventing silences, especially by the free association method, is an important therapist activity while patients are learning about psychotherapy. As patients become accustomed to the treatment process, however, exploring silences takes priority over merely breaking through them, and therapists should begin to replace asking silent patients for associations with a fourth way of responding to patient silence.

Fourth and finally, therapists can offer observations and interpretations of a patient's silence. When patients who have had ample opportunity to become acclimated to psychotherapy are extensively silent without displaying a degree of anxiety that appears to call for support, often the most productive response to their silence consists of focusing on it as behavior that needs to be understood. A variety of approaches can be used to introduce such a focus, depending on how fully therapists understand the silence and how much pressure they feel should be placed on the patient.

For example, when therapists have little idea why a patient has fallen silent, they might simply comment, "You haven't said anything for the last several minutes." An observation of this kind puts no pressure on the patient to respond in any particular way, but it does constitute both a suggestion that the silence is worth paying attention to and an invitation for the patient to give some thought to what it might mean. An alternative statement in this situation that puts a little more pressure on patients to reflect on their silence rather than just begin talking again, would be, "I wonder why it is you've stopped talking."

Should therapists sense some relationship between a patient's silence and what the patient was saying prior to falling silent, they might then observe, "You've been sitting silently for a while now, and just before you stopped talking you were describing some feelings you have about your mother." Whereas such a response to silence is more directive than merely commenting on the silence without any reference to content, it still leaves it up to patients to consider whether their silence is in fact saying something about their feelings toward their mother.

In still other situations, therapists may be fairly certain that a patient's silence is the result of upsetting thoughts or feelings stirred up by the subject under discussion. They can then choose to offer a direct interpretation on the order of, "There's something about talking about your mother that is upsetting to you." In this manner of responding to silence, the therapist puts direct pressure on the patient to explore further an apparently difficult subject, and the silence is used as partial evidence for a content interpretation rather than as the focus of an observation.

HANDLING PATIENT DISCOMFORT

If psychotherapy is proceeding in productive directions, patients will inevitably experience moments of psychological discomfort. In fact, if a person presumably engaged in uncovering psychotherapy rolls along session after session in unmitigated good spirits and without transient indications of being angry, anxious, or depressed, it behooves the therapist to look closely at whether anything constructive is taking place. Consistently comfortable patients are either not being helped to explore anything about themselves that they are not already familiar with, or they are rigidly defending against any emotional involvement in the treatment process. In such cases, therapists must take steps to help patients confront new material and relax their defenses, or else the treatment will bounce around ineffectually on the surface of the patient's psyche and produce little benefit.

When patients are emotionally involved in expanding their self-awareness, on the other hand, they do become upset from time to time, perhaps to their dismay. Having entered psychotherapy in hopes of feeling better, patients need time to adjust to the fact that learning about themselves may on occasion make them feel worse. Until they have made this adjustment, there is some risk that becoming upset may discourage them from talking or even suggest to them that they have little to gain from continuing in the treatment. It is at these points that therapists must be prepared to recognize and handle patient discomfort.

The most useful way of handling such discomfort in the early stages of psychotherapy is to explain it. For example, therapists can point out that when people begin to look at aspects of themselves they have not previously been aware of, some uneasiness is to be expected. They can furthermore indicate that it is usually the things that are going well in a person's life that are most pleasant to talk about, whereas people who set out to explore aspects of their lives that trouble them can anticipate some discomfort with the subjects that arise.

Such comments serve only to relieve or circumvent patient discomfort, and as therapy progresses, they should be gradually replaced with interpretation of patient discomfort. Early in the treatment, however, when the therapist's attention should be focused more on helping patients talk than on interpreting what they say, education in psychotherapy takes precedence. Not until patients have come to accept psychological discomfort as an inevitable by-product of their quest for greater self-understanding are they ready to profit from the therapist's shifting from an instructive to an interpretive stance.

Offering an explanation of patient discomfort in the early stages of psychotherapy is not inconsistent with the recommendation in Chapter 6 that therapists should avoid telling patients in advance that there will be times when they find talking difficult. Anticipating difficulty before it occurs is different from responding to it after it has appeared, and telling uncomfortable patients that they are apparently dealing with a subject that is troubling to them does not dilute their discomfort or strip it of any uniquely personal significance.

ARRANGING THE PHYSICAL SETTING

As noted in Chapter 6, seeing patients in the same room for each session fosters a sense of familiarity with the surroundings and makes talking easier for them. There are additional ways in which therapists can arrange the physical setting so as to make patients comfortable and promote their talking productively, especially with regard to the style and placing of furniture in the interviewing room.

For example, interviews should be conducted without any large physical barrier interposed between patient and therapist. Therapists ensconced behind a desk are less likely to be seen as warm, open, genuine people than therapists who allow themselves to be seen and could even be reached out to and touched. Whether patients actually experience or act on a wish to touch their therapist, there is something much more engaging in talking with someone who could be touched than with someone so far removed or so sheltered behind furniture that he or she is untouchable. Therapists who use a desk will do well to have patients sit at its side rather than directly across from them, and they might do even better to consider changing to a seating arrangement that puts no furniture between themselves and their patients.

As for the style of furniture used, both patient and therapist should obviously be comfortable, and therapists may justifiably feel that their long hours of sitting call for a particularly comfortable chair. What needs to be avoided, however, is any use of furniture that might convey disadvantageous surplus meaning. Consider, for example, the possible implications of the therapist's settling into a comfortable easy chair while the patient perches on a hard, straight-backed model; or of having patients buried deep in the folds of an overstuffed chair with therapists in their regular desk chair towering several inches above them. Although there are no uniform ways in which such features of the seating arrangement can be expected to affect all patients, they are likely to generate feelings that can inhibit productive talking, such as of being in a subservient position, of being judged, of being accorded second-class status, and so forth. Approximate equality of seating, on the other hand, contributes to demonstrating therapist respect for the patient and minimizes any unintended significance that might be injected into the treatment relationship by an insensitive choice of chairs.

ELICITING FURTHER INFORMATION ABOUT THE PATIENT

When patients have become reasonably acclimated to psychotherapy and able to talk productively in their sessions, the treatment is ready to progress from its initial, preparatory phase to its middle, interpretive phase. What remains initially is for therapists to fill in the picture they have of the patient's personality structure and dynamics, because they cannot begin to interpret effectively until they have sharpened their earlier working formulations.

Hence this last part of the initial stage of psychotherapy is a time when therapists should concentrate on eliciting and absorbing further information about a patient. As they become increasingly confident that they have a full and accurate grasp of the patient's lifestyle, past experiences, and current difficulties, they can gradually shift their focus from gathering information to interpreting it. In the process, the treatment itself will gradually shift from the initial to the middle phase. As discussed earlier, no specific length of time or number of sessions can be specified as necessary or sufficient for this shift to be accomplished; how easily patients talk about themselves and how sensitively therapists can listen are among the many factors that determine the duration of the initial phase of treatment. Ordinarily, however, therapists can sharpen their formulations and shorten this initial phase by employing tactics that probe the patient's personal dimensions, call attention to what is not stated, and encourage a balanced expression of thoughts and feelings.

PROBING THE PATIENT'S PERSONAL DIMENSIONS

One can learn a great deal about other people simply by finding out how they define the dimensions of their experience, that is, what things mean to them. For example, a woman may say, "I feel happy today." What does feeling happy mean to this person? In what ways does she experience the feeling of happiness? What things generally tend to make her feel more or less happy? And how does she feel about feeling happy?

Is she surprised at feeling happy or is it something she takes for granted? Is happiness a totally pleasant experience for her or one that is bittersweet because she feels undeserving or anticipates a rude letdown? The answers to such questions would provide considerable information about this woman, and similar amplification of what other feeling states mean to her could paint a revealing picture of her personality style.

In the psychotherapy situation, then, therapists should listen closely for words that have idiographic meaning and encourage patients to elaborate on them. Adjectives such as "happy" and "sad" illustrate only one part of speech that provides a basis for therapists to probe patients' personal dimensions in this way. Colorful nouns and verbs offer similar opportunities. When a man says his wife is "a real shrew," the therapist may have a fairly good idea what he means. However, the opportunity should not be missed to question the meaning of "shrew" to this man (e.g., "What do you mean by a shrew?" or "Your wife is a *shrew?*") and thereby encourage him to elaborate on his marital relationship and on what there is about his wife that bothers him.

Suppose in responding, this patient describes an incident in which he "chewed out" his wife. What does "chewing out" consist of for him, how does he feel about doing it, and is it a common or uncommon thing for him to do? Suppose he contrasts his wife with someone else whom he regards as a more "sympathetic" person. What does being sympathetic consist of in his mind, in what circumstances and from what people in his life is he likely to feel sympathy being extended to him, and how does he usually react to receiving sympathy?

Therapists should not take for granted the use of slang expressions or metaphors by patients, especially if they are unsure what patients mean by them. While being careful not to discourage patients' spontaneity by inquiring into their every use of colorful language, therapists should pose such questions as "How do you mean?" often enough to ensure that they understand what is being said. As an additional benefit of such inquiry, asking patients to elaborate the feelings and attitudes reflected in their choice of words helps to communicate that the focus in psychotherapy is not on what things mean in general, but on what they mean specifically to the patient.

CALLING ATTENTION TO WHAT IS NOT STATED

Calling attention to what patients have not said often provides an effective way of leading an interview without appearing to, and it is a tactic that can be adapted to serve strategic purposes in different phases of the treatment. In the initial assessment phase of psychotherapy, saying, "You haven't mentioned anything about your work" can help to open up discussion of this diagnostically important topic. Later, in the middle phase of psychotherapy, a modified version of this observation ("You're not saying anything about your work") can be utilized not so much to elicit general information about a patient's work situation as to focus on what reasons there might be for the person's omitting to talk about this subject.

At the intermediate point being discussed now, when therapists are moving from the initial into the middle phase of psychotherapy, observations of what is not being said should be intended to elicit specific information rather than just open a subject for discussion. However, the therapist's focus should still be limited to *what* is being said or not said (which defines the *content* of psychotherapy) and not yet extend to *why* something is said or not (which is an aspect of the *process* of psychotherapy and is best reserved for the middle phase of treatment). As an example of phrasing statements to serve this intermediate purpose, a therapist who has learned from earlier interviews a fair amount about the nature of a patient's work and how it relates to his or her difficulties might observe at an appropriate point, "You've been talking about your job, but you haven't said anything about how you got into your line of work."

ENCOURAGING A BALANCED EXPRESSION OF THOUGHTS AND FEELINGS

Psychotherapy progresses best when patients express both thoughts and feelings; conversely, therapy usually founders when it is limited either to an emotionally detached discussion of ideas and events or an unbridled outpouring of affect. People can understand themselves and realize their full human potential only by accessing both ideational and affective aspects of their lives, and excessive emphasis on one at the expense of the other almost always proves maladaptive. Accordingly, therapists can usually promote the progress of their patients by helping those who are primarily "thinkers" to feel more, and those who are primarily "feelers" to think more.

The transition period between the initial and middle phases of psychotherapy is a good time for beginning to help patients strike an adaptive balance between thinking and feeling. As a useful tactic in implementing this strategy, therapists can comment at appropriate points on which aspect of their experience patients are omitting to mention: "You've given me a detailed description of what went on in that situation, but you haven't said anything about how you felt"; "You've told me a lot about the feelings you experienced in the situation, but you haven't given much of a description of what actually took place." Comments of this kind elicit additional information that supplement the therapist's picture of a patient's personality, and they also subtly convey that both thoughts and feelings need to be recognized and explored. Later in treatment, therapists' observations that thoughts or feelings are not being expressed can serve the same purpose as observations of what is not stated, that is, to call attention to process aspects (why) rather than merely content aspects (what) of the material.

A concluding general guideline for using the psychotherapy interview tactics suggested in this chapter is that therapists should avoid relying too heavily on any one of them. Whenever therapists slip into a mode of repeating certain kinds of statements automatically, the treatment loses its spontaneity and becomes a stilted and formal exercise in a patient's eyes. To avoid the pitfalls of routinization, therapists should employ a varied repertoire of methods for helping patients talk and eliciting items of information, and they should keep these methods as natural and as unobtrusive as possible.

NOTES

1. Hasty, premature, and undisciplined interpretation of a patient's unconscious mental life is known as "wild analysis" (S. Freud, 1910/ 1957d). Practiced usually by inexperienced or inadequately trained therapists who regard psychotherapy as a flashy and sensational lunge for the psychic jugular, rather than as the painstaking pursuit of understanding it needs to be, wild analysis seldom serves a patient's best interests. Buckley, Karasu, and Charles (1979) found in this regard that premature interpretations are among the most common mistakes made by novice therapists in training.

2. The free association method was devised by Freud, who considered it the "fundamental rule" of psychoanalysis (S. Freud, 1913/1958a, pp. 134–135). Although various types of psychotherapy can be differentiated in terms of how therapists respond to a patient's productions, they share the basic concept that patients should talk about themselves as freely as they can. Thus in all types of psychotherapy, regardless of how supportive they are intended to be or how structured the sessions are, therapists depend on what patients are able to report as their basis for assessing the progress of the treatment and selecting strategies and tactics to pursue. For fuller discussions of free association, see Busch (1995, Chapter 3), Kanzer (1961), A. Kris (1982, 1992), Singer (1965, Chapter 8), and Spacal (1990).

3. Numerous authors have elaborated on how these aspects of the therapist's stance acclimate patients to the treatment process and help them talk productively, beginning with a series of papers on technique published by

Freud between 1911 and 1915 (see Ellman, 1991). Of particular note is the contribution of Schafer (1983), who describes Freud's recommendations in this regard as being concerned with "establishing an atmosphere of safety" in the treatment situation. Schafer delineates such features of what he calls "the analytic attitude" as therapists being consistently attentive, nonjudgmental, responsive in terms of patients' needs rather than their own, and dedicated to providing help through enhanced understanding rather than advice or exhortation.

4. Wachtel (1993) provides detailed and well-conceived guidelines for phrasing therapist statements in ways that promote effective communication while minimizing patient distress. His apt terminology includes the sound advice that therapists learn to practice "the art of gentle inquiry" so that their interviews comprise "exploration, not interrogation": "Effective inquiry increases the likelihood that the patient will experience their therapist's comments as an invitation to explore rather than take them as a challenge to be warded off or as a signal to hide" (p. 88).

PART THREE

THE MIDDLE PHASE
OF PSYCHOTHERAPY

CHAPTER 8

Communicating
Understanding: Interpretation

T HE MIDDLE phase of psychotherapy is the period during which therapists concentrate on communicating understanding to a patient.
As noted earlier, there is no fixed number of sessions necessary to
reach this middle phase of treatment. Therapists may require anywhere
from a few sessions to a few months to complete their evaluation and assessment, establish a treatment contract, accustom a patient to therapy,
and arrive at a solid grasp of the patient's personality style. Sooner or
later, however, therapists will feel prepared to begin shifting their emphasis from efforts to learn about patients to efforts to help patients learn
about themselves.

The main tool for communicating understanding in psychotherapy is
interpretation. To use this tool effectively, therapists need to be familiar
with the nature of the interpretive process and with specific aspects of offering interpretations, including (a) what to interpret, (b) when to interpret, (c) how to interpret, (d) judging the effectiveness of interpretations,
and (e) working interpretations through.

THE NATURE OF INTERPRETATION

Interpretations are statements that refer to something patients have said or
done in such a way as to identify aspects of their behavior of which they
have not previously been fully aware. Interpretations are intended to expand patients' awareness of their thoughts and feelings and thereby enhance their understanding of themselves. Accordingly, interpretations

serve their purpose when they help patients achieve some adaptive restructuring of their cognitive and affective experience and some advantageous modification of their behavior patterns. Clinical observations have consistently demonstrated the therapeutic benefit of increased self-knowledge generated by the interpretive process (Levy, 1990, Chapter 9; Meissner, 1991, Chapter 13), and research findings confirm that skillful application of interpretations contributes to favorable outcome in psychotherapy (Orlinsky et al., 1994).[1]

In a sense, any therapist intervention can be regarded as an interpretation, because even the most noncommittal remark can influence what patients are attending to and thereby result in some cognitive or affective restructuring. A simple observation ("You seem a little restless today") may direct patients to an aspect of their behavior they had not been conscious of, such as crossing and uncrossing their legs repeatedly; a soft "Mm-hmm" or even a nod of the head may communicate that what a patient is saying is interesting, important, or commendable. However, such a broad concept of interpretation eliminates any systematic differentiation among kinds of therapist intervention and muddles matters both for clinicians conducting psychotherapy and for researchers studying the psychotherapy process.

Alternatively, there are advantages for both clinical and research purposes of adopting a relatively narrow definition of interpretation; namely, that interpretation constitutes an attempt to expand patients' conscious awareness of themselves by pointing out unconscious determinants of their behavior. This definition excludes comments on patients' observable behavior, although observations such as "You seem a little restless today" may be a prelude to suggesting some unconscious significance of the behavior ("It seems that you often get restless this way when you're feeling angry about something"). Similarly, incidental comments that are not intended to expand a patient's self-awareness are best not considered interpretations, even though they may have some interpretive effect. This definitional guideline is a corollary of the point made in Chapter 1 that psychotherapy should be defined by what a therapist is attempting to do and not by whatever happens to have a psychotherapeutic effect.

To distinguish further between interpretations and other kinds of therapist interventions, therapist behavior can be classified into the following five categories of increasing potential impact:

1. *Questions*. The simplest and most superficial way for therapists to intervene is by asking patients questions about themselves and their experiences. Although direct questioning can elicit useful information, it is not a particularly productive technique in the psychotherapy situation, as elaborated in Chapter 7.

2. *Clarifications.* Clarifications are statements intended to emphasize some aspect of patients' manifest productions. This emphasis can often be achieved simply by inviting further attention to something a patient has said and thereby implying its possible importance ("I wonder if you could tell me a little more about that"; "Could you go over that incident again so I can be sure I have a clear picture of what it was like for you?"). At other times, clarification consists of recapitulating a patient's remarks, perhaps in somewhat different language but without any elaboration or attempt to draw inferences ("As I hear it, then, you were feeling fine all the time you were watching the movie up to the point when someone sat down in the seat next to you, and then you began to feel so nervous and edgy that you had to leave the theater"). Expressed in either way, clarifications do not present patients with any ideas or possibilities that are not already in their conscious awareness, although they may initiate a sequence of interventions that leads to such new material.

3. *Exclamations.* Exclamations are brief therapist utterances that let patients know they are being listened to and encourage them to continue talking. Like clarifications, exclamations lend emphasis to what a patient is saying, even when they consist of no more than "Mm-hmm" or "I see." More so than clarifications, however, exclamations convey endorsement of a patient's comments as well as interest in them. Remarks such as "Mm-hmm" and "I see" imply not only "I'm listening" and "I understand," but also "I agree" and "I approve." Exclamations can of course be disapproving as well as approving, as in "Uh-uh" or "No way." However, should therapists intend to challenge or disagree with what a patient is saying, their interventions, no matter how brief, will have more in common with confrontations than with exclamations, which are meant to be at least relatively noncommittal.

4. *Confrontations.* In contrast to clarifications and exclamations, both of which address patients' manifest productions, confrontations call attention to something patients could be talking about but are not. By observing that patients have described an incident without mentioning any of their feelings about it, for example, or that the incident is notably similar to some previous episodes in their life, or that they seemed on the verge of tears while relating the incident, the therapist focuses on some potentially significant data that might otherwise have gone unnoticed.

Although confrontations bring new material to a patient's attention, they refer to observable events that should be obvious to the person once they are pointed out. Therapists may sometimes fail to keep their facts straight; for example, they may misjudge the similarity of a current incident in a patient's life to experiences in the person's past. With allowances for therapist error, however, confrontations are meant to be factual statements of how things are or how they were, not hypotheses about how they could be or might have been. Because confrontations refer to observable facts of which patients can readily become aware, they address the level of preconscious awareness. They go beyond what patients are immediately attending to but not so far as to introduce possibilities from their unconscious.

5. *Interpretations.* Interpretations identify possible aspects of patients' personality or behavior of which they are not fully aware and, without the therapist's help, are unlikely to become so. In contradistinction to other therapist interventions, interpretations (a) deal with unconscious material rather than manifest productions, (b) seek to explain rather than merely describe the patient's behavior, and (c) consist of inferences, probabilities, and alternative hypotheses rather than observations, facts, and certainties. Interpretations also have two distinctive characteristics that often make patients uncomfortable.

First, because interpretations convey something new to people about their inner life or their behavior, they inevitably take something away from their previous conceptions of themselves. To entertain new ways of thinking, feeling, or acting, a person must contemplate giving up old ways; the restructuring of experience and modification of behavior toward which interpretation aims can be achieved only through changes in existing structures and behavior patterns. Asking people to give up familiar aspects of their psychic functioning to which they have long been accustomed, even if these psychic processes have proved maladaptive, is thus asking them to endure a sense of loss. This consideration led Tarachow (1963, p. 20) to posit that the principal consequence of interpretation is object loss and that correct interpretations are therefore likely to be followed by momentary mild depression.

Second, because interpretations imply that a patient's current modes of doing or looking at things are not as effective or as realistic as they might be, they always constitute an attack. Suggesting to people that there are alternative ways for them to think, feel, or act, and furthermore that these alternatives are likely to direct them toward a richer and more rewarding life, tacitly conveys that there is something bad, wrong, or misguided in how they have been conducting their lives. Even mild interpretations tend to challenge patients' integrity, deflate their self-esteem, and mobilize defensive reactions.[2]

WHAT TO INTERPRET

In typical psychotherapy sessions, therapists form many more hypotheses about the meaning of patients' thoughts, feelings, and actions than they can or should express. Time is never sufficient to interpret every pertinent feature of an interview, and some priorities are therefore necessary to guide therapists in deciding what kinds of patient behavior should be interpreted.

Because interpretations are intended to communicate understanding, a first step in establishing priorities for what to interpret consists of recognizing that increased self-understanding is not uniformly beneficial across all areas of a person's life. Consider, for example, a male attorney who is successful and happy in his work, even though he is not fully aware of why he chose a career in law, and who has come for help because he is depressed about a perceived or actual decline in sexual potency. Although expanded self-awareness concerning his career choice might be of some interest to him, it would have minimal impact on his lifestyle and feeling of well-being, whereas learning more about his sexual attitudes could make considerable difference in how he feels and acts. On the other hand, if this attorney has sought help not because he is concerned about sexuality but because he feels frustrated and unfulfilled in the practice of law, the benefit he derives from increased self-understanding is likely to be much greater in the area of occupational choice than in the area of sexual behavior.

This hypothetical instance identifies a general principle that should govern decisions about what to interpret: Interpretations should focus on those aspects of patients' lives that are causing them difficulty. To this end, therapists should constantly ask themselves the following three interrelated questions as they listen to a patient and think about offering interpretations:

1. *What is making the patient anxious?* As a corollary of focusing psychotherapy on problematic aspects of people's lives, interpretations should be addressed to experienced or recollected events that patients find upsetting. There is little to be gained by pursuing the nature and origins of matters that are of little concern to patients and do not appear to be playing any role in the problems that have brought them for help. On the other hand, any circumstance that either by direct patient report or therapist observation seems to be generating manifest anxiety should be identified as a potentially fruitful target for appropriate interventions.

2. *What is the patient handling ineffectively?* Whether because of anxiety or faulty learning, people sometimes handle aspects of their lives in ways that are less satisfying and self-fulfilling than they could be. Such ineffectiveness usually generates additional anxiety that leads in turn to even further ineffectiveness. Interpretations addressed to ineffective coping strategies can help patients replace them with more rewarding ways of dealing with their experiences and concurrently reduce their susceptibility to becoming anxious.

3. *What is the patient perceiving in a distorted fashion?* Although clinicians tend at times to regard distorted perceptual functioning as associated only with severe disturbance, various needs and attitudes cause all people to misperceive themselves and their environment from time to time. When people are misconstruing the nature and significance of their experiences, they become at risk for developing psychological problems and managing them ineffectively. Hence, whatever patients are perceiving inaccurately constitutes a third major focus for interpretations.

To summarize this general principle, therapists should direct their interpretations toward sources of difficulty in patients' lives as they become apparent in what is unusual, ineffective, inappropriate, contradictory, irrational, self-defeating, or anxiety-arousing in their actions, thoughts, and feelings. Conversely, nonproblematic events and recollections that are not upsetting and in which patients appear to have exercised accurate perception and effective coping should usually be allowed to pass without comment. In addition to this general principle, deciding which among apparent sources of difficulty to select for interpretation and which to defer can be guided by two priorities that help sustain a systematic and effective interpretive effort: (a) Interpretation of defense should take precedence over interpretation of conflict, and (b) interpretation of process should take precedence over interpretation of content.

CONFLICT AND DEFENSE

As described in Chapter 4, unresolved conflicts tend to generate anxiety that in turn evokes defenses against anxiety. Whenever people are motivated more by needs to avoid anxiety than by pursuit of self-fulfillment, they become likely to engage in ineffective and unrewarding behavior. Hence, the underlying conflicts and the defenses they evoke are both potential sources of difficulty in a person's life that warrant being interpreted in psychotherapy.

In terms of priority, however, there are benefits to interpreting patients' defenses against anxiety before attempting to interpret the conflicts that are giving rise to their anxiety. If interpretations of underlying conflicts and sources of anxiety are offered before patients have been helped to recognize and modify their defensive style, these interpretations tend to be integrated within their existing defensive framework and to add little to their self-understanding. On the other hand, the more people have previously been helped to identify and alter how they use defenses, the more likely they are to learn something from interpretations of conflict rather than ward them off with their habitual defenses against anxiety.

As an example, patients whose preference runs to ideational defenses may thoughtfully mull over an interpretation but intellectualize it into an abstract personality description devoid of personal significance. The following response was made by an only child female college student whose therapist had just told her that her failing grades were probably related to feelings she had about being pressured by her father to fulfill his expectations of the son he never had:

> Yes, Doctor, I think that's a very good point. I can easily see how somebody who is resentful about being pressured by a father to achieve something he had in mind for somebody else might end up not working to capacity in school. It makes good sense, and I can think of a number of other students I know who probably have the same problem.

The conflict interpretation made in this instance had not been preceded by adequate attention to the patient's intellectual defensive style, and the result was the above sterile intellectualization. The patient praises the therapist's acuity, comments on how "somebody" who is resentful toward a father might act, and claims increased understanding of the behavior of other students who have the same problem. Absent from the response are any emotional reactions or relevant associations to indicate that the interpretation has been taken personally, as by expressing surprise ("Do you really think so?"), dismay ("That's a disturbing thought"), or involvement (by references to "I," "me," and "my father"). Instead, the anxiety that might accompany such emotions or associations is warded off by an intellectualization of the interpretation and by taking distance from personal involvement, and no increment in self-understanding takes place.

To illustrate further what can happen when conflict is interpreted before defense, consider how this same college student might have responded to the same interpretation if, instead of being an intellectualizer, her preference was for repressive defenses:

> I don't see how that could be. I know my father wants only the best for me, so I don't have to worry about his feelings, and I know I've never been afraid of doing well. You must be on the wrong track.

Assuming that the therapist in this example is not on the wrong track, this second response demonstrates characteristic uses of repression and denial to avoid the anxiety an interpretation might stir up. Nothing is wrong with my father or me (denial), the response indicates, and furthermore the whole thing is not worth looking into (repression). Interestingly, when patients are responding to a conflict interpretation defensively, the accuracy of the interpretation may be of little account.

The therapist's attempt to probe beneath the surface by itself provokes sufficient anxiety to lead an ideational patient to endorse intellectualized versions of interpretations and a repressing patient to discount interpretations completely, regardless of whether they are correct.

Whatever their preferred defenses may be, patients continue to use them to ward off possible sources of anxiety until they have become capable of doing otherwise. This capability is fostered by helping them recognize and identify the behavior patterns by which they typically seek to protect themselves against anxiety. Defenses do not promptly disappear on being interpreted, never again to characterize a patient's behavior or hamper the person's adjustment. Identified and understood, however, defenses become more subject than before to voluntary control and hence more flexible and adaptive in how they are employed. As patients in psychotherapy gain control over their defenses, they become increasingly capable of relaxing or suspending them in the face of conflict interpretations.[3] For this reason, interpretations of underlying concerns are more likely to enhance self-understanding if they follow, rather than precede, relevant interpretations of defense, especially defenses that are characterological rather than situational in nature.

Situational and Characterological Defensive Operations

In listening for and responding to indications of defensive behavior, it is helpful to distinguish between *situational* and *characterological* defensive operations. Situational defensive operations consist of specific steps people take to reduce their anxiety in circumstances they find threatening, whereas characterological defensive operations comprise the ways people generally conduct their lives to avoid feeling threatened and thereby minimize the likelihood of their becoming anxious.

Situational defensive operations typically become apparent in psychotherapy when patients are describing how they responded to some past anxiety-provoking event or are reacting to an anxiety-provoking aspect of the treatment session. Consider, for example, a male patient who reports developing a headache and having to leave work after being criticized by his boss, or who tells the therapist he is pressed for time and wants to end his session early. Both statements suggest situational defense by leaving the field, and an appropriate interpretation in either case might be, "Your way of handling that [this] situation was [is] apparently to run away from it."

Characterological defensive operations become evident in the attitudes, values, and preferred behavior patterns that make patients the kind of people they are. Therapists need to appreciate, however, that not all the attitudes, values, and preferred behaviors that define characterological style are defensive operations generated by and serving to ward off anxiety. Many features of a person's characterological style are likely to be positively motivated, self-fulfilling, and unrelated either to experiencing or defending against anxiety. Interpretation of characterological style should accordingly be focused for the most part on persistent patterns of avoiding anxiety at the expense of self-fulfillment, rather than on characterological dispositions that are effectively promoting a patient's best interests. Each of the following observations refers to a fairly common pattern of self-defeating behavior used by people seeking psychological help. These therapist statements illustrate ways to express interpretations of characterological defensive operations:

- You apparently try to organize everything in your life down to the last detail.
- You seem to have a tendency to do or say whatever comes into your mind, without taking much time to think over the consequences.
- Whenever you start to get into a close relationship with someone, you find some reason for breaking it off.
- When something goes wrong, your first tendency is to blame yourself and feel that the fault lies with your not being as good a person as you should be.
- Your usual way of deciding what to do in a situation seems to be based on what you think other people would like you to do, rather than on what you yourself would really like to do.

*The Particular Importance of Interpreting Characterological
Defensive Operations*

Dynamic psychotherapy as originally formulated by Freud concentrated on tracing maladaptive aspects of current behavior to specific sources of anxiety lying deep in the unconscious and related to events occurring early in life. Subsequent to the influence of Wilhelm Reich's (1933/1949) work on character analysis and Anna Freud's (1936/1946) contributions on ego mechanisms, however, the emphasis on origins of conflict became balanced by an equal or even greater emphasis on the handling of conflict. Reich explained the necessity of characterological interpretations ("the loosening of the character armor") as a prelude to interpretations of underlying conflicts, while Anna Freud described how specific defense mechanisms, if unchallenged by the therapist, can prevent patients from coming directly to grips with their underlying concerns. As one result of their work, it became generally recognized that effective interpretation of characterological defensive operations can by itself bring psychotherapy to a satisfactory conclusion in many cases.[4]

To elaborate this point, it may not always be possible or necessary to help patients understand the early origins as well as the nature of their personality style. In the first place, because the conflicts that lead to the emergence of characterological defenses have usually occurred in the developmental years, adults may have difficulty recapturing them in vivid detail. The more intensive psychotherapy is and the longer it lasts, the more likely patients are to reexperience early life events that placed them in conflict, made them anxious, and influenced their choice of defensive operations. On the other hand, psychotherapy should be conducted with an eye to the point of diminishing returns, when further uncovering no longer promises sufficient increments in self-understanding and self-satisfaction to justify the time, effort, and cost it would entail. At such a point, patient and therapist may concur that termination rather than further exploration will best serve the patient's interests.

Second, conflicts originating in early experiences may be so remote from patients' current concerns and life style that they have little impact in the present, even if they are able to become aware of them. Characterological patterns of defensive operations that have persisted over many years tend to become autonomous and provide their own rewards, as a consequence of which reexperiencing and reworking the events that evoked them exerts little influence on current behavior, defensive or otherwise.[5] On the other hand, being able to grasp how they are presently using defensive operations to cope with their experience has considerable potential for helping people modify their defensiveness and increase the effectiveness of their coping style. Hence, the interpretation of defense can constitute a significant end as well as a means to an end in psychotherapy.

CONTENT AND PROCESS

As indicated earlier, the content of psychotherapy interviews consists of what patients are saying; the process refers to how and why they are saying it and why they are not saying something else. Accordingly, content interpretations typically focus on connections between current concerns and events outside the psychotherapy session, whereas process interpretations focus on connections between current concerns and ongoing behavior within the interview. Content interpretations establish continuity between what people are at the moment and what they have been and might be, whereas process interpretations help patients see their personality style in action right at the present moment, here and now. Although both kinds of interpretation serve important functions in psychotherapy, there are two reasons for giving preference to process over content interpretations when possibilities for both are equally compelling.

First, process interpretations are generally more vivid and incisive than content interpretations, because they address currently observable behavior rather than recollected or reported events. Second, whereas interpretable items of content are likely to be mentioned again by a patient or can be reintroduced by the therapist, interpretable aspects of process are one-time affairs that rarely recur in exactly the same fashion. This means that missed opportunities to interpret sources of difficulty apparent in content can usually be recouped, whereas lost occasions to make constructive use of ongoing process are lost for good.

To distinguish process from content in psychotherapy interviews, therapists need to observe patient behavior closely. When patients are talking, are they stammering, squirming, perspiring, or in some other way manifesting more anxiety than they are admitting to, or are they instead being more casual or flippant than seems consistent with the seriousness of what they are saying? While patients are saying what they are, do they appear more concerned with making some kind of impression on the therapist than with talking about matters that trouble them, or is there perhaps something about the sequence of the subjects they are mentioning that seems to say more about their underlying concerns than about these subjects themselves? Whenever the answer to such questions is in the affirmative, interpretations addressed to process rather than content may be indicated.

Finally with respect to why patients are not saying something, therapists will find it helpful to identify four content alternatives in psychotherapy interviews: (a) Patients can talk about relatively current events ("Yesterday I . . .") or relatively remote events ("When I was much younger I . . ."); (b) they can talk about themselves in the abstract ("I have a bad temper") or in reference to actual behavior ("This morning I lost my temper"); (c) they can talk about their life independently of the treatment or in specific relation to the role of the therapy and the therapist in their life; and (d) they can either report thoughts or express feelings. Repeated focus on any one of these pairs of content alternatives to the exclusion of the other is an aspect of the psychotherapy process that should be interpreted when it occurs.

Many of these process aspects of patients' behavior in psychotherapy involve elements of resistance and transference. As noted in Chapter 4, resistance is a paradoxical reluctance on the part of patients to participate in the treatment, and transference refers to feelings and attitudes that patients develop toward their therapist. Resistance and transference frequently account for patients having difficulty talking, attempting to impress their therapist, and emphasizing some subjects to the exclusion of others. Hence interpretations of resistance and transference can be very productive in opening up lines of communication and, like process interpretations in general, they usually take precedence over interpretations of content.

Despite their key role in the treatment process, however, resistance and transference should still be interpreted selectively, when they constitute a source of difficulty for the patient. That is to say, indications of resistance and transference do not always call for an interpretation, but mainly when they become so marked or repetitive as to interfere with communication. Therapist guidelines in this respect are elaborated in Chapters 9 and 10. In the present context, the distinction between *near derivatives* and *remote derivatives* is an additional concept that can help therapists decide whether to call attention to an aspect of the psychotherapy process.

A near derivative is an instance of behavior that is relatively clearly and closely tied to some underlying concern it reflects; a remote derivative, by contrast, consists of behavior that is relatively distant in time and in psychological relatedness from conflicts that have engendered it.[6] For the same reasons that interpretations of defense and process take precedence over interpretations of conflict and content, interpretations of near derivatives are more likely to be productive than interpretations of remote derivatives: they are more vividly and easily grasped by a patient, they bear more directly on the patient's current concerns, and they initiate a potential sequence of interpretations (from near derivatives to remote derivatives) that cannot readily be initiated in the opposite direction (from remote to near derivatives).

To illustrate the distinction between near and remote derivatives, suppose that a female patient is telling a male therapist about being envious of her more attractive sister, and suppose that she is sitting with her legs spread apart. Her posture could conceivably be a sexual overture reflecting transference feelings of wanting to love or be loved by the therapist. In the absence of strong supporting evidence for such transference feelings, however, her way of sitting is a remote derivative: there is neither a previous basis for connecting her open legs with love for the therapist, nor does the content of what she is saying (envy of her sister) provide much current basis for a transference interpretation of her posture. Some tortuous reasoning could construct such a basis if, for example, it were speculated that her concern about being less attractive than her sister means that she wants to prove she can attract men, which means that she wants the therapist to be attracted to her. However, such complex chains of logic dangling from remote derivatives seldom result in useful interpretations. They are subject to multiple errors of inference, because of the multiple suppositions they involve, and, even if correct, they may be too complex for patients to unravel without losing their sense of personal engagement.

By contrast, suppose this same woman sitting with her legs apart is saying, "I enjoy talking with you so much I wish I could see you every day." Although a wish for more therapist time can mean many things, including a felt need for additional help or a general belief that the more therapy the better, explicit statements such as "I enjoy talking with you so much I wish I could see you every day" are almost certain to reflect strong positive transference feelings. In addition, the manifest content of the statement, with its "I-you" emphasis, refers directly to the patient-therapist relationship.

Because of its clear connection to underlying feelings toward the therapist and its manifest relevance to the nature of these feelings, this expressed wish for additional sessions would constitute a near derivative and lend itself well to being interpreted. In the course of using this near derivative (i.e., the patient's expressed wish to see the therapist every day) as a basis for exploring possible feelings of wanting to love and be loved by the therapist, there might be opportunities to allude to the remote derivative (her inviting posture) as related or supportive evidence. Beginning instead with the remote derivative, however, would be to lead from weakness (a less certain connection) rather than from available strength (the more certain connection).

Lest this example suggests that what patients do will always be a remote derivative in relation to what they say, consider the following situation. A male patient stalks into the office for his session, slams the door, drops heavily into his chair banging it against the wall behind him, crosses his legs with a kick to the therapist's desk, scowls, and then says, "I've been having dreams about beating people up." Such behavior leaves little room for doubt that the patient is angry at his therapist, and in this case what has been said, not the accompanying behavior, constitutes the relatively remote derivative. The patient's comment reflects an aggressive theme, but it concerns dreaming rather than waking fantasy and refers to "people" in general. On the other hand, what he is actually doing—beating up on the therapist's office—approaches being a direct assault on the therapist and constitutes a relatively near derivative of probable negative transference feelings. In light of his behavior, an appropriate interpretive response to this patient's statement that "I've been having dreams about beating people up" might well be "It looks like you're beating me up right now."[7]

Distinguishing between near and remote derivatives can help therapists avoid becoming sidetracked by process details, which at times are given more attention than they warrant. Such overvalued process details often involve the kinds of behavior described by S. Freud (1901/1960) in *The Psychopathology of Everyday Life,* including forgetting, slips of the tongue, mistakes in reading and writing, and various types of accidental behavior and "erroneously carried-out actions." Because of its dramatic flair and apparent simplicity, interpreting slips and errors has at times been popular among inadequately trained therapists and self-anointed amateur "analysts" intent on demonstrating their wizardry. The fact is, however, that even slips and errors whose meaning is transparently clear tend to be remote derivatives that rarely provide prime subjects for interpretation in psychotherapy.

For example, consider a female patient who "accidentally" refers to her husband as her father ("I said to my father just the other night—er, I mean my *husband* of course—that we should take a vacation") or who repetitively "forgets" her purse or umbrella in the therapist's office. The therapist may be fairly certain that the first behavior reflects some unresolved paternal attachment and the second some longing for a closer patient-therapist relationship. Despite the certainty of such connections in the therapist's mind, however, for the patient they involve remote derivatives: the chain of evidence linking the overt behavior to the underlying wish it indirectly expresses is long, complex, and only loosely anchored in the content of what the patient is saying.

On the other hand, suppose that in the first of the preceding examples the patient, instead of talking about taking a vacation, is describing some problem in her marriage. Suppose further that these problems appear to derive from her acting more like a child than a wife, and suppose that her slip occurs in this context ("I keep telling my father—I mean my husband—that he expects too much of me"). She then would be describing a near and readily interpretable derivative of an unresolved attachment to her father (a wish to have her husband baby her or, at a deeper level, perhaps a wish to receive paternal love through the person of her husband), and the remote derivative included in her statement (the husband-father slip) could be adduced secondarily as evidence to support such an interpretation.

Patients' slips and errors, together with their gestures, mannerisms, posture, and other peripheral interview behaviors, are usually too distant from the underlying concerns they reflect and too discontinuous with the content of an interview to be interpreted fruitfully. Moreover, repetitive focusing on such process details can make patients so self-conscious and preoccupied with observing themselves that they become incapable of reporting their thoughts and feelings spontaneously. Should some detail of the psychotherapy process seem to provide the only available avenue for gaining access to an area of concern that is being strongly resisted, an interpretation of it may be called for. By and large, however, process details are useful mainly as supporting evidence for interpretations of less remote derivatives and should be assigned low priority for interpretation in their own right.

WHEN TO INTERPRET

Deciding when to offer interpretations is primarily a matter of attending to their *timing* and *dosage*. The timing of interpretations pertains to the specific moment when they are made, and their dosage concerns how many interpretations are being made. As noted earlier, interpretations challenge a person's existing ways of doing or looking at things, and because they often dredge up unwelcome thoughts and feelings, they almost always evoke some defensiveness. However, proper timing and dosage can help to minimize patients' aversion to interpretations and promote their openness to learning from them.

TIMING OF INTERPRETATIONS

Interpretations are most timely when patients are prepared to receive them and therapists are prepared to offer them. For patients to be prepared to receive an interpretation, they should have a level of awareness bordering closely on the content of what is to be interpreted, and they should be in a reasonably positive frame of mind regarding the therapist and the treatment process. For therapists to be prepared to offer an interpretation, they should be reasonably certain that the interpretation is accurate and that they have adequate information to document it.

Patient Level of Awareness

Interpretations are most useful in communicating understanding when patients are verging on becoming aware of them and ready to do so. This does not mean that therapists should sit passively waiting for patients to work themselves into psychological proximity to an underlying concern, which can then be safely interpreted. Rather, the therapist's task is to use questions, clarifications, and confrontations as part of an interpretive sequence that leads up to an interpretation by gradually bringing patients into near-awareness of some previously unrecognized aspect of themselves or their behavior.

Interpretations made before patients have been helped to approach awareness of them have negligible prospects for enhancing their self-understanding. Learning new things about oneself requires experiencing them as personally meaningful, not just having them pointed out, and people have difficulty experiencing as personally meaningful anything that is remote from their conscious awareness. S. Freud (1910/1957d) observed in this regard that, if knowledge about the unconscious were important in its own right, it would be sufficient for patients to read books or go to lectures, and he noted further that descriptions of the unconscious have as much influence on neurotic symptoms as "a distribution of menu-cards in a time of famine has upon hunger" (p. 225).

Thus it is not psychological knowledge in the abstract, but learning about uniquely personal aspects of one's underlying concerns and experiencing them as relevant to one's past and current behavior, that enhances self-understanding. For interpretations to facilitate such learning and experiencing, they must be deferred until the matters they involve have been brought to a point close to the patient's awareness. Busch (1995, Chapter 2), borrowing on Freud's observations, describes the important practice guideline of interpreting "in the neighborhood" of what patients already dimly recognize or have been helped to the brink of doing so. Research reported by Hill, Thompson, and Mahalik (1989) provides empirical confirmation that effective interpretations are typically of moderate depth, being neither blinding glimpses of the obvious nor penetrating commentaries on matters far removed from a patient's conscious awareness.

In addition to being of limited usefulness, interpretations offered before patients are prepared to receive them may also mobilize resistance to the treatment process. Like a plunge into cold water, interpretations are potentially bracing but also nerve-jangling, and careful preparation of patients for an interpretation readies them for the icy waters with a sequence of progressively cooler immersions. Without having been thus prepared, gradually and with consideration, patients are likely in knee-jerk fashion to shrug off startling and unwelcome interpretations and to resent the therapist's having laid them on without warning. Hence, premature interpretations not only fail to promote self-understanding but also foster negative feelings toward the treatment process and toward the therapist. Levy (1990, Chapter 1) notes similarly that excessively deep interpretations, by taking patients off-guard and exceeding their capacities for understanding them, prevent any learning from taking place and also cast the therapist more as a magician than as a collaborator in an exploratory process.

Such negative consequences of premature interpretations are almost inevitable if therapists compound their error by insisting that patients come to grips with them. Sometimes therapists allow themselves to become overly impressed with their omniscience and with the staggering significance of their insights, and they may then come mistakenly to believe (a) that it is essential for a patient to accept and integrate every interpretation they make and (b) that any disinterest or disagreement on the patient's part reflects resistance rather than their having offered an incorrect or poorly timed interpretation. Despite the importance of recognizing resistance, therapists must guard against holding patients responsible for every interpretive sequence that goes awry. The infallible therapist does not exist, and therapists with pretensions to such status will frequently fail to sustain a positive working relationship with their patients. Busch (1995) offers the following succinct observation:

One is impressed with how many interpretations seem based less on what the patient is capable of hearing and more on what the therapist is capable of understanding. We too often confuse our ability to read the unconscious and the patient's ability to understand it. (pp. 24–25)

Premature interpretations have the further disadvantage of diluting the impact that the interpretation might have had later on, when the patient was prepared to receive it. Interpretations are more likely to be effective when they state fresh ideas than when they repeat possibilities that have previously been considered and found wanting. Such reduced effectiveness of an accurate interpretation becomes particularly likely when a premature presentation has mobilized strong defenses against the ideas it contains. In this sense, premature interpretations are analogous to opening fire at too great a distance to hit anything; by the time the range has been closed, the quarry has had sufficient warning to take evasive action. For accurate interpretations to have their full impact on a patient who is prepared to receive them, they should not come compromised by prior fittings in which they have been tried on and felt to be the wrong size.

Patient Frame of Mind

With regard to their frame of mind, patients benefit most from interpretations when they are experiencing relatively little resistance to the treatment process and relatively positive attitudes toward the therapist. Resistance is a means of defending against the anxiety generally stirred up by psychotherapy, and resistant patients have limited tolerance for the additional anxiety that specific interpretations often generate. Resistance and receptivity are mutually exclusive, because patients who are wrestling with concerns about participating in the treatment do not have an open mind for learning more about themselves as people. Interpretations during periods of marked resistance should therefore be limited to interpretations of the resistance itself and aimed at helping patients understand and resolve their aversive reaction to the treatment process.

Feeling positively toward the therapist, on the other hand, like low resistance to the treatment process, creates a climate of receptivity to interpretations. When patients feel that their therapist respects them and is interested in helping them, they are likely to consider interpretations carefully, even if they cause them distress. Conversely, patients in the throes of reservations about how much their therapist respects them or is devoted to helping them will be inclined to take interpretations as criticisms and to respond to them defensively rather than open-mindedly.[8]

The positive feelings necessary to sustain patients' receptivity to interpretations consist of trusting their therapist and appreciating his or her efforts, but they do not include liking or loving the therapist. Although some aspects of positive transference can facilitate progress in psychotherapy, as discussed in Chapter 10, patients do not need to like or love their therapists to tolerate having them interpret their behavior; they need only to feel that the therapist genuinely respects their integrity and is sincerely trying to help them. Furthermore, because interpretations provide concrete evidence of therapists' work on their patients' behalf, they can aid in building and sustaining positive patient regard. Hence well-timed interpretations, even though challenging, can help to maintain an effective working alliance and facilitate receptivity to subsequent interpretations.

Therapist Certainty

Turning next to the preparation of the therapist, well-timed interpretations require therapists to be reasonably certain of their accuracy and to have adequate evidence to document them. The value of accurate interpretations is self-evident: They help patients learn something new about themselves, and they demonstrate that their therapist is capable of understanding them. Incorrect interpretations, on the other hand, because they lack congruence with the patients' past and current experiences, add little to their self-knowledge and give them cause to question the therapist's capacity to understand and help them.

The potential disadvantage of inaccurate interpretations does not mean that therapists must refrain from making any interpretive statements until they are absolutely certain of their validity. What it does mean is that more certain interpretations should be favored over less certain ones and that interpretations should be couched in language commensurate with the certainty they embrace. Interpretations that therapists have good reason to believe are correct might be introduced by saying, "It seems clear now that you . . ." Having some expectation but less certainty that an interpretation is accurate, therapists could begin with "It may be that . . .", or "It seems to me that . . .", or "Could it be that . . . ?" Wanting merely to explore a hunch based only on suggestive evidence, they might best opt for "Is there any possibility that . . . ?" or "I just had a thought I want to check out with you."

Nevertheless, research by Silberschatz and his colleagues has documented a "goodness of fit" relationship in which therapists' interventions are most helpful when they accurately address patient's conscious and unconscious needs and concerns (Silberschatz, Curtis, & Nathans, 1989; Silberschatz, Curtis, Sampson, & Weiss, 1991; Silberschatz, Fretter, & Curtis, 1986). Crits-Christoph and his colleagues have similarly shown that the degree to which interpretations correspond to independently derived clinical formulations concerning patients relates positively to the benefit these patients derive from their treatment, and furthermore that accuracy of interpretation enhances the quality of the therapeutic alliance as well as prospects for a favorable treatment outcome (Crits-Christoph, Barber, & Kurcias, 1993; Crits-Christoph, Cooper, & Luborsky, 1988). Studies of the relationship between the quality of interpretation and the outcome of psychotherapy are also reported by Piper, Joyce, McCallum, and Azim (1993).

Luborsky (1996) concludes from the available research findings that accuracy of interpretation is among the "curative factors" most related to psychotherapy outcome, and there are clear empirical indications that the competency with which therapists deliver interpretations carries curative weight beyond benefits accruing merely from the therapeutic alliance (Barber, Crits-Christoph, & Luborsky, 1996).

Therapist Documentation

The final guideline for deciding whether an interpretation that seems accurate should be offered at a particular time consists of whether there is sufficient information available to document it. Documentation is almost always required to make an interpretive sequence effective, because patients seldom greet even correct and well-timed interpretations with an enthusiastic surge of insight. In fact, prompt and ecstatic endorsement of interpretations ("Of course, you're absolutely right; that explains exactly what's been going on, and I can see it all clearly now") often serves as a way of warding off rather than exploring whatever connections are being suggested and should be regarded with suspicion. Patients who immediately express unequivocal acceptance of interpretations are in effect saying that the therapist's suggestions have been so precise, comprehensive, and conclusive that there is no need to consider them further—which is hardly ever the case.

By contrast, when patients are prepared to work on rather than ward off an interpretation, they typically respond to it not with unqualified agreement, but with some combination of increased attention ("I never thought of that before"; "I had a real pang of anxiety when you said that, so it must have some important meaning for me"), self-reflection ("I wonder if that could be why I'm so afraid to meet new people?" "That makes me think of having had the same feelings toward one of my teachers when I was in school"), and questions about what has been proposed ("I'm not sure how you came to that conclusion"; "How would that account for the feelings I have toward my wife?").

It is in relation to questions patients raise about an interpretation that therapists should be able to provide documentation based on the previous content of the therapy. Such questions may be turned back to the patient ("What ideas do you have?"), and they may also be taken at times as manifestations of resistance rather than genuine requests for information. However, resistance should not be presumed to lurk behind every minor hesitation in patients' progress toward understanding themselves better, and patients who appear about to come to grips with an interpretation should be given information to help them with their task when they raise relevant questions about it. Consider the following example of a female patient to whom it has just been suggested that she seems to place herself in subservient roles to men, whom she then resents:

PATIENT: I'm not sure how you came to that conclusion.

THERAPIST: The same pattern has been apparent in your relationship with three different men we've discussed, first your father, then your husband, and now me.

PATIENT: I'm beginning to see what you mean. [pause] Yes, I'm like that. But how can this account for my getting more irritable with my husband when he is doing so well?

THERAPIST: He's a man, and you tend to downgrade yourself in relationship to men and then resent them for being in a superior position to you.

PATIENT: So I resent him. (pause) And that could explain why the more successful he is, the more I resent him. And it's my own doing, because I feel I have to be subservient to a man in order to please him, like with my father. That's it, isn't it?

Note in this example that the answers to this patient's questions about an interpretation do not spell out every detail of the therapist's reasoning. Rather, they call to the patient's attention bits of additional information intended to demonstrate some basis for the interpretation and stimulate her exploration of its implications. Further questions would be answered with further, more detailed documentation, as long as the questions did not become so numerous or tangential as to suggest that the patient was trying to avoid rather than wrestle with what the interpretation might mean to her.

If therapists cannot document an interpretation with information they and the patient have previously shared, the interpretation may best remain unvoiced, except in the most tentative of ways. Otherwise, therapists risk creating the same treatment disadvantages as result from premature interpretations. Presenting with some certainty an interpretation they cannot subsequently justify makes therapists seem careless and inconsiderate, and both the quality of the treatment relationship and the potential effectiveness of a better-timed interpretation suffer in the process. The undisciplined offering of interpretations that cannot be adequately documented exemplifies the previously mentioned "wild analysis" approach that therapists should carefully avoid.

Of particular significance is the distinct possibility that misapplication of interpretive techniques, particularly in the various forms that wild analysis takes, will lead to poor treatment results for which some presumed ineffectiveness of the interpretive method is mistakenly held responsible. To avoid this mistaken impression, therapists in both their clinical practice and in their reading of the literature should base their conclusions concerning the effects of interpretive psychotherapy on instances in which it is appropriately conducted; inappropriately conducted psychotherapy, on the other hand, should be regarded as testimony to the inexperience or inadequacy of the therapist and not as a basis for drawing evaluative inferences about the method.

DOSAGE OF INTERPRETATIONS

Effective interpretation requires keeping dosage, which refers to the number of interpretations offered per unit of time, at a level patients can tolerate. As pointed out, interpretations typically generate anxiety and evoke defensiveness. Interpretations offered in rapid-fire succession cause patients to become increasingly anxious, which interferes with their attention to the interpretations, and increasingly defensive, which interferes with their participation in the treatment process. Interpretations should be made only when the patient appears able to tolerate the anxiety likely to be aroused, and one interpretation should not follow another until the patient has adequately worked through any defensiveness evoked by the first one. Research reported by Langs, Bucci, Udoff, Cramer, and Thomson (1993) confirmed in this regard an inverse relationship between frequency of therapist interventions and extent of patient communication; the more interpretation therapists made, the less involved their patients were likely to become in exploring them.

The effects of interpretation also indicate that the dosage of interpretations can be regulated according to the type of patient response that seems desirable to elicit. Thus if therapists feel it would be useful for a patient to talk less or respond less fully, they should consider offering interpretations. If, on the other hand, they would like a patient to become more discursive and spontaneous, they should consider limiting their interventions to observations and clarifications and avoid interpretations. Similarly, if therapists think it would be helpful for a patient to express understanding, to manifest anxiety or defensiveness, or to talk about the treatment relationship, interpretation should be their intervention of choice; but if they prefer to have a patient talk freely with minimal anxiety or defensiveness, then they should employ interventions other than interpretation.

An advantageous dosage of interpretations is therefore relative to the needs of each patient at specific points in his or her treatment. However, as a further general guideline for dosage, therapists should avoid offering interpretations whenever there will be limited opportunity for a patient to respond to them. An interpretation made during the early and middle portions of an interview allows patients time to explore its implications and work through whatever discomfort it causes them, whereas an interpretation delivered in the waning moments of an interview leaves patients hanging, unable to discuss it with the therapist and uncomfortable about it until the next session.

A case can certainly be made for the importance of patients' having to explore the implications of an interpretation on their own and having to endure the distress that inevitably accompanies exposure to the interpretive process. Nevertheless, patients' reflections on interpretations should occur in addition to, not instead of, adequate opportunity to reflect on them jointly with the therapist, and their discomfort should arise as a natural consequence of their decision to look closely at themselves, not as painful affect artificially and unnecessarily stimulated by poor timing of interpretations.

Therapists should avoid interpretations that crowd the latter part of a treatment session, and they should be similarly circumspect about major interpretive efforts just prior to some interruption of the treatment. When vacations or other anticipated breaks in the treatment routine occur, the last session prior to the interruption should be used more for review and consolidation than for breaking ground in new areas. Patients themselves often sense that the session preceding an interruption is a poor time to stir up new problems and concerns, and they accordingly limit their conversation to mundane and uncomplicated matters. Therapists do well to follow such leads from their patients just before a break in the treatment, and they should particularly avoid interpreting a patient's superficiality in this circumstance as resistance. The major exception to this guideline involves instances in which patients give evidence of some unexpressed feelings toward a therapist who is responsible for interrupting the treatment. To prevent such feelings from building into a negative transference reaction that will interfere with the resumption of the treatment, they should be identified and brought forward promptly, even if there is insufficient time to explore them fully. Recognizing and responding to transference in this circumstance is discussed further in Chapter 10.

HOW TO INTERPRET

To sustain an effective interpretive style, therapists must prepare a patient for any interpretations they plan to offer, encourage the patient's participation in developing and evaluating interpretations, and phrase their interpretations as concisely and incisively as they can. Adhering to these guidelines, as elaborated in this section, enhances the likelihood of offering interpretations in a manner that capitalizes on accurate prior judgments about what and when to interpret.

PREPARING THE PATIENT

The previous discussion of timing emphasized the importance of offering interpretations when a patient is on the verge of becoming aware of them. To be most effective, therapists should direct their interpretations at material that is just below the surface, or just outside the patient's conscious awareness. Accordingly, effective interpretive technique requires therapists to take steps to bring aspects of a patient's thoughts, feelings, or actions that they believe should be interpreted into close awareness where they can be interpreted usefully. Simply listening and waiting for patients to bring themselves to the brink of expanded self-awareness provides relatively few opportunities for well-timed interpretations. Instead, therapists must work systematically to guide their patients toward interpretations that appear indicated.

Guiding a patient toward an interpretation is usually accomplished with a sequence of increasingly penetrating interventions, beginning with questions and clarifications, proceeding with confrontations, and ending with the interpretation to be made. The following exchange illustrates how such a sequence often unfolds:

PATIENT: We had a salesmen's meeting, and a large group of us were cramped together in a small room, and they turned out the lights to show some slides, and I got so jumpy and anxious I couldn't stand it.

THERAPIST: So what happened? (question)

PATIENT: I just couldn't stand it, I was sweating and shaking, so I got up and left, and I know I'll be called on the carpet for walking out.

THERAPIST: You became so anxious and upset that you couldn't stand being in the room, even though you knew that walking out would get you into trouble. (clarification)

PATIENT: Yeah . . . What could have bothered me so much to make me do a dumb thing like that?

THERAPIST: You know, we've talked about other times in your life when you've become upset in close quarters with other men, once when you were in the army and again in your dormitory at college. (confrontation)

PATIENT: That's right, and it was the same kind of thing again.

THERAPIST: And if I'm correct, this has never happened to you in a group of men and women together, no matter how closely you've been cramped together. (further confrontation)

PATIENT: Uh . . . Yes, that's right.

THERAPIST: So it appears that something especially about being physically close to other men, and especially in the dark, makes you anxious, as if you're afraid something bad might happen in that kind of situation. (interpretation)

PATIENT: (pause) I think you're right about that . . . and I know I'm not physically afraid of other men. Do you think it might be sexual, that I might get worried about something homosexual taking place?

This sequence illustrates several typical features of the interpretive process. First, note that it does not end with a dramatic conclusion delivered by the therapist to the accompaniment of the patient's adulation and gratitude. Clinicians seeking such drama will rarely find it in the practice of psychotherapy. Instead, the sequence proceeds gradually from a reported experience (the patient's anxiety in the dark, crowded, all-male environment), through clarification of the experience and confrontation with its similarity to other experiences in the patient's life, to an interpretation that takes the patient one small step ahead in understanding himself more fully than before (the apparent fact that he fears something bad might happen in situations of close proximity to other men).

Second, note that the interpretation serves not only to summarize what has previously been said but also to stimulate new lines of inquiry ("Do you think it might be sexual?"). Once an interpretation of connections or relationships heretofore outside a patient's conscious awareness has been made and accepted, it can function in turn as a confrontation that helps pave the way for further interpretations. In the preceding example, the therapist goes only so far as to point out the patient's apparent fear of being too close to other men. Then the patient, having agreed with this interpretation, uses it as a basis for suggesting a new topic, possible homosexual concerns, that can provide the subject for an additional sequence of questions, clarifications, confrontations, and interpretation.

Third, note the extent of the patient's activity in pulling the interpretation together and beginning to explore its implications. In light of the suggestive information available, the therapist might have extended the interpretation to include, "Could it be that you have some concerns about homosexual activity that cause you to become anxious in such situations?" To have done so, however, would have been to take more of an interpretive leap than would have been necessary or productive. An effectively managed interpretive sequence prompts patients to take the next step on their own, as happened in this instance. If an interpretive sequence is too far off the mark or is generating too much anxiety for a patient to pursue it spontaneously, then efforts by the therapist to push the patient further are more likely to increase resistance than to promote progress. Furthermore, should therapists "succeed" in pushing the implications of an interpretation beyond where a patient was prepared to go, they will have abrogated rather than fostered the patient's participation as a respected partner in the interpretive process.[9]

FOSTERING THE PATIENT'S PARTICIPATION

Active participation by patients in the interpretive process is necessary to keep both the nature of interpretations and the nature of the treatment relationship in proper perspective. Interpretations are, after all, alternative hypotheses. They suggest different ways in which patients might look at themselves and their experiences; if apt, they prove more congruent with patients' basic personality, present emotional state, and past history than their current views. However, it is not the therapist's expressing it that makes an interpretation effective; rather, what makes interpretations effective is patients articulating how they have some personal meaning to them and how they have helped them know themselves better. Effective interpretations rarely occur in psychotherapy absent patient participation in developing and evaluating them.

In the same way as interpretations comprise alternative hypotheses and not oracular pronouncements, psychotherapy patients are not students to be lectured, but instead partners in an exploratory venture. In addition to being entitled to judge the accuracy and usefulness of interpretations, they also should share responsibility for arriving at interpretations. Contributing actively to an interpretive sequence enhances patients' sense of being able to generate self-understanding and to become masters rather than victims of their fate. Interpretations that patients can be helped to formulate for themselves tend to have more impact and a more lasting effect than interpretations set before them in finished form. To excuse patients from responsibility for arriving at interpretations demeans and patronizes them while depriving them of valuable opportunities to construct their own new ideas about themselves.

The patient's role in the interpretive process can be understood and illustrated further in terms of the distinction drawn in Chapter 4 between a person's experiencing self and observing self. To recapitulate this distinction, people differ from each other and from one moment to the next in whether they are oriented primarily toward experiencing or observing themselves, and a rewarding lifestyle usually requires a flexible balance between both modes of operating. Too much self-observation produces paralyzing self-consciousness and eliminates spontaneity, so that a person cannot enjoy thinking, feeling, or doing anything simply for its own sake. Too much self-experiencing fosters mindless, uncritical immersion in thoughts, feelings, and actions for their own sake, without concern for their consequences or implications. For interpretation in psychotherapy to achieve personal meaning to patients and to generate understanding that takes firm root in their consciousness, patients must have both the experiencing and the observing parts of their personality available for the therapist to call on alternately, as the situation demands.

In preparing for an interpretive sequence, the therapist needs to emphasize patients' experiencing self, as a way of helping them feel and report the life events that will be the subject of clarifications, confrontations, and interpretations to come. When fertile grounds for interpretation have been prepared, however, the therapist needs to shift focus and establish an alliance with patients' observing self, to ensure their participation in the interpretive process.

To establish such an alliance, therapists need first to communicate that they have formed certain impressions of the experiences reported to them. Having made this clear, they need next to indicate that the patient, by putting part of him- or herself where the therapist is sitting and joining the therapist as an observer, will be able to share in evaluating these impressions. By thus encouraging the patient to function as both an observing and an experiencing person in the psychotherapy session, the therapist actively promotes participation in the interpretive process. The following exchange with a female patient illustrates such an effort to activate and engage her observing self:

PATIENT: I wish I could understand why people are always taking advantage of me, so that I end up doing things their way instead of how I would like to.

THERAPIST: From what you've been telling me, it sounds to me not so much that you're taken advantage of, but that you always go along with what other people say, without saying what you would like to do or how you would like to see things done. I wonder if you can see it that way? (an invitation to the patient to separate her observing self from her experience of being taken advantage of, so that she can join the therapist in looking at it)

PATIENT: Well, I haven't thought of it that way before, but I suppose I am that way. I sort of ask for people to make decisions for me by not making them for myself.

THERAPIST: So you're not a passive victim. (an invitation to the patient to consider further that she may be actively bringing about some of the interpersonal difficulties she previously thought she was undergoing passively)

PATIENT: No, I guess if you look at it that way I get myself into these situations that aggravate me by avoiding expressing any strong opinions or trying to influence what is decided on. But why would I want to avoid telling people, especially my friends, what I really feel or want?

THERAPIST: What thoughts do you have about that? (the patient's observing self has been activated in this sequence to help her participate in learning something new about herself, namely, that her subordination to others is at least in part her own doing; she is now on the verge of recognizing that her interpersonal passivity may serve some defensive purposes, in that she avoids asserting himself to avoid anxiety associated with being assertive, and the stage is set to begin exploring a conflict-defense sequence in this area)[10]

As an additional technique for promoting patients' participation in the interpretive process, therapists will often find *partial interpretation* useful. Partial interpretation consists of offering an abbreviated version of an interpretation and thereby encouraging the patient to provide the rest of it. In the preceding example, the therapist's statement, "So you're not a passive victim," constitutes such a partial interpretation. A full interpretation at this point might have been, "In other words, you're not a passive victim of what other people do to you; you avoid expressing strong opinions or trying to influence decisions that are made, and it is because you avoid being decisive that other people end up making decisions for you." What actually happened, however, was that the therapist went only so far as to make the somewhat elliptical statement, "So you're not a passive victim," and the patient, her participation having been engaged, formulated the rest of the interpretation in her own words.[11]

Partial interpretation is not always as successful as it was in this case, even when the full interpretation toward which it points is accurate and timely. Sometimes patients' reluctance to confront the full interpretation causes them to dig in their heels a bit, and sometimes dependent or manipulative needs lead them to shirk their responsibility and wait for the therapist to do more of the work. In these circumstances, a partial interpretation may have to be buttressed with additional statements intended to prod the patient toward the full interpretation. The preceding interaction might then have taken the following course:

Therapist: So you're not a passive victim.

Patient: What do you mean? (therapist remains silent) Oh, you mean I may be bringing some of this aggravation on myself. But how do you see me doing that?

Therapist: Someone has to make decisions.

Patient: You mean it's my own doing, that because I don't express strong opinions other people end up making the decisions. But why don't I express strong opinions?

Therapist: Why indeed?

Patient: Oh, now I see what you're getting at; it's like for some reason I'm avoiding telling people what I really feel or want.

Therapist: What thoughts do you have about that?

This second, hypothetical version of the example provides some instructive contrasts with the first, actual version. The patient appears equally sensitive to her behavior and equally prepared to explore its defensive aspects. However, whether due to elements of resistance or aspects of the transference, she seems just not ready to move as fast; she needs or wants the therapist to help her through the interpretation. The therapist provides such help, but not at the cost of sacrificing the patient's active participation. The therapist follows the partial interpretation first with silence and then with two other elliptical statements ("Someone has to make decisions"; "Why indeed?"), and thus gradually elicits the same response that emerged more quickly in the example as it actually happened.

The partial interpretation technique offers much to gain and virtually nothing to lose. If it provokes an immediate and full response, as in the first of these two versions, some time is saved and the patient has the beneficial experience of formulating her own self-understanding. If it does not promptly strike a responsive cord, as in the second version, it is merely necessary to supplement it with further comments or explanations. The latter process of gradually eliciting an interpretation through a series of elliptical statements requires therapists to be patient, but no more so than is generally necessary to minimize patients' resistance and promote their active participation in the treatment. Furthermore, should an interpretation be incorrect or poorly timed, approaching it with partial statements can provide therapists some opportunities to recognize and correct their error before they have already put the hook in their mouth with a comprehensive, elaborate statement of an interpretation that is off the mark.

Phrasing of Interpretations

Interpretations constitute reasonable but not incontrovertible inferences about the patient, and their effectiveness, as just noted, usually depends on how actively the patient participates in arriving at them. Accordingly, interpretation should be tentative, couched in the language of possibilities and probabilities rather than certainties, and they should be concise, consisting of no more words than are necessary to communicate the intended message and elicit the patient's reaction to it.

Phrasing Interpretations Tentatively

The overriding consideration in phrasing interpretations effectively is to make them tentative statements rather than pronouncements. Pronouncements leave no room for error and imply that the therapist is omniscient; moreover, by allowing no opportunity for shared participation in their formulation, they relegate patients to being passive recipients. To avoid having interpretations foster either of these unprofitable roles, therapists need regularly to precede them with some qualifying remark indicating possibility or probability: "It's as if . . ."; "Perhaps . . ."; "I get the feeling that . . ."; "I wonder if . . ."; "Could it be that . . ."; "Apparently, then, . . ."; "Maybe it's because . . ."[12]

Interpretations introduced in this way leave the door open to alternatives and invite a patient to weigh any such alternatives against what is being suggested as possible or probable. At times, patients may not hear that an interpretation is being made tentatively, or they may not recognize that they are being invited to evaluate it. If so, their response may imply the message, "If that's the way it seems to you, I guess that's the way it is." Any such response to an interpretation, whether direct or implicit, calls for immediate intervention to prevent the patient from drifting into an inactive role. Depending on the circumstances, this intervention may be directed either at process features of patients' behavior (perhaps their acquiescence reflects submissiveness to the therapist or sullen resistance to the treatment) or at the content of their response. At the content level, a therapist whose patient responds passively to a tentative interpretation ("If that's the way it seems to you, I guess that's the way it is") should consider reemphasizing the active role expected of a psychotherapy patient: "My thinking it doesn't make it so." This elliptical comment implies (a) that the therapist is not omniscient, (b) that conclusions can be drawn about the patient only in light of his or her estimate of these conclusions, and (c) that the next step in exploring the accuracy of the interpretation that has been offered is up to the patient. Should such an elliptical comment not immediately elicit all the points it is intended to make, therapists can lead patients through them one at a time at whatever pace they can follow.

Because such elliptical statements and partial interpretations are usually made bluntly and without hedging ("My thinking it doesn't make it so," or, from the previous example, "So you're not a passive victim"), they differ from interpretations, which need to be offered tentatively. Elliptical statements and partial interpretations consist of information about which the therapist is almost totally certain, and they are intended to stimulate patients' observations of their experience. Interpretations are inferences intended to suggest some meaning of experiences that patient and therapist have shared in observing. Therapists may be very emphatic and uncompromising in guiding patients toward increased self-understanding by encouraging them to observe themselves more fully. When the time comes for attempting to communicate such understanding, however, therapists should opt for restrained suggestion rather than unequivocal pronouncement.

In striving to phrase their interpretations tentatively, therapists should also take care to vary their style. If they precede every interpretation with "Could it be that .. ?" or "It's as if . . .", their work will take on an automatic, stereotyped quality. Stereotyped therapist behavior can make patients more conscious of their therapist's technique than of what the therapist is saying. Additionally, the more therapists are perceived by their patients as playing out a formalized role, the less they are seen as being interested in and sensitive to their patients' individual needs. Therapists too can suffer from falling into repetitive speech patterns because such routine responses create a risk of their becoming bored and inattentive. Hence there are advantages in therapists alternating among suitable ways of expressing themselves, whether in offering interpretations or conducting some other aspect of the treatment.

Phrasing Interpretations Concisely

Turning next to the number of words used in phrasing an interpretation, considerable attention has already been given in principle and through example to the utility of therapists saying no more than is necessary to help their patients talk meaningfully about themselves. Therapists' words have no importance in their own right; they are important only to the extent that they aid patients to achieve the goals of their treatment. Erudite exposition belongs in the lecture hall, not in the treatment room. The less therapists say about a subject being discussed, the more their patients will say about it, because (a) there will be more time for them to talk and (b) there will be more left for them to say. And it is what patients say that gives them their sense of participating in the treatment and learning to understand themselves better. Because of the extent to which it limits patients' participation in the treatment process, therapist wordiness is with few exceptions antithetical to progress in psychotherapy.[13]

JUDGING THE EFFECTIVENESS
OF INTERPRETATIONS

When interpretations are effective, patients accept them, understand them, and use them as a stimulus to additional self-exploration. Of these three indications that an interpretation has been effective, the first is the most crucial. Only if the content of an interpretation is experienced by patients as a part of the self can they derive any lasting benefit either from reconstructing the evidence for it or from projecting its implications into their present and future life. Unless such acceptance occurs, any professed understanding or apparent use of an interpretation amounts to little more than an abstract exercise in personality dynamics, without an accompanying increment in personal self-understanding.

Is the Interpretation Accepted?

Whether patients have accepted an interpretation is usually revealed by, but not always obvious from, how they respond to it. For example, consider a patient who responds to an interpretation with "Yes, I think you're right," or "As you say that, it feels right to me." Such comments ordinarily indicate agreement with the interpretation, and the second type of comment in particular suggests the experience of an interpretation as congruent with oneself. On the other hand, such agreeable responses are sometimes encountered in psychotherapy for two other possible reasons.

First, patients who are characterologically submissive or momentarily concerned with courting the therapist's favor may be motivated to acquiesce to whatever he or she says. A "yes" in these circumstances does not necessarily mean that patients agree with the interpretation, but only that they do not want to disagree with their therapist. Second, patients who find an interpretation particularly threatening may agree with it in order to close the issue, just as someone may seek to end an unpleasant argument simply by agreeing with whatever the other person says. Thus, particularly before they have had sufficient experience with the treatment process to appreciate the therapist's patience and tenacity, patients may agree with an unwelcome interpretation not because they have accepted it, but because they expect by so doing to end discussion of the subject it concerns.

The indications that patients who say "Yes" really mean something else are usually to be found in process aspects of their behavior. Sometimes an endorsement of an interpretation simply does not ring true, as when agreement comes too readily without reflection, or too grudgingly without enthusiasm. In other instances, therapists may sense attitudes in patients that are probably influencing them to agree without being in agreement, such as a wish to court the therapist's favor.

Along with process clues, what patients say next also bears on the genuineness of their expressed agreement with an interpretation. Interpretations that are experienced and acknowledged as congruent can be expected to stimulate fresh associations and guide patients into previously unexplored territory. When patients agree to an interpretation but then drop it, without spontaneously reporting some ideas or events related to or suggested by it, the interpretation has probably not been genuinely accepted, whether because of the patient's resistance to it or because it was ill conceived, poorly timed, or awkwardly phrased.

As a further demand on the therapist's alertness, there are also times when patients disagree with an interpretation that they recognize as being accurate. Patients who are characterologically obstinate or counterdependent, for example, or who feel negatively toward the therapist, or who are upset by the implications of what is being said to them may reject an interpretation because they dislike having to agree with others, or because they resent giving the therapist the satisfaction of having been perceptive, or because they want to avoid any further discussion of the subject involved. Evidence that such motives are present make it likely that a rejected interpretation has in fact struck home, especially when patients who have rejected an interpretation proceed to reflect on it in ways that leave little doubt about its having been meaningful to them.

IS THE INTERPRETATION UNDERSTOOD?

Turning to the second criterion for judging the effectiveness of interpretations, patients need to understand an interpretation in order to learn anything from it. Understanding an interpretation means being able to recognize how the evidence for it fits together and how it could account for some thoughts, feelings, or actions that have previously been puzzling or unaccountable. Patients who have understood an interpretation can usually demonstrate their understanding by recapitulating it in their own words:

> Let me think about that for a minute . . . yes, I see it now. I turned him off by being nasty to him and yet I wasn't angry at him, just worried he might put me down if I gave him a chance; and this must be the fourth or fifth time the same thing has come up in our sessions. So you must be right—I've got some fear of having people not like me or reject me, and I protect myself by rejecting them first, and that would explain a lot about why I do such a poor job of trying to make and keep friends.

Therapists should listen for such glimmers of understanding as a patient responds to an interpretation, and they should try to elicit them if they do not emerge spontaneously ("I wonder what thoughts you have about that possibility"; "You haven't said anything about the meaning such a connection might have to you"). It has already been noted that professed understanding in the absence of basic acceptance of an interpretation is a hollow accomplishment. Likewise, inability to demonstrate understanding of an interpretation, no matter how enthusiastically it has been accepted, indicates that more work needs to be done to make it effective.

Limited understanding of an interpretation that has been accepted may mean that factors other than a true experience of its being accurate have motivated a patient to agree with it, as just illustrated. If so, then therapists need to defer further consideration of the interpretation until they have been able to explore why the patient said "Yes" to it when the true response was "No." As another possibility, however, inability to understand an accepted interpretation may occur when patients' experiencing self has temporarily outstripped their observing self; that is, they have had a sudden flash of experiencing the interpretation as truly characteristic of themselves, as "feeling just right," even though they cannot yet put their finger on why it feels so right.

Although the experiencing of an interpretation as "feeling just right" provides strong evidence of its accuracy, interpretations cannot be fully effective until a patient's powers of reasoning and observation are also brought to bear on them. An emotional experience, no matter how powerful, is a thing of the moment. For people to learn from their experience, they must not only experience but also understand why they experience as they do, what their experiences mean, and what implications the experiences of one moment have for experiences of the next. At times, therapists may have to use additional questions, clarifications, and confrontations to promote understanding of an interpretation that appears to have been accurate, well timed, and nicely phrased. As a basic guideline, therapists should not consider interpretations effective until patients have been able to supplement their acceptance of it with indications that they understand it as well.

IS THE INTERPRETATION USED?

The third clue to the effectiveness of interpretations is the extent to which they stimulate patients to generate new ideas about themselves or to begin exploring aspects of their life not previously touched on in therapy. Once accepted and understood, interpretations should lead to new avenues of self-understanding, and patients should enter these avenues with some mixture of curiosity, perplexity, anxiety, and enthusiasm. Accordingly, therapists should listen for the following kinds of comments from a patient who has agreed with and recapitulated an interpretation: "You know, that reminds me of something I haven't thought of before"; "I really feel good about that, because I think its going to help explain a number of things"; "Now that I understand a little better how I've been handling that type of situation, I'd really like to know more about how I got to be this way"; "Knowing that makes me a little uneasy about the kind of person I'm finding myself to be."

If patients do not respond in some such manner, indicating that an interpretation is leading them in some new direction, the interpretive effort will have been less than fully effective. Whereas therapists can help their patient understand an interpretation, they can no more force an interpretation to lead somewhere than they can compel agreement with it. The acceptance and utilization of interpretations must come from the patient; when such positive responses are not forthcoming from patients who seemed to be in a receptive frame of mind, the interpretation has probably been inaccurate or inadequately presented. Therapists' only recourse in these circumstances is to drop the matter and do a better job the next time they undertake an interpretive sequence.

For readers who are interested in research as well as practice in psychotherapy, a concluding comment is necessary in this section to clarify what otherwise might appear to be a circular approach to judging the effectiveness of interpretations. If the preceding paragraphs are read as stating that an effective interpretation is one that patients accept, understand, and make use of, and that the effectiveness of interpretations is judged from the extent to which they are accepted, understood, and generative, then we are left with a tautological definition of effectiveness that precludes an adequate research strategy. An interpretation accompanied by the criteria of effectiveness is defined as effective, and one that is not is defined as ineffective, and there is no way to disprove hypotheses about the impact of effective interpretations.

However, there is no need to tie the concept of effective interpretation to the same criteria for defining it as for assessing its impact, which would hopelessly contaminate the independent and dependent variables in relevant research studies. The point is simply that accurate, well-timed, and carefully conceived interpretations are likely to be effective, as measured by patient agreement, understanding, and subsequent productivity. Utilizing this distinction, research studies of the effectiveness of the interpretive process can employ separate measures of the characteristics of an interpretation and of the patient's response to it.

WORKING THROUGH INTERPRETATIONS

Just as learning in general rarely occurs on the basis of a single trial, learning about oneself in psychotherapy seldom becomes established with the initial offering of an interpretation. Even interpretations that are accepted and understood attain little more than the status of a likely possibility the first time patients hear them. After holding certain views of themselves and their experiences for many years, people rarely embrace alternative views as soon as they are suggested. Instead, the alternative views need to be repeated on several occasions, each time helping patients understand better some aspect of themselves or their behavior. In this way alternative views develop a cumulative plausibility that gradually allows them to supplant previous views completely. This process is called *working through.*

Working through, then, consists of the regular repetition of interpretations (a) to establish their validity in accounting for the events that first suggested them and (b) to extend their applicability to new events that come under consideration. Such repetition allows patients both to reassess interpretations in their original context and to test them out in new contexts where they should be relevant. In common with other aspects of the interpretive process, working through is the shared responsibility of patient and therapist. On some occasions, patients spontaneously undertake their own working through, on other occasions therapists must instigate it, and on all occasions, no matter which party initiates the working through, patients must end by understanding interpretations in their own words.[14]

To illustrate the process of working through, consider a male patient who has been discussing his awareness of never having aspired to anything that might stretch or even approach the limits of his potential, and who with the therapist's help has come to realize that he is so afraid of failing that he avoids any situation where he cannot be absolutely certain of success. Several sessions after first arriving at this new perspective of himself, he states that he was offered a promotion at work but turned it down because it involved changing to a department where he thought he would enjoy the work less. He then says, "I've been doing some hard thinking about it since it happened; do you suppose it could be that my not liking the different kind of work was just a lame excuse, and that what really was involved was my being afraid of being a failure, like we talked about a while ago?"

With this statement, the patient has initiated the process of working through the interpretation of his fear of failure, which he is now observing in a new situation beyond the experiences that introduced it into the therapy. Appreciation of the full extent to which this underlying concern about failure is influencing his behavior and preventing him from utilizing his potential will strengthen both his understanding and his ongoing awareness of it. It is the ongoing awareness of what people learn about themselves from an interpretation, achieved by working through, that allows them to modify their behavior in light of the interpretation.

Without such ongoing awareness to mediate between interpretation and behavior change, interpretations are usually doomed to run a barren course.

To take the preceding example one step further, suppose the patient had not initiated his own working through, that is, suppose he had reported turning down the promotion at work because of not liking some of the changes it entailed but had not said anything more to relate his behavior to previous work in the therapy. Therapists must guard against being disappointed or irritated when patients describe maladaptive behavior clearly related to a recent interpretation but do so with no apparent recognition of either the maladaptiveness or its relationship to the interpretation. Such lack of awareness may reflect some resistance on a patient's part, but it does not mean that the patient is dense or insensitive, or that the therapist has not been conducting the treatment properly, or that interpretive psychotherapy is an ineffective procedure.

What it does mean when patients act as if a previously accepted and understood interpretation never existed is that they have not yet worked it through. Because virtually all interpretations have to be worked through (except in those rare instances when a particularly powerful interpretation results in one-trial learning), therapists must be prepared for patients to display minimal behavior change and even minimal recollection following the initial offering and acceptance of an interpretation. Hence, as in the preceding example, the patient may do just what he would have done before (decline the promotion) but subsequently begin to think about how his behavior may have been influenced by underlying concerns previously interpreted to him. If patients do not begin to generate some connections in such circumstances, it falls to the therapist to use a blend of elliptical statements and partial interpretations to lead them into a reexperiencing of the interpretation:

PATIENT: I was offered a better paying job with more responsibility, but I would have had to switch from the accounting to the advertising department, and I didn't think I would like it there as well so I turned it down.

THERAPIST: I think there may be more to it than that.

PATIENT: Like what?

THERAPIST: Like this isn't the first time you've backed off from a chance to take on something more demanding.

PATIENT: Uh . . . you mean this could be like what we were talking about a while back . . . a situation where I don't do something I really could do and that would get me ahead, because I'm afraid of not succeeding at it. As I think about it now, I'm sure that's what it was again, which means I screwed myself for no good reason.

Second, in addition to helping patients reexperience an interpretation in contexts similar to the one in which it originally emerged, therapists should also help them extend the interpretation to other contexts in which it is applicable. Continuing with the example, this patient's fear of failure in work situations could also be contributing to maladaptive handling of social situations, leading to the following exchange:

PATIENT: I would like to become involved with a woman I could really admire and look up to. But somehow the only ones I end up trying to date are ones who don't have much going for them and who look up to me, and I don't enjoy their company very much.

THERAPIST: There's a familiar theme to that.

PATIENT: I'm not sure what you mean.

THERAPIST: You're not taking any chances.

PATIENT: In a way, I suppose. I'm not taking any chances of being unimpressive because the woman's as sharp as I am or sharper, so there's not much risk of—oh, I see what you mean by the same theme. I'm hedging my bets, not risking failure, just as I've been doing in my work.

When patients have an opportunity to work through the context of an interpretation in this way, seeing it repetitively relevant to understanding their behavior in a variety of situations, they become increasingly able to integrate their new knowledge of themselves. Concurrently with working through an interpretation, patients gradually become capable of using it to alter their behavior. Initially, they may continue to display some maladaptive or self-defeating behavior pattern that has been the subject of an apparently effective interpretation and be able to recognize how this behavior relates to the interpretation only with the aid of reminders from the therapist. Later, after some working through has taken place, they may persist in the ill-advised behavior but begin to recognize on their own that they could and should have acted in a more constructive and self-actualizing manner. Over time, the lag between their behaving in a neurotic fashion and their recognizing the neurotic determinants of their behavior will continue to shrink, and finally, when the new understanding of themselves has been fully worked through, they will realize its implication for situations in which they have been behaving maladaptively as they encounter them, and before they respond, and they then will have achieved full capacity to master their conflicts and control their behavior in those situations.

The necessary role of working through in translating interpretations into potential for behavior change is an important note on which to conclude this chapter, because it bears on the function of insight in dynamically oriented psychotherapy. Interpretive psychotherapy has at times been regarded as a treatment method in which interpretations produce insight, which consists of increased understanding of why one has been behaving in certain maladaptive ways, and this insight in turn produces behavior change. In truth, however, interpretation in dynamically informed psychotherapy is not aimed at insight alone, nor is insight alone expected to result in behavior change. Rather, the interpretive process is intended to bring thoughts and feelings of which people have little or no awareness, and over which they consequently have no control, into their awareness, to allow the person to examine them, consider their relationship to other thoughts and feelings, and exert some conscious control over the extent to which they influence the person's behavior.

Thus the interpretive process in psychotherapy is above all an effort to liberate patients from psychological influences previously outside their control and thereby free them to think, feel, and act in ways they find gratifying and self-fulfilling. In this process, an after-the-fact understanding of why they behaved in certain ways is not what allows people to change their behavior, even though such understanding is an essential ingredient in this form of treatment and does constitute what is called "insight." Only after people have worked through something new they have learned about themselves, to the point where they can recognize its potential influence on their behavior before they act, do they become free to exercise self-determination and behave in different ways. Coming to a similar conclusion, Wachtel (1993) observes, "It is likely that the most common cause of therapeutic failure is not a failure to achieve some degree of insight but rather the failure to carry through with that insight into new ways of experiencing oneself and relating to others" (p. 236).

NOTES

1. For additional discussion of the nature and utility of interpretation, readers are referred to Chessick (1994), Messer (1989), Oremland (1991), and Strachey (1934).

2. Strupp (1989) has urged psychotherapists to avoid confronting or challenging patients as much as possible by limiting interpretations to statements of empathic understanding intended to help them "come to terms with a troubled past" and not to explain how and why they became the kind of people they are. This well-reasoned and research-based suggestion is consistent with the emphasis in the present chapter on using interpretation as a tool for communicating understanding. Even so, however, despite a full measure of therapist gentleness and consideration, people being helped to learn new things about themselves cannot be fully

spared from the unsettling and sometimes painful realization that some of their prior beliefs were mistaken.

3. Papers by E. Kris (1954) and Loewenstein (1954) provide two classical statements concerning the modification of defenses subsequent to their being interpreted.

4. To place these observations in broader perspective, the emergence of attention in psychotherapy to interpreting characterological defensive operations paralleled a shift from an id emphasis to an ego emphasis in psychoanalytic theory and practice, as recounted by Lorand (1972/1973). The psychodynamic map has subsequently been redrawn further by the addition of object relations formulations, as illustrated by the work of Kernberg (1976), and the notions of self-psychology, as propounded by Kohut (1971). In a book titled *Drive, Ego, Object, and Self,* Pine (1990) provides an excellent overview of these four "psychologies" and their implications for psychotherapy. For an encyclopedic source of information concerning these developments in psychoanalytic thinking, readers are referred as well to Wallerstein's (1995) *The Talking Cures.* As for the present book, the text attends to instinctual and relational issues but exemplifies primarily an ego-analytic perspective that approaches them as aspects of conflict and defense.

5. The distinct possibility that cumulative life experiences will minimize or transcend the importance of connections between characterological defenses and the conflicts that engendered them relates closely to Gordon Allport's (1937) classical concept of the "functional autonomy of motives." Allport's point, subsequently subscribed to by most behavioral scientists, was simply that a person's behavior can become an end or a goal in itself, independent of the original reasons for engaging in it.

6. This distinction originates in classical psychoanalytic notions that repressed material tends to seek outlets in the form of events that permit some discharge of energy. In a detailed elaboration of this id-analytic formulation, Fenichel (1941, pp. 148–150, 193–194) indicated that the displacement of energy in this way produces a wide variety of *derivatives,* including dreams, daydreams, screen memories, and neurotic symptoms. Whether one embraces the psychoanalytic model of energy flow, the concept of some behavior being derived from and indirectly expressing conflict is very useful in deciding what to interpret in psychotherapy, especially if distinctions are made between near and remote derivatives.

7. As remote derivatives, dreams themselves can vary in how closely they are related to the thoughts and feelings that elicit them. Whether dreams reported by patients in psychotherapy are relatively near or relatively remote derivatives depends on the extent to which the "dream work," consisting of condensation, displacement, symbolization, and secondary revision (see S. Freud, 1900/1953c) has intervened between their

latent and manifest content. The less disguised the meaning of a dream, the more suitable it is for interpretation in psychotherapy. Yet S. Freud (1911/1958c) cautioned that therapists should not become so preoccupied with dreams that they lose sight of a patient's current thoughts and emotions. Once undertaken, dream interpretation proceeds according to the same general principles of interpretation being outlined in the present chapter. The technique of utilizing dream material in psychotherapy is elaborated by Conigliaro (1997), S. Freud (1923/1961), Grinstein (1983), Hill (1996), Mendelsohn (1990), Weiss (1986), and Wolberg (1988, pp. 671–685).

8. Spence (1995) presents extensive case material demonstrating greater effects of interpretation during sessions in which the patient is relating to the therapist in a relatively close and involved manner than in sessions when the patient appears detached and distant from the treatment relationship. The research of Hill et al. (1989) has confirmed that the characteristics of effect interpretation include their being offered in the context of a positively toned patient-therapist relationship.

9. The utilization of an interpretive sequence of progressively more penetrating interventions, as described here, has long had a place in psychodynamic psychotherapy and is discussed in further detail by Bibring (1954), Glover (1955), Greenson (1967), and Oremland (1991). In research reported by McCullough and Winston (1991), careful listening and clarification in preparation for interpretations was found to help patients respond less defensively and with more affective engagement than they otherwise would have.

10. This illustration is based in part on guidelines for the interpretation of defenses provided by Fenichel (1941, p. 77), who was among the first writers to stress the importance in uncovering psychotherapy of isolating a patient's observing self from what he or she is experiencing.

11. The nature and potential utility of partial interpretations are discussed by Glover (1955) under the designation of "incomplete interpretation" and by Blanck and Blanck (1994) as "piecemeal interpretation."

12. Research reported by Jones and Gelso (1988) confirms that patients are generally inclined to view tentatively delivered interpretations more positively than interpretations expressed in absolute terms. Similarly, Bischoff and Tracey (1995) found that directive therapist behavior tends to increase resistance behavior on the part of patients. Nevertheless, as mentioned earlier in this chapter and as also noted by Oremland (1991, Chapter 3) among others, there are occasions when therapist certainty about an interpretation and its having been aired previously warrant expressing it in fairly certain terms.

13. As in Chapter 7, attention should be called to the valuable contribution of Wachtel (1993) to effective communication in psychotherapy. His

text explains and illustrates numerous guidelines for felicitous phrasing of therapist interventions. As for empirical data, Sachse (1993) reports research in which brevity, clarity, and simplicity of therapist statements increased the likelihood of patients utilizing these statements effectively. In particular, short statements were found to have an enabling effect on the treatment process, whereas long statements had severely negative effects.

14. For extended discussion of the general topic of working through, readers are referred to Brenner (1987), Fialkow and Muslin (1987), S. Freud (1914/1958e), Greenson (1965a), and Wolberg (1988, pp. 819–832). Luborsky (1996) provides some relevant research findings that show how patients' gains in mastery of their core interpersonal conflicts are facilitated in psychotherapy as part of the working-through process, and Hill et al. (1989) have similarly confirmed that repetition of interpretations enhances their effectiveness.

CHAPTER 9

Interference with Communication: Resistance

R ESISTANCE IN psychotherapy constitutes a paradoxical reluctance of patients to participate in the treatment process. Patients who are resisting become temporarily unwilling or unable to fulfill the terms of the treatment contract. Despite continuing to want help and believing in the potential benefit of the therapist's efforts to provide it, resistive patients conduct themselves in ways that undermine or interfere with the therapeutic process. Resistance differs from situations in which patients truly feel that they have had all the help they want or need, or in which they have adequate basis for concluding that psychotherapy has little to offer them. In these latter situations, reluctance to collaborate in the treatment process represents a rational decision, not a paradox, and cannot be construed as resistance. Once an appropriate treatment contract has been entered into and interpretive work has begun, however, reduced participation by a patient typically reflects resistance rather than any genuine conviction that therapy is no longer necessary or beneficial.[1]

Resistance interferes with both the sending and receiving aspects of patient communication. Patients who are resisting ordinarily talk too much about inconsequential matters, too little about important matters, or perhaps not at all. Either way, they cease to communicate freely the thoughts and feelings that bear most directly on the concerns that have brought them for help. At the same time, resistive patients stop receiving communications, so that they no longer listen to the therapist, or if listening do not hear, or if hearing do not lend credence to what is being said.

Because resistance always disrupts communication in psychotherapy, it was originally viewed solely as an obstacle to treatment progress. Freud in his early work depicted resistance as a force so antithetical to the aims of psychotherapy that it must be overcome by drawing on almost any available means" by which one man can ordinarily exert psychical influence on another" (Breuer & Freud, 1893–1895/1955, p. 282). Included among these means were hypnosis, insistence, exhortation, and even a procedure in which the therapist presses on a patient's forehead and instructs the person that this pressure will elicit previously unrecollected images and associations that should then be communicated.[2] Within a few years, however, Freud began to regard resistance as being itself an important subject for interpretation, to be explored and understood rather than merely removed (S. Freud, 1904/1953b). The interpretation of resistance has ever since been recognized as a key ingredient of dynamically oriented psychotherapy, and some psychoanalytic scholars, such as Gray (1994) and Weinshel (1984, 1990), view the understanding and resolution of resistance phenomena as the centerpiece around which uncovering therapy revolves.

There are several reasons why resistance plays a major role in psychotherapy. First, resistance inevitably accompanies a patient's efforts to come to grips with interpretations and their implications for behavior change. As noted previously, psychotherapy confronts people with unpleasant aspects of themselves and their lives, and it further requires them to consider adopting new and unfamiliar ways of doing and looking at things. Few people can sustain participation in such a process without some waxing and waning of their enthusiasm and tolerance. Indeed, patients who coast merrily along in psychotherapy without intercurrent periods of reluctance to participate usually lack meaningful engagement in the treatment process. Boesky (1990) has wryly noted that successful analytically oriented therapy can be defined as "just one damned resistance after another" (p. 557).

Second, the therapist's help in reducing or eliminating resistance allows patients to work more comfortably in the treatment and hastens their progress toward self-understanding and behavior change. Whatever else may be said about resistance, it does in fact interfere with being able to talk about oneself in psychotherapy, and the easing of resistance usually allows thoughts and feelings to emerge that would not otherwise have been expressed.[3]

Third, in addition to what patients may learn from interview content that emerges following the reduction of some resistance, careful consideration of resistance behavior in its own right can enhance self-understanding. Why has the resistance occurred at a particular point? What is the patient resisting and for what reason? How has the patient

156 INTERFERENCE WITH COMMUNICATION: RESISTANCE

chosen to manifest the resistance? What relationships exist between the resistance behavior seen in the treatment and the patient's behavior outside psychotherapy? Pursuit of answers to these questions can help patients gain increased awareness of what makes them anxious and how they typically cope with anxiety.

Fourth, as a subject for interpretation in its own right, resistance often proves more fruitful than a patient's recollected experiences. Resistance behavior is an aspect of *process* in psychotherapy, which was identified in Chapter 8 as usually taking precedence over the *content* of what patients are saying as a subject of interpretation. As process, resistance is occurring right at the moment, and its manifestations can be directly observed and its impact vividly experienced. By contrast, recollected events in a patient's life are an aspect of content and, as such, seldom serve as well as events transpiring during a treatment session in providing reliable samples of personality style and vivid opportunities for patients to observe themselves in action.

To help therapists recognize resistance behavior and respond to it effectively, it is useful to distinguish four types or sources of resistance to the treatment process: *resistance to change, character resistance, resistance to content,* and *transference resistance.*[4] These four types of resistance are elaborated in the sequence in which they are likely to make their first appearance during the course of psychotherapy. Following this discussion of the origins of resistance, the remainder of the chapter delineates common manifestations of resistance behavior and alternative ways of responding to them.

RESISTANCE TO CHANGE

It has long been recognized that emotional and behavioral disturbances are often accompanied by a reluctance to give them up. In some instances, such resistance to change stems from an anticipation that recovery will put an end to certain advantages of being disturbed, in which case patients are said to display *secondary gain resistance.* At other times, change is seen as a source of specific new disadvantages, the most common of which are reflected in *neurotic equilibrium resistance, resistance to patienthood,* and *superego resistance.* Whatever form it takes, resistance to change involves feelings and attitudes that predate the patient's entering psychotherapy and exist independently of the treatment. Although resistance to change may become exacerbated at various points during psychotherapy, especially when visible progress occurs, it can make its presence felt by interfering with a patient's communication from the first moment of the first session.

SECONDARY GAIN RESISTANCE

Secondary gain consists of a variety of rewards, benefits, or gratifications that people accrue as a consequence of being psychologically incapacitated and that influence them to resist any significant change in their condition.[5] This is not to say that emotionally disturbed people become disturbed because they enjoy it. To see secondary gain as a source of psychological problems is to conceive behavior as arising because of its consequences, as in suggesting that people develop emotional problems in order to enjoy having others sympathize with them. Such teleological hypotheses contribute little to comprehending the origins of psychological disturbance and erroneously imply that disturbed individuals can voluntarily give up their psychopathology anytime they decide to forgo the advantages stemming from it.

Correctly speaking, secondary gain serves to reinforce already established patterns of disturbed behavior, not to elicit them, and to hinder change, not prevent it. Secondary gain emerges because a person who is perceived by others as suffering an ailment or affliction is likely to receive sympathy, to be exempted from responsibilities, and to have allowances made for outlandish, inconsiderate, and self-indulgent behavior that would not otherwise be tolerated. People cannot easily avoid becoming attached to having their needs catered to, their feelings spared, and their energies freed to serve only purposes that please them, and these potential advantages of being incapacitated in turn resist being relinquished. Additionally, resistance to change associated with such secondary gain may become bolstered by some tangible benefits contingent on being incapacitated, such as a disability pension, extended paid sick leave from a job, or the assistance of a full-time housekeeper.

Yet not everyone who experiences psychological difficulties basks in supportive responses from others, accompanied by special privileges and a reprieve from responsibility. Instead of sympathy and forbearance, others' impatience and irritation may be the lot of people who become disturbed, which means that they will realize little secondary gain from persistence of their problems, unless they happen to delight in irritating others and trying their patience. Similarly, having psychological difficulties may not lead to being excused from responsibilities at home, in school, or on the job, but rather to having to carry on despite the burden of one's problems. In such a case, the burden usually constitutes a stronger motive to overcome the problems than any source of secondary gain is to persist in them.

Furthermore, even when sympathy and freedom from responsibility accompany psychological incapacitation, there is a limit to how long most people enjoy being dependent and cared for. Not having to work, make decisions, confront delicate interpersonal situations, or be held account-able for one's behavior has a certain temporary appeal, like going on a va-cation. Over the long haul, however, human nature makes most people feel best about themselves when doing something meaningful with their lives and being treated by others as worthwhile and responsible individ-uals capable of making their own decisions. Hence secondary gain ema-nating from emotional problems tends to be short-lived, except in those relatively few instances in which it becomes entrenched as part of a chronic, intransigent disorder that produces psychological invalidism.

Secondary gains associated with emotional disturbance may on occa-sion become sufficiently important to inhibit participation in psychother-apy, but they are usually outweighed by patients' motivation to overcome their emotional distress and by intrinsic pressures toward positive per-sonality growth. Nevertheless, therapists need to be prepared to recog-nize and deal with secondary gain resistance in every patient they see. No matter how limited the benefits a patient appears to be reaping as a result of having psychological problems, some resistance to change due to sec-ondary gain is bound to develop during the treatment. At the very least, the therapist's interest and respect provide patients a rewarding experi-ence that will last only so long as they require treatment. For this reason, patients who seem fully capable of implementing desirable behavior change may resist changing to prolong their relationship with the thera-pist. This particular pattern of resistance to change has obvious implica-tions for termination in psychotherapy and is elaborated in Chapter 12.

Neurotic Equilibrium Resistance

Whereas resistance to change associated with secondary gain involves re-luctance to give up aspects of their condition that are providing patients some advantages, other important sources of resistance to change are based as previously noted on the anticipation of new and distinct disad-vantages. Most common in this regard are concerns that change will dis-rupt current patterns of interpersonal relationships constituting what is known as a *neurotic equilibrium.*

In a neurotic equilibrium, the people with whom patients interact at home, in school, on the job, or in leisure activities have adapted to their behavioral problems and idiosyncrasies, so that patients feel accepted or at least tolerated in others' company and can anticipate how they will re-spond to them from one day to the next. Patients in a neurotic equilib-rium may even be valued by significant people in their lives because their shortcomings gratify the needs of these other people in some complemen-tary way. For example, a man who is psychologically handicapped by a reluctance to assert himself may be married to a domineering woman who thrives on having him defer to her. As another example, people whose failures and misadventures seem to be the bane of their family's existence may also be providing family members a scapegoat on whom they can blame their other individual and collective difficulties and toward whom they can direct negative feelings they would otherwise direct toward each other.

Either because they and their environment have become accustomed to how they are, even if disturbed, or because their difficulties are meeting the needs of others, people with psychological problems may be reluctant to change at the risk of disrupting the equilibrium in their lives. Early in treatment, such reluctance often appears in the form of vague apprehensions about the unknown, as if the patient were musing as follows: "I don't like the way I am, but at least I know what to expect of myself and what other people expect of me; if I were to change, what would I be like, how would other people react to me, and what new kinds of experiences would I have to face?" The charting of unexplored psychological waters inevitably provokes anxiety, even for venturesome people determined to extend their life horizons. Accordingly, psychotherapy may from its beginning include moments when a patient's wish to change is temporarily opposed by a wish to avoid uncertainty, and therapists must be prepared to help patients recognize this source of resistance.

As treatment proceeds and behavior change begins to occur, resistance related specifically to sustaining previous patterns of interpersonal relationships may come to the fore. In particular, progress toward the goals of the treatment may have the adverse effect of alienating key figures in patients' lives, whose needs they are no longer gratifying. Should the passive man just mentioned become more assertive, for example, he may annoy and disappoint his domineering wife to the point where she feels unappreciated, unfulfilled, and perhaps even undecided about continuing in the marriage. Should a chronically unsuccessful or irresponsible patient deprive his or her family of a scapegoat by attaining admirable goals or becoming a respectable member of society, the result may be increased family disharmony and decreased family interest in the person's activities.

In such circumstances, patients may feel tempted to persist in their behavior problems and retain the interpersonal equilibrium associated with them, rather than change their behavior and risk disrupting the equilibrium. If so, the therapist will have to ponder whether to encourage continued treatment. Would the patient do better to become more self-actualizing and let the interpersonal chips fall where they may? Or is the person so locked into his or her current interpersonal context that equilibrium-disrupting behavior change, no matter how apparently desirable, would be psychologically deleterious?

Whether to change and bear the consequences or remain the same and avoid taking chances is in the end a decision for patients to make; barring emergency situations, a therapist should not presume to make it for them. Yet therapists can and should influence a patient's choice between remaining in a neurotic equilibrium or working to change it, according to their estimate of where the patient's best prospects lie for finding satisfaction in life. It can be hoped that this estimate will have been accurately made during the assessment phase of the treatment, so that patients engaged in psychotherapy will have been correctly identified as having more to gain than to lose by modifying their behavior. On the basis of their prior assessment that psychotherapy is appropriate, then, therapists should ordinarily work to keep a patient in it when a dissolving neurotic equilibrium produces resistance to change.

Assessments are not perfect, however, nor are therapists perfect in their judgments. Information emerging in the course of psychotherapy, including untoward disruption in a patient's life subsequent to behavior change, may indicate that the treatment was a path not wisely taken. Therapists must be prepared to recognize instances of apparent resistance to change that are not paradoxical at all, but instead reflect these patients' well-founded conclusion that they would be better off not to continue in psychotherapy. Needless to say, such well-founded decisions should be distinguished from resistance and respected for the reality they represent.

RESISTANCE TO PATIENTHOOD

In some cases, resistance to continuing in or benefiting from treatment stems from negative attitudes toward being in the patient's role. Even before beginning treatment, as discussed in Chapters 2 and 5, prospective patients may be repelled by what it means to them to receive professional psychological help. If they perceive entering psychotherapy as evidence that they are a weak, worthless, inadequate, or dependent person, their threatened self-esteem may generate a *resistance to patienthood*, in which the negative connotations of being in psychotherapy exceed the appeal of any gains expected from it.

After treatment has begun, resistance to patienthood sometimes originates in or is intensified by the very kinds of behavior change toward which the patient has aspired. In these instances, a desired change occurs and is then immediately tarnished by the patient's awareness that the change was achieved with professional help. Having needed professional help to change makes the person feel even more worthless, inadequate, and dependent than he or she felt about entering psychotherapy; further change is then resisted because being helped by the treatment will be more damaging to the person's self-esteem than just talking with the therapist but not changing at all.

Unlike neurotic equilibrium resistance, which protects a comforting interpersonal context against the inroads of behavior change, resistance to patienthood provides little benefit beyond some illusory bolstering of self-esteem. Failing to take advantage of available opportunities to receive needed help, simply because of negative attitudes toward receiving such help, is analogous to letting one's teeth decay rather than face up to the dentist's drill. Therapists must be alert to resistance associated with the patients' reservations about being in treatment and take pains to resolve resistance to patienthood before it endangers the viability of the treatment.

SUPEREGO RESISTANCE

As patients begin to experience gratifying behavior change in psychotherapy, they may fall prone to another source of resistance to change derived from self-attitudes—*superego resistance.* Superego resistance is spawned by a demanding conscience and nourished by a propensity to feel guilty. People ruled by conscience attribute their misfortunes to their own failings and misdeeds, regard hardship and disappointment as their just desserts, and renounce any claims to a more pleasurable existence. People burdened with a harsh superego consequently tend to view any improvement in their lot with suspicion or even alarm. Success and happiness come bittersweet for them, marred by nagging inner whisperings: "It's too good to be true"; "Don't let yourself enjoy it because it won't last and you'll only be let down"; "You don't deserve to have such a good thing happen, and if you go along with it, there will be some price to pay later on."

For people struggling with such harsh attitudes toward themselves, apparent progress in psychotherapy generates skepticism and anxiety. Such patients doubt that the beneficial changes are real or permanent, and should events begin to suggest that they may indeed be so, they fret about some future time when they will have to make a Faustian accounting for their enhanced success and pleasure in life. Anxiety emerging on this basis inevitably produces resistance to change in psychotherapy and accordingly needs to be recognized when it arises.

CHARACTER RESISTANCE

Character comprises the customary and preferred ways in which people deal with their experience. The attitudes and habits that define people's characterological style often serve positively to foster their productivity and enhance their satisfaction in life. On the other hand, as indicated in Chapter 8, some aspects of character constitute defensive operations aimed more at reducing anxiety than at seeking self-fulfillment. Considerable emphasis was placed in Chapter 8 on the importance of helping patients in psychotherapy understand and modify characterological defensive operations, both as an end in itself and as a prelude to increased understanding of the underlying concerns that have given rise to these defensive operations. Relevant to the present chapter is that the behaviors people characterologically use to ward off anxiety will also be used by them to ward off psychotherapy as a potential source of anxiety, which means that characterological defensive operations may inhibit participation in psychotherapy and constitute a source of resistance.

Several ways in which characterological style can interfere with communication in psychotherapy were illustrated in the earlier discussion of interpreting characterological defensive operations. In the present context, potential sources of character resistance can be classified in three levels of specificity. First, there may be instances in which reliance on some specific defense mechanism, such as isolation, repression, or reaction formation, prevents direct access to the concerns that would be most useful for a patient to talk about. Second, there may be times when broader aspects of coping style, such as a markedly active or passive approach to life or a predominantly concrete or abstract style of thinking, restrict the range of a patient's conversation in the treatment. Third, there may be patients in whom generalized characterological problems, such as a masochistic personality disorder or a success neurosis, pose particular obstacles to establishing and sustaining the basic treatment contract.

SPECIFIC DEFENSE MECHANISMS

Defense mechanisms are psychological strategies employed by people to avoid conscious recognition of thoughts or feelings that would make them anxious. Because a core strategy in psychotherapy consists of increasing conscious awareness of matters that cause people anxiety, as a way of allowing them to deal with these matters more effectively, defense mechanisms always interfere with implementing the aims of treatment. People who frequently utilize isolation as a mechanism of defense tend to skirt spontaneous expression of emotion by a careful cognitive filtering of affective experience that separates ideas and events from the feelings associated with them. When angered, they do not explode with "You sonofabitch, I'll get you for this!" but are more likely to intone, "I want you to know I'm getting very irritated with you." When in love they are less likely to say "I love you" than "You mean a great deal to me."

In psychotherapy, the characteristic schism between affect and ideation that marks isolation produces excessive attention by patients to what they think rather than what they feel. Emotions are stripped of their immediacy, events are described with pallid objectivity as if from a scenario involving strangers, and efforts by the therapist to elicit feelings produce only grudging, impersonal allusions to affect: "I'm sure I must have been very angry"; "It seems to me right now that I'm feeling pretty good"; "I didn't think I needed to mention feeling sad, since it's obvious anyone would be unhappy in a situation like that." Because such difficulty in experiencing affect directly and expressing it spontaneously inhibits the communication of feelings in psychotherapy, it constitutes a resistance to the treatment. Accordingly, effective interpretation of isolation serves not only to expand a patient's self-awareness, but also to facilitate the emergence of affect-laden material that might otherwise have remained submerged and unavailable for discussion.

Some examples of repression and reaction formation will illustrate further the manner in which specific defense mechanisms produce resistance in psychotherapy. Repression, which consists of excluding mental contents from conscious awareness, can be directed toward either thoughts or feelings, just as isolation can be used to disconnect two thoughts that belong together as well as thoughts from the feelings that correspond to them. However, whereas isolation promotes a predominantly ideational focus on experiences, repression as a generalized defensive mode fosters an immersion in affect and immediacy at the expense of thought and reflection. People who rely heavily on repressive defense have relatively little difficulty experiencing feelings directly and expressing them spontaneously, but they are seldom inclined to reflect on the meaning of their experience and actions.

Repressing individuals as psychotherapy patients freely indicate how they feel but give little attention to why they feel that way. If asked why they feel as they do, they are more likely to brush the question off ("I don't know"; "Just because"; "The important thing is that I *do* feel this way") than they are to undertake any analysis of their reactions. Similarly, repressing individuals frequently recount their affective reactions to events without including sufficient factual detail for the therapist to know what actually took place. Subsequent requests for such details try their patience, because they attach much less significance to facts than to feelings; these requests may also exceed their capability to respond, because repressors tend not to note or remember the factual details necessary for clear reconstruction of an event. Hence, though in quite an opposite manner from isolation, prominent repressive defenses also contribute to resistance in psychotherapy, and their modification can expand the amount of information that becomes available to work with in the treatment.

Reaction formation involves an overemphasis on certain manifest attitudes or behavior patterns directly opposite to underlying feelings and impulses that would be anxiety provoking to recognize or express. When reaction formation holds sway, what is totally unacceptable is reversed 180° into something that is perfectly acceptable, even if maladaptive. Enmity becomes transformed into self-sacrificing adoration ("How can I resent my mother when she has been so good to me?"), and aggressive urges into extreme meekness ("Being a good person means taking care never to offend anyone"). Whenever the process of psychotherapy begins to unearth underlying feelings or impulses that evoke fear, guilt, shame, or embarrassment, patients who use reaction formations seek to disguise them with a deluge of self-reports attesting just the opposite kinds of feelings and impulses—they protest too much. In the face of reaction formation, then, as in instances of isolation and repression, interpretive easing of the patient's defenses allows information to come into the therapy that would otherwise remain outside awareness.[6]

COPING STYLES

Coping styles comprise abiding dispositions or traits that influence how people organize and respond to their experience. Although defense mechanisms similarly influence how people organize and respond to experience, coping styles refer to a broader set of behaviors that differs from defensive operations in two respects. First, individual preferences for mechanisms of defense are determined primarily by experiences in anxiety-provoking situations, whereas individual coping styles are influenced not only by experiential factors but also largely by aspects of temperament that are constitutionally determined.

Second, defense mechanisms are protective measures activated to ward off or bind anxiety that would otherwise be experienced in situations a person cannot handle effectively; while thus minimizing anxiety, they also inhibit personality functioning and direct an individual away from coming constructively to grips with the source of the anxiety. Coping styles, on the other hand, constitute modes of dealing with experiences of all kinds, whether anxiety provoking or not; although they may at times be defensive or maladaptive, they also include constructive and self-fulfilling ways of behaving and meeting challenge.

Because coping styles consist of certain ways of organizing and responding to experience, to the exclusion of other ways, they can narrow a person's behavioral repertoire sufficiently to produce resistance in psychotherapy. For example, some people are by nature relatively active in their approach to life, whereas others are temperamentally passive. Active people are likely to expect constant interchange, cascading insights, and rapid change in psychotherapy, and for them a process of sober reflection and gradually expanding self-awareness may be difficult to tolerate. Passive people frequently look to psychotherapy as a treatment that will do something to them, if only they bring their body regularly into the shop, and for them the responsibility for introducing subjects for discussion and helping to explore and learn from them may be difficult to shoulder.

Manifestations of resistance associated with this activity-passivity dimension of temperament take characteristic forms. Active patients bridle at the slow pace of the treatment, complain that little or nothing is being accomplished, and talk about other treatment methods they have heard or read about that really get things moving quickly. Passive patients grumble about the lack of direction they are receiving from the therapist, argue that if they could do what is apparently expected of them in the treatment they would not have needed it in the first place, and ask about the possibility of drugs, hypnosis, or other treatment adjuncts that similarly minimize a patient's responsibility for doing anything.[7]

GENERALIZED CHARACTEROLOGICAL PROBLEMS

In some instances character resistance in psychotherapy results not from specific defense preferences or broader aspects of coping style, but from generalized characterological problems that pose particular obstacles to effective treatment. Two such problems that merit special attention are *masochistic character disorder* and *success neurosis*, both of which have been mentioned briefly in previous chapters.

People with masochistic character disorder thrive on psychological pain, no matter how much they complain about it, and typically shrink from or "overlook" opportunities to improve their fortunes in life. In psychotherapy, such people present an exaggerated and pervasive picture of the superego resistance pattern described earlier. Convinced that they do not deserve to be any happier or self-satisfied than they are, they mistrust and are made uneasy by indications of progress in their treatment. Seen through the lenses of masochism, undeserving people who prosper are doomed to be stripped of their unrightful gains and punished for having presumed to accept them. As is obvious, then, a masochistic orientation to life can generate unusually refractory resistance to pursuing potentially helpful discussions in psychotherapy.

Individuals with a success neurosis similarly resist progress toward becoming more effective people, not because they prefer pain to pleasure but because they feel threatened by the prospect of accomplishing too much. A success neurosis does not usually preclude enjoying a rich and rewarding social life, but it does inhibit people from fully utilizing their capacities to achieve in academic, occupational, and creative pursuits. Harboring irrational fears of the consequences of surpassing others, success neurotics hold back in competitive endeavors and avoid accomplishment in such challenging situations as attempting to improve themselves in psychotherapy. Like masochism then, fear of success creates specific obstacles to the work of the treatment that must be identified and surmounted for significant progress to occur.[8]

RESISTANCE TO CONTENT

In contrast to resistance to change and character resistance, both of which involve personality characteristics that patients bring with them into psychotherapy, *resistance to content* refers to obstacles to progress that are elicited by and exist uniquely within the treatment situation. Of all the forms of resistance, resistance to content is the least complex in its origin and the least difficult to comprehend. When psychotherapy focuses as it should on the aspects of people's lives that are causing them difficulty, attention will regularly be drawn to subjects that are embarrassing, frightening, aggravating, depressing, or in some other way unpleasant for a patient to think or talk about. Hence the treatment process inevitably evokes content that makes patients averse to participating fully in it.

Because resistance to content often motivates patients to avoid certain subjects by keeping them out of their conscious awareness, Freud originally referred to it as "repression resistance," defined as "the persistent, automatic, normative tendency of the ego to try to control dangerous tendencies by blocking them off" (Menninger & Holzman, 1973, p. 108). In view of subsequent advances in conceptualizing ego functioning and neurotic personality styles, however, it seems useful to distinguish between repression as a normative tendency to resist content in psychotherapy, which is present in all patients, and repression as a preferred defensive style that produces specific kinds of resistance in some patients but not others. Accordingly, resistance stemming from a generalized preference for repressive defenses was discussed in the previous section on character resistance, and the resistance that all patients display from time to time by avoiding awareness of content is being considered here under the generic label of resistance to content.

The relative ease of recognizing resistance to content derives from its close ties to the ongoing interchange in treatment interviews. Resistance to change and character resistance, although exacerbated by psychotherapy, have their origins in life events outside the treatment. Transference resistance, to be considered next, originates in the treatment situation but is a complex function of the patients' relationships with their therapist and with other current and past figures in their lives. Content resistance, on the other hand, is both a unique product of psychotherapy and a fairly simple, transparent reaction to here-and-now events occurring in the treatment.

More specifically, resistance to content emerges either concurrently with the discussion of some topic that is difficult for a patient to pursue or when such a topic appears about to come up for discussion.[9] Suppose that a woman who has been discussing some marital problems has become visibly upset while describing concerns about being unattractive as a sex partner. She might then attempt to drop the subject, either by saying nothing further about it or by stating that the matter is too distressing or humiliating for her to talk about further. The source and meaning of this emergence of resistance would be apparent. The patient's motivation to escape the psychological distress associated with talking about her perceived sexual unattractiveness has temporarily overridden her motivation to work toward resolving her marital problems and produced a reluctance to continue discussing content very likely to be relevant to these problems.

As for resistance to anticipated content, suppose the patient in this example had been elaborating nonsexual aspects of her marital relationship and then volunteered, "I better get into telling you what goes on in regard to sex." Instead of doing so, however, she falls silent, or talks about something other than sex, or begins discussing sex in a general way unrelated to her personal concerns. Her behavior would then reflect anticipatory resistance to content, and the onset of her resistance just at the time when the topic of her sexuality is about to surface would leave little doubt as to the origin and significance of her having become resistive at this point.

TRANSFERENCE RESISTANCE

In the course of psychotherapy, all patients experience various kinds of positive and negative feelings toward their therapists as a result of displacing onto them attitudes they have held toward other important people in their lives. Transference phenomena are of considerable importance in psychotherapy, and Chapter 10 is broadly concerned with their origins, manifestations, and utilization in the treatment. The following discussion in the present chapter is intended merely to identify transference as a possible source of resistance in psychotherapy and to indicate that transference reactions typically give rise to resistance behavior.

To understand how transference produces resistance, it is helpful to review briefly the manner in which psychotherapy generally fosters positive and negative feelings toward the therapist. In response to receiving appropriate amounts of therapist genuineness, warmth, and empathy, patients customarily come to appreciate their therapist's nonjudgmental interest and admire the therapist's personal sensitivity and dedication to a helping profession. Such attitudes initially cultivate eagerness to participate in the treatment process, but sooner or later they intensify to a point where patients begin to idealize their therapists and to crave relationships with them that transcend the boundaries of the treatment contract. Patients often fantasize specifically about how wonderful it would have been or would be to have this person (the therapist) as a mother or father, a son or daughter, a spouse, a lover, or a close friend. Accompanying these positively toned fantasies are wishes or images involving patients being dependent on therapists or taking care of them, becoming important people in their lives, seeing them socially, exchanging expressions of love and admiration with them, or having sex with them.

As time passes and such positive feelings are not reciprocated in kind, disappointment and frustration set in. Now therapists cease to be admirable and lovable in a patient's eyes. Instead, as callous agents of the patient's disappointment and frustration, they are revealed as cold, insensitive, unresponsive, inconsiderate, uncaring individuals unworthy of adulation or respect, and positive feelings toward therapists consequently give way to negative ones. Because therapists in reality are neither quite so remarkable nor quite so despicable as their patients perceive them to be, these positive and negative feelings both involve transference elements.

The specific form that transference reactions take and the circumstances that elicit them are determined by each patient's prior interpersonal experiences, as are the readiness with which transference feelings develop and the manner in which they are expressed (see Chapter 10). For all patients, however, both positive and negative transference reactions interfere with communication in psychotherapy and hence constitute resistance.

Positive transference interferes with communication by fostering undue concern with the therapist's opinions. People can talk most freely about themselves when they attach no significance to what their listeners think of them; the more they ponder a listener's impression of what they have to say, the less spontaneous they can be in saying it. Accordingly, because positive feelings toward therapists motivate efforts to court their fancy, they usually distort patient communication in two respects. First, they incline patients to censor their remarks, excluding anything they fear might detract from the favorable impression they want to create. Second, they encourage patients to embellish what they say with thoughts, feelings, self-descriptions, and narratives chosen not so much for their accuracy as for their anticipated likelihood of stirring their therapist's interest and gaining the therapist's approval. In both respects, positive transference reactions impede candid communication and thereby result in resistance.

Negative transference feelings lead to resistance by causing reactions similar to those that accompany unrequited love. Some patients, in their frustration and disappointment at not having their wishes for a closer, more intimate relationship with their therapist gratified, respond in a primarily depressive fashion, either passively or actively. Passive depressive reactions associated with negative transference result in patients talking in a subdued and desultory manner, becoming listless and discouraged about their progress, and perhaps expressing reservations about continuing in the treatment. In the latter case, seeing therapists in the knowledge that the desired relationship with them will never come to pass resembles the experience of rejected suitors, who may prefer never to see their loved one again rather than endure the agony of being in the person's presence but denied his or her love.

Depressed but relatively active patients reacting to ungratified positive wishes toward their therapist are less likely to fall silent or contemplate leaving therapy than they are to hang in there, sullen, pouty, and complaining, in an effort to wheedle the therapist into gratifying them. Without visible anger, they plead with, reprimand, and admonish the therapist: "If only you could tell me more about yourself or we could get together outside this office, so that I could get to know you better, I would be able to talk to you more easily and you could be of more help to me"; "If you really cared about me, you wouldn't be so remote and distant"; "I wouldn't be surprised if I just slid back into all the problems I was having before if I can't get any more feeling that I'm a person and not just a patient to you." Such statements from patients require carefully conceived responses in which therapists avoid either retreating behind a caricatured shell of therapist "objectivity" or stumbling into an interpersonal morass that gratifies patients for the moment but limits their prospects for eventually benefiting from the treatment (see Chapter 10).

Continuing with patterns of transference resistance, some patients react angrily rather than with depression to therapists' frustration of their positive wishes toward them. Patients thus angered typically seek not to prod therapists into some desired relationship, but to punish them for not reciprocating their positive feelings. Commonly, then, negative transference is expressed through maneuvers that complicate a therapist's task, such as failing to appear for sessions, coming late, or refusing to talk. Also frequent are more direct expressions of negative transference couched in (a) criticisms of the therapist's perceived nonresponsiveness ("You're such a cold person, you must have ice water in your veins"; "I've said all I can, it's time for you to do some work for a change"); (b) criticism of the therapist's conduct of the treatment ("You never seem to have anything useful to say"; "I don't think you're experienced enough to help me with the problem I have"); or (c) criticisms of the therapy itself ("I don't think this treatment is doing me much good"; "From what I've heard, the evidence for psychotherapy's being worthwhile isn't all that good").

Faced with such remarks, therapists need to consider two questions: First, how much of what the patient is saying has a basis in reality and how much is a distortion of reality determined by aspects of the transference? Second, whatever the mixture of reality and transference in the patient's behavior, which elements of each would be most useful to pursue at the particular moment? Deferring to Chapter 10 the discussion of how to answer these questions, the key point to emphasize in the present context is that all these manifestations of negative transference draw patients' attention away from the problems that brought them for help and interfere with their talking about themselves, and hence they inevitably function as resistance behavior.

Finally, transference feelings can lead to resistance not only by making patients more intent on impressing or punishing their therapist than they are on pursuing the original goals of the treatment, but also by making them anxious or uncomfortable. When transference feelings are embarrassing or frightening to admit, as feelings of love or hate toward the therapist may often be, they evoke resistance to their content. Thus patients who are generally loath to express affection directly tend to deny or suppress positive feelings toward their therapist, even if doing so means not talking freely and openly with him or her, and patients who shrink from feeling or venting anger tend to ward off negative transference, even at the price of narrowing their range of self-awareness and self-report. In this way, transference feelings that are themselves not expressed, either directly or indirectly, can participate in resistance behavior in the form of content that is difficult for a patient to think about or report.[10]

INDICATIONS OF RESISTANCE

Many ways of manifesting resistance have been illustrated in the preceding discussion of its origins. However, not all indications that patients are experiencing some reluctance to participate in the treatment are as obvious as the prior examples used, nor are cumulative examples as helpful in learning to identify resistance as a categorization of the kinds of behavior that are likely to reflect it. The following five categories of patient behavior in psychotherapy encompass most of the ways in which resistance is manifested: (a) reducing the amount of time spent in the treatment, (b) restricting the amount or range of conversation, (c) isolating the therapy from real life, (d) acting out, and (e) flight into health.

Reducing the Amount of Time Spent in the Treatment

The simplest way for patients to resist the impact of psychotherapy without overtly renouncing the treatment contract is for them to find "reasons" for reducing the amount of time they spend in it. In particular, patients who arrive late for sessions, ask to leave early, cancel or miss appointments, or prematurely propose termination are likely to be resisting full participation in the treatment through the simple medium of limiting their exposure to it.

However, despite the straightforward way in which reducing the time spent in psychotherapy can serve the purpose of resistance, it is not always easy to distinguish resistance from reality when patients cancel or come late for a session. "I got caught in traffic," apologizes a woman dashing in 10 minutes late for her session, or "He's home sick in bed," says a wife calling to cancel her husband's appointment. How is the therapist to interpret these events? Everyone gets caught in traffic on occasion and arrives late for an appointment, even when highly motivated to be on time. But could this woman have anticipated heavy traffic and allowed extra driving time? Or could her lateness be due not to any usual traffic congestion but to her having left home later than usual? Or could she have arrived on time despite heavy traffic had she not stopped to talk with an acquaintance she met in the parking lot?

As for the man's cancellation because of being sick in bed, this could certainly constitute reality and not resistance. But is the patient's illness really serious enough to prevent him from keeping his appointment? Or could the "illness" be an anxiety or phobic reaction, perhaps manifested in headache, abdominal pain, or some other physical complaint, symptomatic of some aversion to the treatment? Or could the whole illness story have been contrived to spare the patient from having to tell the therapist directly that he preferred not to keep the appointment?[11]

How much resistance and how much reality underlie such events depends then on the specific context in which they occur. As therapists attempt to make this judgment in the individual case, neither trusting naivete nor relentless skepticism will serve them in good stead. They should be sufficiently suspicious of whatever reasons patients give for limiting the time of their participation in the treatment to consider whether elements of resistance are involved. At the same time, they should be sufficiently cognizant of reality and of the distinction between near and remote derivatives to accept some explanations at face value and defer exploring others, even when they appear somewhat lame.

Explanations of missed or abbreviated sessions will usually strike a therapist in one of three ways. Some explanations will appear so realistic and far removed from resistance as to suggest little reason for pursuing them further. Patients who cancel a session because of illness and arrive for the next interview still obviously suffering the effects of a bad cold, for example, or who arrive late but give a credible account of having been unavoidably detained should not be pressed for possible resistance elements in their behavior.

A second group of explanations are those that seem ambiguous and call for open-ended exploration. Suppose a man cancels a session because he will be out of town on a business trip. Being out of town on business is seemingly a justifiable reason for missing a session, but is there more to the situation than meets the eye? Was it necessary for the patient to be out of town on the particular day of his session, or did he in fact have some latitude in scheduling his trip that he chose not to exercise? Or, if the day of his trip was inflexible, would it still have been possible for him to leave at noon and keep his morning therapy appointment? In such ambiguous circumstances, where the truth of the matter could lie either in resistance or in reality, the details of the patient's explanation need to be explored until they point clearly in one direction or the other.

A third group of explanations leaves little doubt from the beginning that patient behavior reflects resistance and should be responded to accordingly. Either patients' actions have been too transparently resistive to permit a reasonable explanation, or their initial explanation of otherwise ambiguous behavior rings so false as to strip it of any ambiguity. With respect to transparency, failing to appear for an uncanceled appointment and asking to end a session early are almost always manifestations of resistance, because nothing short of a major crisis in a patient's life can justify such behavior in reality. Thus a woman who misses a session without calling because her son fell out of a tree and required emergency medical treatment can hardly be perceived as resisting the treatment, whereas a woman who begins a session by saying she has to leave early to take her son to the dentist (for an appointment that presumably could have been scheduled at some other time) is very probably resisting. As for the quality of the explanation offered, patients who arrive late and say, "I just couldn't get myself moving today," or who cancel an appointment because "I'm not in the mood to talk with you," are almost certainly resisting, even though their behavior might have been more ambiguous if they had attempted to justify it in terms of some mitigating circumstances.

Special attention should be paid to prematurely proposed termination, because it may foreshadow an irreversible reduction in the amount of time spent in the treatment. Patients who raise the question of termination usually do so by indicating either that they can no longer continue in the treatment, due to circumstances such as a move out of town, or that they are disinterested in continuing, because they no longer feel a need for psychotherapy. As a third alternative, patients may simply stop appearing for appointments, without having mentioned an inability or unwillingness to continue. However, such drastic action is rarely taken unannounced once a patient and therapist have passed a period of working together constructively.

Each of these three approaches to termination can embrace elements of resistance and reality. Patients who state they are unable to continue may in fact be moving several hundred miles away, to attend school or to take a new job. But perhaps they are just moving to a different neighborhood and facing only a slightly longer trip to the therapist's office, or perhaps they are merely taking on new commitments that will make their regular appointments somewhat less convenient. Whereas the first circumstance seems realistic, the latter two smack of an excuse to limit the therapy and warrant being explored for possible resistance elements. Similarly, patients who say they feel they no longer need or want therapy may be manifesting resistance or may be presenting an accurate appraisal of their progress in the treatment, in which case their proposal for termination would be appropriate rather than premature. Even patients who drop out of treatment, and who are therefore very likely to be resisting the impact of further psychotherapy, may in some cases be reluctant only to tell their therapist that they have achieved their treatment objectives and no longer need to continue (which would imply that, by being more alert and perhaps less possessive, the therapist would have recognized the patient's progress and suggested the termination).

Hints of premature termination are perhaps the most critical resistance behavior for therapists to confront promptly and effectively, primarily because there may not be a second chance. Should overlooked or unresolved resistances rupture the treatment contract, there will be no subsequent opportunities to recognize them more quickly or respond to them more usefully; the patient will have dropped out of therapy and canceled the therapist as a helping agent. The important distinction between appropriate termination based on realistic considerations, and premature termination, which indicates resistance, is discussed further in Chapter 12.

RESTRICTING THE AMOUNT OR RANGE OF CONVERSATION

Whereas reducing the amount of time spent in psychotherapy is the simplest way to minimize its impact, the most common manner in which patients resist the treatment is by restricting the amount or range of their conversation. Reducing the time spent involves the interface between a patient's life inside the therapist's office and the person's life outside it, and whether time reduction constitutes resistance depends on whether there are mitigating factors in reality. Restriction of conversation, on the other hand, exists totally within the context of the psychotherapy situation, and any effort by patients to limit what or how much they say can automatically be taken as a manifestation of resistance (except possibly in the case of laryngitis). To recognize when such limits are being imposed, therapists should listen for what may be called three kinds of language: the language of *silence*, the language of *fixation*, and the language of *avoidance*.

Silence

Whenever patients talk noticeably less freely than usual or stop talking altogether, it can be inferred that a wish to avoid discomfort has temporarily usurped their commitment to the treatment process. Because not talking serves effectively to avoid uncomfortable subjects and limit change in psychotherapy, relative or absolute silence is frequently employed as a means of resisting treatment and points to resistance when it occurs.

When patients who are talking sparingly comment on their behavior, either spontaneously or in response to being confronted with their silence, they may attempt to account for it with such statements as "I just don't feel much like talking today" or "Not much has happened so I haven't much to say." Whatever form such statements take, the therapist must not be misled into accepting them as realistic explanations of relative silence. The treatment contract to which patients have explicitly agreed (assuming the treatment has been properly initiated as described in Chapter 6) calls for them to talk regardless of how they feel about talking and to say what comes to their mind independently of how little is happening in their lives. This does not mean that therapists should hasten to rap patients' knuckles whenever they express a disinclination to talk. What is needed in this circumstance is recognition that something beyond the obvious is interfering with a patient's ability or willingness to communicate, followed by constructive effort to help the patient identify and resolve the particular source of this resistance.

On occasion, silent patients may report that they simply have nothing to say or that "My mind is a blank." However, there is reason to question whether in normal circumstances the waking mind ever becomes totally "blank," without conscious awareness. Patients who say their mind is empty are in all likelihood either dissembling to avoid airing their thoughts or feelings, or struggling to keep their mind free to provide justification for their silence. Either way, claiming to have nothing to say is as much an indication of resistance as a patients' frank admission of reluctance to say what is on his or her mind.

Fixation

As noted in Chapter 8, patients in psychotherapy can vary the content of what they say along four dimensions. They can talk about past or about present events, in concrete or in abstract terms, about thoughts or feelings, and in specific regard to the treatment process or independently of it. Overemphasis on either pole of these content dimensions provides grist for confrontations that call attention to the omitted pole, that is, what a patient is not talking about. By applying the concepts developed in the present chapter, any such overemphasis can now be identified as a *fixation* that serves the purpose of resistance by restricting the range of a patient's conversation. Busch (1995, Chapter 5) notes similarly that anything can be used as a resistance, including whatever patients say or do and also what they do not say or do.

When patients are talking freely, they ordinarily touch on both past and present events, employ both abstract and concrete frames of reference, report both thoughts and feelings, and discuss experiences both internal and external to the treatment situation. Whenever therapists hear patients narrow the focus of their conversation in ways that reduce or eliminate any of these ways of talking, they are hearing the language of fixation. Thus patients who talk endlessly about their childhood but rarely volunteer information about their current life are resisting; no matter how poignant their childhood recollections, their apparent reluctance to alternate memories of the past with reports of current events suggests that the present may be more difficult for them to talk about and more pertinent to the problems for which they have sought help.

Likewise, patients who never refer to the treatment relationship are resisting, as are those who can hardly talk about anything else, and the same significance attaches to fixations involving the abstract-concrete and thought-feeling dimensions of content. In using the language of fixation as a clue to resistance, however, therapists should be careful to avoid concluding that whatever patients choose to talk about signifies resistance because they are choosing not to talk about something else. The fixation clue goes only so far as to indicate that prolonged or exclusive engagement in certain ways of talking to the exclusion of other ways often reflects elements of resistance.

Avoidance

Whereas content fixations constitute a form of avoidance behavior, there is also a more specific language of avoidance in psychotherapy that pertains primarily to what patients are not talking about rather than to how they are not talking about it. A patient who is fearful of interpersonal intimacy may be describing this fear only with respect to past events, for example, or only in abstract terms, or without any expression of feelings, or without any reference to the treatment relationship with the therapist. In each case, the person is fixating on some ways of talking about the

problem and probably resisting other ways. Should this patient not mention fears of intimacy at all, not along any of the four dimensions of content, then resistance is being manifested through the language of
avoidance.

The language of avoidance is sometimes easy to hear, when patients
constantly talk around rather than about some topic that is obviously central to their concerns. Consider again the example of a woman patient
with marital problems who discusses many aspects of her relationship
with her husband but who stops talking, changes the subject, or drifts off
into some digression whenever she seems on the verge of getting into
their sex life. Any such avoidance or skirting of a potentially important
subject signals resistance at work.

At other times, the language of avoidance may be less obvious, especially when patients are comfortably filling interviews with fluent accounts of their thoughts, feelings, and experiences and do not appear to
be omitting anything. What needs to be kept in mind at such times is that
psychotherapy is intended to direct attention at least in part to problematic matters that are unpleasant to think or talk about. Accordingly, patients who are participating openly in the treatment process, without
resistance, typically talk easily at some points but haltingly at others, and
are comfortable during some sessions but anxious, depressed, or irritable
during others. When no such variation occurs, patients are likely to be resisting despite their apparent openness. Even without the slightest
inkling of what matters are being avoided, therapists can infer from persistent breeziness that some potentially important thoughts or feelings
are being censored.

Nevertheless, therapists should guard against seizing on every instance
of resistance manifested in the language of avoidance. Psychotherapy cannot accomplish much if it deals only with matters patients enjoy talking
about, but it is also unlikely to be maximally effective if it dwells without
respite on a patient's anxieties, embarrassments, regrets, and failures.
Like all learning, learning about oneself in psychotherapy proceeds best if
there is some spacing in the introduction of new material and some opportunity for consolidation of the old. Patients need time to ponder alternative ways of looking at themselves and their experiences, and they also
need time to recover from the distress of being confronted with such
alternatives.

Patients in psychotherapy typically see to these needs by following their
work on an interpretive sequence with a period of pulling back or re-
grouping in which they limit their conversation to relatively mundane
matters. Although such limitations constitute resistance, strictly speaking, they should be recognized as an expectable way of "taking a breather"
during the interpretive process. This momentary recess differs from

avoidance behavior that emerges independently of interpretive work or persists longer than seems necessary to regroup following an interpretive sequence. Interventions should be reserved for these latter patterns of avoidance, whereas taking a breather constitutes a necessary, expected episode of coasting that should be allowed to pass without comment.

ISOLATING THE THERAPY FROM REAL LIFE

One of the most effective means by which patients can resist the impact of psychotherapy consists of minimizing the extent to which anything that transpires in the treatment generalizes to their life outside the therapist's office. This pattern of resistance is easily identified in retrospect, because it sooner or later becomes obvious that the apparent progress patients are making in understanding themselves is not being translated into more effective or rewarding ways of living. In the present tense of psychotherapy, however, current manifestations of this form of resistance consist only of subtle efforts by patients to divorce their experience as a psychotherapy patient in the interview room from their experience in other roles in other places.

Patients seeking to isolate the therapy from their real lives usually strive to maintain two separate and noninteractive relationships with the therapist, a "psychotherapy relationship" and a "real-life relationship." In the psychotherapy relationship, they fill their role as prescribed in the treatment contract, whereas in the real-life relationship they attempt to carve out blocks of time in which they can interact with the therapist in ways that transcend or are irrelevant to the treatment contract. The more they succeed in maintaining such a separation, the more they erect artificial boundaries between their lives as psychotherapy patients and their lives outside the treatment, and the more they can resist allowing progress in the former to influence behavior change in the latter.

Some illustrations of how patients sometimes seek to establish these two separate relationships with a therapist can help to clarify this concept of isolating therapy from real life. Consider a male patient who enters the office and, while he and the therapist are still standing, says with good humor, "How's life treatin' ya, doc?" Then, after he and the therapist are seated, he becomes somber and subdued and says, "Today I want to talk with you about something really bad that happened to me." Who is the real patient in this excerpt? Is it the exuberant, high-spirited person who began so informally, or is it the concerned and troubled person who opened with a formal preview of his subject for the day? Obviously, it cannot be both, and what we have is a patient who is presenting one face to the therapist in the form of a greeting and another face as he gets down to business. Certainly the greeting can be understood simply as a forced effort at gaiety intended to cushion the impact of the disturbing incident to be reported—but herein lie the seeds of resistance. If the patient feels that his real-life troubles and depressed affect should not intrude on his relationship to the therapist, so that even while being upset he must face the therapist with a smile, then he will just as easily shield his behavior outside the treatment relationship from the impact of what he learns in it.

Similar efforts to isolate psychotherapy from life by maintaining two separate relationships with the therapist emerge in the following examples: a patient stops the therapist on their way from a waiting room to the therapist's office and says, "Before we go *in there* [with some ominous emphasis on the "in there"], there's something I have to ask you about"; a patient in the middle of a session says "I'd like you to stop being a therapist for a minute and tell me how you really feel"; a patient heading for the door after an uneventful session stops and says with more feeling than has been evident in the preceding 50 minutes, "Now that our time is up, there's something important I want to mention to you"; a patient calls on the telephone and says, "I know we don't do this kind of thing in our sessions, but I need your advice right now on whether I should take a new job I've been offered." In each of these examples, the patient is attempting to divorce some matter from the psychotherapy relationship by casting it beyond the boundaries of time, place, or role behavior defined by the treatment contract.

To identify isolation of psychotherapy from real life, then, therapists must be alert to any tendency of patients to compartmentalize the treatment relationship, so that certain topics, styles of talking, or role behaviors arise only in the beginning or the end of sessions, or only outside the confines of the therapist's office, or only on the telephone, or in some other arbitrary disjunction of time or place. On the other hand, the treatment relationship as elaborated in the next two chapters is in fact a complex distillate of reality factors, transference elements, and the "working alliance" between patient and therapist. Patients can alternately emphasize one or another of these three facets of the treatment relationship, with marked shifts in what they choose to say and how they choose to say it, without necessarily compartmentalizing them. These shifts in emphasis follow naturally from the course of the treatment and do not involve any arbitrary sectioning off in time, place, or role behavior.

By contrast, when psychotherapy is being isolated from real life, differing role relationships to the therapist are maintained on an arbitrary basis, so that some subjects are broached only at certain times or in certain ways. Moreover, patients who are resisting by attempting to isolate the therapy from their lives go beyond merely being a party to real aspects of the psychotherapy relationship. Instead, they make a deliberate effort to create "real-life" interactions with their therapist that they explicitly structure as not being part of the psychotherapy relationship.

Oremland (1991, Chapter 3) appropriately warns therapists against inadvertently fostering such compartmentalizing of the treatment relationship by their manner of informing patients of such matters as an interruption in their schedule of sessions. He points out that making such announcements by saying, "Before we begin, I need to tell you that ..." conveys that there is material "inside" and "outside" the session and encourages artificial boundaries between patient-therapist interactions that are grist for the therapeutic mill and interactions that are not. Even though changes in schedule have an undeniable reality component, how patients respond to them is part of the treatment process, and therapists in their choice of words should not suggest that the treatment relationship comprises any totally unrelated components.

ACTING OUT

Acting out refers to the resolution of psychological conflict by direct translation of anxiety-provoking impulses into behavior that discharges these impulses. Because acting-out behavior alleviates intrapsychic grappling with conflicts, it is temporarily anxiety reducing. However, because acting-out behavior is typically impulsive and poorly planned, it tends to generate new sources of anxiety. People who act out usually behave in ways that make them feel guilty or ashamed, that incur the wrath or derision of others, and that in other ways prove self-defeating.

Acting-out behavior interferes with the process of psychotherapy in a manner that constitutes resistance. In the first place, people who are acting out are rejecting both reflection on their thoughts and openness to their feelings in favor of action. Precipitous behavior forecloses opportunities to experience and observe oneself, and the behavior itself involves a minimum of self-awareness. Hence acting out is by nature antithetical to the process of psychotherapy, because it involves substituting immediate behavior for efforts to plan more effective behavior on the basis of enhanced self-understanding. Acting out a problem obviates talking about it, and acting-out behavior in a psychotherapy patient suggests that important concerns are not coming up for discussion because they are being translated directly into action.

Levy (1990) observes in this regard that "acting out should be understood and interpreted as a particular form of resistance in which the behavior functions both as a means of avoiding the direct introduction of certain material in the treatment as well as an indirect means of communicating the presence of such material" (p. 142). Thus the content of resistance behavior can be especially revealing when it takes the form of acting out, and therapists being able to recognize and respond to the message contained in patient acting out can help put an end to such ill-advised behavior patterns or at least prevent them from escalating.[12]

As a second possible source of interference, acting out may appear specifically in response to anxiety stimulated by discussions in the treatment. Thus patients reviewing a thorny problem in their lives or working through some anxiety-provoking interpretations of their previous ways of handling it may be tempted to take some action that will "end" the problem and thereby abort discussion of it. Returning again to the example of a woman with marital problems who is on the verge of discussing some distressing sexual aspect of the problem, suppose she were suddenly to report that she and her husband had decided on a trial separation and that he had already moved out and rented an apartment for himself. "I've solved my marital situation for the time being," her actions would imply, "so we don't need to talk about it anymore."

When patients respond in this way to distressing aspects of the treatment, it can usually be demonstrated that the actions taken were hastily conceived and have as many drawbacks as advantages. Acting out—an attempt to resolve a problem by precipitous action—will have occurred, and the resistance purposes served by the acting out will be evident. To generalize from the preceding example, whenever acting out occurs in the context of a treatment focus on a sensitive or upsetting topic, the patient is very probably attempting to resist further attention to the topic by rendering it passé.

One fairly common variant of acting out in psychotherapy merits special comment because, at times, it may provide the only clear indication that a patient is resisting participation in the treatment. This pattern of resistance consists of talking to people other than the therapist about problems and concerns germane to the therapy. People who enter treatment are, of course, not expected to break off their normal social and interpersonal relationships; indeed, psychotherapy frequently aims to help people extend the circle of acquaintances with whom they can discuss mutual interests and concerns. What should not occur, however, are regular rehearsals or reviews of the content of psychotherapy sessions with a spouse, relative, or friend, especially when these conversations include information that is not shared with the therapist.

Such use of "ancillary" therapists as sounding boards interferes with communication in psychotherapy by diluting both what comes into and what emerges from treatment interviews. The more patients are airing their problems in conversations outside psychotherapy, the less spontaneous they will be in the treatment and the less opportunity the therapist will have to work with fresh ideas and vivid affects; the treatment, in

S. Freud's words, will have "a leak which lets through precisely what is most valuable" (1913/1958a, p. 136). Likewise, the more patients are soliciting responses from other people to their thoughts and feelings, the less impact their therapist's comments and observations are likely to have.

Any intimation that a patient is regularly discussing the treatment with someone other than the therapist, or has sought outside opinions on matters being considered in the treatment, or is reporting pertinent information to other people but not to the therapist should be pursued as a likely manifestation of resistance. In some instances, it may even emerge that the patient is contemplating or has entered into another professional relationship concurrently with the psychotherapy. Without having mentioned it, for example, the patient may have begun seeing a marriage counselor, sought personal guidance from a clergyperson, or asked his or her family doctor for some psychotropic medication.

People with psychological problems can certainly be helped by a variety of approaches, and some patients may profit most from a treatment program that combines individual psychotherapy with group or family sessions, marital or vocational counseling, pastoral guidance, or medication management. When individual psychotherapy is the primary treatment mode, however, care must be taken to avoid situations in which such other relationships dilute rather than sustain the impact of the primary treatment, and these other modalities should be endorsed by both patient and therapist as necessary adjuncts to their work together. Patients who unilaterally seek other forms of psychological help with their problems are resisting psychotherapy by taking actions that will buffer its impact.

FLIGHT INTO HEALTH

Patients in psychotherapy commonly begin feeling better or behaving more effectively during the initial stages of their treatment. Such early benefits derive not so much from the work of the treatment itself, which is just underway, as from positive attitudes the patient has toward being in psychotherapy. In response to the therapist's commitment to work with them and indications of the therapist's capacity to be helpful, most people gain some optimism about being able to resolve their psychological difficulties. Patients are in addition often pleased with themselves for having taken the steps necessary to receive professional help, and their self-esteem may be bolstered further by the therapist's interest in them. Flushed with high expectations and spurred by enhanced self-regard, beginning patients may experience sudden symptom relief and increased control over problematic behavior.

In some cases, such rapid improvement takes place during the evaluation period, before a treatment contract has been made, and it may even occur between the time a patient schedules a first appointment and is actually seen for evaluation. For some people, in other words, just the opportunity to discuss their concerns and have them evaluated professionally, or just having made an appointment for this purpose, proves to be supportive and reassuring. The initial contacts, even if limited to a telephone call setting up an appointment, signify to patients that they have taken some definitive action to do something about their problems and that help is on the way. The hopeful expectations and sense of accomplishment associated with these pretherapy contacts may alone be sufficient to ease people's concerns and help them function more effectively, at least on a temporary basis.

In some cases, however, rapid improvement early in psychotherapy indicates resistance to treatment rather than any real benefit derived from being engaged in it. Patients who feel reluctant to continue in psychotherapy may suddenly find themselves feeling much better or behaving much more effectually. When such improvement is reported to their therapist, the implied message is clear: "See, I'm doing much better already, and I don't really need to continue with this treatment." Used in this way, as grounds for escape, prompt symptom relief constitutes what originally was termed *flight into health* and serves the purpose of resistance (see Oremland, 1972; Train, 1953).

Needless to say, careful distinction must be drawn between actual, enduring improvements, produced by the initiation of treatment, and illusory, short-lived improvements, based on a flight into health. Therapists should not overlook the possibility of meaningful early gains in psychotherapy and should not risk undermining such gains by interpreting them as resistance. Yet they should also be alert to possible resistance elements responsible for apparent early improvement, so that they can bring them to a patient's attention before they jeopardize the continuity of the treatment.

Resistance elements in early improvements can be identified by observing the kind of improvement reported, the timing of its occurrence, and the implications attached to it. The more modest, credible, and durable the improvement appears to be, the more likely it is to represent a real gain and not a flight into health. On the other hand, a dramatic report ("Suddenly I'm a new person") of an implausible change ("I've completely lost the self-consciousness that has plagued me for 20 years") that quickly evaporates ("For a while last week I thought I was all straightened out, but now I'm feeling as self-conscious as ever") points to illusory improvement and probably reflects resistance to continuing in the treatment.

Concerning the timing of early improvements, the more they seem to have occurred in the normal course of patients' lives, independently of the content of their psychotherapy sessions, the more likely they are to constitute reality. If instead, the reported improvement seems to follow on the heels of a session in which some anxiety-provoking subjects have come up for discussion and the therapist has offered some telling confrontations or interpretations, resistance elements in the behavior change should be strongly suspected. For this particular form of resistance, Wheelis (1949) coined the term "flight from insight."

As for the implications attached to early improvement, patients who report their improvement to the accompaniment of increased enthusiasm for the treatment are likely to have experienced some real gain. The changes they have noted in themselves have heightened their long-range expectations of benefiting from psychotherapy, and the interviews immediately following the reported improvement are likely to be remarkably free of indications of resistance. When, on the other hand, patients seem to be concluding from their improvement that they no longer need treatment or that the rapidity of their improvement indicates treatment was unnecessary to begin with, the improvement probably represents resistance through a flight into health.

In concluding this section, it merits mention that the rejection of interpretations has not been included as an indication of resistance. Therapists are often tempted to regard refusal to accept an interpretation as resistance behavior. To be so tempted, however, is to regard the therapist as omniscient and the patient as ever culpable. Interpretations exist only as alternative hypotheses, not as absolute truths; as stressed in Chapter 8, it is not therapists saying something that makes it so, but patients finding it congruent with their experience. When patients reject an interpretation, it is because the interpretation has either been inaccurate, poorly timed, or badly presented, and therapists should direct their attention not to possible resistance elements in the patient's behavior, but rather to improving their own sensitivity or their technique in preparing the patient to receive the interpretation.

RESPONDING TO RESISTANCE BEHAVIOR

The manner in which therapists respond to resistance behavior bears significantly on the course and outcome of psychotherapy. Responding to resistance is not synonymous with interpreting resistance however and whenever it occurs. Instead, selective decisions about when and how to interpret resistance should be made, following the general principles of interpretation presented in Chapter 8. Within the framework of these principles of interpretation, four alternative modes of responding to resistance behavior are available: (a) allowing the resistance to build,

(b) circumventing the resistance, (c) exploring the resistance, and (d) breaking through the resistance.

ALLOWING RESISTANCE TO BUILD

Just as therapists should refrain from making interpretations in the absence of sufficient information to document them, they should not respond actively to resistance behavior until they feel confident they can demonstrate its presence. No matter how certain they are of how and why a patient is resisting, therapists will make little progress in communicating this understanding unless they can first help the patient appreciate that he or she is in fact resisting.

Solid evidence is usually necessary to help patients recognize that some aspect of their behavior is serving the purpose of resistance. Turning again to the prototypical example of a patient's being late, suppose once more that a usually prompt patient arrives 5 minutes late for a session because of traffic. Such an isolated instance of mild tardiness provides flimsy support for an interpretation of resistance, which even if accurate could be construed by the patient as picayune and unreasonable. The same could be said for a patient who hesitates slightly in bringing up a new subject or on one occasion asks "How are you?" on entering the office. By contrast, a patient who arrives 15 minutes late for three successive interviews "because of traffic," or who refuses to say anything further about a subject, or who asks numerous detailed questions about the state of the therapist's health—in short, patients whose manifestations of resistance are blatant or repetitive—can be shown relatively easily that their behavior is probably motivated by a wish to avoid participating fully in the treatment process.

Hence, the first step in responding to resistances is to allow them to build to a point where a patient can readily be made aware of them and they can then be profitably explored. If some suggestive behavior such as arriving slightly late dissipates quickly without escalating into marked or repetitive tardiness, the patient's possible reluctance to participate in the treatment has been inconsequential and would have been difficult to document. Resistance that is substantial does not dissipate quickly, but tends instead to generate increasingly repetitive and pronounced resistance behavior that can be readily demonstrated and explored.

By allowing resistance to build, therapists sacrifice little and improve their prospects for being able to interpret resistance behavior effectively. To this end, they need to refrain from jumping on every hint of resistance behavior they detect, just as they generally guard against offering interpretations prematurely or too often. Careful attention to timing and dosage help in the exercise of such restraint, as does keeping in mind that the therapist's task calls more for being helpful than for being clever.

CIRCUMVENTING RESISTANCE

When resistance reaches a point where its manifestations are obvious and demonstrable, therapist passivity becomes an error of omission. Therapists who ignore marked resistance, waiting and hoping for it to evaporate while they carry on with available interview content, are abdicating their responsibility. Marked resistance left alone tends to fester and may soon infect a patient's commitment to remaining in the treatment or the person's expectations of benefiting from it. Should the resistance happen to pass of its own accord without inducing the patient to drop out or lose confidence, an opportunity will still have been lost to explore a meaningful process aspect of the psychotherapy. Whether because further progress in the treatment would otherwise have been scuttled or because an opportunity to facilitate progress would have been lost, resistance behavior requires the therapist's active attention whenever it becomes pronounced.

Responding actively to resistance does not preclude attempting to circumvent it, however. On some occasions, therapists may feel that efforts to help patients understand and learn from their resistance will be less fruitful than helping them pursue a particular subject of concern to them. Usually these occasions involve content resistances that are too pronounced to be ignored but can most usefully be responded to either by providing support, to decrease anxiety about the subject on the patient's mind, or by calling attention to the resistance, as a means of encouraging the patient to proceed despite the anxiety.

Providing Support

When resistances arise because patients are too embarrassed, ashamed, or hesitant to report what is on their mind, some reassurance from the therapist may be all that is necessary to relieve their hesitancy and avert any escalation of resistance. Reassuring comments to circumvent content resistance can be addressed sometimes to the nature of psychotherapy, as in the first of the following two examples, and at other times to the nature of human behavior, as in the second example:

PATIENT: I just thought of a sexual thing I did once, but it's awfully hard to talk about.

THERAPIST: It's the hard things to talk about that we need to focus on. The things that are easy to talk about are not the ones that are likely to be causing you any problems.

PATIENT: I just can't tell you about the horrible thoughts I've had about harming my children. You'll think I'm a terrible person.

THERAPIST: It's what people do that makes them good or bad, not what they think.

As both of these examples indicate, resistances that can be responded to supportively are also usually open to a variety of other approaches. Thus, instead of attempting to encourage elaboration of content, the therapist might have focused attention on the patient's difficulty in talking about sexual matters in the first of the preceding examples, and on the patient's concern about being regarded as a terrible person in the second example. So long as care is taken not to ignore the resistance in such instances, the decision whether to circumvent or explore it should depend on the therapist's best estimate of which approach will contribute most to patients' learning about themselves at that particular point in the treatment.

Calling Attention to Resistance

Content resistance can often be circumvented simply by calling attention to it, without providing support or attempting to explore the origin and meaning of the resistance. The therapist needs only to make a statement such as, "I get the feeling there's something on your mind that you're reluctant to talk about." If accurate, such observations may give patients all the encouragement they need to plunge into a difficult subject: "Well . . . yes, you're right . . . there is something . . . well, okay, let me tell you." Or, instead of going directly into content when their resistance is noted, patients may reflect on how or why they are resisting: "I usually talk a lot when I'm trying to hide something"; "I'm afraid if I tell you what I'm thinking you won't have much respect for me." Merely calling attention to a resistance has the advantage of leaving patients this choice of pursuing either the content with which they are struggling or the nature and origins of their struggle.

Nevertheless, because just calling attention to possible resistance may go beyond a patient's current level of awareness and hence constitute an interpretation, therapists must be prepared to document their observation. Should a patient ask, "What makes you think there's something on my mind I'm reluctant to talk about?" the therapist should be able to point to firm evidence of such reluctance: "This is the second session in a row you've sat silently for several minutes at a time, whereas you usually have no difficulty finding something to say." Unless such documentation is at hand, even a noncommittal effort to call attention to possible resistance behavior will risk all the disadvantages of a premature interpretation.

EXPLORING RESISTANCE

When there is no compelling reason for focusing on the content of what a patient is saying or could be saying, resistance that has reached demonstrable proportions should be explored rather than circumvented. To explore resistance effectively, therapists should follow closely the guidelines presented in Chapter 8 for constructing an interpretive sequence. In particular, interpretations of resistance should be the culmination of a series of clarifications and confrontations that have gradually prepared the patient to recognize that some aspects of their behavior reflect reservations about participating in the treatment process.

The interpretive exploration of resistance accordingly begins with helping patients perceive discrepancies between how they are behaving and how they agreed to behave in endorsing the treatment contract. Unless resistive patients can acknowledge that their behavior diverges in certain ways from what might be expected of them and is thereby opposing progress in the treatment, no exploration of the origins and implications of their resistance will be possible. Thus the first step in initiating an interpretive sequence aimed at resistance consists of encouraging patients to observe their own unusual behavior, as in the following confrontations:

- You're talking much less today than usual.
- It seems that whenever we have a session in which you get upset, you have a long talk with your wife just afterward.
- I've noticed that you begin each session with several minutes of small talk, about the weather and such things.
- You've canceled a number of sessions in the last couple of months, and before that you hardly ever missed a session.

Patients may respond to such observations by acknowledging resistance elements in their behavior, or they may instead attempt some rational explanation of it ("I've just had a lot of extra work to do and couldn't make it, even though I really wanted to"). In the latter case, therapists will then have to draw on supplementary data (which should be available if they have allowed the resistance to reach demonstrable proportions) to refute whatever rationalizations are offered ("But from what you've told me, there have been other times when you've been equally busy at work, yet you never missed any sessions then").

A detailed and laborious review of a patient's "explanations" of resistance behavior may be necessary to expose them as masking an underlying reluctance to participate fully in the treatment. Painstaking dissection of the events involved in such behavior as coming late, canceling an appointment, discussing the therapy with someone else, or experiencing a sudden improvement is well worth the effort if it results in patients clearly recognizing that their behavior derives from resistance. On the other hand, when such efforts fail to elicit acknowledgment of apparent resistance elements in a patient's behavior, therapists should be prepared to recognize that the resistance was either in their imagination or was not yet sufficiently developed to support an effective interpretive sequence.

A fairly common way that patients justify resistance behavior is by invoking a distorted conception of their role in the treatment. For example, patients confronted with being silent may say, "I think I've been doing my share of the talking, and it's your turn now"; or patients asking to leave a session early may indicate that they have said everything they wanted to say that day; or patients who have been canceling appointments may assert, "As I see it, I really should come in to talk with you only when something is really bothering me." All such statements distort the usual terms of a psychotherapy treatment contract, which specify that it is the patient's task to talk and the therapist's to listen, that sessions last for a prescribed length of time regardless of what is being discussed, and that appointments are regularly scheduled independently of how the patient is feeling. To help patients who respond in this way recognize that their behavior is not so immediately explicable, therapists should directly contrast the explanation offered with the terms of the treatment contract ("But we discussed initially in planning the treatment that we would meet each time for 50 minutes, so there must be some reason for your wanting to leave early other than just thinking that the sessions end when you're through talking about a particular subject").

This latter example illustrates two important features of interpretive sequences aimed at resistance behavior. First, as noted in Chapter 6, an explicitly stated and mutually endorsed treatment contract often provides the basis for demonstrating to patients that they are resisting. Without previously specified role behaviors and treatment arrangements to refer to, therapists may be hard put to convince patients that there is anything unusual about ways in which they are limiting their participation in the treatment. To continue with the preceding example, if therapists have not previously clarified that sessions will be of a fixed length, they are on shaky ground trying to attach significance to a patient's asking to leave early. "Oh," the patient may say, "you never told me that we would always meet for 50 minutes, and if I had known I wouldn't have suggested stopping right now." Thus an adequate treatment contract becomes a valuable ally when resistance interpretations depend on obvious discrepancies between patients' current behavior and the role they agreed to play in the therapy.

Second, an interpretive sequence aimed at indications of resistance should usually be initiated by arousing patients' curiosity about their behavior. Although such curiosity may emerge spontaneously, it often must be fostered in gradual stages. In Stage 1, the apparent resistance behavior is called to patients' attention for them to acknowledge as existing ("You're right, I'm not talking as much as usual today"). In Stage 2, the behavior now acknowledged as fact is recognized by patients as being unusual, either because they cannot account for it on a rational basis or because it runs counter to the treatment contract they previously endorsed. In the third stage, the behavior acknowledged as unusual is labeled as a subject worth pursuing:

PATIENT: So there must be other reasons why I'm acting as I am.

THERAPIST: We have to wonder about what you're feeling this way might mean.

Once interpretation of resistance has reached this point, with the resistance behavior recognized as worthy of exploration, patients are prepared to begin working on understanding its origins and meanings. They may already have sensed their resistance and been on the verge of talking about it, in which case an initial observation by the therapist ("You seem very quiet today") proves sufficient to induce their exploration of it ("I've been aware of some things we're getting into that I just don't feel like talking about"; "I'm not saying much because I've been having some feelings about you that I'd be embarrassed to have come out"). More commonly, however, unraveling identified resistance behavior requires more assistance from the therapist than merely arousing a patient's curiosity.

Should therapists have no impressions or hunches about the origins of acknowledged resistance behavior, the interpretive sequence may go no further than simply marking for future reference the fact that some unaccountable behavior opposing the progress of the treatment has occurred. On the other hand, if therapists have some basis for thinking the resistance behavior is related to aspects of a patient's characterological style or the patient's attitudes toward behavior change, the content of the interviews, or the therapist as a person, they can then employ a sequence of clarifications, confrontations, and partial interpretations leading the patient toward sharing in this understanding of the behavior. The following two examples, the first involving resistance to content and the second transference resistance, illustrate such interpretive sequences:

PATIENT: I can see that there must be something more to my coming so late today, but I don't know what it could be.

THERAPIST: It's as if you don't want to talk much.

PATIENT: How do you mean?

THERAPIST: The less time you're here, the less time there is for you to talk.

PATIENT: Okay, but that would seem to mean there's something I don't want to talk about. Could that be it?

THERAPIST: You seemed to have some strong feelings during our last session.

PATIENT: Did I? Oh yes, I remember, I had just started to tell you about what I did behind my husband's back while we were engaged—you know, sexually—and how guilty I feel about it, and . . . well, that must be it. I remember when I left I had the thought that I never wanted to come back if it meant I would have to talk more about that subject.

PATIENT: I know it's different from usual, but I just don't feel like talking today. I suppose there are things I could say, but I'd prefer to keep quiet.

THERAPIST: What does keeping quiet mean to you, what comes to your mind about it?

PATIENT: Oh, I suppose keeping quiet means minding your own business, not getting involved, keeping your feelings to yourself.

THERAPIST: So maybe right here and now you have some feelings you want to keep to yourself, to avoid getting involved.

PATIENT: Uh . . . no . . . uh, I don't think so. Nothing much at all seems to be on my mind. (patient squirms, appears uncomfortable)

THERAPIST: I wonder if you're not having some feelings about me that are difficult to talk about.

PATIENT: Well, if you must know, I had a dream about you, an intimate kind of dream, and coming in here today I had a feeling of anticipation like I was going on a date or meeting a lover, and I don't know what to make of it.

These examples illustrate two useful techniques for helping patients explore resistance behavior, in the first case by reconstructing the events leading up to the onset of the resistance and in the second case by encouraging associations to its possible meanings. If patients can recall when and in what circumstances they experienced some reservations about participating in the treatment, and particularly if they can pinpoint events that were likely to have precipitated these reservations, they will be off to a good start in identifying the origins and meaning of their resistance behavior. Such a reconstruction in the preceding examples, focused by the therapist's reference to the events of the previous interview, paved the way for the patient to recognize the source of her resistance. When patients can associate to the meaning of their resistance behavior, their comments will often contain clues to its underlying significance, which is what occurred in the second example. The therapist's request for associations yielded some behavioral descriptions ("not getting involved, keeping your feelings to yourself") that provided access in the patient's own words to the transference feelings causing the resistance.

When resistive patients have been helped to understand the origins of their resistive behavior, their resistance will usually abate sufficiently for them to resume communicating freely in the treatment. Additionally, as in the second example, the nature of the resistance may itself capture the patient's attention ("I don't know what to make of it"). Why is she uncomfortable or embarrassed to talk about a particular subject? Why, when a situation makes her uncomfortable, does she seek to avoid it in some ways rather than in others? How does her resistance behavior in the treatment relate to other situations in her life in which she has felt uncomfortable and has become maladaptively defensive? Each of these and other similar questions can lead to fruitful areas of exploration, thus illustrating the utility of resistance interpretations not only in helping patients continue with the current content of the treatment but also in providing new topics for discussion.

BREAKING THROUGH RESISTANCE

Exploring resistance, although occasionally providing dramatic breakthroughs, tends like the interpretive process in general to be a deliberate, low-key reconstruction of patients' thoughts, feelings, and actions during which they gradually arrive at an enhanced understanding of their behavior. At times, however, circumstances call for therapists to break directly through resistance behavior with a single, unequivocal interpretive statement. For example, to a patient who has slouched sullenly in a chair for the first 5 minutes of a session, the therapist may say, "You're angry at me today."

The criteria for attempting to break through resistance in so abrupt a manner, without prior inquiry or exploration, are very stringent. Therapists must be quite certain that the patient is in fact resisting and is aware of being reluctant to participate in the treatment; they should be confident that their proffered explanation of the resistance behavior ("You're angry at me today") is accurate and can be readily documented; they should have good reason to expect the patient to accept, understand, and utilize their direct interpretation; and finally, they should be convinced that breaking through the resistance of the moment will be more advantageous than gradually exploring it. Unless therapists have all these strong feelings about the appropriateness of an interpretation that breaks directly through resistance behavior, any such interpretation they make is likely to inject in the treatment the several disadvantages of premature interpretation outlined in Chapter 8.

With few exceptions, the criteria for attempting to break directly through resistance are likely to be met only in instances of repetitive resistance behaviors that have previously been explored and traced to their origins. Consider, for example, a male patient who from time to time has been opening his interviews with how-are-you's and subsequent efforts to make small talk about the therapist's life. Suppose further that careful exploration of his behavior on several occasions has clarified (a) that the patient tends to begin this way when he has some delicate or difficult subject on his mind, and (b) that by beginning in this way he attempts to delay getting into the subject, to shift attention from his life to the therapist's, and to cast the patient-therapist relationship more as a mutual friendship than as a working arrangement focused on his problems. In this context, should the patient then begin a session with "How are you today?" the therapist might usefully respond, "There's something on your mind you're hesitant to talk about."

Although such a direct breaking through of resistance is justified only infrequently, it is an oversight for therapists not to proceed in this way when the criteria just noted are met. As in the general process of working through, repetitions of a resistance interpretation should not begin each time from scratch, with detailed exploration as if the behavior in question had never been previously discussed. Rather, each repetition should build on what has gone on before, so that a decreasing amount of therapist effort is necessary to help patients recapture the probable meaning and implications of a behavior that is being interpreted. In the preceding example, for a therapist continually to treat "How are you?" as a new and unaccountable process aspect of the treatment, as if no previous understanding of it had been achieved, would both prolong the treatment unnecessarily and sooner or later give this patient cause to wonder whether the therapist was really paying attention and understanding him.

Furthermore, like interpretations in general, interpretations of resistance can become worked through to a point where only minimal therapist activity is necessary to revive them. As patients progress from their initial insight into some aspect of their behavior toward being able to use this insight to effect behavior change, breaking through its resistance elements may cease to require such statements as "You're angry at me today" or "There's something you're reluctant to talk about." Instead the therapist's response to "There's nothing on my mind" may be "We've heard that before" or perhaps just a raised eyebrow, following which the patient is able to say, "Oh yes, I know, whenever I say that it usually means I've got something to talk about that's hard to say, and I suppose there is something I need to tell you about today." Eventually, a point should be reached where patients interpret their own behavior as quickly as they report it, even when it involves resistance: "I found myself puttering around today, which would have made me late, and I know that means I'm having some mixed feelings about the treatment; so I got myself to get moving and make it here on time, but I still think it would be important to find out what was bothering me."

Hence, although exploration will remain the most frequently indicated way of responding to demonstrable resistance behavior, resistance interpretations that have been accepted and understood by a patient become part of the working-through process. As such, they may be offered with increasingly direct comments that break through rather than explore the resistance behavior. Over time, then, as the working through of resistance interpretations is accomplished, patients not only learn about themselves from their resistances but also achieve sufficient control of their resistance behavior to eliminate its interference with their communication in the treatment.[13]

NOTES

1. For further elaboration on the paradoxical nature of resistance behavior in psychotherapy, readers are referred to Levy (1990, Chapter 4), McLaughlin (1995), Menninger and Holzman (1973, Chapter 5), and Moore and Fine (1990, pp. 168–169).

2. This procedure is described in Freud's chapter on the psychotherapy of hysteria in *Studies in Hysteria* (Breuer & Freud, 1893–1895/1955, pp. 270–278). This book is usually regarded as marking the inception of the psychoanalytic method.

3. Research reviewed by Orlinsky et al. (1994) confirms that patients' cooperation with treatment procedures is generally associated with favorable outcomes in psychotherapy and resistance with unfavorable outcomes. Consistent with the inevitability of resistance in successful psychotherapy, however, Orlinsky et al. point out that a patient's experiencing or expressing a negative attitude during a treatment session does not signify that the therapy is going poorly. Rather, the data document that therapists can facilitate progress in treatment by recognizing resistance and responding to it in ways that restore a patient's active collaboration in the treatment procedures.

4. This typology of resistance differs in some respects from the traditional classification proposed by S. Freud (1926/1959a, p. 160) and reviewed by such psychoanalytic writers as Glover (1955, pp. 50–78), Greenson (1967, pp. 85–88), A. Kris (1985), McLaughlin (1995), and

Menninger and Holzman (1973, pp. 108–112). The modest revisions involved in formulating the types of resistance discussed in this chapter incorporate the traditional types but place them in the context of a somewhat broader frame of reference.

5. Good descriptions of the nature of secondary gain and its role in perpetuating emotional disturbance appear in several papers by S. Freud (1909/1959b, pp. 231–232; 1913/1958a, p. 133; 1916–1917/1963, pp. 382–385), who first noted the manner in which secondary gain functions as a resistance in psychotherapy (1926/1959a, pp. 98–101, 169). In the contemporary literature, Castelnuovo-Tedesco (1989) elaborates how patients' fears of what they may have to lose can contribute to their resisting change in psychotherapy.

6. Extended discussions of the nature of specific defense mechanisms and their implications for resistance in psychotherapy are provided by Fenichel (1945a, pp. 141–167), A. Freud (1936/1946), Rangell (1983), and Wallerstein (1983).

7. Zeidner and Endler (1996) provide encyclopedic coverage of individual differences in coping styles and their implications for adaptive and maladaptive behavior.

8. Although written over 60 years ago, the best available discussion of masochistic character disorder and the obstacles it erects to progress in psychotherapy is provided by Wilhelm Reich (1933/1949, pp. 208–247), who introduced the notions of "character armoring" and "character resistance" to the literature. Other important contributions concerning this topic include work by Blum (1991), Brenner (1959), Glenn and Bernstein (1995), and Reik (1941). Also recommended with respect to characterological styles and their bearing on response to treatment are a classical paper by Sterba (1953) and books by S. Johnson (1994), Horowitz et al. (1984), Millon (1996), Shapiro (1965, 1989), and M. Stone (1993). The sometimes intractable resistance to psychotherapy among patients who are masochistic or unable to tolerate success has also been referred to as "negative therapeutic reaction" (Jaffe, 1981; Levy, 1990, Chapter 7).

9. Dewald (1980, 1982) elaborates how patients in psychotherapy employ what he calls "strategic resistances" to help them avoid painful thoughts and feelings. In related research, Horowitz, Milbrath, and Stinson (1995) found that patients typically showed increasing signs of defensive control processes at those times when they were communicating conflicted or unresolved themes, and they concluded that such signs of defensiveness may be a useful way of identifying issues that remain unresolved.

10. Gill (1982, Chapter 2) presents a detailed conceptualization and numerous illustrations of how transference reactions can interfere with communication in psychotherapy (transference resistance) and also constitute

themselves distressing experiences that patients seek to avoid recognizing or communicating (resistance to transference). Bauer (1989) comments on ways in which therapists as well as patients may sometimes resist dealing with here-and-now issues in the transference.

11. Echoing the recommendation in Chapter 6 concerning the importance of arriving at explicit contractual agreements during the initial phase of therapy, Gans and Counselman (1996) urge inclusion in the treatment contract of a clear cancellation policy. When cancellation policies have been explicated and are neither too rigid nor too lenient, they point out, missed sessions can provide valuable opportunities for exploration of their significance.

12. "Acting out" has been a loosely used term among mental health professionals and the general public as well. The traditional psychodynamic notion of acting out employed in this discussion was elaborated by Fenichel (1945b), and readers are referred to Abt and Weissman (1965), Boesky (1982), Milman and Goldman (1973), and Roughton (1995) for additional discussions of its characteristics and implications for psychotherapy.

13. For additional discussion of techniques for handling resistance in psychotherapy, readers are referred to Busch (1995, Chapter 5; 1996), Levy (1990, Chapter 4), Milman and Goldman (1987), Rockland (1989b, Chapter 8), Strean (1985), and Wachtel (1982).

CHAPTER 10

The Psychotherapy Relationship: Transference

T RANSFERENCE CONSISTS of the displacement of feelings, attitudes, or impulses experienced toward previous figures in a person's life onto current figures to whom they do not realistically apply. As such, transference participates to some extent in all interpersonal relationships, because the reactions of one person to another are always subject to the influence of prior interpersonal experience. Like resistance, however, transference behavior is exacerbated by the psychotherapy situation and has considerable bearing on its course.

The role of transference in psychotherapy was first elucidated by S. Freud (1905/1953a, 1912/1958b, 1915/1958d), who saw transference reactions both as a useful source of information and a potential impediment to progress in the treatment. As a process aspect of psychotherapy, transference provides vivid clues to the nature of a patient's past and current interpersonal relationships; as a source of resistance, it can cut deeply into a patient's commitment to the treatment contract.

To appreciate the special significance of transference reactions, it is necessary to understand them in the broader context of the psychotherapy relationship. Transference accounts for only part of patients' feelings and attitudes toward their therapist; the psychotherapy relationship is additionally shaped by patients' realistic responses to the therapist as a person (the *real relationship*) and by their adherence to the terms of the treatment contract (the *working alliance*). This chapter first elaborates these three components of the patient-therapist relationship and then describes (a) the origins and fostering of transference in psychotherapy,

(b) variations in the intensity, feeling tone, and expression of transference reactions, and (c) technical considerations in the exploration and interpretation of transference phenomena.

TRANSFERENCE, REALITY, AND THE WORKING ALLIANCE

The relationship of psychotherapy patients to their therapists proceeds simultaneously on the three different levels of transference, reality, and the working alliance. These three components of the patient-therapist relationship differ widely in how they emerge and how they influence the course of treatment, and many aspects of patient behavior in psychotherapy are determined by which component is in ascendance.

TRANSFERENCE

The distinguishing feature of transference is the *displacement* of feelings, attitudes, or impulses. As displacements, transference reactions are always inappropriate to the actual circumstances of the treatment situation. Some transference reactions are unjustified primarily in kind or quality, and others primarily in their intensity; in either case transference "exceeds . . . anything that could be justified on sensible or rational grounds" (S. Freud, 1912/1958b, p. 100).

To illustrate first a reaction of inappropriate quality, suppose a patient in the midst of recounting an event suddenly flushes with anger and exclaims, "It really burns me up, the way you sit there frowning at whatever I say, like you wish I wasn't even taking up your time." Why is the patient angry? Assuming that the therapist has done nothing to incur the patient's wrath except sit and listen, as the treatment contract prescribes and as the therapist has been doing in previous interviews without evoking anger, why does the patient perceive a frowning visage and a begrudging time commitment? Because the answer to these questions does not lie in the reality of the situation, the patient's behavior constitutes a transference reaction unjustified in quality by the circumstances in which it has occurred.

To illustrate a reaction of inappropriate intensity, consider a situation in which the therapist is 5 minutes late in beginning an interview. The patient in this situation might justifiably feel somewhat irritated or disheartened, because the therapist's tardiness cuts into time that is being paid for and also indicates that other matters have been allowed to override the therapist's commitment to the treatment contract. In view of such realistic considerations, therapists who begin late owe their patient an apology and should usually extend the session to its contracted length.

However, suppose that instead of an appropriately mild reaction, this patient flies into a rage and accuses the therapist of unethical practice, or becomes too depressed to talk about anything other than the therapist's "obvious" disinterest. Then the patient's reaction will be appropriate in kind to the actual circumstances but unjustified in intensity, and hence a manifestation of transference.

Implicit in both of these examples is another useful way of conceptualizing transference reactions: Transference represents a distorted perception of a therapist's attitudes and behavior. To see therapists as frowning when they are not, as being disinterested or disapproving when they feel no such way, or as failing to work conscientiously in the patient's behalf when they are doing so, are all instances of inaccurate perception. Sullivan (1954, pp. 25–27) coined the term *parataxic* to label the process by which a person's present interpersonal relationships become distorted by inappropriate generalizations from previous interpersonal experience. Although parataxic distortion has not become a widely used term, it nicely captures the role that misperception of the therapist plays in generating and shaping transference reactions.

REALITY

Patients' real relationships with their therapists comprise their appropriate and reasonable responses to what the therapist is, says, or does. Patients may respect therapists for their educational and professional attainments; they may become annoyed if the therapist interrupts an interview to accept a telephone call or appears to have forgotten some important information from a previous session; or, depending on their tastes, they may like or dislike the way therapists arrange their furniture, comb their hair, select their clothes, display their diplomas, or whatever. Should such reactions become unrealistically intense— should respect for the therapist generate diffidence, or a brief interruption provoke fury, or opinions of the therapist's personal qualities influence what patients choose to talk about—then they will constitute transference. However, so long as they remain within the bounds of how one person might appropriately respond to another, they will be part of the real treatment relationship.

The distinction between transference reactions and the real treatment relationship provides an important guideline for the selection of patient-therapist transactions to interpret. Because transference reactions often contain otherwise unavailable clues to a patient's interpersonal difficulties and may also contribute to resistance, their exploration provides avenues for enhancing self-understanding and at the same time overcoming obstacles to progress in the treatment. The real relationship, on the other hand, seldom interferes with communication in psychotherapy and provides little information about patients beyond what is superficial and readily apparent. Attempts to interpret the realistic behavior of patients toward their therapist therefore contribute minimally to the work of the treatment.

Their differences notwithstanding, transference and reality are rarely exclusive in patients' relationships toward their therapist. Transference reactions are usually triggered by some event in reality, and realistic reactions are often embellished with transference attitudes. Patients who become furious at the therapist for taking a telephone call have after all had their session interrupted, and patients who denounce a youthful therapist as being too young to be competent are correctly perceiving the therapist's age and relative inexperience. Patients who realistically like the way their therapist looks or arranges furniture can leave it at that, but if they weave these opinions into statements that "You're a handsome man" or "You have great taste in decorating," some transference elements, such as a wish to ingratiate themselves with the therapist, are probably participating in their behavior.

Therapists need to determine where the balance lies between transference and reality in a patient's reactions to them and to concentrate their attention on those reactions that appear determined primarily by transference. Aside from there being more to be gained by pursuing the transference, there are some distinct disadvantages to probing the real relationship. For example, a patient may conclude the final session of a calendar year with "Happy New Year," or say to a therapist obviously suffering with a bad cold, "I hope you're feeling better soon." Although such comments may involve transference elements, they also constitute ordinary social amenities that pass between people who have no particular personal relationship.

Such social amenities are best responded to in psychotherapy by taking them at face value. Aside from yielding minimal information, attempts to explore conventional behavior (e.g., "I wonder what thoughts you have about saying that to me") risk making patients feel more an object of study than a person worthy of respect. Patients denied the opportunity for a real relationship with their therapist, so that they cannot wish him or her good health or a happy holiday without having their motives impugned, will feel demeaned in the treatment situation and consequently have less likelihood of benefiting from it (see Chapter 3). Unless they blossom into resistance and impede patients' communication about themselves and their problems, conventional social comments call for a response in kind: "Happy New Year" calls for "Same to you," and "I hope you're feeling better soon" calls for "Thank you." As Schafer (1983) correctly notes, "There is always room in analytic work for courtesy, cordiality, gentleness, sincere empathic participation, and other personal, though not socially intimate modes of relationship" (p. 9).[1]

THE WORKING ALLIANCE

The working alliance consists of those aspects of the patient-therapist relationship that are determined by the treatment contract: the agreement to work in certain prescribed ways toward alleviating the patient's problems. The working alliance is in evidence whenever patients are reporting their thoughts and feelings openly and participating with the therapist in observing them. Although colored by both transference and reality, the working alliance stands separate from each of these other two components of the treatment relationship.

The working alliance differs from transference because it comprises accurate perception of the treatment situation and strict allegiance to the terms of the treatment contract. When the working alliance holds sway, patients do not "forget" the essence of their task or the therapist's role as initially agreed on, nor do they seek an inappropriately extensive or intimate relationship with their therapist, nor do they distort the nature or meaning of the therapist's behavior. Rather, they go about the business of describing and looking at themselves without displacements and without attempts to cast the therapist in any role other than the contracted one as listener and facilitator of self-understanding. In this sense, the working alliance component of the treatment relationship engages a patient's observing ego, as defined in Chapter 4, whereas transference reactions fall within the province of the experiencing ego.

Although the working alliance is reality-oriented and free from perceptual distortion, it has a contrived and nonreciprocal quality that also distinguishes it from a real relationship. Interpersonal relationships in the real world are sustained by mutuality, which means that people interact on a personal basis only so long as they are gratifying each other's needs. In the relationship formed by a working alliance in psychotherapy, by contrast, one person (the patient) agrees to forgo gratification of needs to allow the other person (the therapist) to facilitate increased understanding of these needs. In a real relationship, people who say to a friend, "I really need someone to do it for me," are told, "Don't worry, you can count on me"; in psychotherapy they are encouraged to explore why they cannot do it themselves. In a real relationship, people who ask other people whether they are married expect to be told "Yes," "No," or even "It's none of your business"; in psychotherapy they are asked "What thoughts do you have about it?" or "How would you like it to be?" or "I wonder how it is that you've raised this question right now?"

These examples should suffice to demonstrate that the working alliance, even though it proceeds realistically according to the terms of the treatment contract, bears only a passing resemblance to interpersonal relationships as they exist in the real world outside of psychotherapy. The focus on one person as talker and the other as listener, the emphasis on understanding patients rather than gratifying their needs, and the technique of exploring rather than responding to comments and questions all identify the working alliance as an artificial situation created to serve the purposes of the treatment.[2]

GENERALIZED AND SPECIFIC TRANSFERENCE REACTIONS

The transference component of the treatment relationship is influenced by typical responses of patients to the therapist's role and by the feelings of each individual patient toward the important people in their lives and toward people in general. Typical responses to the therapist's role result in *generalized transference reactions,* whereas the particular interpersonal attitudes of the individual patient contribute to *specific transference reactions.* As elaborated next, this distinction proves helpful in recognizing the origins and significance of transference behavior.

GENERALIZED TRANSFERENCE REACTIONS

Generalized transference reactions comprise the characteristic ways in which almost all patients respond to therapists' performance of their task. In the generalized transference, patients first develop unrealistic positive feelings and later unrealistic negative feelings toward their therapist, and it was this general pattern to which the brief discussions of transference in Chapters 4 and 9 referred.

To recapitulate these previous discussions, psychotherapy patients tend initially to be favorably impressed with therapists' professional position, their tolerance and self-control, their psychological sensitivity, and their dedication to being helpful. These impressions culminate in an idealized image of the therapist accompanied by longings to be loved or admired by him or her and to enjoy a more intensive or extensive personal relationship than is consistent with the boundaries of the treatment contract. Over time, as therapists refrain from expressing love and admiration and keep the real relationship within the boundaries of the treatment contract, patients begin to feel hurt and rejected. Frustrated and disappointed by the therapist's failure to reciprocate their positive feelings, they start to view the therapist in a different light. Instead of seeing him or her as sensitive, interested, and helpful, they regard the therapist as callous, uncaring, and inconsiderate—how else could he or she be so impersonal and unresponsive and be the agent of so much unhappiness?

This prior description of positive and negative feelings in the generalized transference can now be elaborated in terms of the distinction drawn in the present chapter between the real and the transference relationship. The main point to keep in mind is that patients' generalized positive and negative attitudes toward their therapist may involve reality as well as transference. Generalized attitudes toward therapists constitute transference reactions only when they are inappropriate, as when patients use therapists' unflagging commitment to the working alliance as the basis for idealizing them as perfect people or denigrating them as heartless automatons. When generalized attitudes toward the therapist are appropriate to the circumstances, they represent reality, rather than transference, and they may appear either independently of transference reactions or concurrently with them.

For example, patients who appreciate their therapist's being a good listener and sensitive observer, but do not exaggerate the therapist's worth as a person on this account, have a positive feeling toward their therapist based on a realistic impression of the therapist as carrying out his or her prescribed role in the treatment.[3] Such realistic positive responses to therapist competence and dedication can exist without being embellished into positive transference reactions, and they can also persist even in the face of negative reactions based on transference. Patients exploring a negative transference reaction not uncommonly offer the following kind of observation:

> I don't know why I'm angry at you for not saying more. I know in my mind that you're doing your job the way it's supposed to be done [reference to working alliance], and I appreciate your trying to be helpful [reference to realistic positive feelings]. But I still feel mad at you and I think I'm going to stay mad until I get more feedback from you about what you think of me [negative transference].

Generalized negative feelings toward the therapist can also exist either as real or as transference reactions, but they are less likely to be justified in reality than positive feelings and are more consistently likely to indicate transference. Although it is possible for realistic events to trigger negative transference reactions, therapists who are doing their jobs competently should provide little basis in reality for patients to become upset with them. Thus therapists should not frequently cancel or arrive late for sessions, should not be psychologically insensitive to what is said to them, and should not bludgeon their patients with poorly conceived, ill-timed, and hypercritical interpretations, all of which give just cause for patients to be upset with them. Conscientious and adequately trained therapists will rarely be guilty of such irresponsibility, obtuseness, and technical blundering.

Recognizing the role of reality elements in patients' generalized attitudes toward their therapist makes it possible to amplify the typical course of feeling tone in the treatment relationship. Because most patients agree to enter into a treatment contract only when they have already formed some respect for the therapist's competence and some belief in his or her ability to help, psychotherapy usually begins in the context of *positive realistic* attitudes toward the therapist. As patients subsequently begin to idealize their therapist, they develop *generalized positive transference* feelings that coexist with the positive feelings they have previously developed on a reality basis. After a time, *generalized negative transference* feelings typically arise in response to the nonreciprocal nature of the working alliance. These negative transference feelings submerge positive transference feelings, but they do not necessarily cancel out realistic positive attitudes toward the therapist. For this reason, patients who are angry at their therapist for not reciprocating intimate personal feelings (transference) can still appreciate the therapist's effort to be helpful (reality), as in the example just given. Moreover, exploring and interpreting negative transference reactions may enhance patients' realistic positive attitudes toward their therapist, because this process demonstrates further the therapist's empathic capacity and willingness to use this capacity on the patient's behalf.

Generalized positive and negative transference feelings alternate and coexist not only with realistic attitudes toward the therapist, but also with each other. With respect to alternation, generalized transference seldom progresses through a single positive-to-negative sequence. Patients vary from session to session in how they are disposed to feel, and sessions vary in the extent to which they leave patients feeling uplifted or put down. Consequently, although generalized positive transference reactions almost always appear earlier in treatment than generalized negative ones, both tend to recur in alternating cycles throughout the middle phase of psychotherapy.

As for the coexistence of positive and negative transference, ambivalence is a well-known characteristic of human emotions. Just as one person can love and hate another person at the same time, patients in psychotherapy can simultaneously hold unrealistic positive and negative attitudes toward their therapist. Ordinarily, the set of attitudes that is stronger or more fully conscious determines the manifest tone of a generalized transference reaction, although a patient's transference behavior may sometimes reflect a more or less balanced mixture of positive and negative attitudes.

A final point to be made about generalized transference reactions is that they are less uniquely influenced than specific transference reactions by the displacement of feelings, attitudes, and impulses onto the therapist. Displacements participate in generalized transference as relatively predictable and uniform features of how patients respond to the helping but frustrating role therapists play in sustaining the working alliance. In specific transference reactions, on the other hand, displacements occur as unique reflections of an individual patient's prior interpersonal experience and are triggered more by details of how therapists appear and behave than by their general performance of their prescribed role.

SPECIFIC TRANSFERENCE REACTIONS

Specific transference reactions consist of displacements onto the therapist of thoughts, feelings, and impulses patients have held toward certain important people in their life or hold toward people in general. Displacements onto the therapist from important people in a patient's life constitute the classical form of transference reaction originally described by S. Freud (1905/1953a, p. 116) as a repetition or reenactment in the therapy of previous interpersonal relationships. Most often, these reenactments reflect patients' relationships to their parents, primarily because parental figures are the people most likely to have been involved in a person's basic psychological conflicts and to have etched indelible images on his or her mind. When patients who experience such specific transference reactions become able to verbalize and comment on them, the following kinds of informative self-observations tend to occur:

> Sometimes I find myself getting very uneasy while we're talking. I think it's the way you clear your throat now and then. My mother had a habit of clearing her throat like that, usually just before she was going to give me a lecture about something.

> I have the feeling you're laughing up your sleeve at me, just like my father always did. He had the most irritating way of being patronizing, with a sort of quizzical, mocking expression on his face, and you're doing the same damn thing to me.

You may not understand this, but it bothered me just now to see another patient leaving your office as I was getting here for my appointment. I know it can't be, but I feel like I don't want you to have any other patients—I want you all to myself. It's like when I was a kid, and my parents were always wrapped up with my brothers and sisters and never seemed to have enough time for me.

This is embarrassing to say, but I'm just thinking how nice it would be to go over to you and curl up in your lap. I used to curl up in my father's lap when I was a little girl, and those were some of the happiest moments of my life.

In this way, then, lingering hopes, fears, resentments, and longings experienced originally toward parents during the formative years may become transferred onto the therapist during the course of treatment. In some instances, parental surrogates, such as an aunt or uncle or much older sibling who played a parental role in a patient's youth, may be the key figures in such specific transference reactions. Similarly, patients can displace onto their therapist feelings and attitudes they are experiencing toward people who are currently important in their lives, such as a spouse or employer. However, because feelings and attitudes toward currently important people usually have more access to direct expression than feelings and attitudes from the past, they are less likely than past feelings and attitudes to be expressed in displacements.

Nevertheless, current interpersonal relationships often influence displacement onto the therapist of feelings and attitudes held toward people in general. Transference reactions of this type were first described by Sullivan, who saw them as an inevitable consequence of the previously mentioned "parataxic distortions" to which all people are prone. Sullivan observed that all patients come to psychotherapy with certain interpersonal dispositions determined by their prior experience—fear or resentment of authority figures, dependent or counterdependent needs, readiness or reluctance to divulge intimate concerns, trust or mistrust of the motives of others, and so forth. Through parataxic distortion, therapists become inaccurately perceived as a specific instance of people in general, and patients transfer onto them the feelings, attitudes, and impulses toward others that constitute their interpersonal orientation.[4]

When patients can verbalize transference attitudes they hold toward people in general, the following kinds of remarks are likely to emerge:

I can see that I've been irritated with you for no good reason, at least not for anything you've done. It's just that you seem to be successful in your work and to enjoy it, and I resent anyone who seems to be getting more out of life than I am. And now that I think about it, I guess I see most people that way, and maybe that's why I go around resenting everybody.

This must be the third or fourth time you've pointed out to me that I act as if you won't be interested in hearing what I have to say. I think that's just the way it is with me—I always expect that people won't find me interesting or pay much attention to me, and if I don't say anything, at least I don't give them a chance to ignore me or brush me off.

I suppose I know I can trust you, but it's still not that easy for me to open up. I'm always afraid that if I really let people know what my feelings are, they'll have me in the palm of their hand, so to speak, and be able to take advantage of me. So I always play it close to the vest.

As you say, there must be some reason why I ask you so many personal questions and why I've tried to learn as much as I can about your life outside this office. I just can't know people at a distance. When I know people I have to know everything about them, so that I can really feel close to them. I suppose that's why I keep being accused by people of being a busybody and being too possessive.

These examples illustrate ways in which envy and resentment, inferiority feelings and anticipated rejection, mistrust and fear of exploitation, and exaggerated needs for intimacy—all as specific attitudes held toward people in general—can become displaced onto the therapist. When patients' transference reactions allow such attitudes to be assayed in the crucible of the treatment relationship, considerable progress can be made in helping them recognize the motives that influence their interpersonal behavior.

Two additional points merit mention in concluding this discussion of specific transference reactions. First, much of Freud's thinking about this aspect of the psychotherapy relationship has received empirical confirmation in a series of research studies reported by Luborsky and Crits-Christoph (1991). In these studies, 22 of Freud's observations about transference were examined and found in 17 instances to correspond with treatment interaction data, with the remaining five observations yet to be studied thoroughly.

Of particular importance in the available research data are findings by Luborsky, Crits-Christoph, and Barber (1991) and by Gelso, Kivlighan, Wine, and Jones (1997) that confirm clinical expectations regarding the course of transference attitudes during psychotherapy. Specifically, the research data indicate that transference typically builds to a peak during approximately the first three-quarters of a successful treatment relationship and then gradually diminishes. Even though diminished, however, transference attitudes developed during successful therapy typically persist beyond termination and rarely dissolve completely until patients have had some time away from the therapist to work them through. In unsuccessful treatment cases, by contrast, transference attitudes are found to continue increasing throughout the therapy, without passing a peak point of intensity and diminishing thereafter.

The second point concerns observations by Comas-Díaz and Jacobsen (1991) regarding the possible impact on transference reactions of ethnocultural similarities and differences between patient and therapist. These authors suggest that patients being treated by therapists from ethnic backgrounds different from theirs may show specific transference attitudes ranging from overcompliance and friendliness to suspicion and hostility. When seeing a therapist from the same ethnic background as theirs, patients may show idealization of their therapist in some cases and devaluation, prejudice, and ambivalence in other cases. Comas-Diaz and Jacobsen go on to elaborate treatment implications of such ethnoculturally influenced transference reactions.

THE FOSTERING OF TRANSFERENCE REACTIONS

Whereas transferred feelings and impulses can participate in any interpersonal relationship, the psychotherapy situation tends uniquely to foster transference reactions and bring them into bold relief. This fostering of transference in psychotherapy derives from the unsymmetric and nonreciprocal nature of the working alliance. Therapists encourage patients to talk, listen to them permissively and without passing judgment, and concentrate on helping them understand the implications of what they say. Therapists do not talk about themselves, express their own views, or become personally involved with their patients, except insofar as they believe that doing so will strengthen the working alliance and serve a patient's best interests.

The therapist is consequently a moderately ambiguous stimulus, someone whose personal history, tastes and preferences, philosophy of life, sources of pleasure and displeasure, and unresolved concerns become only slightly more apparent to patients after many months of treatment than they are at the beginning of therapy. Reducing the amount of external structure provided by a perceptual field is generally known to increase the extent to which it is structured in terms of the perceiver's internal needs and dispositions. Therapists in their ambiguity assume the dimensions of a projective test, leaving patients considerable latitude to form impressions of them based on their own fears, wishes, expectations, and prejudices.

In conceptualizing the manner in which psychotherapists foster transference reactions, Tarachow (1963, Chapters 2–3) has drawn a useful distinction between the therapist's roles as a *real* object and an *as-if* object.
Therapists are always a real object to some extent by virtue of their appearance, their manner, their way of speaking, their response to social
amenities, and their professional identity. As stated earlier, however, sustaining a helpful treatment relationship requires therapists to emphasize
the working alliance between themselves and their patients and to keep
any real relationship between them at a carefully controlled minimum. It
is in their commitment to the working alliance that therapists act as an as-
if object in reaction to their patients, taking on a role intended to benefit
the patient but differing from how they would ordinarily behave in interpersonal situations:

> The therapist imposes a barrier to reality. . . . The *real* situation is trans-
> formed into an *as if* situation demanding attention and comprehension.
> . . . Nothing in the interaction is permitted to be regarded as real, and
> everything is subjected to the scrutiny of both parties. (Tarachow, 1963,
> p. 9)

In their relative anonymity, their noncommittal stance, and their emphasis on understanding rather than responding in kind to what is said to
them, therapists become a screen onto which patients project their interpersonal orientation. The utility of being such a screen was first described
by S. Freud (1912/1958b), who recommended that the therapist "be
opaque to his patients and, like a mirror, should show them nothing but
what is shown to him" (p. 118). Regrettably, this "opaque mirror" recommendation has sometimes been interpreted to mean that the therapists
should keep themselves aloof, impersonal, and emotionally unresponsive
at all times, in the manner of a blank screen. Yet there is no way therapists
can effectively demonstrate the warmth, empathy, and genuineness that
contribute to favorable outcomes in psychotherapy without becoming
deeply engaged in discussing patients' concerns and responding to their
needs for help.[5]

Properly construed, being a mirror means that, without becoming in-
different or detached, therapists should minimize their participation
with patients as a real object to concentrate on their role as an as-if object
and thereby sustain the working alliance. If a patient's needs for help
could be met solely by a real relationship, then these needs could be met
by the person's friends and loved ones, and the patient would not require
professional assistance. If, on the other hand, their personal relationships
have proved insufficient to help patients resolve their difficulties, then
something more than or different from another friendship is called for.

Psychotherapy, with its emphasis on understanding rather than exchanging information and on meeting patients' needs for help rather than establishing mutually gratifying relationships with them, constitutes such an alternative arrangement.

Although transference reactions provide information that can facilitate progress in the treatment, the fostering of transference should not be conceived as a special activity undertaken by the therapist. Conscious efforts to provoke or manipulate transference reactions will be perceived by patients as ungenuine, and their response to them will lack sufficient spontaneity to be informative. By merely adhering to their role as prescribed in the treatment contract, therapists will create an interpersonal climate that in the natural course of events will foster the emergence and expression of transference reactions.

Faithful allegiance to the treatment contract can thus be seen as a way of safeguarding the transference, by sustaining an atmosphere in which transference reactions are likely to occur with sufficient spontaneity, frequency, and clarity to aid the progress of the treatment. Because of the complex nature of the treatment relationship, however, care must be taken to safeguard the real relationship and the working alliance as well, which means that therapists need to recognize how and when to protect all three components of the relationship.

Safeguarding the Transference

Therapists need to safeguard the transference by providing as few opportunities as possible for patients to form feelings, attitudes, and impulses toward them on a reality basis. The less basis there is in fact for patients' reactions to their therapist, the more these reactions are likely to involve transference and the more information they will provide about a patient's unique or neurotic dispositions. If patients conclude that a therapist is bored after observing the therapist stifle several yawns, or begin to regard the therapist as a parental figure after learning that he or she has several children, they are reacting in a conventional way to objective data and revealing very little about their individual needs and attitudes. On the other hand, patients who perceive their therapist as bored without there being any telltale yawn, or as parental without knowing anything about his or her family life, may well be displaying a propensity for seeing themselves as being disinteresting in the first instance and seeking parental figures on whom to depend in the second instance.

Unless the transference is adequately safeguarded, reality factors may act to contaminate it. When such contamination occurs, real and transference elements may become so intertwined in patients' reactions to their therapist as to obscure the inappropriate aspects of these reactions and preclude any fruitful exploration of them. For this reason, therapists should ordinarily not yawn or tell patients how many children they have, nor should they express any other emotions or provide any other information about themselves unless they have specific and carefully thought out reasons for doing so. Instead, they should uniformly and consistently concentrate on being an as-if object. In this way, they will minimize the basis for a real relationship in the treatment and maximize the possibility of being able to trace a patient's reactions to them to clinically meaningful displacements.

Deciding on whether and when to provide information about themselves touches on the general issues of *therapist self-disclosure,* concerning which some additional guidelines are helpful. An influential book by Jourard (1964) fostered the notion that personal self-revelation by therapists would increase their appearance of humaneness and encourage patients to be similarly disclosing. Although this notion remains widely discussed, subsequent research has indicated that therapist self-disclosure does not consistently influence how much patients are likely to say about themselves and has little bearing on improvement or outcome in psychotherapy (see Orlinsky et al., 1994; Watkins, 1990; M. Weiner, 1978). With specific respect to therapists disclosing feelings of being attracted to patients, clinical observations and research findings indicate that such disclosures are likely to be less therapeutic than a noncommittal stance (Gabbard, 1996; Goodyear & Shumate, 1996).

At present, survey data and the weight of the literature indicate widespread agreement that therapists' talking about themselves has the dual disadvantages of diverting patients' attention from their own self-observations and detracting from the information value and therapeutic utility of their transference reactions (Lane & Hull, 1990; Levy, 1990, Chapter 6; Mathews, 1988; Wachtel, 1993, Chapter 11). However, even in the absence of reason to expect that personal revelations by therapists will lead to any therapeutically beneficial exchange of intimacies, there is also widespread agreement concerning circumstances in which self-report can be helpful and should not be sacrificed on the altar of unswerving anonymity.

In particular, when therapists are disclosing reactions they are having to sessions while they are in progress, rather than life experiences unrelated to the treatment, and when they are doing so as a way of helping patients understand themselves better, they have good reason for engaging in these self-disclosing interventions. As an example of such within-sessions self-disclosure intended to enhance patients' self-understanding, therapists may give feedback concerning the impression patients are making on them as a way of helping patients recognize how they are likely to affect and be perceived by people in general. These final points have implications for therapists' management of their countertransference reactions to patients, which is discussed in Chapter 11, and for steps they should take to safeguard the real relationship as well as the transference.

Safeguarding the Real Relationship

In their zeal to safeguard the transference and thereby facilitate the interpretive work of the treatment, therapists should be careful not to douse all sparks of the real relationship between themselves and their patients. Failure to interact with a patient on a real rather than an as-if basis at certain times can detract from a therapist's genuineness, undermine a patient's feeling of being respected as a person, and hinder the eventual resolution of transference reactions.

With regard to genuineness, first of all, therapists need to acknowledge obvious facts about themselves and to allow some of their emotional reactions to be expressed. If a patient says "I gather from the diploma on your wall that you went to the University of Michigan, isn't that right?" the appropriate response is "Yes, that's right." To attempt to explore the significance of the patient's questions before or instead of answering it directly, as by responding with "How would you like it to be" or "I wonder what it would mean to you either way" when the facts are hanging squarely on the wall, is to engage in a strained, ungenuine, and probably unproductive subjugation of reality to the as-if relationship.

Whether such an expression of interest in the therapist has emerged as a resistance to talking about the patient's problems is another matter, to be pursued in its own right (see Chapter 9). With respect to the treatment relationship, however, the point is that obfuscation in the face of obvious fact serves no constructive purpose and may prove disadvantageous. Likewise, there will be times when therapists should smile at a humorous remark or show sympathy with an unfortunate event in a patient's life. Although they may go on to inquire about why the patient has said something funny or what part the patient may have played in the unfortunate event, they will have responded first as a real person in a situation that called for real rather than as-if behavior. Unless therapists acknowledge facts and expresses emotions in circumstances when it would be natural to do so, patients will have cause to doubt their genuineness and their three-dimensionality as a feeling, caring, and responsive person.[6]

With regard to respect, neglect of the real relationship inevitably deprives patients of their due as a person. As illustrated earlier, a patient who says "Happy New Year" in a conventional fashion deserves a similarly conventional "Same to you." Like patients who find their therapist ungenuine, patients who doubt that their therapist regards them as worthy of personal consideration have fewer prospects for benefiting from psychotherapy than patients who perceive their therapist as both genuine and respectful (see Chapter 3). In a study in which Grunebaum (1986) interviewed 47 patients who believed that they had had a harmful psychotherapy experience, he found that the most common reason they gave for their bad experience was their therapist being distant and uninvolved. In a similar vein, patients dropping out of psychotherapy early in treatment were found by Mohl, Martinez, Ticknor, and Huang (1991) to feel less well-liked and less respected by their therapist than patients continuing in treatment.

As for the resolution of transference reactions, two previously mentioned considerations to keep in mind are (a) that the treatment relationship proceeds on multiple levels during the course of psychotherapy and (b) that successful treatment involves the gradual diminution of transference in the latter stages of therapy and increasing reality in the interaction between patient and therapist. This does not mean that patient and therapist end their work together on a dramatically different note from before, passing the time of day as acquaintances rather than as parties to a treatment contract. The treatment contract remains in effect and, as described next, the working alliance receives its share of safeguarding. Nevertheless, as successful treatment nears termination, interpretive work concerned with matters other than issues of termination is largely finished, and the therapist becomes less involved than previously in probing areas of underlying concern as an as-if observer.

For the real patient-therapist relationship to be available to replace the transference partially near the end of treatment, it has to be nurtured and kept alive during the middle phase of psychotherapy, while the therapist is focusing primarily on transference elements in the relationship. For these three reasons, then—to maintain the therapist's genuineness as a three-dimensional person, to sustain the patient's feeling of being respected rather than merely studied or treated in the psychotherapy situation, and to nourish realistic aspects of the treatment relationship that can eventually replace transference reactions—the real relationship must be safeguarded concurrently with the therapist's efforts to safeguard and learn from the transference relationship.

Safeguarding the Working Alliance

The working alliance is implicitly safeguarded by steps therapists take to prevent transference reactions and the real relationship from intruding on it. Whenever therapists point out the inappropriateness of transference reactions or avoid participating in a mutually intimate relationship, they direct their patients toward the role behaviors prescribed by the treatment contract. At times, however, such implicit support for the working alliance requires some bolstering through explicit reaffirmation.

Consider, for example, a patient who says, "It's not fair, the way I talk and you listen, and I have to tell you all about myself and you never have to open yourself up at all." Safeguarding the transference in response to this complaint would involve regarding it as unwarranted and setting out to explore its latent meanings in terms of the treatment relationship. However, because this complaint accurately describes the treatment situation, declining to take it at face value and imputing some hidden significance to it would be likely to ring most hollow.

Furthermore, categorizing realistic comments on the nature of the working alliance as interpretable transference behavior denies patients their rights as informed and voluntary participants in the treatment contract. Just as patients have the right to accept or reject the contract initially, they have the right to suggest reviewing or modifying it during the course of therapy. Perhaps patients have good reasons for wanting to change the time of their appointment, or alter their goals in the treatment, or criticize some of the procedures being used by the therapist. Unless patients are accorded objective discussion of these and similar matters pertaining to the treatment contract, whether or not they contain transference elements, their commitment to the working alliance may become seriously frayed.

On the other hand, safeguarding the working alliance does not mean that matters pertaining to the treatment contract should be considered solely at the level of the real relationship. To respond realistically to the previously illustrated complaint about the nonmutuality of the treatment relationship, the therapist would have to say, "Yes, it is unfair, so we won't operate that way any more." Such capitulation to reality would compromise the interpretive approach that characterizes the working alliance and that distinguishes psychotherapy from other interpersonal relationships.

To protect the working alliance against reality, therapists need instead to respond to questions and comments about the treatment contract in ways that acknowledge a patient's right to raise these issues but sustain the nonreciprocal relationship that has been established to accomplish the aims of the treatment. Thus to a complaint about nonmutuality, the therapist might answer, "Yes it is unfair, in a way, just as you say; but it is a way of working together in psychotherapy that gives us the information we need in trying to help you understand yourself and your problems."

VARIATIONS IN THE INTENSITY, FEELING TONE, AND EXPRESSION OF TRANSFERENCE REACTIONS

Whereas transference reactions develop in all psychotherapy patients, they differ widely in their intensity, in the balance of positive and negative feelings that accompany them, and in the extent to which they are directly or indirectly expressed. Variations in these three dimensions of transference account for a wide range of individual differences in how particular patients respond at particular times to the impact of the treatment relationship.

THE INTENSITY OF TRANSFERENCE REACTIONS

Because the psychotherapy situation fosters transference reactions, the intensity of these reactions usually increases in direct relationship to how long and how frequently patients are seen. If treatment sessions are frequent enough and the treatment continues long enough, transference reactions may build into what is known as a *transference neurosis.* A transference neurosis is said to exist when patients are reenacting in the treatment relationship a panorama of neurotic conflicts, including many that are rooted in their childhood experiences, and when their cumulative transference reactions have become so pervasive as to make therapy and the therapist the central concerns in their lives.[7]

General principles notwithstanding, the relationship between frequency and duration of psychotherapy on the one hand and intensity of transference reactions on the other is a highly individual matter. People who give free rein to their feelings, who make friends quickly and become intimate on short notice, and who lean more toward experiencing than observing themselves are relatively prone to forming transference reactions in psychotherapy. Conversely, people who characteristically keep their emotions in check, who relate to others at a distance and become intimate only after prolonged acquaintance, and who incline more toward observing than experiencing themselves tend to be relatively insulated against transference reactions.

Such personality differences in transference proneness influence both the rapidity with which patients develop transference reactions and the intensity of these reactions in response to a particular frequency and duration of psychotherapy. For relatively transference-prone individuals, such as patients with a borderline or hysterical personality style, once-weekly psychotherapy may be sufficient to generate pronounced transference reactions in the first few months of treatment. For people relatively insulated against transference reactions, such as patients with an avoidant or obsessive personality style, once-weekly sessions may elicit only faint whisperings of transference, insufficiently pronounced to support effective interpretation, and two or more sessions per week for several months or longer may be required to foster the emergence of therapeutically useful transference reactions.

Also relevant is the likelihood that interpersonal affect will peak sooner and dissolve more readily in people who become affectively engaged with others quickly than in those whose engagements develop more slowly. Hence the rapidly emerging transference reactions of the hysterical patient, although sometimes dramatic, tend to be superficial rather than intense and to give way easily to appropriate interpretation. By contrast, the slowly developing transference reactions of the obsessive patient, although often expressed in muted fashion, tend to be intensely felt and to yield only to a lengthy process of interpretation and working through.[8]

These individual differences explain why psychotherapy with patients who are transference prone may require not only fewer sessions per week but also less total time than similar treatment for patients who are insulated against transference. Such considerations should enter into the original treatment planning because patients' apparent transference propensities will provide some basis for determining how frequent their sessions should be and for estimating how long their treatment will last. Such initial assessments are imperfect, however, and it may become evident after treatment is underway that sessions have not been scheduled frequently enough to elicit transference reactions in a particular patient, in which case session frequency may have to be increased.

As a distinctly different possibility, psychotherapy may in some cases mobilize transference reactions of such intensity as to interfere with a patient's capacity to function effectively either in the treatment or outside it. In their sessions, such patients may become so overwhelmed by their transference feelings that they can no longer distinguish them from reality or sustain the working alliance, despite the therapist's best efforts to help them do so. Outside the treatment, they may become so preoccupied with fantasies and ruminations about the therapist that they cannot attend to their customary responsibilities or carry on in their usual social roles.

When transference reactions become so prepotent that patients insist they are real, can no longer observe and discuss them in ways that further the goals of the treatment, and are prevented by them from continuing to carry on in their usual roles and responsibilities, they are said to be suffering a *transference psychosis.* With few exceptions, transference psychotic reactions make themselves painfully evident to therapists who have evoked them. Patients express intense feelings of love and hate toward their therapist and refuse to consider that these feelings may not be justified in reality; they make impossible demands ("You've got to see me every day and not see any other patients") and become furious or deflated when these demands are not met; and they report frequent periods of anxiety, inability to think clearly, or loss of self-control associated with fantasies and daydreams about the treatment relationship.

These and other manifestations of psychotic transference signify deterioration in a patient's personality organization, because they involve decreased capacity to modulate affective experience and to separate fantasy from reality, and they bring progress in the treatment to a halt, because they represent a total suffusion of patients' observing self by their experiencing self. Hence psychotic transference reactions are inevitably a damaging turn of events in psychotherapy, and they must accordingly be averted wherever possible and reversed whenever they occur.

Susceptibility to psychotic transference reactions usually derives from personality impairments that can be identified during the initial assessment phase of treatment and should alert therapists undertaking expressive psychotherapy to proceed very cautiously. Particularly in work with borderline patients, however, underlying problems in modulating affective experience and maintaining appropriate distance in interpersonal relationships may, at times, be masked by superficial displays of adequate personality integration. Propensities for intense transference reactions can then go unsuspected until such reactions actually begin to emerge. Should this occur, the treatment strategy may need to be shifted to a more supportive and less uncovering approach, one that would have been selected in the first place with benefit of a more accurate initial evaluation.

Adjustments may also be indicated for patients who can tolerate and benefit from a relatively uncovering approach, but whose transference intensity in response to the initially selected frequency of sessions appears greater than can be accommodated within the working alliance. Then a particularly transference-prone patient who is being seen twice weekly, for example, might be continued in uncovering psychotherapy but changed to once-weekly sessions to keep transference reactions from reaching a disruptive level of intensity.[9]

POSITIVE AND NEGATIVE ATTITUDES IN THE TRANSFERENCE

Every transference reaction involves some degree of positive or negative feelings toward the therapist. Although psychotherapists customarily speak in shorthand terms of "the positive transference" and "the negative transference," the positive-negative distinction refers in fact only to the kinds of attitudes patients hold toward their therapist and not to any global feature of their transference. All transference reactions are essentially negative phenomena, in the sense that they always represent distortions of reality and invariably produce resistance. Hence, as elaborated by Singer (1965, pp. 270–278), the phrases "positive transference" and "negative transference" are best used and interpreted as referring only to positive or negative attitudes in the transference.

As a function of their previous experiences and the dispositions they bring to the treatment situation, patients vary in the average or typical feeling tone of their transference reactions. Surly and suspicious patients who harbor considerable ill will toward the important people in their lives are likely to manifest predominantly negative attitudes in the transference, whereas patients whose interpersonal style revolves around idealizing or ingratiating themselves with others tend to display primarily positively toned transference reactions. Accurate monitoring of such differences in the emotional tone of patients' reactions to their therapist provides useful clues to the positive-negative balance of their feelings toward other people in their past and current life. Furthermore, to the extent that unrealistically positive or negative interpersonal attitudes constitute part of a patient's psychological problem, shifts in the prevailing tone of the person's transference reactions over time can serve as an index of progress toward more balanced emotional relationships with others.

Therapist appraisals of whether patients' transference reactions involve primarily positive or primarily negative attitudes can also guide decisions concerning how best to intervene, if at all. Positive and negative transference reactions call for different treatment strategies, particularly because there is generally some advantage to concentrating interventions on negative transference reactions and being somewhat circumspect in the exploration and interpretation of positive attitudes in the transference.

DIRECT AND INDIRECT EXPRESSION OF TRANSFERENCE

Transference reactions vary considerably in how directly they are expressed, and the behaviors by which patients reveal positive or negative feelings toward their therapist on a transference basis range from the very subtle to the patently obvious. First and most indirectly, patients experiencing transference attitudes may without comment display suggestive alterations in their behavior or appearance. Under the influence of positive transference attitudes, for example, patients may begin coming early for sessions or lingering around after them, perhaps striking up an acquaintance with the therapist's receptionist or secretary, as if by this means to gain a more intimate relationship with him or her. They may start appearing for sessions particularly well dressed and groomed, in an effort to elicit the therapist's commendation or sexual interest. Or they may in their posture, gestures, and facial expressions convey a wish to become closer, more attractive, or more responsive to the therapist, for example, by leaning forward in their chair or pulling it closer to where the therapist is sitting, by making seductive body movements, or by frequently smiling or nodding their head agreeably.

Under the influence of negative attitudes, patients may manifest opposite versions of these subtle behavioral indices of transference. They may come late, ask to leave early, and be pointedly uncommunicative with anyone in the reception area, as if to increase their distance from the therapist; they may ignore their dress and grooming, even arriving sloppy and disheveled for their sessions, as if to communicate disdain for the therapist's impressions or to imply that neither the therapy nor the therapist is worth the effort of looking presentable; or they may move their chair away from the therapist and sit back in its farthest recesses, or hold their body rigid and unyielding, or scowl, turn down the corners of their mouth, shake their head from side to side, and otherwise present themselves as dour and disinterested.

As a second and somewhat less indirect mode of expressing transference, patients may begin to comment about the therapist's trappings and his or her profession. With respect to trappings, patients may mention that they like a certain picture in the therapist's office, or that they wish they had as comfortable a chair at home as the one they sit in during their sessions, or that they like the selection of magazines in the waiting room, or that they appreciate the convenience of a bus stop right in front of the therapist's building. Or, if their feeling tone in the transference is primarily negative, patients may produce a litany of veiled jibes or complaints: "I wish you didn't keep it so warm in here"; "There sure are a lot of stairs to climb to get to your office"; "You know, your receptionist isn't very friendly"; "It's too bad you're not located in a more convenient place to get to." Positive or negative, such comments about extensions of the therapist usually mask similarly toned feelings toward the therapist as a person that are not being directly experienced or expressed.

Likewise, implied approval or disapproval of the therapist's profession can be used as an indirect channel for expressing transference. Patients may talk about a friend who profited from psychotherapy, or about society's need for more mental health professionals, or about how interesting and gratifying it must be to listen to people and help them with their problems. Or they may instead give some firsthand accounts of acquaintances who have fared poorly in psychotherapy, or refer to a newspaper article questioning the effectiveness of psychotherapy, or state how dull and unrewarding they would find the therapist's job.

Unlike the transference feelings that such indirect comments express, which involve distortions of reality, the comments themselves may have considerable basis in fact. The therapist's office may indeed be uncomfortably warm or inconveniently located, and certainly there are both successful and unsuccessful outcomes in psychotherapy as well as debate in the literature concerning the effectiveness of this form of treatment. There are accordingly times when such comments call for direct answers that address the real relationship or the working alliance rather than the transference: "I'm sorry about the stairs, but the elevator should be fixed by next week" (real relationship); "There is no guaranteed outcome of the work we're doing together, but there is good reason to expect psychotherapy to be helpful to you, and our agreement involves continuing the treatment only so long as it seems to be beneficial" (working alliance).

For the most part, however, even realistic comments about the therapist's trappings or profession will constitute manifestations of transference that should be explored. A usually helpful way of beginning to identify the probable transference basis of such comments consists of asking oneself, "Why is the patient bringing this up at this time?" Unless reasonable answers to this question indicate a need to bolster the real relationship or the working alliance, the particular comment under consideration should be taken as an indirect expression of positive or negative transference attitudes.

In contrast to the ambiguities of indirect expressions, relatively direct expressions of transference leave little doubt as to their origin in unrealistic feelings and attitudes toward the therapist, even if these feelings and attitudes are not explicitly stated. Most common are evaluative comments patients make about the therapist as a person or about the course of the treatment. If they are feeling positive, they may express interest in or approval of the therapist ("I wonder if you're married"; "You have a nice smile"; "I like the way you handle yourself"); they may report pleasant dreams or fantasies involving the therapist; or they may laud the treatment as a way of pleasing the therapist ("I'm really getting a lot out of this"; "You always seem to know just the right thing to say"). Contrariwise, patients who are feeling negative may find fault with the therapist ("I don't think you're interested in me") or with the treatment ("For all my time and money, I don't see where this is doing me much good"), or they may report dreams and fantasies in which the therapist is an agent or target of hostility or rejection.

Finally, as a fourth level of directness, patients may express transference attitudes openly and explicitly. When expressing positive transference attitudes openly and explicitly, patients do not merely imply their feelings by leaning toward the therapist, admiring the therapist's office decor, or praising his or her skill. Instead, they come right out with words to the effect of "I like you," "I love you," "I wish I could know you better," or "I wish I could have you for a (parent) (spouse) (lover)." When they are expressing negative transference attitudes directly, patients do not beat around the bush with coming late, describing treatment failures they have heard about, or questioning the therapist's competence. Instead, they let the therapist know in so many words, "I'm feeling angry at you," "Everything you do irritates me," or "I don't like talking to you anymore."

Directness of Expression and Awareness of Transference

Appreciating variations in the directness with which transference is expressed helps therapists to recognize its manifestations and also to gauge patients' awareness of their own feelings. When transference is stated explicitly, patients' feelings are as apparent to them as they are to the therapist; as transference manifestations become less direct, the feelings that have given rise to them are increasingly likely to lie outside the patient's awareness.

To illustrate this relationship between indirect expression and lack of awareness of transference, patients who complain about not making progress in the treatment when the facts would suggest otherwise may recognize that they are angry with their therapist and are attempting to punish him or her with this complaint. However, it is also possible for patients to be unaware that negative attitudes they are expressing toward their treatment are unwarranted in reality and reflect negative attitudes they have toward the therapist. Patients commenting only about the uncertain value of psychotherapy in general, and not about their own treatment, or merely assuming a posture of leaning back to increase distance from the therapist, are behaving in ways even farther removed from their origins in underlying transference feelings and probably are even less consciously connected with such feelings.

This is not to say that patients who express transference feelings indirectly are never aware of them. A female patient who wears a particularly short skirt or low-cut blouse to a session may know full well that she has dressed to catch the eye of her male therapist, to whom she feels attracted. As a rule, however, the more indirect their expression of transference, the less likely patients will be to appreciate the meaning and implications of their transference behavior. The distinction between direct and indirect expression of transference thus parallels the distinction between near and remote derivatives drawn in Chapter 8 and suggests similar guidelines for interpretation. Just as near derivatives are more readily interpretable than remote derivatives, relatively direct expressions of transference prove more useful to interpret than relatively indirect transference reactions.

Acting Out of the Transference

A final dimension in the expression of transference that should be recognized when it occurs constitutes a reversal of the usual sequence of events in which transference becomes manifest. Transference reactions, as defined earlier, comprise displacements onto a therapist of thoughts, feelings, and impulses originally experienced toward other people in a patient's life. When powerful affects and attitudes are formed toward therapists in this way, they may be more or less directly expressed in the therapist's presence, or they may in turn be displaced onto people with whom patients interact in their daily life. Thus a man who is angry at his therapist following a session may become unreasonably testy with his wife later that same day, or a woman experiencing sexual feelings toward a male therapist may become attracted to or begin an affair with a man who resembles her therapist in age, appearance, or some other characteristic.

This displacement of attitudes toward a therapist onto people external to the treatment is known as *acting out of the transference* (see Greenson, 1967, pp. 258–263). Although transference feelings can be acted out simultaneously with their being directly or indirectly expressed in the treatment, more commonly such acting out replaces overt manifestations of transference in the therapist's presence. Hence, acting out of the transference always constitutes a resistance to the treatment, because for patients it serves the purpose of preventing their transference attitudes from coming to their therapist's attention.

To circumvent this resistance, therapists need to listen closely for features of patients' behavior that suggest the acting out of transference. In patients who are resisting the emergence of transference during their sessions, some otherwise unaccountable behavior outside the treatment, especially when it is comparable in tone to transference reactions that might have been expected to surface in the sessions, may provide the only clue to the existence of transference reactions that should be identified and explored. Similarly, when patients who are becoming increasingly direct in expressing transference feelings suddenly cease to talk about the treatment relationship and begin engaging in behaviors that are atypical for them and seem to reflect the kinds of feelings they were about to express toward the therapist, acting out of the transference is a likely possibility.

THE EXPLORATION AND INTERPRETATION OF TRANSFERENCE REACTIONS

For reasons noted at the beginning of this chapter, effective exploration and interpretation of transference reactions greatly facilitates progress in psychotherapy.[10] To mount an effective interpretive sequence in response to manifestations of transference, therapists should follow closely the general guidelines for interpretation presented in Chapter 8. These guidelines can be elaborated with particular reference to the interpretation of transference phenomena by turning again to the major questions of *what* aspects of the patient's behavior to select for interpretation, *when* to make these interpretations, and *how* to construct an interpretive sequence.

Selecting Aspects of Transference to Be Interpreted

Although there are no aspects of transference reactions that should always or never be interpreted, there are two priorities in the interpretation of transference. As mentioned earlier, these priorities consist of (a) favoring interpretations of negative attitudes in the transference over interpretations of positive attitudes and (b) favoring interpretations of relatively direct expression of transference over interpretations of relatively indirect expressions.

The favoring of negative over positive transference attitudes as subjects for interpretation is based on some potential disadvantages of interpreting positive feelings toward the therapist. First, because all interpretations are implicitly critical and challenging, interpretations of positive transference can be experienced as demeaning and rejecting. Consider a patient who says, "I'm enjoying coming to see you every week," and who then proceeds to talk in a productive and resistance-free manner about matters relevant to the focus of the therapy. For the therapist to interrupt in an attempt to capitalize on this offhand remark—say by exposing its hypocrisy (patients are after all supposed to be working on personal problems, not enjoying themselves), or by laying bare its hidden meanings (the patient could well be displacing onto the therapist positive feelings that are really felt toward someone else)—is tantamount to a slap in the face. The patient is made to feel foolish, that such pleasantries are frivolous and of no personal interest to the therapist, and that the only value his or her comments have lies in ulterior motives lurking behind them (e.g., "Why did you feel a need to say that to me?").

There is seldom much to be learned from exploring fleeting manifestations of transference, and doing so when they are positively toned can abrade patients' self-respect and diminish their enthusiasm for participating in the treatment. Mild positive transference is too useful an ally in the treatment to be sacrificed by interpretation, especially when the interpretive yield from this effort is insufficient to justify the distress it causes the patient.

Second, because interpretations convey special interest in what patients are thinking or feeling, exploration of positive transference reactions may have a seductive impact. In response to patients who say, "I enjoy coming to see you," for example, therapists who smile pleasantly, lean forward in their chair, and say, "Tell me more about that" cannot help but communicate delight in hearing the patient say nice things about them. Because such delight can imply that a therapist is becoming more than just professionally involved in the treatment relationship, expressions of interest in probable manifestations of positive transference may seduce a patient into continuing to feel and report positive attitudes in the expectation that the therapist will soon be reciprocating them. Seductiveness of this kind has the marked disadvantage of stimulating positive transference to peaks of intensity that generate nonproductive resistance and set patients up for a harder fall and more intense negative transference reactions when they finally realize that the therapist is not going to reciprocate.

On the other hand, the possible disadvantages of calling attention to positive transference feelings do not justify ignoring them at the risk of compromising the working alliance. Consider, for example, a patient who is progressing well in treatment to the accompaniment of numerous manifestations of positive transference; suppose this patient inquires about the therapist's age and indicates that he or she will be very upset if an answer to this question is not forthcoming, or suppose that this patient is obviously skirting some important subject that would probably be painful or embarrassing to discuss. To sustain this patient's positive feelings in the treatment situation, the therapist would have to state his or her age in the first instance and allow continued avoidance of the important subject in the second instance. Taking either course would make concessions that violate the treatment contract; that is, the therapist's actions would be serving primarily to help the patient feel good for the moment, rather than to promote increased self-understanding. Therapists cease to discharge their responsibility if they become so enamored of patients' positive transference feelings that they bend over backward to sustain them.

The potential disadvantages of possibly rejecting or seducing patients by calling attention to their positive transference attitudes have no counterparts in the interpretation of negative transference. Because patients experiencing negative transference are already feeling out of sorts in the treatment relationship, there is little to be lost in the way of enthusiastic patient participation by setting out to explore these negative feelings. Moreover, because accurate interpretations demonstrate therapist interest and empathy, they are unlikely to reinforce negative patient attitudes in the same way as they reinforce positive patient attitudes. To the contrary, when negative transference is producing sticky, unpleasant exchanges in the treatment or threatening to disrupt it completely, timely interpretation of the transference behavior may lead not only to increased self-understanding by the patient but also to a period of convivial affect and renewed dedication to the work of the therapy.

As for favoring direct over indirect expressions of transference as subjects for interpretation, it follows from the discussion on page 220 that interpretive sequences should be preferentially aimed at transference behavior that is relatively clearly and closely tied to the feelings and attitudes underlying it. In reference to the stages of directness delineated earlier, this means that suggestive behaviors and comments about the therapist's trappings and profession will not ordinarily be prime subjects for transference interpretation. Arriving late for sessions or talking about negative outcomes in psychotherapy may become sufficiently pronounced to call for resistance interpretations, but transference sources of such resistance behavior are likely to be relatively remote and provide a less compelling focus for interpretation than possible sources of the behavior in characterological resistance, content resistance, or resistance to change.

On the other hand, personal comments about therapists and open expressions of feeling and attitudes toward them point directly to the existence of transference reactions and usually say a good deal about the precise nature and intensity of these reactions. Transference interpretations of such behavior therefore have relatively good prospects for being accurate, easy to document, and accessible to a patient's conscious awareness. Accordingly, transference interpretations should be reserved for relatively direct expressions of transference attitudes and applied sparingly if at all to its relatively indirect manifestations.

DECIDING WHEN TO INTERPRET TRANSFERENCE

Like interpretations in general, transference interpretations should be made when patients are bordering on awareness of them and are in a receptive frame of mind to consider them, and when the therapist is reasonably certain of the interpretation and prepared to document it. Additionally, transference interpretations should not follow too closely on the heels of prior interpretations and should be followed by an adequate opportunity for discussion. In addition to conforming to these general requirements for good timing and proper dosage in the delivery of interpretations, as discussed in Chapter 8, transference interpretations should be reserved mainly for times (a) when the transference is producing marked resistance, (b) when transference reactions are of moderate intensity, sufficient to be demonstrable but not so intense as to be intolerable, and (c) when significant information is likely to emerge from the interpretive sequence.

When Transference Is Producing Marked Resistance

All transference reactions produce some resistance, by virtue of distracting patient's attention from the problems for which they have sought help. However, just as resistance needs to be allowed to build to a certain point before it can be interpreted effectively, so transference is best interpreted when it is interfering markedly with patients' talking about themselves and their difficulties. To illustrate this consideration in timing, suppose that during a session for which the therapist was late a male patient talks about expecting too much from people and cites as an example an excessive tendency to feel irritated when someone keeps him waiting. Yet suppose further that, after citing this example, he continues to talk freely and meaningfully about his problems in interpersonal relationships.

In this situation, the therapist could with reasonable certainty begin a transference interpretation as follows: "I wonder if you were irritated with me for being late today and keeping you waiting." However, because the patient's irritation had not been sufficiently pressing for him to express it directly or otherwise let it interfere with his continuing to work in the treatment, such an interpretation would have little or no impact. Only if this man had become so irritated with the delay that he had refused to talk at all or had in some other way displayed marked resistance would there be adequate basis for helping him see his transference behavior as unusual and worth exploring.

Timing transference interpretations to coincide with marked resistance is advisable not only because the potential impact of the interpretations is thereby enhanced, but also because there is some disadvantage to interpreting transference in the context of fleeting resistance. Specifically, the more therapists interrupt productive, task-oriented behavior to interpret elements of transference that are producing only minimal resistance, the more patients are likely to perceive them as picky and depreciatory, as more interested in being clever than in being helpful, and as insensitive to the importance of the real-life experience and events they have been attempting to report.[11]

When Transference Is of Moderate Intensity

As already implied, interpretations of attitudes, feelings, and impulses in the transference should ordinarily be deferred until these reactions have become sufficiently intense for patients to be made aware of them readily and helped to distinguish them from real reactions to the therapist. In the case of the man who mentioned being irritated by people who keep him waiting but went right on to talk productively, considerable effort might have been necessary to convince him that he was feeling irritated with the therapist for being late. Even if he were to become so convinced, it could hardly be argued that his mild and nondisruptive irritation in response to the therapist's actual tardiness was inappropriate to the circumstances and therefore worth exploring.

Some degree of intensity, then, usually enough to produce relatively direct behavioral manifestations and result in resistance behavior, is necessary before transference reactions can be effectively interpreted. On the other hand, allowing transference to build to an interpretable intensity should stop short of sitting idly by while transference reactions reach an intensity that overruns the working alliance. Even within a treatment plan intended to allow the formation of a transference neurosis, no single reaction or set of reactions should be permitted to become so intense that the patient can no longer participate in trying to understand them. Patients who only want to make love with their therapist or are so angry at the therapist that they refuse to continue in the treatment have developed a transference intensity that should have been averted by interpretations of these positive and negative feelings when they were still in a more formative stage.

Correct appraisal of the intensity of transference is particularly important whenever transference feelings are being expressed only indirectly and without the patient's awareness. For example, a patient who scrupulously avoids saying anything personal to or about the therapist during sessions but who brings the therapist gifts, "forgetfully" leaves belongings behind in the therapist's office, and begins to affect some of the therapist's mannerisms may be on the verge of uncomfortably intense positive transference feelings. Because of the intensity of feeling they reflect, such behaviors call for interpretation, even though as indirect expressions of positive transference they would ordinarily have low priority as subjects for interpretation. Indirect manifestations of strong negative attitudes should similarly be recognized and responded to before the transference builds to a disruptive intensity.

To summarize the considerations in interpreting transference presented thus far, indirect expressions of mild positive transference attitudes should receive the least interpretive attention and direct expressions of intense negative transference the most. The appropriateness and potential utility of interpreting transference increases as positive transference elements shade into negative ones, as mild transference reactions become moderately intense, and as indirect expressions of transference grow increasingly direct.

When Significant Information Is Likely to Emerge from the Interpretive Sequence

Generally speaking, there is always something to be learned from an accurately conceived, properly timed, and aptly phrased interpretation. In a situation calling for interpretation, however, interpretations addressed to transference elements in patients' behavior may be more or less informative compared with other aspects of their behavior that might be interpreted. Independently of its feeling tone, directness, and intensity, a transference reaction should therefore be weighed for its information value before it is selected for interpretation.

To clarify what is meant by the "information value" of a transference reaction, it is first necessary to emphasize that the interpretation of transference is not itself an end in the psychotherapy process, to be implemented whenever possible. Rather, transference interpretations are a vehicle for facilitating progress in the treatment, to be employed when they will help to alleviate resistances or to identify aspects of patients' interpersonal life that might otherwise escape notice. Because there are resistances in which transference elements play only a peripheral role, and manifestations of transference that reveal nothing about patients beyond what they already recognize, there will be circumstances in which little stands to be learned from selecting transference as the focus of an interpretive sequence, even when it is possible to do so.

The example of the tardy therapist and the patient irritated with being kept waiting can be used to illustrate both kinds of circumstances in which transference interpretations will have negligible information value. The patient in this instance followed his passing reference to being irritated when people make him wait by talking freely and meaningfully about his interpersonal problems, and his working productively in this way obviated any therapist intervention. Suppose, however, that this man had continued as follows: "I remember one time just last week. . . . I don't even like to think about it. . . . I guess it really wasn't the same kind of thing anyway." Then his comments would have suggested resistance and called for an interpretation, but still not an interpretation of transference. The type of resistance most probably involved in "I don't even like to think about it" is resistance to content, not transference resistance. Hence a transference interpretation, even if appropriate to some aspects of the patient's behavior, would contribute little in this instance to understanding or resolving his resistance of the moment.

As for what the patient is already aware of in this example, the major inference to be drawn from his feeling irritated at the therapist for keeping him waiting is that he is generally prone to irritability in interpersonal situations because he expects too much of people—yet this is exactly what he goes on to say without benefit of therapist intervention. When transference reactions thus mirror interpersonal attitudes and dispositions the patient already appreciates full well and can discuss freely, chiming in with interpretations will offer no more than a blinding glimpse of the obvious.

On the other hand, behavior suggesting transference resistance or some previously unmentioned interpersonal attitudes offers considerable potential for something to be learned from a transference interpretation.

Suppose the patient in the example, invited into the therapist's office 5 minutes later than his session was scheduled to begin, had sat silently for a while and then said, "There were some things I wanted to tell you about today, but now I don't feel like it—I'm feeling irritated with you instead." This response would constitute resistance, because it pushes aside the work of the treatment, and it would identify transference as the source of the resistance, since it is the patient's preoccupation with his feelings toward the therapist that is preventing him from taking up his task.

Furthermore, the patient's poutiness in response to a delay of only 5 minutes—as if to say "You were mean so now I'm not going to talk to you"—would suggest that he may overreact to similar situations outside of the treatment. Hence an interpretive focus on his exaggerated, maladaptive response to the therapist could serve both to relieve his resistance and to help him recognize a personality disposition that has been limiting his pleasure and effectiveness in interpersonal relationships.

CONSTRUCTING INTERPRETIVE SEQUENCES AIMED AT TRANSFERENCE

Effective interpretation of transference reactions requires a sequence of interventions intended to help patients clarify, explore, and understand aspects of their behavior that are influenced by unrealistic feelings, attitudes, and impulses toward the therapist. In considering specific procedures for the interpretation of transference, it should be kept in mind that the question of how to interpret transference becomes relevant only when the previously discussed criteria for what and when to interpret are satisfied.

Clarifying Transference Reactions

The therapist's first response to relatively direct expressions of transference otherwise suitable for interpretation should be to clarify that they represent a distortion of reality and accordingly merit the patient's curiosity and attention. As noted earlier, the distortions that underlie transference behavior may involve inaccurate perception of either the therapist or of the treatment contract, and one or both possibilities may have to be addressed as patients are helped to recognize that their transference reactions constitute unusual behavior that needs to be observed as well as experienced.

When a transference reaction involves misperception of the therapist, the therapist's task is to point out how the patient's perceptions diverge from reality. The following two examples, similar in kind and both taken from the beginning of sessions, illustrate such initial clarification of relatively directly expressed transference feelings:

PATIENT: You seem in a sour mood today, like you're ready to bite my head off.

THERAPIST: What suggests that to you?

PATIENT: I don't know. I'm just not getting the right vibes, like you're not in a good mood or you're feeling down on me.

THERAPIST: I'm not aware of being in a bad mood or feeling down on you. I wonder if there might be some reason why you're perceiving me in that way.

PATIENT: (pauses, appears thoughtful) Well, I suppose maybe there is. I've got something I think I should tell you, and I don't know how you'll take it. (pause) I've decided to move in with my boyfriend, and I have the feeling you may disapprove.

PATIENT: (long pause) I don't know what to talk about today. (pause) It seems hard to get started. (pause) You look tense and anxious.

THERAPIST: I hear you saying that *you* are finding it hard to talk, but that *I* look tense and anxious.

PATIENT: (quickly and loudly) Oh I can talk, that's for sure, I wouldn't have any trouble talking—(breaks off, then proceeds more softly) I guess you're right. I am feeling anxious because there's something that's happened that I need to tell you about, and I'm worried what you'll say about it.

Both of these examples are richly revealing in terms of the psychotherapy process. Both illustrate resistance manifested in reluctance to talk; in both the resistance seems clearly derived from transference concerns, namely, apprehension about what the therapist will think or how the therapist will respond; and the transference reaction in each case appears primarily positive, centering around a wish to retain the therapist's approval. Additionally in the first example, the patient's reference to moving in with her boyfriend could be subtly seductive (an attempt to arouse the therapist's jealousy or sexual fantasies) or could signify some acting out of the transference.

When transference distorts the treatment contract, the therapist needs first to contrast the patient's feelings with the relevant terms of the original agreement. Suppose as commonly happens a patient chides the therapist for not talking more, for not giving advice, or for not answering questions. The therapist might then make the following kind of response:

> You say you're upset with me because I'm not telling you what to do, as if I'm not interested in helping you. Yet the basis on which we agreed to proceed in psychotherapy is that I would try to help you understand yourself

better, so that you could make your own decisions about what to do, not that I would advise you. So there must be some other reason aside from what I'm actually doing that is causing you to feel upset with me.

As in the case of resistance behavior, such transference phenomena arising during the middle phase of therapy accentuate the importance of having an explicit and mutually endorsed treatment contract. Therapists operating in the absence of such prior agreements to refer back to will have difficulty helping patients recognize that their transference reactions embody feelings and attitudes inappropriate to the reality of the treatment situation. Only when it can be demonstrated to patients' satisfaction that their transference behavior is unrealistic and hence stems from other than its apparent motives can this behavior be utilized effectively to enhance self-understanding.

Exploring Transference Reactions

Once a transference reaction has been demonstrated sufficiently well for a patient to perceive it as behavior not rooted in current reality and hence worthy of being understood further, the transference behavior should be explored for its possible origins and implications. Consider, for example, a female patient who has angrily and without justification accused her therapist of not being interested in her. What is it like for this woman to feel angry and what fantasies are associated with the experience? In what other situations, past and present, has she experienced anger related to the perceived disinterest of others? Toward what other people has she felt such anger and how has she typically expressed it? The answers to these and similar questions help to elucidate the original instances of interpersonal conflict that are being reenacted in the transference and to identify the underlying feelings and attitudes toward significant people in a patient's life that are being displaced onto the therapist.

Exploring the dimensions, history, and more widespread expressions of a transference reaction can proceed only as far at a particular point in the treatment as patients are prepared to go in their recollection and reporting of events. Partial interpretations and requests for associations may help press the inquiry beyond where it initially seems destined to end, but when patients have exhausted their available ideas bearing on a transference reaction, the exploration will have to be dropped until some further expressions of the particular reaction occur.

Understanding Transference Reactions

When exploration of a transference reaction has yielded sufficient information to support appropriate interpretations, patients should then be helped to understand their transference experience in ways that teach them about their interpersonal experience in general. The key element in this process is assisting patients to generalize from their transference reactions to the previously unrecognized attitudes, feelings, and impulses toward others that have shaped their transference behavior.

Interpretations aimed at helping patients use the treatment relationship to draw inferences about their interpersonal experiences in general may focus on either past or current events in patients' lives. To illustrate use of the transference in recapturing interpersonal experiences from the past, consider the following exchange between a female patient with chronic feelings of inferiority, especially in relation to men, and a male therapist toward whom some negative reactions on her part have just been clarified as transference:

PATIENT: Now that you've pointed it out, I can see that you haven't been acting any different than usual, and you probably had no expression on your face at all. Yet when I started talking today, I did have the impression you had some kind of superior look about you, like you were mocking me, and it really made me feel bad. Where did I get that impression from?

THERAPIST: I wonder what other people in your life may have given you the same impression.

PATIENT: Other people? Let me think a minute. (pause) Hey, you know I haven't thought about this in a long time, and I don't like to think about it now, but my father always used to do that to me. Anytime I wanted to tell him something, or about something I was proud of doing, he'd sit back there with that smug smile on his face, mocking and patronizing as hell, and make me feel like I was an insignificant worm. Boy, did that get to me—I never knew whether to feel more angry or more crushed, and I think I felt a mixture of both.

THERAPIST: So you were reacting to me just now as if I were your father and you were still a little girl.

PATIENT: It seems silly, but that's right.

THERAPIST: So here you are, a grown woman, feeling inferior to men because you still see yourself as an insignificant little girl and men as being superior to you, like your father was.

In this example, then, the transference phenomena were used as a clue to real experiences in the patient's past life that had probably contributed to her psychological problems as an adult, and the therapist was able to help her recall and begin reexperiencing some relevant and unresolved conflicts from her childhood. A possible alternative in the example would have been to encourage the patient to explore further her memories about her father and to vent more of her pent-up affect toward him, rather than move so directly to the transference interpretation that was offered. As with the interpretation of transference, however, the reworking of past experience is not an end in psychotherapy, but only a vehicle for increased self-understanding and positive behavior change in the present. The emphasis in the example was placed first on helping the patient answer her very relevant question ("Where did I get that impression from?") by accounting for her distorted perception of the therapist, and second on helping her appreciate that similar distortions in her present experience, based on childhood feelings and attitudes lingering beyond the time when they were justified in reality, probably participate in her current difficulties in relationships with men.

Transference reactions can be used in much the same fashion to generalize directly to current interpersonal relationships outside the treatment, without necessarily proceeding through a recollection of past events. Suppose in the preceding example the therapist instead of saying, "I wonder what other people in your life may have given you the same impression," had said, "If you've had this kind of impression here, there must be other situations in which you have a similar reaction without there being any real basis for it." The patient might then have begun talking about some of her current relationships with men, recognizing in the process that she was indeed prone to feeling patronized and inferior without sufficient cause, just as she had in relation to the therapist.

In this latter version of the example, the patient is helped to recognize *how* she is distorting her current interpersonal experience, whereas in the original version, which involves tracing back the origins of transference feelings before attempting to generalize from them, the patient is helped to understand *why* as well as how she tends to misperceive the attitudes of others. The choice between a past or current focus in the interpretation of transference will depend on the salient content of the interviews and on the intensity of the treatment. With regard to interview content, a focus on either past or present concerns may be closer to a patient's awareness and hence more timely to pursue. If the woman in this example had been talking about childhood experiences, perhaps describing members of her family but pointedly omitting to mention her father, there would have been good reason to direct the interpretation of her transference reaction toward her earlier experiences with people, with particular expectation that previously repressed thoughts about her father might emerge. If on the other hand she had not been talking about childhood at all but had been complaining at length about current interpersonal difficulties, then an effort to generalize directly from the transference to those ongoing situations would have been indicated.

Regarding the intensity of the treatment, it should be kept in mind that the origins of transference reactions are usually more remote from a patient's awareness than their implications for his or her current behavior. Hence in a relatively uncovering treatment approach, it is likely to be appropriate to trace the past origins of transference as well as to elucidate its current impact, whereas in a relatively supportive approach it may be appropriate to limit the interpretation of transference to a focus on current events only.

Yet in planning their strategy therapists should recognize that some patients' needs may be adequately met by generalizations from transference reactions to current interpersonal behavior, whether or not they have the interest and capacity to unravel the origins of their interpersonal attitudes. Merely realizing from their experiences in the transference that they are currently misperceiving other people in their life may be sufficient to help people gradually bring their perceptions into better tune with reality and thereby resolve the problems that have brought them into treatment. Therapists must be prepared to appreciate such improvement as meaningful and avoid insisting that the causes of a patient's problems must all be traced to their earliest origins. When the goals of the treatment, as expressed in desired changes in behavior or self-attitudes, are met within the context of a contemporary focus on transference reactions, there is little reason to push for a historical accounting of their origins. This point of view concerning the interpretation of transference has obvious implications for deciding on when to terminate psychotherapy, which is the topic considered in Chapter 12 following discussion in Chapter 11 of the therapist's side of the treatment relationship.

NOTES

1. It should be noted that clinicians over the years have conceptualized transference in many different ways. However, most dynamically oriented therapists concur that transference reactions are ubiquitous in interpersonal relationships, although especially likely to emerge and become intense in the psychotherapy situation, and that these unwarranted reactions can be usefully distinguished from real aspects of the treatment relationship (Blanck & Blanck, 1994, Chapter 17; Gelso & Carter, 1994; Greenson & Wexler, 1969; Luborsky, Barber, & Crits-Christoph, 1990; Oremland, 1991, Chapter 3; L. Stone, 1995). For other reviews concerning the evolution and status of the concept of transference

readers are referred to Abend (1993), A. Cooper (1987a), Macalpine (1950), and Panken (1996).

2. As noted by Ellman (1991, pp. 47–48), the concept of the working alliance, although not formulated by Freud, is an extension of what he termed the "unobjectionable" part of the transference and regarded as comprising the patient's positive attitudes toward collaborating with the therapist. Current appreciation of how the working alliance functions as an integral part of the patient-therapist relationship was shaped in contributions of Bibring (1954), Zetzel (1956), Greenson (1965b, 1967, pp. 190–216), and Bordin (1979), whose further elaboration of this concept was noted in Chapter 3.

3. Like positive attitudes toward collaboration in the treatment, positive feelings toward the therapist were embraced by Freud (1912/1958b) within his concept of the "unobjectionable transference," because they facilitate rather than hinder the work of the treatment. Strictly speaking, however, these reality-based feelings are not transferential at all because they do not involve any distorted perception of the therapist or any attribution to the therapist of qualities he or she does not possess.

4. Sullivan's concept of parataxic distortion and its implications for transference are nicely summarized by Singer (1965, pp. 258–264). The notions presented at the beginning of this chapter, of transference as a pervasive interpersonal phenomenon rather than a phenomenon unique to the treatment situations, and of transference as reflecting attitudes toward people in general as well as attitudes toward specific people, emerged largely from the writings of Sullivan.

5. As observed by numerous authors, a "blank screen" approach to conducting psychotherapy differs substantially from the warm, personal, and engaged manner in which Freud himself actually interacted with his own patients (Blanton, 1971; Gay, 1988; Lipton, 1977; Wortis, 1954).

6. Therapists' relationships with their patients, particularly with respect to how much reality can and should pass between them, may be complicated by circumstances that prevent them from totally avoiding dual or even multiple relationships. These complicating relationships can range from chance encounters in social or business situations that require therapists to conduct themselves in "real" ways, to the daily experiences of therapists practicing in small or tightly knit communities in which they must of necessity interact with and become personally known to their patients well beyond the confines of psychotherapy sessions in their office. The nature of possible role conflicts in these circumstances and guidelines for dealing with them in an ethical and psychotherapeutically

constructive manner are discussed by Borys and Pope (1989), Faulkner and Faulkner (1997), Gody (1996), and Schank and Skovholt (1997).

7. The usefulness of the transference neurosis concept is limited by the lack of any more precise criteria for identifying when it has come into being. Nevertheless, transference neurosis is commonly used as a synonym for intense transference reactions, and the formation of an intense transference has often been proposed as a phenomenon differentiating psychoanalysis from other forms of dynamically oriented psychotherapy. Discussions of psychoanalytic views concerning how transference neurosis develops and the role it plays in the therapeutic process are provided by A. Cooper (1987b), Little (1981), Reed (1994), and Wallerstein (1995, Chapter 14).

8. The previously cited books by S. Johnson (1994), Millon (1996), Shapiro (1989), and M. Stone (1993) elaborate on these contrasting personality styles and their implications for individual differences in the handling of interpersonal affect. Also informative in this regard are books by Horowitz (1991), Mueller and Aniskiewicz (1986), and Salzman (1968).

9. For additional reading and case illustrations concerning the emergence and resolution of psychotic transference reactions, contributions by Little (1981) and Wallerstein (1967) are recommended. The nature of borderline personality organization, including the intense transference propensities of people with this condition, is elaborated by Chessick (1983), Goldstein (1996), Kernberg (1967), Kernberg et al. (1989), and Rockland (1992).

10. Research documenting the effectiveness and beneficial impact of well-conceived transference interpretations is reported by Joyce and Piper (1993); Luborsky et al. (1990); and Piper, McCallum, Azim, and Joyce (1993). In the opinion of Strupp (1996a), a salient lesson learned from research and practice in psychotherapy has been the critical role in all successful cases of skillful therapist management of the patient-therapist relationship.

11. Not all therapists agree concerning the timing of transference interpretations to coincide with manifestations of marked resistance. Gill (1982), for example, encourages interpreting resistance implications of what patients say and do at virtually every possible opportunity, beginning early in the treatment and regardless of whether resistance elements are clearly manifest. Partly as a result of Gill's influence, as observed by Kernberg (1993), contemporary practice of dynamically oriented psychotherapy involves greater focus on and earlier interpretation of transference phenomena than had traditionally been considered advisable. Nevertheless,

there remains substantial endorsement of the view presented here, that transference interpretations can be presented and utilized most effectively in the context of resistance that has built to substantial proportions, and that early transference interpretations should be employed only in a superficial manner, to legitimize such attention to the treatment relationship, rather than as an in-depth effort to unearth powerful underlying feelings (see Levy, 1990, Chapter 5).

CHAPTER 11

The Psychotherapy Relationship: Countertransference

C OUNTERTRANSFERENCE IN psychotherapy consists of inappropriate or irrational reactions by therapists to a patient's behavior. Countertransference reactions parallel transference in reverse, in that they comprise displacements by the therapist onto a patient of thoughts, feelings, and impulses that are not justified in reality by anything the patient has said or done.

Like transference, countertransference was originally viewed solely as a hindrance to psychotherapy that must be avoided for progress to occur. Freud (1910b/1957a) admonished each therapist to "recognize this countertransference in himself and overcome it," because "no psycho-analyst goes further than his own complexes and internal resistances permit" (p. 145). However, subsequent experience has indicated that countertransference reactions can at times be turned to advantage, because they have the potential for teaching therapists something about themselves and about unverbalized feelings and attitudes of their patients.

In further parallel with transference, countertransference interacts with real aspects of the treatment relationship and with the working alliance between patient and therapist. Additionally, as with transference, the ways in which countertransference develops and becomes manifest can be described by distinguishing between generalized and specific reactions and by elaborating individual differences in the intensity, feeling tone, and directness with which these reactions are expressed.[1]

THE NATURE AND CONTROL OF
COUNTERTRANSFERENCE REACTIONS

Because countertransference reactions mirror transference reactions, virtually everything said in Chapter 10 about inappropriate or irrational reactions of patients to therapists (transference) applies equally to inappropriate or irrational reactions of therapists to patients (countertransference). Without reiterating each parallel between these phenomena, the following discussion translates the nature and control of transference reactions into the language of countertransference.

COUNTERTRANSFERENCE, REALITY, AND THE WORKING ALLIANCE

Defining countertransference as *inappropriate* or *irrational* reactions by therapists to a patient's behavior implies that the treatment relationship is complex and multifaceted from the therapist's as well as from the patient's point of view. Although some clinicians have suggested that all therapist feelings toward a patient constitute countertransference, it is generally considered more accurate and useful to distinguish countertransference both from realistic reactions to a patient's behavior and from attitudes based on the working alliance (see Blum & Goodman, 1995).[2]

The Real Relationship

As people in their own right, all therapists carry a set of values with them into the treatment room. They may feel personal dislike toward patients who are racially bigoted or anger toward patients who have been abusive to their children. They may feel more sympathy for a patient who has suffered financial reversals than for one who has been disappointed in love, or vice versa. They may find some patients physically attractive, consider some particularly admirable for their talents or achievements, and regard some as people they would enjoy knowing socially had they met them in that context.

Such reactions, stemming as they do from congruities between therapists' values and their patient's actual characteristics or conduct, constitute reality. Unlike countertransference, they do not involve distorted perceptions of patients or displacements onto them of approval or opprobrium that has not been merited. Although there is accordingly little to be learned from exploring these real reactions, therapists need to be sufficiently aware of them to prevent them from diluting their commitment to the working alliance. Whenever real reactions threaten to impair therapist effectiveness, as for example when a therapist finds it difficult to respect a particular patient as a person, serious consideration should be given to transferring the patient to another therapist.[3]

Similarly inevitable are realistic reactions to specific bits of patient be-havior during treatment sessions, especially expressions of transference. Therapists may feel irritated with a patient who tracks mud into the of-fice; they may take pleasure in being complimented for their perspicacity and offense at being assailed for a lack of understanding; they may feel gratified when patients are progressing well in the treatment and disap-pointed when progress comes to a standstill. Whereas these kinds of re-actions may escalate into countertransference, they can also remain at the level of the real relationship between therapist and patient, as long as the therapist's feelings remain appropriate in kind and intensity to the patient's behavior.

To elaborate this last point, a therapist may realistically be annoyed at having mud tracked into the office; if the therapist becomes furious, he or she is probably experiencing a countertransference reaction. A therapist may realistically enjoy compliments and resent criticisms; therapists who are thrilled by patient's praise or devastated by their censure are experi-encing countertransference. Therapists may realistically feel better about a course of the treatment when it is progressing well than when it is not; if their dedication to the treatment ebbs and flows with the tides of its progress, however, they are experiencing countertransference. Weisman (1991, p. 118) summarizes such clues to the boundary between reality and countertransference by pointing out that it is "when we find ourselves angry, disappointed, exasperated, gratified, especially frustrated, or in some other way imposing our individual imperatives" that therapists are likely to feel toward and respond to patients in ways that reflect counter-transference distortions.

In addition to reacting emotionally to patients on a realistic basis, ther-apists (as described in Chapter 10) also initiate or respond to certain aspects of a patient's real relationship to them. They say "Hello" and "Goodbye," they respond to "Happy New Year" with "Same to you," they smile at humorous events, and they express condolences should tragedy cross a patient's life. When appropriately modulated, these expressions of humanity sustain a patient's belief in the therapist's wish and capacity to be of help, and they participate in distinguishing the real relationship between therapist and patient from either countertransference or the working alliance.

The Working Alliance

From the perspective of therapists, the working alliance comprises how they feel and behave toward patients as a function of their commitment to the treatment contract. They are dedicated to helping their patients understand themselves better, resolve their psychological difficulties, and more fully realize their human potential. They are obliged to respect their patients' integrity and their right to be themselves, even as they are attempting to help them find more effective and rewarding ways of being themselves. They are required to listen in a relatively nonjudgmental manner, to respond primarily for the purpose of deepening a patient's self-understanding, and to refrain from using the treatment relationship to gratify their own personal needs.

The therapist's behavior in these respects, being rational and appropriate, does not constitute countertransference. Nonetheless, the working alliance is no more a real relationship for the therapist than it is for the patient. Unlike real interpersonal relationships, which involve a measure of spontaneity and mutual need gratification, the working alliance invokes an asymmetrical, nonmutual relationship and specific guidelines for how and when the parties to it shall interact. In keeping most of their personal feelings to themselves, in passing no judgments, in seeking satisfaction only for their professional needs, in responding interpretively to what is said to them, in setting a schedule of appointments, and in continuing the relationship for as long as the patient requires, therapists are behaving in a manner contrived to serve the aims and goals of psychotherapy and not as they would ordinarily behave in conducting their interpersonal affairs.

Countertransference

When therapists feel or act toward patients in ways that are neither part of the real relationship, rationally justified by the circumstances, nor part of the working alliance, appropriate to the terms of the treatment contract, they are manifesting countertransference. More than from the real relationship or the working alliance, it is from these countertransference aspects of their relationships with patients that therapists have an opportunity to increase their understanding of themselves and of the people they are trying to help. Whereas they must be sufficiently attentive to their parts in the real relationship and the working alliance to modulate the former and sustain the latter, neither will provide them much information beyond what is already explicit in content of the treatment. On the other hand, because countertransference reactions are inappropriate or irrational reactions of the therapist to a patient's behavior, they often furnish otherwise unavailable clues to both the therapist's and the patient's underlying motives and concerns.

The ways in which a therapist's distortions can provide information about a patient's personality may initially be difficult to conceive. However, countertransference, like transference, always has some foundation in reality on which the edifice of unjustified feelings or attitudes is built. Patients who observe a therapist stifling a yawn and accuse the therapist of not caring about the treatment are overreacting to the situation (transference), but they have after all seen the therapist behave in a manner usually indicative of boredom or disinterest (reality). Similarly, searching out the real features of a patient's behavior that have triggered a countertransference reaction can often reveal previously undetected aspects of the patient's personality.

Suppose, for example, that a therapist begins to feel drowsy during a session, despite having had ample sleep the night before and sitting with a patient who is talking freely. Because there is no realistic basis for this therapist being drowsy, and because the working alliance calls for being attentive at all times, his or her apparently flagging interest in what the patient is saying is irrational and inappropriate and constitutes a countertransference reaction. But why should the therapist be inattentive, and what could the patient be doing to precipitate the therapist's inattentiveness at this particular time? The answer may be that the patient, despite talking freely about seemingly important matters, is in fact talking around issues central to the work of the treatment rather than about them. Should this be the case, the therapist's difficulty in paying attention may serve as a clue to such resistance behavior.

In a similar vein, therapists may find themselves getting annoyed with a particular patient, out of proportion to any real circumstances and contrary to their prescribed nonjudgmental role. Why are they becoming inappropriately irritated and what is the patient doing to irritate them? Could the patient have some underlying motivation for wanting to be irritating? Could this be a manifestation of resistance unconsciously intended to terminate the treatment by provoking the therapist into discharging the patient, or does the patient have masochistic needs that he or she is seeking to gratify by goading the therapist into being punitive? Asking such questions and considering such possibilities can often help therapists utilize their countertransference reactions to identify needs and impulses that patients are not verbalizing.

CONTROLLING THE COUNTERTRANSFERENCE

As discussed in Chapter 10 it is important to "safeguard" the transference component of the treatment relationship, which dictates that therapists be circumspect in how much they reveal about themselves in order to maximize what can be learned from how patients perceive them. However, such safeguarding is neither possible nor desirable for countertransference. Therapists need to discover as much as they can about a patient, not remain in shadowy ignorance to avoid contaminating their impressions with fact. The more effectively they function in this task, identifying the true nature of patients' feelings and attitudes, the less opportunity there will be for them to misperceive these feelings and attitudes on a countertransference basis.

Although therapists should therefore do nothing to safeguard the countertransference, they do need to prevent countertransference reactions from interfering with their commitment to the working alliance, just as they strive to prevent patients' commitments from being eroded by transference reactions. To exert such control over their countertransference reactions, therapists must be able to recognize them when they occur and abort any untoward influence they might have on their conduct of the treatment.[4]

Suppose, for example, a therapist is feeling unusually sympathetic or solicitous toward a patient and allowing sessions to run several minutes overtime. Suppose further that the additional time is being offered not in response to some crisis or emergency in the patient's life, but only because the patient asked for it or the therapist found the sessions "too interesting" to cut off. In such a situation, the therapist is probably experiencing positive countertransference that he or she should immediately bring under control by returning to the prescribed session length. Whenever therapists continue out of insensitivity to their countertransference to give more of themselves than is called for by the treatment contract or by some urgent circumstances, they risk seducing a patient into unrealistic positive expectations about their relationship and thereby complicating resolution of the transference.

As another example of controlling countertransference, consider a session in which the patient mentions a concern that has previously been the subject of several detailed interpretive sequences. The patient says, "I just don't have any idea of what that could relate to," and the therapist barks in return, "We've been over that a dozen times, but you just don't seem to be making any use of our work together." Although the patient's behavior in this example may indeed reflect resistance or even an inability to profit from uncovering psychotherapy, neither possibility justifies the therapist expressing such pique. Disappointment and frustration may realistically be the therapist's lot in such situations, but anger toward the patient has no appropriate place here, should be recognized as countertransference, and ought to be kept from entering into either the therapist's words or tone of voice. Otherwise therapists risk responding in ways that gratify their own needs more than they meet their commitment to helping patients understand themselves.

Thus countertransference is important in psychotherapy not only because of what therapists may learn from it, but also because recognizing and controlling countertransference is a necessary part of the therapist's commitment to maintaining a constructive working alliance and providing patients a therapeutic climate. In their zeal to restrain expressions of countertransference, however, therapists should be careful not to suppress appropriate responses in the context of the real relationship. As discussed in Chapters 9 and 10, therapists who hold all of their personal comments and reactions firmly in check fail to demonstrate the human qualities essential to sustaining the real relationship, and total suppression of freedom in therapists' reactions to their patients isolates the treatment from real life in a manner that is as disadvantageous for the therapist as for the patient.

ORIGINS AND MANIFESTATIONS OF COUNTERTRANSFERENCE

Countertransference originates when a patient's personality characteristics and behavior impinge in an affect-arousing manner on the underlying needs and concerns of the therapist. Depending on the nature of this interplay, countertransference reactions may be generalized or specific, positive or negative in feeling tone, and directly or indirectly felt and expressed.

GENERALIZED AND SPECIFIC COUNTERTRANSFERENCE REACTIONS

All therapists are prone to countertransference reactions based on the needs and attitudes that generally characterize their interpersonal relationships. Therapists with strong needs to be nurturant, for example, may be particularly attracted to patients who become dependent on them and put off by patients who resist a dependent relationship. Therapists with voyeuristic needs may feel more enthused about their work with patients who readily relate details of their sex life than with those who do not. Therapists with unresolved problems with authority figures may be more prone to feeling irritated and defensive while conducting psychotherapy with a pompous and overbearing patient than while treating someone who is humble and deferential.

Interactions of this kind between therapists' personality and patients' attributes constitute generalized countertransference and pose potential obstacles to progress in the treatment. A highly nurturant therapist who fails to control countertransference may become inordinately supportive of a dependent patient, while offering fewer interpretations than the patient could have benefited from. A voyeuristic therapist may become preoccupied with ferreting out details that satisfy his or her own curiosity but contribute little to enhancing the patient's self-understanding. And a therapist with unresolved concerns about authority may devote more time to reacting in a defensive or retaliatory manner to a patient's pomposity than to helping the patient appreciate the nature and implications of the over-bearing behavior.

By recognizing and controlling any such potential influences of their personality on the performance of their task, therapists can prevent generalized countertransference from impairing their capacity to be helpful. Additionally, by identifying early in the treatment relationship any patients toward whom their generalized countertransference tendencies are likely to exceed their ability to control them, therapists can improve their judgment of whom they should attempt to treat and whom they should refer to another therapist. Virtually any abiding personality characteristic of a therapist can spawn generalized countertransference in relation to a patient's personality style; to such attributes as the patient's age, sex, socioeconomic status, physical appearance, and mannerisms; or to how the patient responds and progresses in the treatment. The better therapists understand themselves and the more experience they have had with different kinds of patients, the more adept they become in anticipating their generalized countertransference and controlling it when it occurs.[5]

Specific countertransference reactions comprise inappropriate or unjustified thoughts, feelings, or actions toward a patient in response to something the patient says or does that touches on problems the therapist has faced or is still facing. For example, a therapist with unresolved concerns about being able to stand up to and deal effectively with authority figures may become anxious listening to a patient describe encounters with a browbeating supervisor, and a therapist struggling with marital problems may have difficulty attending with equanimity to a patient recounting difficulties in his or her marriage.

Unless such countertransference reactions are recognized and controlled, therapists may in some circumstances inadvertently project their own limitations onto a patient and think poorly of the patient for not being able to handle some problem more effectively; they may become angry at the patient for having brought up a subject that has made them feel anxious; or, without realizing the source of their anxiety, they may intervene in ways that discourage the patient from continuing with the anxiety-arousing topic, such as changing the subject or suggesting that the patient is resisting talking about something else. In other circumstances, countertransference may induce therapists to think well rather than poorly of a patient, to become kindly disposed toward the patient for making them feel good, or to encourage the patient to pursue some pleasurable topic further than the needs of the treatment would dictate. Under the influence of specific countertransference, then, therapists may think, feel, and act toward patients in ways that have more to do with defending or gratifying themselves than with understanding or being helpful to the patient.

Specific countertransference reactions tend to be short-lived, arising and dissipating as a patient begins and finishes talking about the subject matter that provokes them. Hence, they have fewer long-term implications for the course of psychotherapy than do generalized countertransference reactions and fewer implications for the kinds of patients a particular therapist can or cannot treat effectively. Yet it should be obvious that moment-to-moment recognition and control of specific as well as generalized countertransference reactions is necessary for therapists to maintain effective commitment to the working alliance in the face of material that impinges on their personal concerns.

POSITIVE AND NEGATIVE COUNTERTRANSFERENCE

Countertransference reactions always involve a prevailing feeling tone that casts the patient in either a favorable or unfavorable light. As in the case of positive and negative transference, however, positive and negative countertransference refer only to the primary attitudes in therapists' reactions to their patients, not to two separate forms of reaction. Like transference reactions, all countertransference reactions are essentially negative, in that they distort reality and suspend a therapist's attention to helping a patient toward increased self-understanding. Singer (1965) expressed this communality of positive and negative transference-countertransference as follows: "A distortion, whether perpetrated by patient or by therapist and regardless of its overt form—irrational admiration or irrational dislike—is inevitably negative and pathological in the sense that it bespeaks a reduction of personal awareness and simultaneously does violence to the other person" (p. 295).

Nevertheless, differentiating the prevailing feeling tone of countertransference reactions can facilitate controlling them, especially because inappropriate positive and negative feelings toward a patient contribute to different kinds of therapist error. A therapist influenced by positive countertransference may tend to be oversolicitous, to back off from making interpretations, to allow sessions to run overtime or the treatment to last too long, or in other ways to be seductive or ingratiating with patients. A therapist influenced by negative countertransference may tend to be patronizing or unresponsive, to bludgeon the patient with interpretations, especially interpretations of resistance and transference, to be overly casual about tardiness or missed sessions, and to seize prematurely on possibilities for termination.

The more alert therapists are to these and other common manifestations of positive and negative countertransference, the better prepared they are to anticipate and reverse their influence. Thus therapists aware that their own needs are causing them to feel positively toward a patient should caution themselves in advance against being so solicitous or seductive as to preclude being helpful; conversely, therapists aware of feeling negatively toward a patient should be prepared to guard against being too cold and distant or using interpretations as a tool to vent their anger rather than as a means of communicating understanding.

DIRECT AND INDIRECT EXPRESSIONS OF COUNTERTRANSFERENCE

Countertransference reactions vary in the directness with which they are expressed and correspondingly in the degree to which their meaning is obvious. Most direct among countertransference reactions are consciously experienced feelings toward a patient of love, hate, anger, jealousy, repugnance, sexual arousal, pride, parental fondness, and the like. The countertransference basis for such strong affects is usually apparent, as long as the therapist does not mistakenly consider them a justifiable part of the real relationship. The psychotherapy interaction—asymmetrical as it is, confined at most to only a few hours of contact per week, and constrained within a set of prescribed role behaviors—provides neither patient nor therapist with the kinds of mutually shared experiences from which one person can develop genuinely strong feelings toward another. Patient and therapist do not really know each other, and any strong feelings of like or dislike should be regarded as transference if a patient has them and as countertransference if they emerge in the therapist.

This point is emphasized because even experienced therapists can fall prey on occasion to believing that strong positive or negative feelings they develop toward a patient are realistically based on the patient's being a marvelous or despicable person. In fact, however, no matter how marvelous or despicable patients may be in their impact on others, they cannot be either in their relationship with the therapist. The relatively limited amount of time they spend with their therapist and the extent to which this time is devoted to the work of the treatment allow patients little opportunity to intrude either marvelously or despicably on the therapist's personal life. Likewise, because the reality of the treatment relationship provides insufficient basis for therapists to develop strong positive or negative feelings toward their patients, the origin of such feelings should always be sought in countertransference, no matter how tempted a therapist might be to regard them otherwise.

Somewhat less direct but also fairly obvious expressions of countertransference comprise feelings or fantasies concerning a patient that imply but do not spell out positive and negative therapist attitudes. Dreaming about a patient constitutes clear evidence that the patient is affecting the therapist in more ways than could be expected from either the real relationship or the working alliance. If correctly understood, the content of their dreams about a patient can tell therapists a good deal about their countertransference reactions to the person, as can the theme and emotional tone of any waking fantasies they have about the patient, whether during or outside treatment sessions.

Countertransference feelings may also appear in thinly disguised form as positive or negative attitudes toward the treatment. For example, therapists may experience mounting or waning interest in their work with a particular patient, or they may find themselves looking forward eagerly or unhappily to sessions with the patient, or they may feel uneasy, depressed, elated, or relieved following sessions with the person. Similarly indirect but obvious manifestations of countertransference are present when, as noted earlier, therapists take great satisfaction in a patient's praising their sensitivity and helpfulness or become markedly upset at having their competence or dedication impugned. With allowance for the satisfactions and disappointments to which therapists are entitled as a professional person observing the success or failure of their efforts, strong positive or negative emotional reactions to a patient's comments on these efforts indicate that they are attaching special importance to a patient's opinion of him.

Another and less obvious type of countertransference expression consists of therapist behaviors that are not accompanied by feelings or attitudes toward a patient or the treatment but that, on closer inspection, seem very likely to derive from such feelings or attitudes. For example, therapists who experience negative countertransference may become careless about their obligations to a patient, "forgetting" an appointment, giving discourteously short notice of an impending vacation, losing track of details from one session to the next, or letting their mind wander during an interview.

Countertransference may also come subtly into play when therapists are inclined to discuss with colleagues their treatment of a particular patient. Although informal sharing of experiences among psychotherapists can contribute to their continuing professional growth, it may also be used as a vehicle for the indirect expression of attitudes toward a patient of which the therapist is not otherwise aware. In speaking with relish and enthusiasm about their work with a patient, for example, therapists experiencing positive countertransference may in effect be telling the world, "Look at what a wonderful patient I have, and how much progress this patient is making, and how well I am conducting the therapy." If countertransference is primarily negative in tone, communication to colleagues may instead focus on the difficulty of the treatment, on the strength of the patient's resistances, or on "humorous" aspects of the patient's problems. Any such complaining about patients or laughing at their foibles in discussions with colleagues bears close scrutiny for its possible origins in negative countertransference. As a general principle, all discussions among therapists of their ongoing treatment cases should be examined with respect to whether they represent solely a collegial consultation or academic sharing of clinical experience, or whether they are additionally expressing countertransference feelings to which one or more of the participating therapists should be alerted.

Least directly indicative of countertransference are variations in the conduct of the treatment that can easily be rationalized and hence escape notice as countertransference manifestations unless therapists are vigilant to them. As described earlier, for example, therapists may at various points in the treatment provide unnecessary reassurance or insufficient emotional support; they may offer too few interpretations, couched in exceedingly tentative terms, or an excessive number of interpretations phrased with undue certainty; they may prematurely encourage consideration of termination or inappropriately defer such consideration; and they may alternate between feeling confident in their plan of action and uncertain about how best to conduct the treatment.

Therapists' judgments in these and similar respects should be guided by their understanding of how best to conduct effective psychotherapy. However, if countertransference is distorting their perception of the treatment situation, they may have difficulty identifying the indications for one or another technical procedure. Is the patient really ready to begin thinking about termination, or is the therapist in negative reaction to a difficult patient seizing too eagerly on some slight references to the possibility of discontinuing treatment? Is the patient really presenting bland information that does not call for interpretation, or is the therapist in hopes of being liked by the patient overlooking appropriate interpretations that might make the patient anxious or angry?

These kinds of questions should be constantly on therapists' minds, to help them address their behavior in the therapy to the needs of their patients rather than to countertransference distortions of what these needs may be. Whenever therapists cannot satisfy themselves that their actions are fully justified by the reality of the treatment situation, they should suspect some countertransference basis for their behavior and take steps to mitigate its influence.

RECOGNIZING AND LEARNING FROM COUNTERTRANSFERENCE REACTIONS

What therapists must do first and foremost with their countertransference reactions is recognize them when they occur. Only with such recognition can there be prospects for controlling countertransference and learning from it. To hone their sensitivity to countertransference, therapists should anticipate that they will develop some countertransference reactions toward every patient with whom they work in a conscientious and dedicated fashion. Furthermore, drawing on their understanding of themselves and their cumulative clinical experience, they should come to anticipate the kinds of countertransference reactions they are likely to form toward patients in general and toward some types of patients in particular.

It is in this latter regard that self-awareness becomes particularly important to a therapist's effectiveness. As noted in Chapter 3, trained professionals do not have to be paragons of psychological adjustment, free from all neurotic concerns, to function effectively as psychotherapists. However, they do have to be sufficiently aware of their own personal concerns and unresolved issues to prevent them from interfering with their clinical work and to guide them in determining which psychotherapy patients they are most likely to benefit and which they should refer to a colleague. For example, therapists should be aware of qualities within themselves that tend to impair their effectiveness with patients of a particular age, sex, social class, cultural background, or personality style, and they need to know in advance whether they are likely to feel intimidated by an overbearing patient or exasperated with a timid one, gratified by a highly dependent patient or impressed with a highly independent one, aroused or alienated by a sexually seductive patient, envious or captivated by an intellectually brilliant one, and so on.

Awareness of their own dispositions to generalized and specific countertransference reactions and knowledge of the ways countertransference is expressed prepare therapists to recognize feelings and attitudes in themselves that are not justified in reality or by the working alliance. The more promptly countertransference is recognized, the more adequately therapists can prevent it from impairing their sensitivity to a patient's communications, from blurring their perspectives on the implications of the patient's behavior, or from inducing them to act in ways that impede progress in the treatment. They can become more careful about scheduling appointments, for example, or concentrate harder on paying attention, or offer fewer interpretations, or give additional attention to possibilities for terminating, or do whatever else is necessary to reverse features of their behavior that, as products of countertransference, have been serving their needs and not the needs of the patient.

When therapists can readily identify their countertransference reactions, they can often learn a good deal about themselves and their patients. With respect to generalized countertransference, therapists cannot help but acquire from their clinical experience knowledge of their own interpersonal attitudes and how they dispose these to react to various kinds of patients and patient problems. Clinicians who assume responsibility for providing psychotherapeutic services should already have attained a large measure of self-understanding, so that they will not need to look on conducting psychotherapy as a major growth experience for themselves; psychotherapy is, after all, intended for the benefit of the patient, not the therapist.

On the other hand, genuine involvement as a participant observer with their patients has considerable potential for adding to therapists' self-understanding. It is partly for this reason that experience contributes to competence in doing psychotherapy. The more patients with whom therapists have worked, the more opportunities they have had to identify interpersonal dispositions that are likely to affect their conduct of psychotherapy and to learn which types of patients are most likely to profit from being in therapy with them.

In terms of specific countertransference reactions, therapists can use any intercurrent anxiety or other discomfort they experience during the treatment to identify unresolved areas of conflict in themselves. If, for example, they feel uneasy or find themselves changing the subject when a patient describes problems in being assertive or sexually responsive, they probably have some unresolved concerns in these areas. As just noted, therapists should bring to their clinical work a fairly thorough understanding of any such areas of conflict in their own personality that might untowardly influence their conduct of the treatment. Yet it is to be expected that the diverse pathways of psychotherapy will from time to time cross areas of conflict that therapists have not previously recognized in themselves, and what they learn from observing the countertransference reactions they experience in these instances will enhance their self-understanding and make them better therapists, better prepared to anticipate and control such reactions in the future.

Sensitivity to countertransference brings with it increased potential for therapists to understand the patient as well as themselves. Although most clinicians consider the recognition and control of countertransference as more important to effective psychotherapy than any clues it offers to the nature of a patient's personality, prevailing opinion nevertheless agrees with the view presented here that countertransference can alert the therapist to important unverbalized attitudes and impulses in the patient.

To use countertransference reactions in this way, therapists need first to understand their inappropriate feelings or attitudes toward a patient and then to seek in the patient's behavior themes that might have triggered the particular countertransference reaction. Suppose, for example, that a therapist becomes anxious during a session in which a patient talks about how much progress has been made in the treatment, and suppose further that the therapist is aware of having become attached to or gratified by the patient in ways that will make termination a personally unhappy experience. Although it may seem fairly obvious that a patient talking contentedly and realistically about considerable progress may be contemplating termination, sensitivity to countertransference can help therapists recognize this implication of a patient's remarks more quickly or clearly than they might otherwise, especially if they harbor an attachment to the treatment relationship that is not in the patient's best interest.

Should a patient's comments or actions be less apparently reflective of unverbalized themes or impulses than in the preceding example, countertransference can be particularly instrumental in bringing these themes or impulses to a therapist's attention. Suppose the patient is not doing or saying anything seemingly related to thoughts about termination, but the therapist is nevertheless experiencing some anxiety that strikes him or her as associated with an imminent rupture of the treatment relationship. The therapist might then have adequate basis for at least raising the topic for exploration: "I wonder if you've been having some thoughts about how much longer we should continue to work together."

Whenever therapists' countertransference reactions sensitize them in this way to unverbalized attitudes or impulses in a patient, they are likely to begin recognizing other subtle clues to these attitudes and impulses that they have previously overlooked. Continuing with the same example, patients satisfied with their progress may find few things to talk about in their sessions, require minimal help to explore and understand what they do say, and display little concern about circumstances that require cancellation of sessions. Although any of these behaviors should signal therapists that a patient may be nearing termination, a countertransference investment in continuing to work with the patient could cloud their vision of them. Then only their anxiety, compensating for their insensitivity to the other available clues, could alert them that the patient may be considering termination.

Countertransference thus provides a barometer of patient feelings and attitudes that can help therapists keep abreast of the climate of the treatment relationship when other indices are unavailable or escape their notice. However, countertransference should not be equated with all the subtle or indirect clues to patients' concerns and motivations that therapists may detect in the treatment situation as a consequence of their being sensitive and knowledgeable observers. Such an equation would make countertransference synonymous with empathy and strip it of its unique significance.[6]

To illustrate this important distinction between countertransference and empathy, suppose a therapist talking with a seriously disturbed patient in a hospital setting suddenly feels apprehensive and steps back just in time to evade a well-aimed punch to the chin. Or suppose a therapist listening to a male patient describing repetitive clumsiness in spilling his drinks at cocktail parties, especially while he is talking to a woman, has an association to premature ejaculation, which is a form of spilling, and it turns out on exploration that premature ejaculation is an important concern of the patient he has not yet been able to verbalize.

In these instances, empathy and not countertransference has determined the therapist's subthreshold communications. Anticipating that the first patient was about to strike out could have been based on sensitivity to a number of visible clues, such as a slight clenching of the patient's teeth or fist or a change in the intensity of the patient's facial expression. Whatever stimuli may have triggered the therapist's apprehension, the therapist was accurately perceiving the patient's impulse, and both the fear and the drawing back were appropriate responses to the situation. As a reaction based on reality, then, independently of any perceptual distortion influenced by prior dispositions or unresolved personal conflicts, the therapist's behavior would have constituted empathic understanding, not countertransference.

Similarly in the second example, the therapist's association from the spilling of a drink to the spilling of semen, which contributed to identifying the patient's unverbalized concerns about premature ejaculation, would have involved accurate rather than distorted perception and conflict-free utilization of the therapist's fantasy to serve the purpose of the treatment. This latter type of sensitivity, in which therapists use their own associations to a patient's productions to enrich their understanding of them, is discussed at length in Reik's (1948) previously mentioned *Listening with the Third Ear*, the third ear being the one that therapists tune in to their own inner voices. However, as long as therapists' emotional reactions are appropriate to the reality of the treatment situation and their associations are not disturbed by their own unresolved conflicts, attention to minimal clues and listening with the third ear constitute empathy and not countertransference.

NOTES

1. Formulations of countertransference as a phenomenon paralleling transference in the opposite direction, and being similarly ubiquitous and inevitable in psychotherapy, are elaborated by Giovacchini (1989, Chapter 2), Loewald (1986), Renik (1993), and L. Stone (1995).

2. For further discussion, past and present, of the definition and nature of countertransference reactions, readers are referred to contributions by Abend (1989), Gabbard (1995), Gorkin (1987, Chapters 1–3), Racker (1968), A. Reich (1951, 1960), and R. Tyson (1986).

3. Research reported by Henry and Strupp (1991) and McClure and Hodge (1987) has confirmed that strong personal reactions of dislike can lead therapists to regard patients as being more different from themselves than they really are, to make unfavorable clinical judgments concerning them, and to fail to communicate with them in an empathic manner.

4. Powell (1995) presents case examples of failures in psychotherapy that appeared due in part to countertransference thoughts and feelings that adversely affected the therapist's behavior. In a study by Robbins and Jolkovski (1987), greater awareness by therapists of their counter-transference reactions was associated with decreased likelihood of their inadvertently manifesting such countertransference behavior as reduced involvement in a patient's treatment.

5. Roth (1987, Chapter 3) provides some good illustrations of how general personality characteristics of patients can interact with a therapist's basic nature to foster potentially disadvantageous countertransference reactions. Numerous authors call special attention in this regard to the frequency with which borderline patients often evoke particularly potent countertransference feelings of anger, hostility, and frustration that challenge therapists' capacities to recognize and subject to appropriate control (Brody & Farber, 1996; Gabbard & Wilkinson, 1994; Masterson, 1983). As for therapist experience, Brody and Farber (1996) found in a survey of 336 therapists that those still in training reported greater concerns about having strong emotional reactions to patients that needed to be defended against than those who were fully trained practitioners.

6. Preference for a narrow definition of countertransference that preserves a distinction from therapist empathy is amplified by Glenn (1992) and Moore and Fine (1990). For further guidelines on translating their countertransference reactions as well as their empathic understanding into therapeutically beneficial interventions, readers are referred to Blum and Goodman (1995), Levy (1990, Chapter 6), and Tansey and Burke (1989).

PART FOUR

THE FINAL PHASE
OF PSYCHOTHERAPY

CHAPTER 12

Termination

T HE FINAL phase of psychotherapy is exceeded perhaps only by the
initial phase in its importance for determining the amount of help
patients receive. The middle phase of treatment, involving as it
does the communication of understanding through interpretation and the
utilization of resistance, transference, and countertransference phenomena for this purpose, constitutes the main work of therapy. Yet this work
becomes possible only if therapists are able first to assess accurately a patient's likelihood of benefiting from psychotherapy and then implement
an adequate treatment contract for engaging in it. Similarly, the manner
in which psychotherapy is brought to a close determines in large measure
whether self-learning during the middle phase of treatment persists as a
life-enriching resource or pales into a transiently interesting but no
longer meaningful experience.

To bring psychotherapy to an effective close, therapists must be able to
judge when an appropriate point of termination has been reached and
what procedures will serve best to consolidate the gains that have been
made. To complicate this task, there ordinarily are no fixed criteria for
when psychotherapy should end, and there are often circumstances external to the treatment that mandate termination. However, several considerations relating to the necessary duration of psychotherapy can guide
therapists in evaluating the appropriateness of termination, and a number of procedures can be specified for conducting the final phase of treatment under conditions of both voluntary and forced termination.

THE NECESSARY DURATION
OF PSYCHOTHERAPY

It is deceptively simple to say that psychotherapy should last until the goals of the treatment have been achieved. In actual practice, the goals of psychotherapy are seldom sufficiently delineated for either patient or therapist to identify precisely when they have been achieved. If the initial treatment contract was aimed toward the resolution of psychological problems through increased self-understanding, then how completely should patients resolve their problems and how thoroughly should they understand themselves before psychotherapy is considered to have achieved its goals? If treatment began with specific objectives in mind, such as relief from symptoms of anxiety or depression, improved functioning in social work situations, or better control of certain impulses or emotions, how much symptom relief, improved functioning, or better self-control must be achieved to meet the objectives of the treatment? Even if treatment is started with clearly delineated goals that should leave little doubt as to when it has served its purpose, such as resolving a marital problem or graduating from college, patients who enter psychotherapy to achieve such narrow goals more often than not become interested during the course of the treatment in pursuing broader concerns they have about themselves. Hence, they too will face ambiguities in deciding when the treatment has gone far enough.

It may seem possible to eliminate these ambiguities by positing complete self-understanding, total symptom relief, full self-actualization, and perfect self-control as indications that psychotherapy has achieved its goals. However, such perfection rarely characterizes the human condition; it exists mainly as an abstraction when measured against the quest for realization of one's potential and satisfaction in one's interpersonal relationships. S. Freud (1937/1964), in one of his last and most memorable papers, "Analysis Terminable and Interminable," cautioned that if therapists continue treatment until the patient is "cured" or has reached a state of complete freedom from neurotic inhibitions or concerns, the treatment will never end. More realistically, therapy will have reached its necessary duration when the patient's freedom from symptoms, anxieties, and inhibitions has been "approximately fulfilled" (p. 219):

> Our aim will not be to rub off every peculiarity of human character for the sake of a schematic "normality," nor yet to demand that the person who has been "thoroughly analysed" shall feel no passions and develop no internal conflicts. The business of the analysis is to secure the best possible psychological conditions for the function of the ego; with that it has discharged its task. (p. 250)

Successful psychotherapy, in other words, should be conceived as making progress toward goals, not necessarily as reaching these goals in all their ramifications. Extending treatment until all its objectives have been realized could bind patients to lifelong psychotherapy, which only in the most unusual circumstances would be in their best interest. Psychotherapy is after all an unreal relationship, in which certain contrived and nonmutual roles are prescribed for the participants (see Chapters 10 and 11), and no matter how much responsibility patients assume for the conduct of their treatment, being in psychotherapy still places them in a dependent relationship rather than on their own two feet. Psychotherapy is a means by which people can help themselves live more fully, but it should never be allowed to become itself a way of living life to the full.

The fact that the work of psychotherapy is never fully completed, and that termination accordingly occurs at a point of progress toward its goals rather than on full attainment of these goals, does not mean that therapists should denigrate the fruits of their efforts or regard psychotherapy as a seriously limited procedure. One of the most important accomplishments of psychotherapy consists of teaching patients a method of looking at themselves. In addition to whatever degree of self-knowledge, self-control, or symptom relief they attain during treatment, patients bring away from therapy some education in ways of thinking and feelings about themselves and some training in ways of observing past and current experiences to learn from them more effective ways of dealing with future experience.

The education and training patients receive in psychotherapy, particularly with respect to skills in self-observation, allow them to make continued progress toward the goals of their treatment, even after the treatment has been terminated. Interpretations that have been fairly well worked through prior to termination continue to be worked through as patients encounter new situations in which these interpretations help them understand and modify their behavior. Self-esteem that has been enhanced during psychotherapy continues to increase following termination as patients realize personal ambitions made possible by their gains in the treatment. Thus psychotherapy constitutes a process that, once set in motion, can help patients sustain progress toward a richer and more rewarding life even after the formal treatment relationship has come to a close.[1]

In this same vein, termination does not need to be deferred until therapists feel certain that patients will never again encounter the difficulties that brought them for help. Although substantial progress toward a more effective and rewarding lifestyle should have occurred before termination is seriously considered, the possibility of new or recurrent psychological problems does not contraindicate a decision to terminate. Just as perfection is an ideal, so psychological problems can never be avoided completely, and termination of psychotherapy should not be taken to signify that patients have received all the help they will ever need. Future and unforeseen circumstances may cause them difficulties for which some return visits with the therapist or another course of therapy would be helpful. Like booster shots, such follow-up periods of treatment help sustain improved functioning and should neither be discouraged nor interpreted to mean that the original psychotherapy was unsuccessful.

Just as there are no fixed criteria for when psychotherapy should end, there are no clinically sound and empirically documented guidelines for determining in advance exactly how much psychotherapy a patient should receive. There is clear evidence that the longer patients remain in therapy and the more sessions they have, within limits, the more benefit they are likely to derive from their treatment. This relationship between duration and outcome in psychotherapy is not linear in nature. Most patients who benefit from psychotherapy begin to do so early in their treatment and achieve a substantial portion of their eventual benefit during the first 6 months of therapy, following which further improvement comes more slowly and in smaller amounts. Nevertheless, the available data confirm that continued improvement can and does occur over 2 or more years of psychotherapy. Moreover, patients who have received more than 6 months of psychotherapy report substantially more improvement in their presenting symptoms, their functioning in work and social situations, and their interpersonal relationships than patients who have received less than 6 months of psychotherapy (see Lambert & Bergin, 1994; Orlinsky et al., 1994; Orlinsky & Howard, 1987; Seligman, 1995, 1996; Whiston & Sexton, 1993).

As valuable as they may be, these research findings speak to psychotherapy and psychotherapy patients in general and do not by any means indicate that the optimum length of treatment in every case is as long as possible. Instead, therapists need to be guided in the individual case by certain factors that affect how long a course of treatment should last. Additionally, even though successful outcome must usually be measured in terms of progress toward various goals rather than attaining them, some definite minimum criteria for beginning to consider the appropriateness of termination can be applied during the course of psychotherapy.

FACTORS AFFECTING THE DURATION OF PSYCHOTHERAPY

The duration of psychotherapy in the individual case is typically influenced by three factors internal to the treatment: (a) the depth and intensity of the therapy, (b) the orientation and skill of the therapist, and (c) the needs and capacities of the patient.

Depth and Intensity of the Therapy

Uncovering psychotherapy proceeds by evoking thoughts and feelings of which patients have not been fully aware and that bear on the problems for which they have sought help. The more intensively the treatment is pursued, as measured by the frequency of the sessions, the more numerous these uncovered thoughts and feelings become and the more time is necessary to discuss them adequately. Furthermore, the more intensive the treatment is, the more deeply involved the treatment relationship is likely to become and the more time will be required to explore and resolve its transference elements. Because any increase in session frequency thus broadens and deepens the scope of treatment, with a corresponding increase in its intensity, it is generally the case that the more intensive psychotherapy is, the longer it will need to last.[2]

There are two exceptions to this general relationship between frequency of sessions and duration of psychotherapy, both of which involve primarily supportive treatment. In crisis intervention, first of all, the treatment plan may involve very frequent sessions but over just a short period, until the crisis has passed. For example, an acutely suicidal patient may be seen daily for only a week or two and then, if the immediate suicide risk has abated, be terminated or placed on a different treatment schedule. Second, in some circumstances supportive treatment may be arranged on a relatively infrequent basis but with the expectation of an extended duration. Especially for patients with chronic psychological problems, psychotherapy on a biweekly or monthly basis over a period of years may be the most appropriate way of sustaining their gradual movement toward a more effective lifestyle or maintaining their psychological equilibrium through a transitional phase in the life cycle. Allowing for these two exceptions, however, a direct relationship will generally hold between the frequency of psychotherapy sessions and the necessary duration of the treatment.

Orientation and Skill of the Therapist

Some psychotherapists approach their work in the tradition of Rogers's (1951) belief that people are innately resilient and remarkably capable of redirecting their lives on the basis of even minimal increments in self-awareness that facilitate their personal growth and self-actualization. Other therapists, though equally dedicated to helping their patients live a fuller life, share S. Freud's (1937/1964) more pessimistic view that neurotic inhibitions and conflicts are stubbornly persistent phenomena that yield, if at all, only to extensive and hard-won increments in self-understanding. Therapists of the first persuasion tend to proceed with the expectation that psychotherapy can be brought to a satisfactory point of termination in relatively short order, whereas those holding the latter view anticipate a much longer period of psychotherapy prior to reaching an appropriate termination point.

In a survey of the beliefs and attitudes of 222 psychologists, Bolter, Levenson, and Alvarez (1990) confirmed that those who preferred long-term approaches in psychotherapy were relatively likely to regard personality as essentially static and immutable and treatment as requiring considerable effort to overcome inertia and resistance to change. Respondents who favored short-term approaches in psychotherapy, by contrast, were relatively likely to endorse an adult developmental perspective in which people are viewed as naturally striving toward personal growth and requiring only modest interventions to help them in this process. Although conceptually valid, this distinction between "long-term values" and "short-term values" brings with it some clinical risks, especially if they are taken not merely as alternative and equally respectable points of view, but as antithetical and diametrically opposed perspectives in only one of which the truth resides.

Miller (1996b) has expressed concern in this regard that extolling the virtues of short-term therapy values while disdaining long-term values may serve as a basis for "rationing" the psychotherapy patients receive and thereby responding less to their needs than to the cost-cutting dictates of managed care companies. Budman and Gurman (1983) in turn have argued that enshrinement of long-term therapy values can unconsciously foster keeping patients in therapy longer than is necessary or helpful to them, as a way of providing financial returns to the therapist rather than psychological returns to the patient. Because patient needs become the sacrificial lamb in either case, psychotherapists are most likely to be helpful when they can provide psychotherapy of whatever length appears clinically indicated and when, if their preferences run strongly to either short-term or long-term values, they can keep humbly in mind that not all the correct answers are theirs.

At any rate, such differences in orientation produce many corresponding differences among therapists in their setting of criteria for termination. Those who are optimistic about their patients' capacities for self-growth are inclined to accept initial symptom relief and beginning progress toward more effective coping as sufficient basis for termination, and they regard prolonging therapy beyond this point as fostering the patient's dependency and discouraging him from seeking his own best destiny. Therapists who are more conservative in their expectations about personality change tend to view such initial progress as only a first step toward improvement and to consider termination based on it as premature and risking reversal of the prior treatment gains.

A noteworthy outgrowth of optimism concerning the possible brevity of psychotherapy has been an effort to specify in the initial contract how many sessions there will be or over how long a period the treatment will continue. Such use of time-limited therapy is believed to create some urgency about the treatment, to encourage both patient and therapist to use their time together more efficiently than they would in the absence of such limitations, and to reduce patient dependence on the therapist.[3] Interestingly, as a reminder not to tie any particular theoretical approach in psychotherapy exclusively to long-term or short-term values, the notion of time-limited therapy goes back in psychoanalytic theory almost as far as Freud himself. Rank (1945) recommended a specific time limit for the duration of analytic therapy as a way of promoting patient progress toward separation and individuation. Psychodynamically oriented clinicians have also generated an extensive array of methods for abbreviating exploratory psychotherapy, beginning with descriptions by Alexander and French (1946, Chapter 4) of insights rapidly achieved by "corrective emotional experience" and extending to numerous detailed techniques and manuals for short-term expressive psychotherapy.[4]

In the absence of specific time restrictions, the pace at which treatment progresses toward a satisfactory termination point in either relatively brief or relatively long-term therapy is influenced by therapists' skill as well as their orientation. The more readily they can understand their patients' communications and the more incisively they can communicate this understanding to the patient, the more rapidly the treatment will yield benefits and the shorter its necessary duration will be. Yet it should be remembered from Chapter 3 that therapist skill is a dyadic variable and not a fixed personality trait of the therapist. Whatever their general level of competence, therapists will prove more skillful in working with certain kinds of patients and patient problems than with others. Each therapist will accordingly require more time to complete a satisfactory course of treatment with some patients than with others.

Needs and Capacities of the Patient

People who enter treatment with relatively serious, complicated, long-standing problems tend to require more prolonged therapy than those seeking help for relatively mild and straightforward problems of recent onset. Likewise, people who wish to achieve sweeping personality changes in psychotherapy usually require a more extended course of treatment than those who seek less ambitious goals. Generally speaking, then, the greater the gap between the seriousness and chronicity of patients' difficulties on the one hand, and the state of improved personality functioning they would like to achieve on the other, the longer their psychotherapy can be expected to last.

This general principle notwithstanding, patients as well as therapists differ in the amount and kind of treatment progress they consider sufficient basis for terminating. Some patients doubt their capacity to change permanently or for the better; in treatment such patients mistrust initial signs of progress, anticipate recurrence of their difficulties, and hesitate to think about termination until there has been extensive working through in the therapy and prolonged improvement outside it. Other patients are optimistic about being able to improve rapidly in therapy and maintain their improvement, if the therapist can get them moving in the right direction; these patients thrive on initial signs of progress, which they see as signifying the beginning of the end of the treatment, and they are reluctant to delay termination once they have begun to cope more effectively with their experience.

The capacities of the individual patient influence the necessary duration of psychotherapy in much the same way as the skill of the therapist. The more freely people can talk about themselves in the treatment situation, the more sensitively they can address their own needs and attitudes, the more perceptively they can draw on the therapist's interventions to expand their self-understanding, and the more readily they can allow the psychotherapy experience to influence their behavior in other situations, the more rapidly they will progress in treatment and the sooner they will complete it.

Adequate attention to the needs and capacities of patients makes distinctions between "long-term" and "short-term" therapy on the basis of some arbitrary number of sessions or months of treatment meaningless, at least from a clinical perspective. Extensive research documents the potential effectiveness of psychotherapy of limited duration in helping patients feel better and cope more effectively with events in their lives (see Anderson & Lambert, 1995; Crits-Christoph, 1992; Koss & Shiang, 1994). However, aside from the previously cited evidence that more therapy produces better results than less therapy, on the average, even such developers of brief treatment methods as Strupp (1996b) point out that time-limited therapy is not for everyone:

> Having developed a manual for time-limited dynamic psychotherapy . . . and having directed a project . . . designed to study the effects of training experienced therapists in it use, I have no doubt that in many cases people can be helped significantly in this way. Moreover, substantial numbers of individuals want no more than a very limited form of professional help. However, as researchers, therapists, and concerned citizens, we should not expect magical returns from minimal efforts. Nor should we ignore the fact that longer and more intensive therapeutic efforts may at times be indicated. (p. 1021)

Consistent with Strupp's point, there is widespread agreement that short courses of psychotherapy lasting less than 15 to 20 sessions are best suited to the needs of patients with mild and situational problems but offer little benefit for severely disturbed patients and those with multiple and characterologically determined problems, who typically require an extended treatment relationship to form an effective working alliance and show improvement (Garfield, 1995, Chapter 11; Hoglend, 1993; Steenbarger, 1994).

Accordingly, the necessary duration of psychotherapy is treatment long enough to meet patients' needs, and ideally, that is how long it should last. Establishing arbitrary numbers to distinguish between brief and extended psychotherapy may serve administrative purposes, including imposed limitations on service delivery, but doing so serves no clinically beneficial purpose. Patients whose needs are minimal and whose treatment goals are modest are likely to be treated successfully in a relatively short period; conversely, treatment of patients with substantial needs and ambitious treatment goals is likely to last a relatively long time. In the end, effective psychotherapy is never too brief or too prolonged if it is tailored to the psychological circumstances of the patient who comes for help.

MINIMUM CRITERIA FOR CONSIDERING TERMINATION

The discussion to this point has clarified that many factors influence the necessary duration of psychotherapy and that there are no fixed criteria for identifying the point at which treatment is complete. However, despite the complexities of deciding whether psychotherapy has lasted long enough and the uncertainties in choosing an ideal time for termination, there are three minimum criteria that should be satisfied before termination is even considered as a possibility.

1. Some substantial progress should have been made toward achieving the goals of the treatment. Although "substantial progress" is open to different interpretations, each patient and therapist should be able to agree on what constitutes progress toward the goals they have set and on whether such progress has taken place. Except when patient and therapist agree to discontinue treatment because *no* progress is being made, then, the principle will generally hold that termination should not be considered until both parties to the treatment contract concur in perceiving substantial progress toward their goals.

2. Patients should appear capable of continuing to work independently on understanding and alleviating their problems. As noted earlier, successful psychotherapy teaches people method as well as substance. They

learn not only about themselves as a person but also about how to observe their own behavior, how to relate their thoughts and feelings to each other and to the actions they take, and how to apply their self-knowledge in pursuing a more effective and rewarding lifestyle. Before termination of psychotherapy is considered, patients should have demonstrated capacity to initiate without the therapist's help such observation, understanding, and realigning of their behavior in situations of conflict and opportunity. Only then will there be sufficient likelihood of their sustaining and building on their treatment gains to justify a decision to terminate.

3. The patient's transference relationship to the therapist should have been resolved sufficiently for the real relationship between them to gain ascendance. As noted in Chapter 10, this does not mean either that transference feelings now totally disappear or that patient and therapist now become personally intimate in ways that transcend their original treatment contract. Rather, it means that fewer transference reactions will occur and that a correspondingly larger part of the treatment interaction will consist of reality-oriented conversations, in which patients recount their experiences with minimal evidence of distortion and therapists listen and comment with minimal utilization of an as-if, interpretive stance. If therapy is terminated before such a resolution of the transference is achieved, patients' unexpressed feelings toward the therapist may trouble them in the future, in the same manner as other unresolved feelings toward important people would trouble them. It is also likely that patients who leave therapy with insufficiently resolved transference feelings probably leave with other inadequately resolved problems as well, for which additional treatment would have been helpful.

These three minimum criteria for considering termination in psychotherapy—substantial progress toward the goals of the treatment, the apparent capacity of patients to continue independently to observe and learn about themselves, and substantial resolution of the transference—is elaborated throughout the rest of this chapter with respect to the specific planning and implementation of termination. In ideal circumstances, termination occurs when a patient and therapist who are working together with few external constraints become fully satisfied that an appropriate stopping point has been reached. Not uncommonly, however, some external circumstances mandate termination of the therapy regardless of what stage of progress has been reached. Because considerations in planning and implementing termination vary with whether it is occurring on a voluntary or forced basis, these two patterns of termination will be discussed separately.

CONSIDERATIONS IN
VOLUNTARY TERMINATION

Voluntary termination of psychotherapy occurs when the parties to a treatment contract come mutually to the conclusion that it should end. Unless an inappropriately conceived treatment contract prompts a decision to terminate shortly after therapy has begun, mutual agreement that psychotherapy should end usually begins to emerge after patients have gone through a period of learning more about themselves and working through the implications of their enhanced self-knowledge. Then the initial suggestion to consider termination may come from either the patient or the therapist, depending on the particular nature of their treatment relationship and the demands of the situation.

TERMINATION PROPOSED BY THE PATIENT

The most desirable way for termination to evolve is for patients spontaneously to report that they believe they have accomplished their objectives in psychotherapy, that they feel capable of handling on their own any further difficulties they might encounter, and that they would like to discuss how much longer the treatment needs to continue. Such a proposal from patients eminently satisfies the minimum criteria for beginning to consider termination: They will have stated in as many words that they have made substantial progress in the treatment, that they have good prospects for sustaining this progress, and that they are prepared to review at the level of the real relationship when and how termination should be implemented.

The therapist's first task in responding to such direct expressions of interest in termination is to consider whether they reflect an accurate estimate of progress or instead mask resistance to further treatment. As noted in Chapter 9, resistance to change, resistance to interview content, and resistance associated with transference attitudes may all contribute to premature suggestions to terminate. When termination is proposed in the context of obvious resistance, the proposal should be interpreted as a manifestation of the resistance; when it is proposed in the absence of obvious resistance but also in the absence of evidence for the improvement the patient claims to feel, the proposal should be explored for its possible origins in resistance that is not otherwise being manifested.

On the other hand, when patients who ask about termination seem not to be resisting and have in fact made substantial progress toward the goals of the treatment, their questions should be taken at their face value. This means that a thorough and reality-oriented review should be initiated of the changes that have occurred during treatment and the extent to which these changes fulfill the treatment goals. The more satisfying both patient and therapist find the conclusions that emerge from such a review, the more clearly the time has come for them to begin planning the termination of their treatment relationship.

If a progress review instituted at a patient's request paints a less positive picture of improvement than the patient has surmised, the opportunity can be utilized to identify what kinds of changes or developments remain to be accomplished before an advantageous termination point will be reached. However, identifying unfinished business does not mean impressing on patients dire consequences of their terminating at the moment. Persuading patients to remain in psychotherapy has no more place in an effective treatment contract than seducing them into beginning it. Rather, therapists need to present as realistically as they can the gaps that still exist between what the treatment set out to accomplish and what has thus far been achieved, after which it is in patients' hands to decide whether they want to continue working toward these remaining goals.

In contrast to situations in which therapists must help patients recognize that progress has not yet been as substantial as they thought, a treatment review initiated at the patient's request may sometimes reveal more progress than the therapist had heretofore recognized. Patients who surprise their therapist with a request to terminate may be resisting and may be overestimating the progress they have made, especially if they have strong needs to bolster their self-image as a competent person. However, it is also possible for them to have made gains considerably beyond what their therapist has appreciated, especially if therapists' personal needs have clouded their judgment. In this latter circumstance, therapists should not hesitate to revise their estimate of a patient's progress and accelerate plans for arranging termination.

Indirect Expression of a Wish to Terminate

Patients who are eager to consider termination may be reluctant to say so directly and instead express their eagerness in some indirect fashion. They may talk at length about how well they are doing, for example, or they may stop bringing pressing problems to the therapist's attention. Assuming they are not trying to please the therapist in the first instance or resist the treatment in the second, such behavior may be their way of attempting to communicate that they regard the work of the treatment as finished. It will then fall to the therapist to recognize and respond to this communication, as by saying, "It sounds as if you feel that therapy has accomplished what you wanted it to accomplish."

Occasionally, patients may indirectly communicate a feeling that the therapy is finished by suddenly dropping out of treatment. Patients who drop out of psychotherapy without discussing their decision to terminate usually do so early in the treatment, prior to the establishment of a firm working alliance. In the event that patients drop out after getting well into the middle of treatment and engaging in some useful interpretive work, their unilateral termination still does not necessarily signify an unsuccessful treatment outcome. Patients who genuinely feel they have derived the full measure of benefit from psychotherapy may decide that, instead of trying to convince the therapist of their progress or going through a drawn-out separation process, they will simply stop appearing for sessions.[5]

Obviously, it is preferable for patients to talk out termination plans before acting on them, and reluctance to do so may indicate some lingering neurotic problems. Why, for example, should patients shrink from reviewing their progress with the therapist, and why should they find it inordinately difficult to say goodbye rather than just drop out of sight? Nevertheless, unilateral terminators may be correct in their estimate that they have achieved their treatment goals, and they may leave therapy considerably improved and with substantial capacity to sustain their improvement.

This possibility that patients who drop out of treatment may have made significant gains merits careful attention, not because therapists should encourage or be fully satisfied with unilateral termination, but because they should avoid automatically regarding it as a negative outcome. There has been an unfortunate tendency in some research studies to label all such patients as "defectors" and to designate them as "failure cases," that is, persons not helped by psychotherapy. Yet aside from the fact that unilateral terminators may have improved before they drop out, the previously cited evidence of posttermination gains demonstrates the unreliability of any such designation. Only careful follow-up investigation can identify which unilateral terminators derived no benefit from psychotherapy and which achieved considerable and lasting improvement.

The Desire to Terminate as a Ceiling Effect

The circumstances discussed thus far in which patients propose termination have been predicated on their feeling satisfied with their progress and no longer in need of help. There are also times when patients ask about discontinuing treatment not because they have made as much progress as they would like, but because they feel they have made as much progress as they can. Although it is preferable to have therapy end because patients believe they have achieved their goals rather than because they anticipate no further progress toward them, the latter circumstances, which can be called a "ceiling effect," may nevertheless signify an appropriate stopping point.

The appropriateness of patients' feelings that they have reached their ceiling in benefiting from psychotherapy depends on the extent to which the treatment goals have in fact been achieved and whether what remains to be accomplished appears within reasonable expectations from continued psychotherapy. Patients who have been making steady gains in the treatment and whose remaining objectives are similar to those that have already been achieved are being unrealistic if they feel they have made as much progress as they can. On the other hand, patients whose gains have become increasingly fewer and farther between may quite accurately perceive that psychotherapy has little more to offer them, even though some of their difficulties persist.

In addition to helping patients appraise whether psychotherapy has reached a ceiling in benefiting them, therapists also need to recognize points at which some other form of help should be instituted to build on what has been accomplished. Thus patients who have learned in psychotherapy to understand themselves and deal with their experiences more effectively may still require marital counseling to resolve some issues with their spouse or vocational counseling to make a career choice consistent with their interests and talents. Or patients who have enhanced their self-image and their capacity to utilize their ability may still be troubled with some focal symptoms, such as a specific phobia, for which a course of systematic desensitization might be helpful.

In evaluating a patient's wish to terminate because maximum progress has been made, the therapist should have in mind that all psychotherapy sooner or later reaches a point of diminishing returns. Consistent with the previously cited research findings concerning a decreasing rate of improvement over the course of psychotherapy, even the most modest of treatment goals can contribute to a ceiling effect, in the sense that substantial progress toward these goals tends to make the remaining increments of gain progressively more difficult to achieve. As current progress and future prospects are evaluated in the individual case, then, it is necessary to weigh the progress yet to be made against the time, effort, and expense that will be necessary to make it. When therapists agree with a patient that little stands to be gained from further psychotherapy, they should simply proceed with plans for termination. When progress has slowed as its apparent ceiling has been approached, but has not yet ground to a halt, patients should have an opportunity to review whether the gains still possible are worth the cost to them of continuing in the treatment.

The realistic weighing of psychotherapy's cost in time, effort, and money against the possible benefits to be derived from it should not be viewed as fatalistic surrender or as any subjugation of the spiritual value of increased self-understanding to practical concerns. Rather, a cost-benefit analysis with patients who ask about terminating serves to emphasize the gains they have made to date and to help preserve them. Because therapy that seeks ultimate aims will be interminable, prolonging treatment beyond a point of diminishing returns risks the erosion of its prior benefits. Patients who are continued in psychotherapy to a point where few additional gains are realizable, and those only with enormous effort, can easily grow disenchanted with the treatment process and with the therapist. Working hard at a task that is no longer as rewarding as it once was can lead people to wonder whether it was ever as rewarding as they thought; being encouraged to continue in this now unrewarding task can lead them to wonder whether the person doing the encouraging really knows his or her job and has their best interests at heart.

As part of allowing patients to participate on an informed basis in deciding whether therapy should continue in light of cost-benefit considerations, therapists should be wary of permitting it to extend into a stage of disenchantment. If patients are to leave therapy not fully satisfied with the progress they have made, it is much better for them to leave with a sense that the treatment worked well as far as it was possible for it to go rather than with a sense that it petered out in a dilatory and unprofitable fashion. It is primarily in the former circumstance that it is reasonable to expect sustained benefits from the treatment and continued engagement by patients in the kinds of self-observation they have learned from it.

TERMINATION PROPOSED BY THE THERAPIST

Whereas most patients monitor their progress closely and sooner or later inquire about how much longer the therapy needs to continue, some either ignore evidence of their own progress or refrain from calling attention to it. Such behavior usually reflects some form of resistance. Patients with characterological resistance who have made substantial progress in therapy may have lingering masochistic or self-depreciatory tendencies that interfere with their accepting their progress as real and taking pleasure in it. Only if their self-abnegation is confronted directly in this regard will they be able to begin appreciating their improvement and considering the work of the therapy accomplished.

In terms of *resistance to change,* some secondary gain elements derived from being in psychotherapy can create as much resistance to terminating the treatment as to entering it in the first place. Patients not uncommonly become very attached to their relationship with the therapist and are loath to give it up. Such resistance to change emerges not so much from any particular feelings patients have had toward their therapist as from the comforting knowledge that, no matter what else happens in their life, continued treatment will provide them regularly scheduled opportunities to meet with a competent and sensitive person who respects, listens to, and stands ever ready to help them.

Secondary gains can also produce resistance to termination in relation to the patient's identified role as being in psychotherapy. Just as patients may hesitate to begin treatment out of reluctance to sacrifice some accrued benefits of being considered psychologically disturbed, they may delay terminating it because doing so will cost them some benefits they have derived from being in treatment. People known to their family, friends, and employers as "being in psychotherapy" or "seeing someone" or "getting some help" may receive special consideration at home, time off from work, and sympathetic encouragement in their social circle, and they may think twice about endangering any of these benefits by becoming a person who has finished treatment and is presumably no longer in need of having allowances made.

Finally, *transference resistance* can make patients reluctant for specific reasons to give up their relationship with their therapist. Particular feelings of liking and respect formed toward the therapist can motivate patients to avoid seeing or saying things about their progress that might hasten the end of the relationship. It is also possible for patients who have not yet resolved their positive transference to be concerned about somehow hurting or offending the therapist by being first to raise a question about terminating the relationship.

Whatever the reasons why patients who have made sufficient progress to consider termination do not spontaneously begin to do so, therapists can explore them only by assuming responsibility themselves for proposing termination and instituting a status review of the therapy. Suppose that a patient who has achieved significant gains in the treatment has for some time been rehashing old material in the sessions while concurrently demonstrating self-sufficiency in thinking through and resolving any new difficulties that have arisen. The therapist should then consider the following kind of remarks:

> For some time now, things have been going along fairly smoothly for you, and any problems you've had you've been working out on your own. There really hasn't been much for us to talk about or that we needed to work on together. So I wonder if we've reached a point where we might consider how much longer we should continue to meet.

As this sample remark illustrates, therapists who decide to broach termination should do so gently, alluding to positive aspects of the progress patients have made and avoiding any criticism of their not perceiving and commenting on these improvements themselves. Therapists furthermore need to speak of these improvements as being just their impression, not yet established fact, and of termination as only a matter for consideration, not an already confirmed implication of the patient's recent conduct. Broaching termination in such a gentle, positively toned, and open-ended fashion encourages patients to participate actively in a progress review, much as if they had been the one to propose terminating. Failure to involve patients in reviewing their progress can complicate termination by giving them cause to think that the therapist is making this decision for the patient or is perhaps overeager to discontinue working with him or her.[6]

Although termination proposed by therapists should therefore consist of no more than raising the topic for discussion, their raising the issue is obviously likely to influence a decision that a good stopping point has been reached. Hence, therapists must attend carefully to the timing of any suggestion they make to discuss termination. In particular, they need to be alert to countertransference feelings that could influence them to be premature or overdue in proposing termination to patients who are disinclined to bring it up themselves. Thus if patients have made frustratingly slow progress, if they have proved difficult to work with, if they are occupying an appointment time the therapist would like to have free for other purposes, or if in some other way they have been personally unattractive or evoked marked negative feelings in the treatment relationship, therapists may rush to judgment in concluding that satisfactory or maximum progress has been made. If patients have been a delight to work with, on the other hand, moving rapidly toward the treatment goals, demonstrating admirable life achievements, or otherwise providing an enjoyable relationship the therapist eagerly renews with each session, then the therapist may inadvertently overlook progress and prolong the treatment beyond a point of diminishing returns. Recognizing such countertransference feelings helps therapists avoid being influenced to act in either of these inappropriate ways.

While ensuring that their decisions to proceed with or defer proposing termination are based on realistic considerations and not countertransference, therapists can often take natural interruptions in the treatment as occasions for suggesting a progress review. Illnesses, vacations, or business commitments inevitably require patient or therapist to cancel sessions from time to time. If patients who seem to have reached a point where termination might begin to be considered sustain their progress during a break in the treatment, the moment may be propitious to comment as follows:

> We haven't met for two weeks now, while I've been on vacation, but from what you've been telling me it was a good two weeks for you and you were able to work things out very well on your own. Perhaps this means we

should give some thought to what has been accomplished in the treatment and how much longer it needs to continue.

As in the previous illustration, the tone here is gentle and open-ended, complimenting the patient on the progress that has been made but not jumping to any conclusions about its implications. Although therapists should avoid using every interruption in the treatment for such review purposes, interruptions at a point where termination might otherwise be considered can provide natural opportunities for proposing to do so.

IMPLEMENTING TERMINATION

When patient and therapist agree that satisfactory or maximum progress has been made, the therapist needs to implement the actual termination of the treatment contract by (a) consolidating the decision to terminate, (b) arranging for either a time-limited or spaced method for proceeding to the final session, (c) reinforcing the patient's self-observational abilities, and (d) fostering the resolution of the transference.

CONSOLIDATING THE DECISION TO TERMINATE

No matter how firmly and unequivocally a review of progress in psychotherapy indicates that a termination point has been reached, time should always be allowed for this conclusion in turn to be reviewed and become consolidated. Although the conduct of psychotherapy is governed largely by relative rather than absolute principles, an absolute prescription can be written with respect to termination: Never terminate psychotherapy with the session in which termination first comes up for discussion, regardless of how appropriate it is agreed to be. There are four compelling reasons for adhering strictly to this principle:

1. The patient or the therapist may be mistaken in his or her initial impression of the patient's readiness to terminate. All the relevant facts may simply not come to mind on the first occasion of a progress review, and further reflection may yield a different perspective on the appropriateness of terminating. Additionally, transference and countertransference attitudes are both capable of influencing a premature conclusion that treatment should end. Patients may claim no further need for therapy either as a means of rewarding the therapist should they feel positively toward him or her, or of escaping the treatment should they be experiencing strong negative transference. Therapists may erroneously decide that the work of the treatment is accomplished because they want the satisfaction of believing they have "cured" the patient or because they want to be

able to justify discontinuing a difficult or distasteful treatment relationship. Only if there is an opportunity in further sessions for both parties to reconsider their wish to terminate will it be possible to identify and adjust for any such transference or countertransference elements.

2. Even if patient and therapist are correct at the time in concluding that the treatment seems no longer necessary or beneficial, they may be failing to anticipate subsequent events that would suggest otherwise. Psychological functioning is cyclical, and it is in the nature of people to feel better about themselves on some days and worse on others, and to deal more effectively with their experience on some occasions than on others. Accordingly, any conviction that psychotherapy has reached its termination point should be tempered by attention to a patient's likely future prospects. Unless patients have already passed an extended period of sustained improvement, special care must be taken to ensure that their apparent improvement of the moment will not succumb to the next life problem they face, nor cycle of its own accord into a state of markedly decreased self-feeling or reduced personal effectiveness. Only by continuing the treatment beyond the session in which termination is first considered reasonable can the therapist adequately determine how enduring a patient's gains have become.

3. Even if a patient's improvement is real and enduring, therapists who suggest terminating treatment the first time such a possibility comes up for discussion risk injecting a note of rejection into the treatment relationship. No matter how gratified patients may be at having completed the work of the treatment, they are unlikely to savor breaking it off at a moment's notice. Indeed, the terminal phase of psychotherapy is a period of separation for patients, often mourned in the same way as other separations from familiar people, places, and activities are mourned. The pain of such separations tends to be eased by opportunities to prepare for them, especially if feelings about the separation can be aired and worked through before it becomes final.

If treatment is terminated as soon as the possibility is considered, patients have no such opportunity to prepare for separation from the treatment relationship, and they also have good reason to wonder about the motives of the therapist's preemptory behavior. It is as if the patient has said, "I don't think I need to see you any more" and the therapist has promptly replied, "Okay, goodbye." Even in the absence of such curtness, therapists' willingness to end the treatment as soon as it begins to seem reasonable to do so can leave a patient thinking the therapist "couldn't wait to get rid of me." Both to allow the patient a gradual separation process and to avoid appearances of rejecting them, it is obligatory to extend psychotherapy beyond the point at which termination is first considered.

4. Even if the three preceding potential disadvantages of hasty termination could be avoided in a particular case, abrupt endings will abort valuable opportunities for a closing burst of activity in the therapy. Very often a mutual decision that psychotherapy has reached a good stopping point motivates effective use by patients of the time between when the decision is made and when it is carried out. Knowing that the treatment is soon to terminate encourages patients to raise issues that have not yet been covered in the treatment and to tie up loose ends of previous discussions. What takes place, then, is the kind of useful integrative summary that occurs in many work situations when a period of time is specified as constituting its final phase. If termination is enacted when it is first considered appropriate, no time is provided for such a concluding period of useful work.

For these four reasons, then, some number of sessions should always be allotted to consolidating the decision to terminate psychotherapy. Because a first impression of progress can be erroneous, because current progress does not necessarily ensure sustained progress, because termination is a separation process, and because an extended summary period can be very useful, therapists should refrain from implementing termination abruptly and should resist any pressure from patients to do so. In this latter regard, suppose a patient follows an initial agreement that the necessary work of the treatment appears completed by saying, "I guess this will be our last session, then, because I don't see any need for me to come again." The therapist should always attempt to defer such decisions with a comment on the order of the following: "Even though everything right now appears to point to your having completed treatment, it is usually helpful to allow a little time to make sure our impressions are correct; so I suggest that we begin now to plan on stopping but arrange for some further sessions between now and when we stop completely." A response of this kind, framed in terms of realistic considerations and inviting patients to begin the work of consolidating their decision to terminate, helps to avert abrupt termination and encourages the patient to work through a termination process.

ARRANGING FOR TIME-LIMITED OR SPACED TERMINATION

The final phase of psychotherapy, between the point at which termination is agreed to be reasonable and the time of the final session, can be arranged in two ways. In *time-limited termination*, a fixed duration of time is set during which sessions continue at their usual frequency and then stop completely. For example, a patient being seen in once-weekly psychotherapy might be scheduled for one additional month of weekly sessions between the time when termination is agreed on and when it is to be implemented. In *spaced termination,* the time between sessions is gradually extended, so that the date of the final session is not set in advance but is approached in measured steps. With spaced termination a patient being seen weekly might be changed first to bi-weekly sessions and then to some monthly visits before the treatment is finally ended.

From the patient's point of view, the most obvious difference between time-limited and spaced termination is that the former method designates when the final session will occur and the latter does not. Thus time-limited termination implies that patients seem fully prepared to go their own way but will find some final period for tying up loose ends helpful. Spaced termination, on the other hand, implies that a wait-and-see period is in order, during which patients will be gradually weaned from the treatment as they are able to sustain their improvements over increasingly longer periods. Even with spaced termination, however, there eventually comes a time when the next regularly scheduled session is intended in advance to be the last ("Let's plan to meet one more time, two months from now, and if things still appear to be going as well for you, we can make that session our last one").

Despite their different implication, neither time-limited nor spaced termination should be considered an irrevocable arrangement. In effective time-limited termination, patients usually pass through a period of tying up loose ends and preparing for separation, following which they find less and less to talk about and the sessions gradually tail off into pleasant but mundane conversation. Should a patient instead continue right into the last scheduled session to bring up new or unresolved issues, then it may behoove the therapist to propose amending the time-limit agreement: "In view of all that has been coming up in the last few weeks, it may be that we set our stopping point too early; perhaps we should allow some additional time to make sure you have an opportunity to finish thinking through the kinds of issues you have been raising recently."

Needless to say, any decision to extend time-limited termination in response to a last-minute flurry of activity must take into account the possibility that the patient's activity level represents resistance to termination. Patients who have completed the work of the treatment but nevertheless want to retain their patient role or their relationship with the therapist may suffer an apparent "relapse" or begin to dredge up "new" or "urgent" matters for discussion as termination approaches. The message in such behavior is "See I've really got a lot of problems yet and a lot to talk with you about, so we better not terminate after all." If on inquiry the reports of relapse prove exaggerated and the problems being presented neither new nor urgent, therapists should then proceed with the time-limited termination as planned, allowing extra sessions only as they seem necessary to help patients work through their specific concerns about ending the treatment.

Spaced termination must similarly be guided by flexibility in deciding which is to be the final session. If patients decrease in a regular progression their use of their treatment sessions for working on continuing issues and concerns, spaced termination may proceed in a corresponding progression toward less frequent sessions and the scheduling of a final follow-up visit. Should new or pressing problems emerge during this spacing-out period, however, it may be necessary to revise the termination plan. Then a therapist who has reduced once-weekly visits to bi-weekly visits may find it necessary to suggest, "Since a number of new things have come up recently that seem useful to talk about, perhaps we should go back to having sessions every week for a while." Similarly, a presumably final follow-up visit may reveal that a patient has had unanticipated difficulty in sustaining prior improvement and that some further follow-up sessions seem in order.

As in the case of time-limited termination, therapists evaluating some apparent continuation or reappearance of difficulties during spaced termination should consider the possible role of resistance to termination in causing a patient to experience or report continuing problems. Yet they must also prevent their wariness from closing their ears to actual continuing problems, and their determination to complete the treatment should not bind them fast to the original termination agreement. At the very least, if they have some reservations about patients' capacities to sustain and build on their improvements but still feel that termination should be implemented, they should make it clear that their door remains open should the patient subsequently experience a need to return.

CHOOSING BETWEEN TIME-LIMITED AND SPACED TERMINATION

The choice between a time-limited and spaced approach to termination depends on the nature and goals of the treatment contract. Generally speaking, time-limited termination works most effectively in uncovering psychotherapy, whereas spaced termination becomes increasingly appropriate the more supportive the treatment has been. Because time-limited termination gives patients a fixed period to finish their business, it presumes considerable capacity on their part to utilize this time effectively and then promptly discontinue the treatment. For patients who have been fulfilling the obligations of participating in uncovering psychotherapy, these demands of time-limited termination are consistent with what has previously been expected of them, and they are furthermore rewarding in the confidence they express in them. The more supportively patients have been seen, on the other hand, the more the requirements of time-limited termination will diverge from their previous role responsibilities in the treatment and burden them with anxiety about being able to meet them.

Hence spaced termination meets the needs of patients in relatively supportive psychotherapy by granting them an initially unspecified length of time in which to extricate themselves gradually from the treatment and to test out in measured steps their capacity to function adequately without it. To offer such an opportunity for gradual weaning from treatment to patients in uncovering psychotherapy would have the disadvantage of appearing to baby them, as if the therapist lacked confidence in their ability to end the treatment as responsibly as they had thus far participated in it. To maintain consistency with the previous tenor of the treatment, then, and thereby promote smooth transit from it, time-limited or spaced termination should be selected according to the relative prior emphasis on uncovering or supportive goals in the treatment.

With either the time-limited or spaced method of termination, the length of the terminal period should be adapted to the frequency and duration of the treatment that has preceded it. In both primarily uncovering and primarily supportive psychotherapy, the more frequent sessions have been and the longer the therapy has lasted, the more patients will have become engrossed in and accustomed to it, and the longer they will require to tie up loose content ends of the treatment and work through their separation from it. Thus the interval set for time-limited termination of uncovering psychotherapy should ordinarily be longer for a patient who has been seen twice weekly than for one seen once weekly, and longer for a patient whose treatment has lasted for two years than for one whose treatment has lasted one year. Similarly in supportive psychotherapy, patients who have been seen weekly for 10 months should have their termination spaced out in more gradual increments and over a longer total period than patients who have been seen biweekly for 5 months.

REINFORCING SELF-OBSERVATIONAL ABILITIES

The decision to terminate psychotherapy should be made with confidence that patients will be able not only to sustain their improvements but also to build on them through continued self-observation. As patients in the final phase of treatment become increasingly capable of self-initiated and adaptive reflection on their experience, they typically bring progressively fewer issues to the treatment sessions that require interpretive comments from the therapist. This means that the less work therapists find to do on a patient's behalf, the more likely it is that patients have become sufficiently capable of sustaining and building on their improvements to justify termination.

On the other hand, in the absence of resistance to termination, the emergence of major new difficulties following an agreement to work toward termination may signify either that the extent of patients' unresolved problems has not been fully appreciated or that their ability to confront problems solely with their own resources is not yet firmly enough established for the treatment to end. In the first instance some new interpretive work may be necessary that will delay termination and continue the treatment in a middle phase, whereas in the second instance the therapist's task will be not so much to engage in new interpretive work as to help patients make better use of their previously developed capacity to understand and modify their behavior.

The techniques for helping patients make better use of their self-observational capacities consist of reinforcing them when they act as their own therapist and confronting them when they do not. To reinforce effective self-observation, therapists in the final phase of treatment should make liberal use of the following kind of comment:

> I think it's important for you to pay special attention to what happened this week. You ran into a problem on Monday that was similar to many of the problems you were having when we began working together. Yet you were able to think it through, without letting it make you anxious, and you were able to find some way of dealing with it that worked out very well. So now on Wednesday, when you come in for your session, you've taken care of the whole thing by yourself, and there's really nothing that we need to discuss about it.

To confront patients with their reluctance or failure to initiate self-observation of which they appear capable, comments of the following kind may be called for:

> It strikes me that the problem you're raising for discussion today is really one that we've talked about a number of times and that you understand pretty well. In fact, I can think of some occasions in the past few months you've handled some similar problems very well on your own, without even finding it necessary to discuss them with me first. So I wonder if perhaps right now you're not using all the ability you have to work through this particular situation on your own.

The first of these illustrative comments is obviously reinforcing and aimed toward consolidating the decision to terminate. The second comment confronts the patient with an apparent failure to utilize self-observational capacities, but note that it also refers to evidence of the person's prior progress. The emphasis, in other words, is less on criticizing patients for what they are not currently doing than on reminding them of how much they have been able to do in the past and engaging their curiosity about what may be preventing them from sustaining their prior accomplishments. If correctly timed and aptly phrased, such confrontation can lead patients into a productive exploration of whatever influences may be suppressing their capacity for independent self-observation.

Fostering Resolution of the Transference

As discussed in Chapter 10, successful psychotherapy is characterized by the gradual diminution of transference reactions in the later phases of the treatment. With termination approaching, transference typically is resolved in great part by the working through of transference interpretations. As patients recognize their dispositions to misperceive the therapist or the treatment situation, they become capable of modifying or at least anticipating and controlling them. As they near completion of the treatment, they accordingly display progressively fewer instances of transference behavior, and these instances are increasingly accompanied by accurate and self-initiated observations about the displacements they involve.

Although resolution of the transference is a process that must emanate from the patient, the therapist can play an important role in fostering and reinforcing it. Attention was given in Chapter 10 to means by which therapists should act to safeguard each of the three components of the treatment relationship, the transference, the real relationship, and the working alliance. In the final phase of therapy, when the time has come for transference to be resolved as much as possible and the real relationship to gain ascendance, therapists can facilitate this change by reducing their efforts to safeguard the transference and concentrating on safeguarding the real relationship.

For therapists to promote the real relationship at the expense of transference, they need to act increasingly as a real rather than as an as-if object. For example, certain questions may now be taken at their face value and answered directly, rather than construed as behavior to be understood. To a patient who says, "I wonder why I didn't realize sooner that I could never make a living as a salesman," the response is no longer "What thoughts do you have about it?" but instead, "As we've learned, for a long time you felt you had to be the kind of brash, back-slapping person you associated with being a salesman." Likewise, the therapist may now express certain personal feelings instead of trying to prevent them from influencing the treatment relationship. To a patient who reports, "I got a promotion at work" or "I got engaged over the weekend," the response is no longer limited to "Tell me about it" but may also include "I'm pleased to hear that" or "Best wishes."

In making such responses, therapists should be striving not to rush headlong into an intimate personal relationship with a patient, but only to change subtly their emphasis within the role prescribed for them by the treatment contract. Instead of constant attention to fostering transference by maintaining their stimulus ambiguity, they should respond in ways that diminish opportunities for patients to form impressions of them on any but a realistic basis.

By becoming somewhat more of a real object in patients' lives, therapists can help them progress toward resolution of their transference reactions and a relatively painless separation from the treatment relationship. Caution is necessary in this process, however, lest the therapist inadvertently suppress unsuspected transference reactions that the patient still needs to work actively on resolving. As with other aspects of consolidating the decision to terminate, there must be some opportunity to assess whether transference is sufficiently resolved for the treatment to end successfully. Should the initial decision to enter a final phase of treatment be followed by an upsurge of transference feelings, further interpretive work may be required, even to the extent of deferring the termination plan.

CONSIDERATIONS IN FORCED TERMINATION

As desirable as it may be for psychotherapy to wind down of its own accord and lead naturally into a final phase, therapists must be prepared for external circumstances that force termination of treatment prior to any substantial realization of its goals. Patients may move out of town to take a new job, get married, go away to school, or enter the military, or they may become realistically unable to sustain the cost in time or money of further sessions. Therapists may also move for personal or professional reasons, and, if they are in training, they may complete an assignment and leave an agency or be rotated to a different service.

Although forced termination does not automatically cancel out the prior benefits of treatment, special care is required to prevent its having a disruptive impact. The closing phase of a course of psychotherapy that must be ended prematurely should, as in voluntary termination emphasize the tying up of loose ends, the diminution of the transference relationship and ascendance of the real relationship, and the encouragement and reinforcement of patients' independent capacity to sustain and build on their improvements. Additionally, forced termination of psychotherapy needs to include a careful review of which goals of the treatment have been fairly well realized and which have not, and also a realistic discussion of patients' future plans, particularly with regard to how they will utilize what they have learned in the treatment and whether they will seek further psychotherapy. The specific techniques for implementing forced termination in this way vary somewhat with whether the termination is being forced by the patient or by the therapist, and these two possibilities are accordingly discussed separately.

TERMINATION FORCED BY THE PATIENT

When patients state that they will not be able to continue in psychotherapy beyond a certain date, the therapist needs first to determine whether this statement reflects real constraints or is instead a manifestation of resistance. Whenever resistance appears responsible for a unilateral decision to terminate, every effort should be made to help patients recognize the origin of their decision and to dissuade them from acting on it until they have given it further thought. However, if circumstances external to the psychotherapy process make it very difficult or impossible for a patient to continue treatment beyond a certain date, then it is necessary to institute terminal work even if the progress to date would not otherwise call for doing so.

To move psychotherapy into a final phase prior to its evolving naturally, therapists can begin with a remark such as the following: "Since with your leaving town it appears we will have only another two months to work together, we should start to review what has gone on in the therapy, especially matters we've considered but haven't finished with." Such an overture sets a review process in motion and also encourages patients to focus on problems and concerns that they feel need further work.

While thus inviting the patient to pursue unfinished business, the therapist needs to be cautious about getting into new problems that cannot be adequately worked through in the time remaining. It is a disservice to patients to allow them to unravel psychological concerns only to send them forth from therapy with these loose ends still flapping. Once therapists have proposed a period of review and consolidation, with forced termination pending, they should concentrate on conducting such a review and discourage patients from opening up major new avenues for exploration.

To this end, therapists in the final phase of forced termination therapy must exchange the relatively noncommittal, unstructured approach by which they have previously encouraged a patient's spontaneous associations for a more focused approach to summarizing and concluding the work of the treatment. Without probing for new areas of concern, they should review at the level of the real relationship the amount and kind of progress that has been made and identify the treatment goals that have not yet been achieved. They should also discuss patients' future plans with them and not hesitate to advise patients about ways in which the finished and unfinished work of the treatment are likely to affect them in the future, as in the following example:

In the time we've worked together, you've been able to overcome much of the work inhibition that was holding you back, and one result of your progress is the promotion you've received that is taking you to a different city. But we've also learned that you have a tendency to doubt yourself at first when you take on a new or challenging task, and we haven't had time to work out that particular problem. So you should keep in mind that you may experience some initial self-doubts in the new job and take care not to let them discourage you or interfere with your keeping at your work.

Such counsel may seem too superficial or gratuitous to provide a patient much protection against continuing neurotic concerns, and indeed it might be in the absence of any prior treatment gains. However, if patients who must terminate have previously been engaged in acquiring and consolidating new learning about themselves, it is reasonable to expect them to draw on parting advice from the therapist to help sustain and enhance their improvements after the treatment ends. Just as patients who terminate voluntarily should continue to build on their gains from therapy, those who must end prematurely should be able to progress on their own following the therapy if the therapist provides them some guidance for doing so.

Considering Further Treatment

A very important consideration in reviewing future plans with patients who must terminate psychotherapy is the advisability of further treatment in the new locale or at some future time. Judgments about further psychotherapy depend on the same considerations that enter into an initial evaluation and assessment, including the extent of the patient's need for help and the likelihood that psychotherapy will provide such help (see Chapter 5). If patient and therapist agree that treatment should be resumed, either with a different therapist in another location or with the same therapist after an unavoidable interruption, then therapists need to curtail somewhat the thoroughness of their progress review and the extent of their emphasis on the real relationship.

With regard to previous progress, otherwise admirable closure in reviewing and summarizing the treatment may seal over areas of concern that should be left exposed if therapy is to resume. The preceding example, in which the therapist explicates for the patient some continuing propensity for self-doubt, represents a helpful procedure primarily when treatment will not be resumed. Yet it is generally the case that patients derive more benefit from participating actively in coming to such understandings of themselves than from having the therapist do the work for them. Hence with patients who will be resuming treatment in the near future, specific advice concerning the handling of likely future problems should be soft-pedaled to allow these matters to emerge spontaneously in the continuing treatment and be worked on independently of prior formulations or judgments about them.

As for the treatment relationship, an emphasis on reality in terminal work with a patient who will be resuming treatment seriously compromises the position of the next therapist. Because of its mutuality, the real relationship is inherently more gratifying and comfortable than the asymmetric working alliance, which patients agree to put up with as the price of learning more about themselves in psychotherapy. Once patients have progressed through a middle phase of psychotherapy, with its stress on the working alliance and on safeguarding the transference, to a terminal phase, with its stress on the real relationship and on resolving the transference, it is very difficult for them to accept a return to nonmutuality. Therapists who attempt to reinstitute exploratory psychotherapy with a patient who has recently completed a final phase of treatment that stressed a real patient-therapist relationship are likely to be seen as harsh, ungiving, and disinterested and to be compared unfavorably with the previous therapist, who is remembered for his or her warm, active, and direct engagement during termination.

For this reason, therapists doing terminal work with patients who will soon be resuming treatment should refrain from becoming too much of a real object in the treatment relationship, lest they pose an unsurmountable challenge for their successor. At the same time, they should work to resolve the patient's pressing transference attitudes toward them as much as possible, to prevent these attitudes from carrying over into the subsequent treatment as a potent source of initial resistance. Ideally, then, patients who must terminate psychotherapy but will soon continue with another therapist should have worked through their transference reactions to their first therapist without having come to interact with this therapist primarily as a real object. The more fully the final phase of the first treatment relationship satisfies both of these aims, the better the patient's prospects will be for participating effectively in and benefiting from continued treatment with a second therapist.

TERMINATION FORCED BY THE THERAPIST

Whereas in private office practice forced termination of psychotherapy tends to be instigated primarily by the patient when it occurs, there are numerous settings in which termination forced by the therapist is a common or even regular occurrence. Most notable in this regard are clinical training centers in which psychotherapy is provided under staff supervision by trainees in mental health disciplines, who leave the center on completion of their assignment to it. Even among practicing clinicians, especially those who hold academic appointments or agency positions, there is sufficient mobility to generate a substantial frequency of therapist-forced termination.

In arranging for terminations they must impose, therapists as in other treatment situations must attend to helping the patient complete unfinished business, resolve transference issues, and plan for the future. Of these, resolution of the transference is most likely to prove problematic, because termination forced by the therapist inevitably foments negative patient reactions. There is no way therapists can avoid having their cancellation of the treatment contract perceived as a hostile and rejecting act. No matter how rational or understandable the patient finds the therapist's action to be from the therapist's point of view, from the patient's point of view it still represents a voluntary decision by the therapist to terminate the treatment relationship. Whatever their intellectual grasp of the therapist's reasons for terminating, emotionally the patient will believe, "If you cared enough for me, you wouldn't be leaving."[7]

There is some reality to patients' feeling this way. Therapists who did care enough about continuing to work with them would turn down a new job opportunity, or refuse to allow supervisors rotate them to a different service, or make whatever other changes in their plans would be necessary to allow continuation of the treatment. Yet it would be both unrealistic and beyond the obligations of the treatment contract for therapists to reverse the normal course of their personal and professional lives to avoid terminating a treatment relationship. Without allowing either guilt or positive countertransference to draw them into extending psychotherapy at the expense of seriously disrupting their own life, therapists need to take account of these inevitable negative reactions to their leaving, in three important respects.

First, they should make certain that patients' reactions to their leaving are aired and discussed as fully as possible. Other efforts at achieving some resolution of the transference prior to termination will go for naught if patients are left with unexpressed anger at the therapist for deserting them. Often patients manifest such anger with sufficient directness for therapists to recognize it promptly and deal with it as they would other transference behavior. Should patients give no hint of emotional reactions to a therapist's leaving, they should be asked specifically about them: "I wonder if you've been having any feelings about my leaving in just a few more weeks." If even this invitation fails to elicit clear-cut expressions of affect, the therapist should go one step further: "It's likely that you've been having some feelings about my leaving, and it would be helpful if we could talk about them."

Such a direct approach is justified by the inevitability of patients' having some feelings about their therapist forcing termination on them and by the importance of having these feelings expressed, even if the therapist must probe for them. Once such feelings are aired, patients can be helped to recognize their transference elements and to reduce their intensity to the level of realistic disappointment at the imminent separation. If the feelings are not aired, their continued rankling may prevent patients from sustaining and building on their gains in the treatment and from resuming treatment effectively with another therapist.

Second, therapists must give patients as much advance notice as possible concerning their having to terminate the treatment, to allow them sufficient time to work through their reactions to termination. Sometimes therapists know in advance that their time for treating a particular patient will be limited, in which case the time limitation should be discussed as part of the treatment contract. For example, therapists who expect to be working for only a year in a particular clinic should tell each patient with whom they consider possible psychotherapy exactly how many months they have remaining in their tour of duty, and a judgment should be made concerning whether this length of time will be adequate to meet the patient's needs. Should either or both parties anticipate that the work of the treatment cannot be accomplished in the time available, referral should be made to a therapist whose availability is less limited.

In other instances, the circumstances that cause therapists to terminate arise during the treatment, without having been anticipated, and it then behooves therapists to share their plans with their patients as soon as they become definite. Exceptions to this principle should be entertained only if the treatment appears certain to reach a voluntary conclusion prior to the time when the therapist will have to leave. For example, therapists who learn they will have to terminate their patients in 8 months' time may elect not to mention this constraint to a patient already in the final phase of treatment with a fixed termination date just one month away. Similarly, therapists beginning a one-year assignment in a clinic may elect not to mention this time limitation to patients they see early in the year who appear to require only brief supportive psychotherapy.

Third, out of respect for the patient as a person and to safeguard the real relationship, therapists need to state candidly their reasons for terminating treatment. "Candor" does not mean the therapist must share all the issues involved in taking a different job or being shifted to a new assignment, but it does mean presenting an accurate and reasonable explanation of the change that will take place:

> I need to tell you of a change in my life that will affect our working together. I've accepted a position in [name of city] beginning next July 1, which means I will be seeing patients here only until next June. That means

we will have about another six months to continue your therapy, and then we'll have to stop.

Although patients vary in their initial response to such an announcement of forced termination, sooner or later their reaction will touch on all three components of the treatment relationship, transference, the real relationship, and the working alliance. On a transference basis, patients may begin to feel angry or dejected as soon as they are told that the therapist will be leaving. Directly or indirectly patients are then likely to communicate hyperbolic beliefs that the therapist is a scheming hypocrite callously dropping them to seek greener pastures elsewhere, or that they themselves are pathetic people unable to sustain anyone's interest in them and doomed to rejection and disappointment in their interpersonal relationships. For therapists, the corresponding task will be to disabuse patients of such distorted perceptions of what their leaving signifies and thereby dilute the patient's transference reactions to the termination.

At the level of the real relationship, patients are likely to be curious about the therapist's plans and ask about many specific details of them: what kind of new job is involved, where is it located, how was the decision made to leave, what kind of patients will the therapist be seeing, and so forth. The number of such questions therapists answer and the amount of detail they provide depend on their judgment concerning an advantageous balancing of the transference and the real relationship. The closer the therapy is to termination and the stronger the emphasis on fostering ascendance of the real relationship, the more directly and fully therapists should respond to inquiries about their future plans, within what they see as the appropriate limits of the treatment contract. If their work with a particular patient suggests they had best be circumspect in talking about their plans, they should still be certain to inform the patient clearly of their reason for terminating and of the origin of this reason in their life rather than in the patient's behavior.

In terms of the working alliance, therapists' announcements that they must terminate the treatment usually evoke numerous questions from patients about the future course of their therapy: will there be enough time to finish treatment, how should they make best use of the time remaining, what should they do if they need more help, and so forth. Most questions of this kind can be answered in terms of the general guidelines for terminating therapy discussed earlier in the chapter. However, special attention may have to be given to helping patients plan for further treatment if their needs for help are likely to extend beyond the time when the therapist must terminate.

Therapists should provide patients who wish to continue treatment with a list of recommended therapists. Usually this list should include more than one name, to spare the second therapist the burden of being the first therapist's designated heir apparent. If the second therapist is a hand-picked successor, patients may come to him or her with underlying resentments at having had the new therapist chosen for them, without having participated in the choice; they may come with an exaggerated expectation that, because the second therapist was the one person from among the entire local professional community selected to continue the treatment, this therapist will be capable of working wonders in bringing it to a prompt and gratifying conclusion; and, if for some reason they are unable to work out a feasible time schedule with this one therapist, or find this therapist difficult to relate to, they will be stranded without anyone else to turn to.

For these reasons, patients being terminated should be given at least two or three names of other therapists who might continue the treatment. Some thought should also be given to the personality style and usual clientele of the therapists being recommended to minimize the likelihood of a poor patient-therapist match. Terminating therapists should also ascertain whether the therapists they would like to recommend have time available to take on new patients. Patients will then have the names of at least a few recommended therapists, each of whom is accustomed to working with people having their type of problem and has time available to devote to them, and they can exercise some choice in deciding which one to contact first.

Patients being offered such a list may ask their current therapist whom he or she would recommend most, in which case therapists should simply emphasize that all the people they have recommended are competent and available. Patients are then free to select among them by any means they prefer, including going alphabetically or flipping a coin. In this way patients make the selection rather than having it made for them; they do not view any of the people on the list as the best person for them to see; and they have some equally recommended alternatives if there is some failure to connect with the first therapist they choose from the list.

When psychotherapy is primarily supportive, therapists who must terminate the relationship may be somewhat more directive in arranging a successor than has been described thus far. To the extent that dependent gratification has participated in the supportive measures of the treatment, for example, or patients lack sufficient personality resources themselves to decide on and arrange for a new therapist, current therapists may specifically designate their successor and even go so far as to arrange the initial appointment with this new therapist. In clinic and hospital settings in which staff in training are being rotated, it is often helpful in supportive work with seriously disturbed or chronic, marginally adjusted patients for departing therapists to invite a designated successor to attend one of their sessions to be personally introduced to the patient.[8]

What remains to be mentioned are those situations in which terminated patients initiate subsequent contact with the therapist through letters or telephone calls. Although such efforts to sustain some relationship with the therapist can occur following any form of termination, they understandably appear to occur primarily in situations where the therapist has forced the termination before the patient would otherwise have been ready for it. Therapists who receive letters or calls from patients they have terminated must be careful to sustain the same level of real relationship with which they concluded the sessions together. They cannot let themselves be dragged into explorations of current problems, lest they interfere with the patient's work with a subsequent therapist or open up issues they are in no position to help the patient resolve. At the same time, they cannot adopt a personally involved style of relating to the patient, as if they are now letting out real feelings previously held in check by the working alliance, lest they be seductive or cause the patient to have second thoughts about the true nature of their previous relationship. Rather, in keeping with their manner of ending the treatment, they should concentrate on being a real rather than a transference object in the patient's life while avoiding any personal engagements that might reflect their lingering countertransference feelings.

NOTES

1. Confirming evidence that beneficial effects of psychotherapy continue to accrue following termination of the treatment comes largely from clinical experience, as illustrated in a conclusion by Kubie (1973) that "for some patients therapy as a process of continuing psychological change and maturation may start only after formal therapy has been terminated" (p. 882). Two relevant research studies of posttermination personality functioning in psychotherapy patients can be noted, however. In one of these studies, Schramski, Beutler, Lauver, and Arizmendi (1984) administered a battery of self-report measures to patients 6 months following termination and concluded that the majority had maintained or continued to make gains during the posttherapy period. Weiner and Exner (1991) administered the Rorschach Inkblot Method to psychotherapy patients at the beginning of their treatment and 12, 30, and 48 months later. As a group, these patients showed steady and significant improvement across a broad range of adjustment indicators during the course of these evaluations, and additional improvements continued to be observed even well

beyond the time when almost all these patients had terminated their treatment.

2. As noted in the discussion of transference proneness in Chapter 10, patients vary in how intensively they become involved in psychotherapy of a given frequency. Thus a relatively expressive person may be engaged in more intensive psychotherapy on a once-weekly basis than a relatively reflective person is with two sessions per week. By and large, however, it is reasonable to expect that, the more frequently patients are being seen, the more intensive their psychotherapy will become and the longer its duration will have to be.

3. The rationale and procedures for time-limited therapy were first elaborated in detail by Mann (1973). Research demonstrating the potentially positive impact of time limitations in accelerating change in psychotherapy is described by Eckert (1993) and Reynolds et al. (1996).

4. Carefully conceived and widely respected methods of dynamically oriented short-term expressive psychotherapy are described in books by Davanloo (1980), Della Silva (1996), Malan (1976), Sifneos (1987), and Strupp and Binder (1984). For general overviews of these methods, readers are referred to Bauer and Kobos (1987), Bloom (1997), Crits-Christoph and Barber (1991), Groves (1996), Messer and Warren (1995), and Wells and Gianetti (1990).

5. Research demonstrating the relationship of an inadequately developing working alliance to increased risk of early dropout from psychotherapy is reported by Beckham (1992) and Tryon and Kane (1993). Data collected by Hynan (1990), on the other hand, confirm that patients who drop out later on in therapy often have a positive involvement in the treatment relationship but decide to stop on the basis of the improvements they have made in the therapy.

6. For further discussion of patient and therapist roles in initiating termination and their importance in the final phase of psychotherapy, readers are referred to Blum (1989), Kramer (1990), Kupers (1988), and P. Tyson (1996).

7. Further discussion of issues surrounding termination forced by the therapist and case illustrations of negative patient reactions to them are provided by Dewald (1965), Glick (1987), Martinez (1989), and Penn (1990).

8. Problems and techniques of transferring patients in psychotherapy training settings are discussed further by Bostick, Shadid, and Blotcky (1996) and Sederer (1975).

References

Abend, S. M. (1989). Countertransference and psychoanalytic technique. *Psychoanalytic Quarterly, 58,* 374–395.

Abend, S. M. (1993). An inquiry into the fate of the transference in psychoanalysis. *Journal of the American Psychoanalytic Association, 41,* 621–651.

Abt, L. E., & Weissman, S. L. (Eds.). (1965). *Acting out: Theoretical and clinical aspects.* New York: Grune and Stratton.

Acosta, F. X., Yamamoto, J., & Evans, L. A. (1982). *Effective psychotherapy for low-income and minority patients.* New York: Plenum Press.

Addis, M. E. (1997). Evaluating the treatment manual as a means of disseminating empirically validated psychotherapies. *Clinical Psychology, 4,* 1–11.

Akhtar, S. (1992). *Broken structures: Severe personality disorders and their treatment.* Northvale, NJ: Aronson.

Alexander, F., & French, T. M. (1946). *Psychoanalytic therapy.* New York: Ronald Press.

Allison, K. W., Echemendia, R. J., Crawford, I., & Robinson, W. L. (1996). Predicting cultural competence: Implications for practice and training. *Professional Psychology, 27,* 386–393.

Allport, G. W. (1937). The functional autonomy of motives. *American Journal of Psychology, 50,* 141–156.

American Psychological Association. (1992). Ethical principles of psychologists and code of conduct. *American Psychologist, 47,* 1597–1611.

Anderson, E. M., & Lambert, M. J. (1995). Short-term dynamically oriented psychotherapy: A review and meta-analysis. *Clinical Psychology Review, 15,* 503–514.

Aponte, J. F., Rivers, R. Y., & Wohl, J. (Eds.). (1995). *Psychological interventions and cultural diversity.* Boston: Allyn & Bacon.

Arnkoff, D. B., Victor, B. J., & Glass, C. R. (1993). Empirical research on factors in psychotherapeutic change. In G. Stricker & J. R. Gold (Eds.), *Comprehensive handbook of psychotherapy integration* (pp. 27–42). New York: Plenum Press.

Austad, C. S., & Berman, W. H. (Eds.). (1991). *Psychotherapy in managed care.* Washington, DC: American Psychological Association.

Barber, J. P., Crits-Christoph, P., & Luborsky, L. (1996). Effects of therapist adherence and competence on patient outcome in brief dynamic therapy. *Journal of Consulting and Clinical Psychology, 64,* 619–622.

Barron, J. W., Eagle, M. N., & Wolitzky, D. L. (Eds.). (1992). *Interface of psychoanalysis and psychology.* Washington, DC: American Psychological Association.

Barron, J. W., & Sands, H. (1996). *Impact of managed care on psychodynamic treatment*. Madison, CT: International Universities Press.

Bauer, G. P. (1989). Use of transference in the here and now: Patient and therapist resistance. *Psychotherapy, 26,* 112–119.

Bauer, G. P., & Mills, J. A. (1987). *Brief therapy: Short-term psychodynamic intervention*. Northvale, NJ: Aronson.

Beckham, E. E. (1992). Predicting patient dropout in psychotherapy. *Psychotherapy, 29,* 177–182.

Beitman, B. D. (1987). *The structure of individual psychotherapy*. New York: Guilford Press.

Beitman, B. D. (1992). Integration through fundamental similarities and some useful differences among the schools. In J. C. Norcross & M. R. Goldfried (Eds.), *Handbook of psychotherapy integration* (pp. 202–230). New York: Basic Books.

Beitman, B. D., Goldfried, M. R., & Norcross, J. C. (1989). The movement toward integrating the psychotherapies: An overview. *American Journal of Psychiatry, 146,* 138–147.

Beres, D. (1995). Conflict. In B. E. Moore & B. D. Fine (Eds.), *Psychoanalysis: The major concepts* (pp. 477–484). New Haven, CT: Yale University Press.

Berger, D. M. (1987). *Clinical empathy*. Northvale, NJ: Aronson.

Bergin, A. E., & Garfield, S. L. (Eds.). (1994a). *Handbook of psychotherapy and behavior change* (4th ed.). New York: Wiley.

Bergin, A. E., & Garfield, S. L. (1994b). Overview, trends, and future issues. In A. E. Bergin & S. L. Garfield (Eds.), *Handbook of psychotherapy and behavior change* (4th ed., pp. 821–830). New York: Wiley.

Berman, J. S., & Norton, N. C. (1985). Does professional training make a therapist more effective? *Psychological Bulletin, 98,* 401–406.

Bersoff, D. N. (1995). *Ethical conflicts in psychology*. Washington, DC: American Psychological Association.

Beutler, L. E. (1997). The psychotherapist as a neglected variable in psychotherapy: An illustration by reference to the role of therapist experience and training. *Clinical Psychology, 4,* 44–52.

Beutler, L. E., & Clarkin, J. F. (1990). *Systematic treatment selection*. New York: Brunner/Mazel.

Beutler, L. E., & Kendall, P. C. (1995). Introduction to the special section: The case for training in the provision of psychological therapy. *Journal of Consulting and Clinical Psychology, 63,* 179–181.

Beutler, L. E., Machado, P. P., & Neufeldt, S. A. (1994). Therapist variables. In A. E. Bergin & S. L. Garfield (Eds.), *Handbook of psychotherapy research and behavior change* (4th ed., pp. 229–269). New York: Wiley.

Bibring, E. (1954). Psychoanalysis and the dynamic psychotherapies. *Journal of the American Psychoanalytic Association, 2,* 745–770.

Binder, J. L., & Strupp, H. H. (1997). "Negative process": A recurrently discovered and underestimated facet of therapeutic process and outcome in the individual psychotherapy of adults. *Clinical Psychology, 4,* 121–139.

Bischoff, M. M., & Tracey, T. J. (1995). Client resistance as predicted by therapist behavior: A study of sequential dependence. *Journal of Counseling Psychology, 42,* 487–495.

Blanck, G., & Blanck, R. (1994). *Ego psychology: Theory and practice* (2nd ed.). New York: Columbia University Press.

Blanton, S. (1971). *Diary of my analysis with Sigmund Freud.* New York: Hawthorne Books.

Blatt, S. J., & Felsen, I. (1993). Different kinds of folks may need different kinds of strokes: The effect of patients' characteristics on therapeutic change and outcome. *Psychotherapy Research, 3,* 245–259.

Blatt, S. J., & Lerner, H. (1991). Psychodynamic perspectives on personality theory. In M. Hersen, A. E. Kazdin, & A. S. Bellack (Eds.), *The clinical psychology handbook* (2nd ed., pp. 147–169). New York: Pergamon Press.

Bloom, B. L. (1997). *Planned short-term psychotherapy* (2nd ed.). Boston: Allyn & Bacon.

Blum, H. P. (1989). The concept of termination and the evolution of psychoanalytic thought. *Journal of the American Psychoanalytic Association, 37,* 275–295.

Blum, H. P. (1991). Sadomasochism in the psychoanalytic process, within and beyond the pleasure principle. *Journal of the American Psychoanalytic Association, 39,* 431–450.

Blum, H. P., & Goodman, W. H. (1995). Countertransference. In B. E. Moore & B. D. Fine (Eds.), *Psychoanalysis: The major concepts* (pp. 121–129). New Haven, CT: Yale University Press.

Boesky, D. (1982). Acting out. *International Journal of Psycho-Analysis, 63,* 39–55.

Boesky, D. (1990). The psychoanalytic process and its components. *Psychoanalytic Quarterly, 59,* 550–584.

Bohart, A. C., & Greenberg, L. S. (1997). *Empathy reconsidered.* Washington, DC: American Psychological Association.

Bolter, K., Levenson, H., & Alvarez, W. (1990). Differences in values between short-term and long-term therapists. *Professional Psychology, 21,* 285–290.

Bongar, B., & Beutler, L. E. (Eds.). (1995). *Comprehensive textbook of psychotherapy: Theory and practice.* New York: Oxford University Press.

Bordin, E. S. (1979). The generalizability of the psychoanalytic concept of the working alliance. *Psychotherapy, 16,* 252–260.

Bordin, E. S. (1994). Theory and research on the therapeutic working alliance: New directions. In A. O. Horvath & L. S. Greenberg (Eds.), *The working alliance* (pp. 13–37). New York: Wiley.

Borys, D. S., & Pope, K. S. (1989). Dual relationships between therapist and client: A national study of psychologists, psychiatrists, and social workers. *Professional Psychology, 20,* 283–293.

Bostic, J. Q., Shadid, L. G., & Blotcky, M. J. (1996). Our time is up: Forced terminations during psychotherapy training. *American Journal of Psychotherapy, 50,* 347–359.

Bowers, K., & Meichenbaum, D. (Eds.). (1984). *The unconscious revisited.* New York: Wiley.

Brenner, C. (1959). The masochistic character. *Journal of the American Psychoanalytic Association, 7,* 197–226.

Brenner, C. (1982). *The mind in conflict.* New York: International Universities Press.

Brenner, C. (1987). Working through: 1914–1984. *Psychoanalytic Quarterly, 56,* 88–108.

Brenner, C. (1996). Psychoanalytic theory of symptom formation and pathological character formation. In E. Nessarian & R. G. Kopff (Eds.), *Textbook of psychoanalysis* (pp. 171–187). Washington, DC: American Psychiatric Press.

Breuer, J., & Freud, S. (1955). Studies on hysteria. *Standard Edition* (Vol. 2, pp. 1–319). London: Hogarth Press. (Original work published 1893–1895)

Brody, E. M., & Farber, B. A. (1996). The effects of therapist experience and patient diagnosis on countertransference. *Psychotherapy, 33,* 372–380.

Buckley, P., Karasu, T. B., & Charles, E. (1979). Common mistakes in psychotherapy. *American Journal of Psychiatry, 136,* 1578–1580.

Budman, S. H., & Gurman, A. S. (1983). The practice of brief therapy. *Professional Psychology, 14,* 277–292.

Burlingame, G. M., Fuhriman, A., Paul, S., & Ogles, B. M. (1989). Implementing a time-limited therapy program: Differential effects of training and experience. *Psychotherapy, 26,* 303–313.

Busch, F. (1995). *The ego at the center of clinical technique.* Northvale, NJ: Aronson.

Busch, F. (1996). The ego and its significance in analytic interventions. *Journal of the American Psychoanalytic Association, 44,* 1073–1099.

Butcher, J. N. (1990). *The use of the MMPI-2 in treatment planning.* New York: Oxford University Press.

Canavan-Gumpert, D., Garner, K., & Gumpert, P. (1978). *The success-fearing personality.* Lexington, MA: Lexington Books.

Carter, R. T. (1995). *The influence of race and racial identity in psychotherapy.* New York: Wiley.

Casas, J. M. (1995). Counseling and psychotherapy with racial/ethnic minority groups in theory and practice. In B. Bongar & L. E. Beutler (Eds.), *Comprehensive textbook of psychotherapy* (pp. 311–335). New York: Oxford University Press.

Castelnuovo-Tedesco, P. (1989). The fear of change and its consequences in analysis and psychotherapy. *Psychoanalytic Inquiry, 9,* 101–118.

Castonguay, L. G., & Goldfried, M. R. (1994). Psychotherapy integration: An idea whose time has come. *Applied and Preventive Psychology, 3,* 159–172.

Cavenar, J. O., & Werman, D. S. (1983). The sex of the psychotherapists. *American Journal of Psychiatry, 140,* 85–87.

Chessick, R. D. (1971). *Why psychotherapists fail.* New York: Science House.

Chessick, R. D. (1983). *Intensive psychotherapy of the borderline patient.* Northvale, NJ: Aronson.

Chessick, R. D. (1994). What brings about change in psychoanalytic treatment? *Psychoanalytic Review, 81,* 279–300.

Chisholm, S. M., Crowther, J. H., & Ben-Porath, Y. (1997). Selected MMPI-2 scales' ability to predict premature termination and outcome from psychotherapy. *Journal of Personality Assessment, 69,* 127–144.

Chodoff, P. (1996). Ethical dimensions of psychotherapy: A personal perspective. *American Journal of Psychotherapy, 50,* 298–310.

Christensen, A., & Jacobson, N. S. (1994). Who (or what) can do psychotherapy: The status and challenge of nonprofessional therapies. *Psychological Science, 5,* 8–14.

Clark, M. M. (1988). Personal therapy: A review of empirical research. *Professional Psychology, 17,* 541–543.

Colson, D. B., Eyman, J. R., & Coyne, L. (1994). Rorschach correlates of treatment difficulty and of the therapeutic alliance in psychotherapy with female psychiatric hospital patients. *Bulletin of the Menninger Clinic, 58,* 393–398.

Comas-Díaz, L., & Greene, B. (1994). *Women of color: Integrating ethnic and gender identities in psychotherapy.* New York: Guilford Press.

Comas-Díaz, L., & Jacobsen, F. M. (1991). Ethnocultural transference and countertransference in the therapeutic dyad. *American Journal of Orthopsychiatry, 61,* 392–402.

Conigliaro, V. (1997). *Dreams as a tool in psychodynamic psychotherapy.* New York: International Universities Press.

Conte, H. R., Plutchik, R., Picard, S., & Karasu, T. B. (1989). Ethics in the practice of psychotherapy: A survey. *American Journal of Psychotherapy, 43,* 32–42.

Cooper, A. M. (1987a). Changes in psychoanalytic ideas: Transference interpretation. *Journal of the American Psychoanalytic Association, 35,* 77–98.

Cooper, A. M. (1987b). The transference neurosis: A concept ready for retirement. *Psychoanalytic Inquiry, 7,* 569–585.

Cooper, S. H. (1992). The empirical study of defensive processes: A review. In J. W. Barron, M. N. Eagle, & D. L. Wolitzky (Eds.), *Interface of psychoanalysis and psychology* (pp. 327–346). Washington, DC: American Psychological Association.

Coster, J. S., & Schwebel, M. (1997). Well-functioning in professional psychologists. *Professional Psychology, 28,* 5–13.

Coursey, R. D., Keller, A. B., & Farrell, E. W. (1995). Individual psychotherapy and persons with serious mental illness: The client's perspective. *Schizophrenia Bulletin, 21,* 283–301.

Craig, R. J. (Ed.). (1989). *Clinical and diagnostic interviewing.* Northvale, NJ: Aronson.

Crits-Christoph, P. (1992). The efficacy of brief dynamic psychotherapy: A meta-analysis. *American Journal of Psychiatry, 149,* 151–158.

Crits-Christoph, P., Baranackie, K., Kurcias, J. S., Beck, A. T., Carroll, K., Perry, K., Luborsky, L., McLellan, A. T., Woody, G. E., Thompson, L., Gallagher, D., & Zitrin, C. (1991). Meta-analysis of therapist effects in psychotherapy outcome studies. *Psychotherapy Research, 1,* 81–91.

Crits-Christoph, P., & Barber, J. P. (Eds.). (1991). *Handbook of short-term dynamic psychotherapy.* New York: Basic Books.

Crits-Christoph, P., Barber, J. P., & Kurcias, J. S. (1993). The accuracy of therapists' interpretations and the development of the therapeutic alliance. *Psychotherapy Research, 3,* 25–35.

Crits-Christoph, P., Cooper, A., & Luborsky, L. (1988). The accuracy of therapists' interpretations and the outcome of dynamic psychotherapy. *Journal of Consulting and Clinical Psychology, 56,* 490–495.

Curtis, J. T., Silberschatz, G., Sampson, H., Weiss, J., & Rosenberg, S. E. (1988). Developing reliable psychodynamic case formulations: An illustration of the plan diagnosis method. *Psychotherapy, 25,* 256–265.

Davanloo, H. (1980). *Short-term dynamic psychotherapy.* New York: Aronson.

Della Silva, P. C. (1996). *Intensive short-term dynamic psychotherapy.* New York: Wiley.

Dewald, P. A. (1965). Reactions to the forced termination of therapy. *Psychiatric Quarterly, 39,* 102–126.

Dewald, P. A. (1967). Therapeutic evaluation and potential: The dynamic point of view. *Comprehensive Psychiatry, 8,* 284–298.

Dewald, P. A. (1971). *Psychotherapy: A dynamic approach* (2nd ed.). New York: Basic Books.

Dewald, P. A. (1980). The handling of resistances in adult psychoanalysis. *International Journal of Psychoanalysis, 61,* 61–69.

Dewald, P. A. (1982). Psychoanalytic perspectives on resistance. In P. Wachtel (Ed.), *Resistance: Psychodynamic and behavioral approaches* (pp. 45–68). New York: Plenum Press.

Dewald, P. A. (1996). The psychoanalytic therapies. In E. Nessarian & R. G. Kopff (Eds.), *Textbook of psychoanalysis* (pp. 455–483). Washington, DC: American Psychiatric Press.

Dobson, K. S. (Ed.). (1988). *Handbook of cognitive-behavioral therapies.* New York: Guilford Press.

Dowling, C. (Ed.). (1991). *Conflict and compromise: Therapeutic implications.* Madison, CT: International Universities Press.

Durlak, J. (1979). Comparative effectiveness of paraprofessional and professional helpers. *Psychological Bulletin, 86,* 80–92.

Eckert, P. A. (1993). Acceleration of change: Catalysts in brief therapy. *Clinical Psychology Review, 13,* 241–253.

Eckert, P. A., Abeles, N., & Graham, R. N. (1988). Symptom severity, psychotherapy process, and outcome. *Professional Psychology, 19,* 560–564.

Eels, T. D. (Ed.). (1997). *Handbook of psychotherapy case formulation.* New York: Guilford Press.

Ellman, S. J. (1991). *Freud's technique papers.* Northvale, NJ: Aronson.

Epstein, S. (1994). Integration of the cognitive and the psychodynamic unconscious. *American Psychologist, 49,* 709–724.

Faulkner, K. K., & Faulkner, T. A. (1997). Managing multiple relationships in rural communities: Neutrality and boundary violations. *Clinical Psychology, 4,* 225–234.

Fenichel, O. (1941). *Problems of psychoanalytic technique.* New York: Psychoanalytic Quarterly.

Fenichel, O. (1945a). *The psychoanalytic theory of neurosis.* New York: Norton.

Fenichel, O. (1945b). Neurotic acting out. *Psychoanalytic Review, 32,* 197–206.

Fialkow, N. J., & Muslin, H. L. (1987). Working through: A cornerstone of psychotherapy. *American Journal of Psychotherapy, 41,* 443–452.

Finn, S. E. (1996). Assessment feedback integrating MMPI-2 and Rorschach findings. *Journal of Personality Assessment, 67,* 543–557.

Frances, E., Clarkin, M., & Perry, S. P. (1984). *Differential therapeutics in psychiatry: The art and science of treatment selection.* New York: Brunner/Mazel.

Frank, J. D., & Frank, J. B. (1991). *Persuasion and healing: A comparative study of psychotherapy* (3rd ed.). Baltimore: Johns Hopkins University Press.

Freedheim, D. S. (Ed.). (1992). *History of psychotherapy: A century of change.* Washington, DC: American Psychological Association.

Fremont, S. K., & Anderson, W. (1988). Investigation of factors involved in therapists' annoyance with clients. *Professional Psychology, 19,* 330–335.

Freud, A. (1946). *The ego and the mechanisms of defense.* New York: International Universities Press. (Original work published 1936)

Freud, S. (1953a). Fragment of an analysis of a case of hysteria. *Standard edition* (Vol. 7, pp. 7–122). London: Hogarth Press. (Original work published 1905)

Freud, S. (1953b). Freud's psycho-analytic procedure. *Standard edition* (Vol. 7, pp. 249–254). London: Hogarth Press. (Original work published 1904b)

Freud, S. (1953c). The interpretation of dreams. *Standard edition* (Vols. 4–5). London: Hogarth Press. (Original work published 1900)

Freud, S. (1953d). On psychotherapy. *Standard edition* (Vol. 7, pp. 257–268). London: Hogarth Press. (Original work published 1904a)

Freud, S. (1957a). The future prospects of psycho-analytic therapy. *Standard edition* (Vol. 11, pp. 141–151). London: Hogarth Press. (Original work published 1910b)

Freud, S. (1957b). On the history of the psycho-analytic movement. *Standard edition* (Vol. 14, p. 66). London: Hogarth. (Original work published 1914)

Freud, S. (1957c). Some character types met with in psychoanalytic work. *Standard edition* (Vol. 14, pp. 311–333). London: Hogarth Press. (Original work published 1916)

Freud, S. (1957d). "Wild" psycho-analysis. *Standard edition* (Vol. 11, pp. 221–227). London: Hogarth Press. (Original work published 1910a)

Freud, S. (1958a). On beginning the treatment (further recommendations on the technique of psycho-analysis-I). *Standard edition* (Vol. 12, pp. 123–144). London: Hogarth Press. (Original work published 1913)

Freud, S. (1958b). The dynamics of transference. *Standard edition* (Vol. 12, pp. 99–108). London: Hogarth Press. (Original work published 1912)

Freud, S. (1958c). The handling of dream interpretations in psycho-analysis. *Standard edition* (Vol. 12, pp. 81–96). London: Hogarth Press. (Original work published 1911)

Freud, S. (1958d). Observations on transference-love (further recommendations on the technique of psychoanalysis-III). *Standard edition* (Vol. 12, pp. 159–171). London: Hogarth Press. (Original work published 1915)

Freud, S. (1958e). Remembering, repeating, and working through. *Standard edition* (Vol. 12, pp. 145–156). London: Hogarth Press. (Original work published 1914)

Freud, S. (1959a). Inhibitions, symptoms, and anxiety. *Standard edition* (Vol. 20, pp. 87–174). London: Hogarth Press. (Original work published 1926)

Freud, S. (1959b). Some general remarks on hysterical attacks. *Standard edition* (Vol. 9, pp. 229–234). London: Hogarth Press. (Original work published 1909)

Freud, S. (1960). The psychopathology of everyday life. *Standard edition* (Vol. 6). London: Hogarth Press. (Original work published 1901)

Freud S. (1961). Remarks on the theory and practice of dream interpretation. *Standard edition* (Vol. 19, pp. 109–121). London: Hogarth Press. (Original work published 1923)

Freud, S. (1963). Introductory lectures on psycho-analysis. *Standard edition* (Vols. 15–16). London: Hogarth Press. (Original work published 1916–1917)

Freud, S. (1964). Analysis terminable and interminable. *Standard edition* (Vol. 23). London: Hogarth Press. (Original work published 1937)

Gabbard, G. O. (1995). Countertransference: The emerging common ground. *International Journal of Psycho-Analysis, 76,* 475–485.

Gabbard, G. O. (1996). The analyst's contribution to erotic transference. *Contemporary Psychoanalysis, 32,* 249–273.

Gabbard, G. O., & Wilkinson, S. M. (1994). *Management of countertransference with borderline patients.* Washington, DC: American Psychiatric Press.

Gans, J. S., & Counselman, E. F. (1996). The missed session: A neglected aspect of psychodynamic psychotherapy. *Psychotherapy, 33,* 43–50.

Garb, H. N. (1997). Race bias, social class bias, and gender bias in clinical judgment. *Clinical Psychology, 4,* 99–120.

García, J. G., & Zea, M. C. (Eds.). (1997). *Psychological interventions and research with Latino populations.* Boston: Allyn & Bacon.

Garfield, S. L. (1994). Research on client variables in psychotherapy. In A. E. Bergin & S. L. Garfield (Eds.), *Handbook of psychotherapy and behavior change* (4th ed., pp. 190–228). New York: Wiley.

Garfield, S. L. (1995). *Psychotherapy: An eclectic approach* (2nd ed.). New York: Wiley.

Gay, P. (1988). *A life for our time.* New York: Norton.

Gelso, C. J., & Carter, J. A. (1994). Components of the psychotherapy relationship: Their interaction and unfolding during treatment. *Journal of Counseling Psychology, 41,* 296–306.

Gelso, C. J., Kivlighan, D. M., Wine, B., & Jones, A. (1997). Transference, insight, and the course of time-limited therapy. *Journal of Counseling Psychology, 44,* 209–217.

Gill, M. M. (1982). *Analysis of transference: Vol. 1. Theory and technique.* New York: International Universities Press.

Giovacchini, P. L. (1989). *Countertransference triumphs and catastrophes.* Northvale, NJ: Aronson.

Glenn, J. (1992). Empathy, countertransference, and other emotional reactions of the therapist. In M. J. Aronson & M. A. Scharfman (Eds.), *Psychotherapy: The analytic approach* (pp. 73–83). Northvale, NJ: Aronson.

Glenn, J., & Bernstein, I. (1995). Sadomasochism. In B. E. Moore & B. D. Fine (Eds.), *Psychoanalysis: The major concepts* (pp. 252–265). New Haven, CT: Yale University Press.

Glick, R. A. (1987). Forced termination. *Journal of the American Academy of Psychoanalysis, 15,* 449–463.

Glickauf-Hughes, C., Wells, M., & Chance, S. (1996). Techniques for strengthening clients' observing ego. *Psychotherapy, 33,* 431–440.

Glover, E. (1955). *The technique of psycho-analysis.* New York: International Universities Press.

Gody, D. S. (1996). Chance encounters: Unintentional therapist disclosure. *Psychoanalytic Psychology, 13,* 495–511.

Goldstein, A. P., & Stein, N. (1976). *Prescriptive psychotherapies.* New York: Pergamon Press.

Goldstein, W. (1996). *Dynamic psychotherapy with the borderline patient.* Northvale, NJ: Aronson.

Gomes-Schwartz, B., & Schwartz, J. M. (1978). Psychotherapy process variables distinguishing the "inherently helpful" person from the professional psychotherapist. *Journal of Consulting and Clinical Psychology, 46,* 196–197.

Goodyear, R. K., & Shumate, J. L. (1996). Perceived effects of therapist self-disclosure of attraction to clients. *Professional Psychology, 27,* 613–616.

Gorkin, M. (1987). *The uses of countertransference.* Northvale, NJ: Aronson.

Gray, P. (1994). *The ego and the analysis of defense.* Northvale, NJ: Aronson.

Greenberg, R. P., & Staller, J. (1981). Personal therapy for therapists. *American Journal of Psychiatry, 138,* 1467–1471.

Greencavage, L. M., & Norcross, J. C. (1990). What are the commonalities among the therapeutic factors. *Professional Psychology, 21,* 372–378.

Greenson, R. R. (1965a). The problem of working through. In M. Schur (Ed.), *Drives, affects, behavior* (pp. 227–314). New York: International Universities Press.

Greenson, R. R. (1965b). The working alliance and the transference neurosis. *Psychoanalytic Quarterly, 34,* 155–181.

Greenson, R. R. (1967). *The technique and practice of psychoanalysis.* New York: International Universities Press.

Greenson, R. R., & Wexler, M. (1969). The nontransference relationship in the psychoanalytic situation. *International Journal of Psycho-Analysis, 50,* 27–39.

Grenyer, B. F. S., & Luborsky, L. (1996). Dynamic change in psychotherapy: Mastery of interpersonal conflicts. *Journal of Consulting and Clinical Psychology, 64,* 411–416.

Grinstein, A. (1983). *Freud's rules of dream interpretation.* New York: International Universities Press.

Groth-Marnat, G. (1990). *Handbook of psychological assessment* (2nd ed.). New York: Wiley.

Groves, J. E. (Ed.). (1996). *Essential papers on short-term dynamic therapy.* New York: New York University Press.

Grunebaum, H. (1986). Harmful psychotherapy experience. *American Journal of Psychotherapy, 40,* 165–176.

Gurman, A. S., & Messer, S. B. (Eds.). (1995). *Essential psychotherapies: Theory and practice.* New York: Guilford Press.

Guy, J. D. (1987). *The personal life of the psychotherapist.* New York: Wiley.

Guy, J. D., & Liaboe, G. P. (1986). The impact of conducting psychotherapy on psychotherapists' interpersonal functioning. *Professional Psychology, 17,* 111–114.

Guy, J. D., Stark, M. J., & Poelstra, P. L. (1988). Personal therapy for psychotherapists before and after entering professional practice. *Professional Psychology, 19,* 474–476.

Halleck, S. L. (1991). *Evaluation of the psychiatric patient.* New York: Plenum Press.

Hare-Mustin, R. T., Marecek, J., Kaplan, A. G., & Liss-Levinson, N. (1979). Rights of clients, responsibilities of therapists. *American Psychologist, 34,* 3–16.

Hattie, J. A., Sharpley, C. F., & Rogers, H. J. (1984). Comparative effectiveness of professional and paraprofessional helpers. *Psychological Bulletin, 95,* 534–541.

Henry, W. E., Sims, J. H., & Spray, S. L. (1971). *The fifth profession: Becoming a psychotherapist.* San Francisco: Jossey-Bass.

Henry, W. E., Sims, J. H., & Spray, S. L. (1973). *Public and private lives of psychotherapists.* San Francisco: Jossey-Bass.

Henry, W. P., Schacht, T. E., & Strupp, H. H. (1990). Patient and therapist introject, interpersonal process, and differential psychotherapy outcome. *Journal of Consulting and Clinical Psychology, 58,* 768–774.

Henry, W. P., & Strupp, H. H. (1991). Vanderbilt University: The Vanderbilt Center for Psychotherapy Research. In L. E. Beutler & M. Crago (Eds.), *Psychotherapy research: An international review of programmatic studies* (pp. 166–174). Washington, DC: American Psychological Association.

Herron, W. G., Javier, R. A., Primavera, L. H., & Schultz, C. L. (1994). The cost of psychotherapy. *Professional Psychology, 25,* 106–110.

Herron, W. G., & Welt, S. R. (1992). *Money matters: The fee in psychotherapy and psychoanalysis.* New York: Guilford Press.

Hersen, M., Kazdin, A. E., & Bellack, A. S. (Eds.). (1991). *The clinical psychology handbook* (2nd ed.). New York: Pergamon Press.

Hersen, M., & Turner, S. M. (Eds.). (1985). *Diagnostic interviewing.* New York: Plenum Press.

Hill, C. E. (1996). *Working with dreams in psychotherapy.* New York: Guilford Press.

Hill, C. E., Thompson, B. J., & Mahalik, J. R. (1989). Therapist interpretation. In C. E. Hill (Ed.), *Therapist techniques and client outcomes* (pp. 284–319). Newbury Park, CA: Sage.

Hilsenroth, M. J., Handler, L., Toman, K. M., & Padawer, J. R. (1995). Rorschach and MMPI-2 indices of early psychotherapy termination. *Journal of Consulting and Clinical Psychology, 63,* 956–965.

Hinze, E. (1987). Transference and countertransference in the psychoanalytic treatment of older patients. *International Review of Psycho-Analysis, 14,* 465–474.

Hoglend, P. (1993). Personality disorders and long-term outcome after brief dynamic psychotherapy. *Journal of Personality Disorders, 7,* 168–181.

Holloway, E. L., & Neufeldt, S. A. (1995). Supervision: Its contribution to treatment efficacy. *Journal of Consulting and Clinical Psychology, 63,* 207–213.

Holmes, D. (1992). Race and transference in psychoanalysis and psychotherapy. *International Journal of Psychoanalysis, 73,* 1–12.

Holt, R. R., & Luborsky, L. (1958). *Personality patterns of psychiatrists.* New York: Basic Books.

Holzman, L. A., Searight, H. R., & Hughes, H. M. (1996). Clinical psychology graduate students and personal psychotherapy: Results of an exploratory survey. *Professional Psychology, 27,* 98–101.

Horowitz, M. J. (1988). *Introduction to psychodynamics.* New York: Basic Books.

Horowitz, M. J. (Ed.). (1991). *Hysterical personality style and the histrionic personality disorder.* Northvale, NJ: Aronson.

Horowitz, M. J., Marmar, C., Krupnick, J., Wilner, N., Kaltreider, N., & Waller-stein, R. (1984). *Personality styles and brief psychotherapy*. New York: Basic Books.

Horowitz, M. J., Milbrath, C., & Stinson, C. H. (1995). Signs of defensive control locate conflicted topics in discourse. *Archives of General Psychiatry, 52,* 1040–1047.

Horvath, A. O., & Greenberg, L. S. (Eds.). (1994). *The working alliance*. New York: Wiley.

Horvath, A. O., & Symonds, B. D. (1991). Relation between working alliance and outcome in psychotherapy: A meta-analysis. *Journal of Counseling Psychology, 38,* 139–149.

Hunt, D. D., Carr, J. E., Dagadakis, C. S., & Walker, E. A. (1985). Cognitive match as a predictor of psychotherapy outcome. *Psychotherapy, 22,* 718–721.

Hurt, S. W., Reznikoff, M., & Clarkin, J. F. (1991). *Psychological assessment, psychiatric diagnosis, and treatment planning*. New York: Brunner/Mazel.

Hynan, D. J. (1990). Client reasons and experiences in treatment that influence termination of psychotherapy. *Journal of Clinical Psychology, 46,* 891–895.

Jacobs, T. J., & Rothstein, A. (Eds.). (1990). *On beginning an analysis*. Madison, CT: International Universities Press.

Jaffe, A. M. (1981). The negative therapeutic reaction. *Psychotherapy, 18,* 313–319.

Johnson, L. D. (1995). *Psychotherapy in the age of accountability*. New York: Norton.

Johnson, S. M. (1994). *Character styles*. New York: Norton.

Jones, A. S., & Gelso, C. J. (1988). Differential effects of style of interpretation: Another look. *Journal of Counseling Psychology, 35,* 363–369.

Jones, E. E., Cumming, J. D., & Horowitz, M. J. (1988). Another look at the non-specific hypothesis of therapeutic effectiveness. *Journal of Consulting and Clinical Psychology, 56,* 48–55.

Jones, E. E., Hall, S. A., & Parke, L. A. (1991). The process of change: The Berkeley psychotherapy research group. In L. E. Beutler & M. Crago (Eds.), *Psychotherapy research: An international review of programmatic studies* (pp. 98–106). Washington, DC: American Psychological Association.

Jourard, S. M. (1964). *The transparent self: Self-disclosure and well-being*. Princeton, NJ: Van Nostrand-Reinhold.

Joyce, A. S., & Piper, W. E. (1993). The immediate impact of transference interpretation in short-term individual psychotherapy. *American Journal of Psychotherapy, 47,* 508–526.

Kanzer, M. (1961). Verbal and nonverbal aspects of free association. *Psychoanalytic Quarterly, 30,* 327–350.

Karon, B. P., & Vandenbos, G. R. (1981). *Psychotherapy of schizophrenia*. New York: Aronson.

Karon, B. P., & Widener, A. J. (1995). Psychodynamic therapies in historical perspective: "Nothing human do I consider alien to me." In B. Bongar & L. E. Beutler (Eds.), *Comprehensive textbook of psychotherapy* (pp. 24–49). New York: Oxford University Press.

Kazdin, A. E. (1990). Psychotherapy for children and adolescents. *Annual Review of Psychology, 41,* 21–54.

Kelly, T. A. (1990). The role of values in psychotherapy: A critical review of process and outcome effects. *Clinical Psychology Review, 10,* 171–186.

Kelly, T. A., & Strupp, H. A. (1992). Patient and therapist values in psychotherapy: Perceived changes, assimilation, similarity, and outcome. *Journal of Consulting and Clinical Psychology, 60,* 34–40.

Kernberg, O. F. (1967). Borderline personality organization. *Journal of the American Psychoanalytic Association, 15,* 641–685.

Kernberg, O. F. (1976). *Object relations theory and clinical psychoanalysis.* New York: Aronson.

Kernberg, O. F. (1993). Convergences and divergences in contemporary psychoanalytic technique. *International Journal of Psycho-Analysis, 74,* 659–673.

Kernberg, O. F., Selzer, M. A., Koenigsberg, H. W., Carr, A. C., & Appelbaum, A. H. (1989). *Psychodynamic psychotherapy of borderline patients.* New York: Basic Books.

Knight, B. G. (1996). *Psychotherapy with older adults* (2nd ed.). Newbury Park, CA: Sage.

Knight, B. G., Kelly, M., & Gatz, M. (1992). Psychotherapy and the older adult. In D. K. Freedheim (Ed.), *History of psychotherapy* (pp. 528–552). Washington, DC: American Psychological Association.

Kohut, H. (1971). *The analysis of the self.* New York: International Universities Press.

Koocher, G. P. (1995). Ethics in psychotherapy. In B. Bongar & L. E. Beutler (Eds.), *Comprehensive textbook of psychotherapy* (pp. 456–573). New York: Oxford University Press.

Kopta, S. M., Howard, K. I., Lowry, J. L., & Beutler, L. E. (1994). Patterns of symptomatic recovery in psychotherapy. *Journal of Consulting and Clinical Psychology, 62,* 1009–1016.

Koss, M. P., & Shiang, J. (1994). Research on brief psychotherapy. In A. E. Bergin & S. L. Garfield (Eds.), *Handbook of psychotherapy and behavior change* (4th ed., pp. 644–700). New York: Wiley.

Kottler, J. A. (1993). *On being a therapist* (Rev. ed.). San Francisco: Jossey-Bass.

Kramer, S. A. (1990). *Positive endings in psychotherapy.* San Francisco: Jossey-Bass.

Kris, A. O. (1982). *Free association: Method and process.* New Haven, CT: Yale University Press.

Kris. A. O. (1985). Resistance in convergent and in divergent conflicts. *Psychoanalytic Quarterly, 54,* 537–568.

Kris, A. O. (1992). Interpretation and the method of free associations. *Psychoanalytic Inquiry, 12,* 208–224.

Kris, E. (1954). Defense mechanisms and psychoanalytic technique. *Journal of the American Psychoanalytic Association, 2,* 318–326.

Krueger, D. W. (Ed.). (1986). *The last taboo: Money as symbol and reality in psychotherapy and psychoanalysis.* New York: Brunner/Mazel.

Kubie, L. S. (1973). The process of evaluation on psychiatry. *Archives of General Psychiatry, 28,* 880–884.

Kuehlwein, K. T., & Rosen, H. (Eds.). (1993). *Cognitive therapies in action.* San Francisco: Jossey-Bass.

Kupers, T. A. (1988). *Ending therapy: The meaning of termination.* New York: New York University Press.

Kushner, M. G., & Sher, K. J. (1991). The relation of treatment fearfulness and psychological service utilization: An overview. *Professional Psychology, 22,* 196–203.

Lafferty, P., Beutler, L. E., & Crago, M. (1989). Differences between more and less effective psychotherapists: A study of select therapist variables. *Journal of Consulting and Clinical Psychology, 57,* 76–80.

Lakin, M. (1991). *Coping with ethical dilemmas in psychotherapy.* New York: Pergamon Press.

Lambert, M. J. (1989). The individual therapist's contribution to psychotherapy process and outcome. *Clinical Psychology Review, 9,* 469–485.

Lambert, M. J. (1991). Introduction to psychotherapy research. In L. E. Beutler & M. Crago (Eds.), *Psychotherapy research: An international review of programmatic studies* (pp. 1–12). Washington, DC: American Psychological Association.

Lambert, M. J., & Bergin, A. E. (1992). Achievements and limitations of psychotherapy research. In D. K. Freedheim (Ed.), *History of psychotherapy: A century of change* (pp. 360–390). Washington, DC: American Psychological Association.

Lambert, M. J., & Bergin, A. E. (1994). The effectiveness of psychotherapy. In A. E. Bergin & S. L. Garfield (Eds.), *Handbook of psychotherapy and behavior change* (4th ed., pp. 143–189). New York: Wiley.

Lane, R. C., & Hull, J. W. (1990). Self-disclosure and classical psychoanalysis. In G. Stricker & M. Fisher (Eds.), *Self-disclosure in the therapeutic relationship* (pp. 31–46). New York: Plenum Press.

Langs, R. J., Bucci, W., Udoff, A. L., Cramer, G., & Thomson, L. (1993). Two methods of assessing unconscious communication in psychotherapy. *Psychoanalytic Psychology, 10,* 1–16.

Levenson, H., Speed, J., & Budman, S. H. (1995). Therapist's experience, training, and skill in brief therapy: A bicoastal survey. *American Journal of Psychotherapy, 49,* 95–117.

Levy, S. T. (1990). *Principles of interpretation.* Northvale, NJ: Aronson.

Lietaer, G., Rombauts, J., & Van Balen, R. (Eds.). (1990). *Client-centered and experiential psychotherapy in the nineties.* Leuven, Belgium: Leuven University Press.

Lipsey, M., & Wilson, D. (1993). The efficacy of psychological, educational, and behavioral treatment. *American Psychologist, 48,* 1181–1209.

Lipton, S. D. (1977). The advantage of Freud's technique as sown in his analysis of the rat man. *International Journal of Psycho-Analysis, 58,* 255–273.

Little, M. I. (1981). *Transference neurosis and transference psychosis.* New York: Aronson.

Loewald, H. W. (1986). Transference-countertransference. *Journal of the American Psychoanalytic Association, 34,* 275–287.

Loewenstein, R. M. (1954). Some remarks on defenses, autonomous ego and psychoanalytic technique. *International Journal of Psycho-Analysis, 35,* 188–198.

Lorand, S. (1972/1973). Historical aspects and trends in psychoanalytic therapy. *Psychoanalytic Review, 59,* 497–525.

Lorion, R. P. (1973). Socioeconomic status and traditional treatment approaches reconsidered. *Psychological Bulletin, 79*, 263–270.

Lorion, R. P. (1978). Research on psychotherapy and behavior change with the disadvantaged. In S. L. Garfield & A. E. Bergin (Eds.), *Handbook of psychotherapy and behavior change* (2nd ed., pp. 903–938). New York: Wiley.

Lowman, R. L., & Resnick, R. J. (Eds.). (1994). *The mental health professional's guide to managed care.* Washington, DC: American Psychological Association.

Luborsky, L. (1996). Theories of cure in psychoanalytic psychotherapies and the evidence for them. *Psychoanalytic Inquiry, 16*, 257–264.

Luborsky, L., Barber, J. P., & Crits-Christoph, P. (1990). Theory-based research for understanding the process of dynamic psychotherapy. *Journal of Consulting and Clinical Psychology, 58*, 281–287.

Luborsky, L., & Crits-Christoph, P. (1991). *Understanding transference: The core conflictual relationship.* New York: Basic Books.

Luborsky, L., Crits-Christoph, P., & Barber, J. (1991). University of Pennsylvania: The Penn psychotherapy research projects. In L. E. Beutler & M. Crago (Eds.), *Psychotherapy research: An international review of programmatic studies* (pp. 133–141). Washington, DC: American Psychological Association.

Luborsky, L., Crits-Christoph, P., McLellan, A. T., Woody, G., Piper, W., Liberman, B., Imber, S., & Pilkonis, P. (1986). Do therapists vary much in their success? *American Journal of Orthopsychiatry, 56*, 501–512.

Luborsky, L., Diguer, L., Luborsky, E., McClellan, A. T., Woody, G., & Alexander, L. (1993). Psychological health-sickness (PHS) as a predictor of outcomes in dynamic and other psychotherapies. *Journal of Consulting and Clinical Psychology, 61*, 541–548.

Luborsky, L., McLellan, A. T., Diguer, L., Woody, G., & Seligman, D. A. (1997). The psychotherapist matters: Comparison of outcomes across twenty-two therapists and seven patient samples. *Clinical Psychology, 4*, 53–65.

Luborsky, L., McLellan, A. T., Woody, G. E., O'Brien, C. P., & Auerbach, A. (1985). Therapist success and its determinants. *Archives of General Psychiatry, 42*, 602–611.

Luborsky, L., Singer, B., & Luborsky, L. (1975). Comparative studies of psychotherapy. *Archives of General Psychiatry, 32*, 995–1008.

Macalpine, I. (1950). The development of the transference. *Psychoanalytic Quarterly, 19*, 501–539.

Maddi, S. R. (1996). *Personality theories: A comparative analysis* (6th ed.). Pacific Grove, CA: Brooks/Cole.

Mahoney, M. J. (Ed.). (1995). *Cognitive and constructive psychotherapies.* New York: Springer.

Mahoney, M. J. (1997). Psychotherapists' personal problems and self-care patterns. *Professional Psychology, 28*, 14–16.

Mahoney, M. J., & Craine, M. H. (1991). The changing beliefs of psychotherapy experts. *Journal of Psychotherapy Integration, 1*, 207–221.

Mahrer, A. R. (1996). *The complete guide to experiential psychotherapy.* New York: Wiley.

Malan, O. H. (1976). *The frontier of brief psychotherapy.* New York: Plenum Press.

Mallinckrodt, B., & Nelson, M. L. (1991). Counselor training level and the formation of the psychotherapeutic working alliance. *Journal of Counseling Psychology, 38,* 133–138.

Mann, J. (1973). *Time-limited psychotherapy.* Cambridge, MA: Harvard University Press.

Marmor, J. (1990). A broad-based definition of psychotherapy. In J. K. Zeig & W. M. Munion (Eds.), *What is psychotherapy?* (pp. 20–23). San Francisco: Jossey-Bass.

Martinez, D. (1989). Pains and gains: A study of forced termination. *Journal of the American Psychoanalytic Association, 37,* 89–115.

Maruish, M. E. (Ed.). (1992). *The use of psychological testing for treatment planning and outcome assessment.* Hillsdale, NJ: Erlbaum.

Masterson, J. F. (1983). *Countertransference and psychotherapeutic technique: Teaching seminars on psychotherapy of the borderline adult.* New York: Brunner/Mazel.

Mathews, B. (1988). The role of patient self-disclosure in psychotherapy: A survey of therapists. *American Journal of Psychotherapy, 42,* 521–531.

Mays, D. T., & Franks, C. M. (1985). *Negative outcome in psychotherapy and what to do about it.* New York: Springer.

Mays, V. M., & Albee, G. W. (1992). Psychotherapy and ethnic minorities. In D. K. Freedheim (Ed.), *History of psychotherapy* (pp. 552–570). Washington, DC: American Psychological Association.

McCallum, M., & Piper, W. E. (1997). *Psychological mindedness.* Mahwah, NJ: Erlbaum.

McClure, B. A., & Hodge, R. W. (1987). Measuring countertransference and attitude in therapeutic relationships. *Psychotherapy, 24,* 325–335.

McCullough, L., & Winston, A. (1991). The Beth Israel psychotherapy research program. In L. E. Beutler & M. Crago (Eds.), *Psychotherapy research: An international review of programmatic studies* (pp. 15–23). Washington, DC: American Psychological Association.

McLaughlin, J. T. (1995). Resistance. In B. E. Moore & B. D. Fine (Eds.), *Psychoanalysis: The major concepts* (pp. 95–109). New Haven, CT: Yale University Press.

McWilliams, N. (1994). *Psychoanalytic diagnosis.* New York: Guilford Press.

Meissner, W. W. (1991). *What is effective in psychoanalytic therapy?* Northvale, NJ: Aronson.

Mendelsohn, R. M. (1990). *The manifest dream and its use in therapy.* Northvale, NJ: Aronson.

Menninger, K. A., & Holzman, P. S. (1973). *Theory of psychoanalytic technique* (2nd ed.). New York: Basic Books.

Messer, S. B. (1989). Must we be action oriented? *Journal of Integrative and Eclectic Psychotherapy, 8,* 246–250.

Messer, S. B., & Warren, C. S. (1995). *Models of brief psychodynamic therapy.* New York: Guilford Press.

Meyer, G. J., & Handler, L. (1997). The ability of the Rorschach to predict subsequent outcome: Meta-analysis of the Rorschach Prognostic Rating Scale. *Journal of Personality Assessment, 69,* 1–38.

Miller, I. J. (1996a). Managed care is harmful to outpatient mental health services: A call for accountability. *Professional Psychology, 27*, 349–363.

Miller, I. J. (1996b). Some "short-term therapy values" are a formula for invisible rationing. *Professional Psychology, 27*, 577–582.

Miller, S. D., Duncan, B. L., & Hubble, M. A. (1997). *Escape from Babel: Toward a unifying language for psychotherapy practice.* New York: Norton.

Millon, T. (1996). *Disorders of personality* (2nd ed.). New York: Wiley.

Milman, D. S., & Goldman, G. D. (Eds.). (1973). *Acting out.* Springfield, IL: Thomas.

Milman, D. S., & Goldman, G. D. (Eds.). (1987). *Techniques of working with resistance.* Northvale, NJ: Aronson.

Mitchell, S. A., & Black, M. J. (1995). *Freud and beyond: A history of modern psychoanalytic thought.* New York: Basic Books.

Mogul, K. M. (1982). Overview: The sex of the therapist. *American Journal of Psychiatry, 139*, 1–11.

Mohl, P. C., Martinez, D., Ticknor, C., & Huang, M. (1991). Early dropouts from psychotherapy. *Journal of Nervous and Mental Disease, 179*, 478–481.

Mohr, D. C. (1995). Negative outcome in psychotherapy: A critical review. *Clinical Psychology, 2*, 1–27.

Mohr, D. C., Beutler, L. E., Engle, D., Shoham-Salomon, V., Bergan, J., Kaszniak, A. W., & Yost, E. B. (1990). Identification of patients at risk for nonresponse and negative outcome in psychotherapy. *Journal of Consulting and Clinical Psychology, 58*, 622–628.

Moore, B. E., & Fine, B. D. (Eds.). (1990). *Psychoanalytic terms and concepts.* New Haven, CT: Yale University Press.

Morrison, J. (1995). *The first interview.* New York: Guilford Press.

Mueller, W. J., & Aniskiewicz, A. S. (1986). *Psychotherapeutic intervention in hysterical disorders.* Northvale, NJ: Aronson.

Murphy, R. A., & Halgin, R. P. (1995). Influences on the career choices of psychotherapists. *Professional Psychology, 26*, 422–426.

Nemiroff, R. A., & Colarusso, C. A. (1985). *The race against time: Psychotherapy and psychoanalysis in the second half of life.* New York: Plenum Press.

Norcross, J. C. (1988). The exclusivity myth and the equifinality principle in psychotherapy. *Journal of Integrative and Eclectic Psychotherapy, 7*, 415–421.

Olfson, M., & Pincus, H. A. (1994). Outpatient psychotherapy in the United States: I. Volume, costs, and user characteristics. *American Journal of Psychiatry, 151*, 1281–1288.

Oremland, J. D. (1972). Transference cure and flight into health. *International Journal of Psychoanalytic Psychotherapy, 1*, 61–75.

Oremland, J. D. (1991). *Interpretation and interaction.* Hillsdale, NJ: Analytic Press.

Orlinsky, D. E., Grawe, K., & Parks, B. K. (1994). Process and outcome in psychotherapy—noch einmal. In A. E. Bergin & S. L. Garfield (Eds.), *Handbook of psychotherapy and behavior change* (4th ed., pp. 270–378). New York: Wiley.

Orlinsky, D. E., & Howard, K. I. (1987). A generic model of psychotherapy. *Journal of Integrative and Eclectic Psychotherapy, 6*, 6–27.

Othmer, E., & Othmer, S. C. (1994). *The clinical interview using* DSM-IV. *Vol. 1. Fundamentals. Vol. 2. The difficult patient.* Washington, DC: American Psychiatric Press.

Panken, S. (1996). The psychoanalytic relationship: Past and present. *Psychoanalytic Review, 83,* 157–179.

Pasternack, S. A. (1988). The clinical management of fees during psychotherapy and psychoanalysis. *Psychiatric Annals, 18,* 112–117.

Patterson, C. H. (1984). Empathy, warmth, and genuineness in psychotherapy: A review of reviews. *Psychotherapy, 21,* 431–438.

Penn, L. S. (1990). When the therapist must leave: Forced termination of psychodynamic therapy. *Professional Psychology, 21,* 379–384.

Perez Foster, R. M., Moskowitz, M., & Javier, R. A. (Eds.). (1996). *Reaching across boundaries of culture and class: Widening the scope of psychotherapy.* Northvale, NJ: Aronson.

Pine, F. (1984). The interpretive moment: Variations on classical themes. *Bulletin of the Menninger Clinic, 48,* 54–71.

Pine, F. (1990). *Drive, ego, object, and self.* New York: Basic Books.

Piper, W. E., Azim, H. F. A., McCallum, M., & Joyce, A. S. (1991). The University of Alberta Psychotherapy Research Center. In L. E. Beutler & M. Crago (Eds.), *Psychotherapy research: An international review of programmatic studies* (pp. 82–89). Washington, DC: American Psychological Association.

Piper, W. E., Joyce, A. S., McCallum, M., & Azim, H. F. A. (1993). Concentration and correspondence of transference interpretations in short-term psychotherapy. *Journal of Consulting and Clinical Psychology, 61,* 586–595.

Piper, W. E., McCallum, M., Azim, H. F. A., & Joyce, A. S. (1993). Understanding the relationship between transference interpretation and outcome in the context of other variables. *American Journal of Psychotherapy, 47,* 479–493.

Ponterotto, J. G., Casas, J. M., Suzuki, L. A., & Alexander, C. M. (Eds.). (1995). *Handbook of multicultural counseling.* Newbury Park, CA: Sage.

Pope, K. S., Sonne, J. L., & Holroyd, J. (1993). *Sexual feelings in psychotherapy.* Washington, DC: American Psychological Association.

Powell, D. H. (1995). Lessons learned from therapeutic failure. *Journal of Psychotherapy Integration, 5,* 175–181.

Power, M. J., & Brewin, C. R. (1991). From Freud to cognitive science: A contemporary account of the unconscious. *British Journal of Clinical Psychology, 30,* 289–310.

Racker, H. (1968). *Transference and countertransference.* New York: International Universities Press.

Ramirez, M. (1991). *Psychotherapy and counseling with minorities.* New York: Pergamon Press.

Rangell, L. (1983). Defense and resistance in psychoanalysis and life. *Journal of the American Psychoanalytic Association, 31,* 147–174.

Rank, O. (1945). *Will therapy and reality.* New York: Knopf.

Raush, H. L., & Bordin, E. S. (1957). Warmth in personality development and in psychotherapy. *Psychiatry, 20,* 351–363.

Reed, G. S. (1994). *Transference neurosis and psychoanalytic experience: Perspectives on contemporary clinical practice.* New Haven, CT: Yale University Press.

Reich, A. (1951). On counter-transference. *International Journal of Psycho-Analysis, 32,* 25–31.

Reich, A. (1960). Further remarks on countertransference. *International Journal of Psycho-Analysis, 41,* 389–395.

Reich, W. (1949). *Character analysis* (3rd ed.). New York: Orgone Institute Press. (Original work published 1933)

Reik, T. (1941). *Masochism in modern man.* New York: Grove Press.

Reik, T. (1948). *Listening with the third ear.* New York: Grove Press.

Reisman, J. M. (1971). *Toward the integration of psychotherapy.* New York: Wiley.

Reisman, J. M. (1986). Psychotherapy as a professional relationship. *Professional Psychology, 17,* 565–569.

Renik, O. (1993). Countertransference enactment and the psychoanalytic process. In M. J. Horowitz, O. F. Kernberg, & E. M. Weinshel (Eds.), *Psychic structure and psychic change* (pp. 135–158). Madison, CT: International Universities Press.

Reynolds, S., Stiles, W. B., Barkham, M., Shapiro, D. A., Hardy, G. E., & Rees, A. (1996). Acceleration of changes in session impact during time-limited therapies. *Journal of Consulting and Clinical Psychology, 64,* 577–586.

Robbins, S. B., & Jolkovski, M. P. (1987). Managing countertransference feelings: An interactional model using awareness of feeling and theoretical framework. *Journal of Counseling Psychology, 34,* 276–282.

Robertson, M. H. (1988). Assessing and intervening in client motivation for psychotherapy. *Journal of Integrative and Eclectic Psychotherapy, 7,* 319–329.

Rockland, L. H. (1989a). *Supportive therapy: A psychodynamic approach.* New York: Basic Books.

Rockland, L. H. (1989b). Psychoanalytically oriented supportive therapy: Literature review and techniques. *Journal of the American Academy of Psychoanalysis, 17,* 451–462.

Rockland, L. H. (1992). *Supportive therapy for borderline patients.* New York: Guilford Press.

Rogers, C. R. (1951). *Client-centered therapy.* Boston: Houghton-Mifflin.

Rogers, C. R. (1957). The necessary and sufficient conditions of therapeutic personality change. *Journal of Consulting Psychology, 21,* 95–103.

Rogers, C. R. (1974). In retrospect: Forty-six years. *American Psychologist, 29,* 115–123.

Rogers, R. (1995). *Diagnostic and structured interviewing: A handbook for psychologists.* Odessa, FL: Psychological Assessment Resources.

Roth, S. (1987). *Psychotherapy: The art of wooing nature.* Northvale, NJ: Aronson.

Roughton, R. E. (1995). Action and acting out. In B. E. Moore & B. D. Fine (Eds.), *Psychoanalysis: The major concepts* (pp. 130–145). New Haven, CT: Yale University Press.

Sachse, R. (1993). The effects of intervention phrasing on therapist-client communication. *Psychotherapy Research, 3,* 260–277.

Salzman, L. (1968). *The obsessive personality.* New York: Science House.

Saunders, S. M., Howard, K. I., & Orlinsky, D. E. (1989). The Therapeutic Bond Scales: Psychometric characteristics and relationship to treatment effectiveness. *Psychological Assessment, 1,* 323–330.

Schafer, R. (1983). *The analytic attitude.* New York: Basic Books.

Schank, J. A., & Skovholt, T. M. (1997). Dual-relationship dilemmas of rural and small-community psychologists. *Professional Psychology, 28,* 44–49.

Schlesinger, H. J. (1969). Diagnosis and prescription for psychotherapy. *Bulletin of the Menninger Clinic, 33,* 269–278.

Schramski, T. G., Beutler, L. E., Lauver, P. J., & Arizmendi, T. A. (1984). Factors that contribute to posttherapy persistence of therapeutic change. *Journal of Clinical Psychology, 40,* 78–85.

Schuster, D. B. (1955). On the fear of success. *Psychiatric Quarterly, 29,* 412–420.

Scott, J. E., & Dixon, L. B. (1995). Psychological interventions for schizophrenia. *Schizophrenia Bulletin, 21,* 621–630.

Sederer, L. (1975). Psychotherapy patient transfers: Secondhand rose. *American Journal of Psychiatry, 132,* 1057–1061.

Seligman, M. E. P. (1995). The effectiveness of psychotherapy. *American Psychologist, 50,* 965–974.

Seligman, M. E. P. (1996). Science as an ally of practice. *American Psychologists, 51,* 1072–1079.

Shadish, W. R., Matt, G. E., Navarro, A. M., Siegle, G., Crits-Christoph, P., Hazelrigg, M. D., Jorm, A. F., Lyons, L. C., Nietzel, M. T., Prout, H. T., Robinson, L., Smith, M. L., Svartberg, M., & Weiss, B. (1997). Evidence that therapy works in clinically representative conditions. *Journal of Consulting and Clinical Psychology, 65,* 355–365.

Shakow, D. (1947). Recommended graduate training program in clinical psychology. *American Psychologist, 2,* 539–558.

Shapiro, D. (1965). *Neurotic styles.* New York: Basic Books.

Shapiro, D. (1989). *Psychotherapy of neurotic character.* New York: Basic Books.

Shapiro, D. A., & Shapiro, D. (1982). Meta-analysis of comparative therapy outcome studies. *Psychological Bulletin, 92,* 581–604.

Shay, J. J. (1996). "Okay, I'm here, but I'm not talking!" Psychotherapy with the reluctant male. *Psychotherapy, 33,* 503–513.

Sherman, M. D. (1996). Distress and professional impairment due to mental health problems among psychotherapists. *Clinical Psychology Review, 16,* 299–315.

Shevrin, H., Bond, J. A., Brakel, L. A. W., Hertel, R. K., & Williams, W. J. (1996). *Conscious and unconscious processes.* New York: Guilford Press.

Sifneos, P. E. (1987). *Short-term dynamic psychotherapy* (2nd ed.). New York: Plenum Press.

Silberschatz, G., Curtis, J. T., & Nathans, S. (1989). Using the patient's plan to assess progress in psychotherapy. *Psychotherapy, 26,* 40–46.

Silberschatz, G., Curtis, J. T., Sampson, H., & Weiss, J. (1991). Mount Zion Hospital and Medical Center: Research on the process of change in psychotherapy. In L. E. Beutler & M. Crago (Eds.), *Psychotherapy research: An international review of programmatic studies* (pp. 56–64). Washington, DC: American Psychological Association.

Silberschatz, G., Fretter, P. B., & Curtis, J. T. (1986). How do interpretations influence the process of psychotherapy? *Journal of Consulting and Clinical Psychology, 54,* 646–652.

Singer, E. (1965). *Key concepts in psychotherapy.* New York: Random House.

Smith, D., & Fitzpatrick, M. (1995). Patient-therapist boundary issues: An integrative review of theory and research. *Professional Psychology, 26,* 499–506.

Smith, M. L., Glass, G. V., & Miller, T. I. (1980). *The benefits of psychotherapy.* Baltimore: Johns Hopkins University Press.

Spacal, S. (1990). Free association as a method of self-observation in relation to other methodological principles of psychoanalysis. *Psychoanalytic Quarterly, 59,* 420–436.

Spence, D. P. (1982). *Narrative truth and historical truth: Meaning and interpretation in psychoanalysis.* New York: Norton.

Spence, D. P. (1995). When do interpretations make a difference? A partial answer to Fliess's *Achensee* question. *Journal of the American Psychoanalytic Association, 43,* 689–712.

Steenbarger, B. N. (1994). Duration and outcome in psychotherapy: An integrative review. *Professional Psychology, 25,* 111–119.

Stein, D. M., & Lambert, M. J. (1995). Graduate training in psychotherapy: Are therapy outcomes enhanced? *Journal of Consulting and Clinical Psychology, 63,* 182–196.

Sterba, R. F. (1934). The fate of the ego in analytic therapy. *International Journal of Psycho-Analysis, 5,* 117–126.

Sterba, R. F. (1953). Clinical and therapeutic aspects of character resistance. *Psychoanalytic Quarterly, 22,* 1–20.

Stone, L. S. (1995). Transference. In B. E. Moore & B. D. Fine (Eds.), *Psychoanalysis: The major concepts* (pp. 110–129). New Haven, CT: Yale University Press.

Stone, M. H. (1993). *Abnormalities of personality.* New York: Norton.

Stone, M. H., Albert, H. D., Forrest, D. V., & Arieti, S. (1983). *Treating schizophrenic patients: A clinical/analytical approach.* New York: McGraw-Hill.

Strachey, J. (1934). The nature of the therapeutic action of psychoanalysis. *International Journal of Psycho-Analysis, 15,* 127–159.

Strean, H. S. (1985). *Resolving resistances in psychotherapy.* New York: Wiley.

Stricker, G. (1995a). Failures in psychotherapy. *Journal of Psychotherapy Integration, 5,* 91–94.

Stricker, G. (1995b). The lessons of failure. *Journal of Psychotherapy Integration, 5,* 183–188.

Stricker, G., & Gold, J. R. (1993). *Comprehensive handbook of psychotherapy integration.* New York: Plenum Press.

Strupp, H. H. (1989). Psychotherapy: Can the practitioner learn from the researcher? *American Psychologist, 44,* 717–724.

Strupp, H. H. (1995). The psychotherapist's skills revisited. *Clinical Psychology, 2,* 70–74.

Strupp, H. H. (1996a). Some salient lessons from research and practice. *Psychotherapy, 33,* 135–138.

Strupp, H. H. (1996b). The tripartite model and the *Consumer Reports* study. *American Psychologist, 51,* 1017–1024.

Strupp, H. H., & Binder, J. L. (1984). *Psychotherapy in a new key: A guide to time-limited dynamic psychotherapy.* New York: Basic Books.

Strupp, H. H., & Butler, S. F. (1990). Psychotherapy. In A. S. Bellack & M. Hersen (Eds.), *Handbook of comparative treatments for adult disorders* (pp. 3–16). New York: Wiley.

Strupp, H. H., Hadley, S. W., & Gomes-Schwartz, B. (1977). *Psychotherapy for better or worse: The problem of negative effects.* New York: Aronson.

Stubbs, J. P., & Bozarth, J. D. (1994). The Dodo bird revisited: A qualitative study of psychotherapy efficacy research. *Applied and Preventive Psychology, 3,* 109–120.

Sue, S., Fujino, D. C., Hu, L., Takeuchi, D. T., & Zane, N. W. S. (1991). Community mental health services for ethnic minority groups: A test of the cultural responsiveness hypothesis. *Journal of Consulting and Clinical Psychology, 59,* 533–540.

Sullivan, H. S. (1953). *The interpersonal theory of psychiatry.* New York: Norton.

Sullivan, H. S. (1954). *The psychiatric interview.* New York: Norton.

Sussman, M. B. (1992). *A curious calling: Unconscious motivations for practicing psychotherapy.* Northvale, NJ: Aronson.

Tansey, M. J., & Burke, W. F. (1989). *Understanding transference.* Hillsdale, NJ: Analytic Press.

Tarachow, S. (1963). *An introduction to psychotherapy.* New York: International Universities Press.

Teri, L., & Logsdon, R. G. (1992). The future of psychotherapy with older adults. *Psychotherapy, 29,* 81–87.

Thompson, A. (1990). *Ethical practice in psychotherapy.* New York: Wiley.

Tracey, T. J., Hays, K. A., Malone, J., & Herman, B. (1988). Changes in counselor response as a function of experience. *Journal of Counseling Psychology, 35,* 119–126.

Train, G. F. (1953). "Flight into health." *American Journal of Psychotherapy, 7,* 464–483.

Tryon, G. S., & Kane, A. S. (1993). Relationship of working alliance to mutual and unilateral termination. *Journal of Counseling Psychology, 40,* 33–36.

Trzepacz, P. T., & Baker, R. W. (1993). *The psychiatric mental status examination.* New York: Oxford University Press.

Tuckfelt, S., Fink, J., & Warren, M. P. (1997). *The psychotherapists' guide to managed care in the 21st century.* Northvale, NJ: Aronson.

Turner, S. M., Calhoun, K. S., & Adams, H. E. (1992). *Clinical behavior therapy* (2nd ed.). New York: Wiley.

Tyson, P. (1996). Termination of psychoanalysis and psychotherapy. In E. Nessarian & R. G. Kopff (Eds.), *Textbook of psychoanalysis* (pp. 501–524). Washington, DC: American Psychiatric Press.

Tyson, R. L. (1986). Countertransference evolution in theory and practice. *Journal of the American Psychoanalytic Association, 34,* 251–274.

Wachtel, P. L. (Ed.). (1982). *Resistance: Psychodynamic and behavioral approaches.* New York: Plenum Press.

Wachtel, P. L. (1993). *Therapeutic communication.* New York: Guilford Press.

Wachtel, P. L., & Messer, S. B. (Eds.). (1997). *Theories of psychotherapy.* Washington, DC: American Psychological Association.

Wallerstein, R. S. (1967). Reconstruction and mastery in the transference psychosis. *Journal of the American Psychoanalytic Association, 15,* 551–583.

Wallerstein, R. S. (1983). Defenses, defense mechanisms and the structure of the mind. *Journal of the American Psychoanalytic Association, 31,* 201–225.

Wallerstein, R. S. (1986). *Forty-two lives in treatment.* New York: Guilford Press.

Wallerstein, R. S. (1989). The psychotherapy research project of the Menninger Foundation: An overview. *Journal of Consulting and Clinical Psychology, 57,* 195–205.

Wallerstein, R. S. (1995). *The talking cures: The psychonalyses and the psychotherapies.* New Haven, CT: Yale University Press.

Watkins, C. E., Jr. (1990). The effects of counselor self-disclosure: A research review. *Counseling Psychologist, 18,* 477–500.

Weinberger, J. (1993). Common factors in psychotherapy. In G. Stricker & J. R. Gold (Eds.), *Comprehensive handbook of psychotherapy integration* (pp. 43–56). New York: Plenum Press.

Weinberger, J. (1995). Common factors aren't so common: The common factors dilemma. *Clinical Psychology, 2,* 45–69.

Weiner, I. B. (1991). Theoretical foundations of clinical psychology. In M. Hersen, A. E. Kazdin, & A. S. Bellack (Eds.), *The clinical psychology handbook* (2nd ed., pp. 26–44). New York: Pergamon.

Weiner, I. B. (1992a). *Psychological disturbance in adolescence* (2nd ed.). New York: Wiley.

Weiner, I. B. (1992b). Rorschach assessment. In M. E. Maruish (Ed.), *The use of psychological testing for treatment planning and outcome assessment* (pp. 249–278). Hillsdale, NJ: Erlbaum.

Weiner, I. B., & Bordin, E. S. (1983). Individual psychotherapy. In I. B. Weiner (Ed.), *Clinical methods in psychology* (2nd ed., pp. 333–388). New York: Wiley.

Weiner, I. B., & Exner, J. E., Jr. (1991). Rorschach changes in long-term and short-term psychotherapy. *Journal of Personality Assessment, 56,* 453–465.

Weiner, M. F. (1978). *Therapist disclosure: The use of self in psychotherapy.* Boston: Butterworth.

Weinshel, E. M. (1984). Some observations on the psychoanalytic process. *Psychoanalytic Quarterly, 53,* 63–92.

Weinshel, E. M. (1990). Some further observations on the psychoanalytic process. *Psychoanalytic Quarterly, 59,* 629–649.

Weisman, A. (1991). Confrontation, countertransference, and context. In G. Adler & P. G. Myerson (Eds.), *Confrontation in psychotherapy* (pp. 97–122). Northvale, NJ: Aronson.

Weiss, L. (1986). *Dream analysis in psychotherapy.* New York: Pergamon Press.

Weisz, J. R., & Weisz, B. (1993). *Effects of psychotherapy with children and adolescents.* New York: Sage.

Wells, R. A., & Gianetti, V. J. (1990). *Handbook of brief psychotherapies.* New York: Plenum Press.

Werman, D. S. (1984). *The practice of supportive psychotherapy.* New York: Brunner/Mazel.

Westin, D. (1990). Psychoanalytic approaches to personality. In L. A. Pervin (Ed.), *Handbook of personality: Theory and research* (pp. 21–65). New York: Guilford Press.

Wheelis, A. B. (1949). Flight from insight. *American Journal of Psychiatry, 105,* 915–919.

Whiston, S. C., & Sexton, T. L. (1993). An overview of psychotherapy outcome research: Implications for practice. *Professional Psychology, 24,* 43–51.

Wiens, A. N. (1991). Diagnostic interviewing. In M. Hersen, A. E. Kazdin, & A. S. Bellack (Eds.), *The clinical psychology handbook* (2nd ed., pp. 345–361). New York: Pergamon Press.

Wierzbicki, M., & Pekarik, G. (1993). A meta-analysis of psychotherapy dropout. *Professional Psychology, 24,* 190–195.

Willick, M. S. (1995). Defense. In B. E. Moore & B. D. Fine (Eds.), *Psychoanalysis: The major concepts* (pp. 485–493). New Haven, CT: Yale University Press.

Wolberg, L. R. (1988). *The technique of psychotherapy* (4th ed.). New York: Grune and Stratton.

Wortis, J. (1954). *Fragments of an analysis with Freud.* New York: Simon & Schuster.

Yutrzenka, B. A. (1995). Making a case for training in ethnic and cultural diversity in increasing treatment efficacy. *Journal of Consulting and Clinical Psychology, 63,* 197–206.

Zarit, S. H., & Knight, B. G. (1996). *A guide to psychotherapy and aging.* Washington, DC: American Psychological Association.

Zayas, L. H., Torres, L. R., Malcolm, J., & DesRosiers, F. S. (1996). Clinician's definitions of ethnically sensitive therapy. *Professional Psychology, 27,* 78–82.

Zeidner, M., & Endler, N. S. (Eds.). (1996). *Handbook of coping.* New York: Wiley.

Zeig, J. K., & Munion, W. M. (Eds.). (1990). *What is psychotherapy?* San Francisco: Jossey-Bass.

Zetzel, E. R. (1956). Current concepts of transference. *International Journal of Psycho-Analysis, 37,* 369–375.

Author Index

315

Subject Index

DATE DUE